SHOULD PARENTS BE
LICENSED?

Contemporary Issues

Series Editors: Robert M. Baird
Stuart E. Rosenbaum

Volumes edited by Robert M. Baird and Stuart E. Rosenbaum unless otherwise noted.

SHOULD PARENTS BE
LICENSED?

DEBATING THE ISSUES

edited by PEG TITTLE

 Prometheus Books
59 John Glenn Drive
Amherst, New York 14228-2197

Published 2004 by Prometheus Books

Inquiries should be addressed to
Prometheus Books
59 John Glenn Drive
Amherst, New York 14228–2197
VOICE: 716–691–0133, ext. 207
FAX: 716–564–2711
WWW.PROMETHEUSBOOKS.COM

08 07 06 05 04   5 4 3 2 1

Library of Congress Cataloging-in-Publication Data

Should parents be licensed? : debating the issues / edited by Peg Tittle.
        p. cm. — (Contemporary issues series)
    Includes bibliographical references.
    ISBN 1-59102-094-8 (pbk. : alk. paper)
    1. Parenting—Government policy. 2. Parents—Legal status, laws, etc.
3. Parenthood—Moral and ethical aspects. 4. Human reproduction—Moral and ethical aspects. I. Tittle, Peg, 1957– II. Series: Contemporary issues (Amherst, N.Y.)
HQ755.8.S5326 2003
649'.1—dc21

                                                                              2003010923
2003018602

Printed in the United States of America on acid-free paper

CONTENTS

INTRODUCTION

*W*ould-be teachers are generally required to study full-time for at least eight months before the state will allow them the responsibility of educating children for six hours a day once they become six years of age. Many would say we have set the bar too low. And yet we haven't even set the bar as high—in fact we haven't set a bar at all—for parents. Someone can be responsible not only for a child's education but for virtually everything about the child for twenty-four hours a day until that child is six years of age—that is, for the duration of the critical, formative years—and he or she doesn't even have to so much as read a pamphlet about child development. How many children have been punished because they could not do what their parents mistakenly thought they should be able to do at a certain age—remember X, carry Y, say Z? How many have been disadvantaged because they grew up on junk food—for their bodies as well as their minds? How many have been neglected because their parents didn't notice the seeds of some talent? And how often have parents "undermine[d] a girl's attempt to be strong and independent? Or repeatedly punishe[d] a boy for crying or for allegedly sissy interests?"[1] As philosopher Hugh LaFollette points out, "Parenting is an activity potentially very harmful to children."[2] And as psychologist Roger McIntire notes, "We already license pilots, salesmen, scuba divers, plumbers, electricians, teachers, veterinarians, cab drivers, soil testers, and television repairmen. . . . Are our TV sets and toilets more important to us than our children?"[3]

Perhaps we have not taken parenting seriously because, traditionally,

9

women have been most responsible for it. It's in our history: when men do X, X is important; the quickest way to devalue a profession is to "admit" women (consider bank tellers, for instance). Or perhaps, as psychiatrist Jack Westman claims, "Parenting is depreciated because it is not regarded as having economic value in our capitalist society."[4]

Certainly the proposal to license parents goes against the prevailing attitude that children are the private property of their parents. But as philosopher Jeffrey Blustein notes, "The public has a legitimate concern with the selection of child rearers and with the way in which children are reared, because a society's children are its future citizens and the future contributors to its material, cultural, and moral advancement."[5]

The proposal also challenges the prevailing attitude of pronatalism, that "having children" is such an assumed good, it is an expectation—an *unqualified* expectation. But having children is not always a good thing. (And a woman "without kids" is not necessarily selfish, and a man is still "grown-up" even if he doesn't support a family.)

There are those who consider such challenges to be warranted: psychologist Katherine Covell and political scientist R. Brian Howe, directors of the Children's Rights Centre in Cape Breton, Canada, say that [a]buse and neglect in various forms will continue until we as a society value parenthood; until we regard parenting as a privilege, rather than as a by-product of sexual intercourse, a route to adult identity, or a route to social assistance."[6] Westman agrees: "The way children are parented plays a vital role in the quality of all of our lives. We no longer can afford to avoid defining and confronting incompetent parenting."[7]

While this desire to license parents may be motivated in part by an increasing number of "bad kids" who are a danger not only to themselves but also to others, it is important to recognize and assess the implicit assumption that bad kids are the result of bad parenting: while this may be true at least to some extent, perhaps some of the blame should be put on the schools that have the kids, albeit *after* their critical formative years, for several hours each day, and on the society that promotes, through its pervasive entertainment media, the consumption of goods detrimental to the child's well-being (for example, we make a plastic gun and call it a *toy*).

SOCIAL PARENTING

Parenting (as opposed to parentage—which refers to the biological element of reproduction rather than this element of "rearing" or "raising," and which will be discussed later) includes the nurturing of a child's physical, cognitive, emotional, and social development; thus, a competent parent would be one who understands and can indeed nurture those aspects of development. But what exactly does that translate into when we set the requirements for obtaining a license?

Requirements

Covell and Howe recommend the model proposed by Westman: first, prospective parents must have attained adulthood (to be determined by age and completion of high school), thus "demonstrating the ability to be responsible for their own lives before being allowed to assume responsibility for a child's life";[8] second, they must sign an agreement to care for and nurture the child and to refrain from abusing and neglecting the child; third, they must complete a parenting course.[9]

A more detailed proposal might include the examination of prospective parents according to the following categories:

(1) **Physical:** Not only might there be a minimum age requirement, there could be a maximum: Lynda Fenwick, author of *Private Choices, Public Consequences*, points out that perhaps people who want to be parents should be young enough to live long enough (barring something unexpected) to raise the child to adulthood.

(2) **Cognitive:** As mentioned above, an understanding of child development should be required. This might disqualify not only mentally challenged adults, but also members of various religions that "[create] serious barriers to the development of [the child's] capacities for autonomous decision-making,"[10] because they are irrationalist and/or sexist.

(3) **Emotional:** Perhaps prospective parents should be patient, affectionate, and emotionally mature.

(4) **Social:** Evidence of previous abusive behavior should certainly disqualify applicants; other criminal behavior may also be relevant. Given our understanding that abusive parents are apt to have been abused children, perhaps applicants who have been so abused should be disqualified; however, Westman argues that "children who have experienced incompetent parenting can break the vicious cycle of continuing incompetent parenting through interventions that improve their life circumstances and through their personal efforts."[11]

(5) **Financial:** Applicants should have an income adequate for the provision of food, shelter, clothing, and other basic necessities. Perhaps, especially if the education system has eliminated extracurricular athletics or arts programs, the provision of some minimal enrichment should also be required of prospective parents.

Robert Hawkins describes several attributes of a good parent, derived no doubt from his teaching experience and work as a clinical child psychologist: a good parent "is an astute observer of behavior and is sensitive to his child's spoken and silent messages . . . , makes conscious and rational decisions about what to teach his child, and . . . has a large repertoire of sound behavior-modification techniques."[12] Like Westman, and Covell and Howe, he suggests parent training courses, but which include a practicum component: "Educators must see their students engage in child-rearing behavior with real children, and they must see them face child-rearing tasks that resemble the ones they will encounter as parents."[13] He suggests further that "[a]fter reading basic material, [the student] might watch a movie or videotape of a behaviorally disturbed child interacting with his parents. He could observe the ways in which parents inadvertently maintain such undesired behavior as tantrums, disobedience, excessive crying, dependency, or social isolation."[14]

Assuming the inclusion of an educational component in the licensing program, content is not the only issue. Would the requirement be mere completion of the course or the achievement of some minimum grade? Perhaps attendance should be mandatory as a measure of commitment: if someone can't find the time and/or energy and/or desire to show up for a class in parenting one night a week for a year, perhaps that person's potential commitment to a child should be questioned. A further issue is whether equivalency measures should be established that would enable specific applicants to waive the course requirement.

In addition to those already mentioned, another criterion for assessing parent license applicants might be current number of children: sociologist Edgar Chasteen suggests that "prolific parenthood" be considered a type of unfitness[15]—one could argue that after a certain number of children, the ability to care adequately for each one of them diminishes.

Prospective parents might also be screened for intent. Many people find it morally unacceptable to produce a child (merely) as a means to an end, such as to create a bone marrow donor, but perhaps we should as well examine for moral acceptability the many other motives for reproduction: to strengthen an ailing relationship; to imitate peers or fulfill others' expectations (perhaps most often those of a partner or a parent); to carry on the family name or genes; to prove one is able to have a child; to produce an heir (for a business or property), a cheap laborer, a playmate, a caretaker for old age, and so forth.[16]

Deciding what's relevant is important; so, too, is deciding what's *not* relevant. There is certainly potential here for unjustified discrimination. Skin color is uncontroversially irrelevant, except perhaps to racists; sexual orientation should be equally so (but see Christine Overall's essay for a discussion of this requirement in the context of access to so-called new reproductive technologies [NRTs] that indicates that it is, unfortunately, not so uncontroversially irrelevant). Coparent arrangements should also be irrelevant since individuals rather than couples would be licensed; this would enable parenting by same-sex couples, mixed-sex triples (perhaps intergenerational), and so on.

One might suggest that all we're really after is proof of parental love: "a passionate, unconditional commitment to nurture one's child, providing it with the care, affection, and guidance it needs to develop its capacities to maturity."[17] Unfortunately, many children have been abused in the name of "love."

Certainly this element of assessment is bound to be problematic, but as LaFollette says, we don't have to license only the *best* parents—we just have to *not* license the *worst*. Lawyer Claudia Pap Mangel argues that we can indeed do just that: there are accurate and reliable measures of the potential for child abuse. And, as Westman comments after he lists signs of incompetent parenting (e.g., insufficient clothing; disease due to inadequate hygiene; inadequate physical growth due to insufficient nutrition; overdoses and accidents due to inadequate supervision; lack of affectionate holding, touching, and talking; instability of household composition), "These signs . . . do not require subtle techniques or tests to detect."[18]

There are three contexts in which we already make decisions about who can and cannot parent: custody, foster care, and adoption. Examination of these contexts might help us clarify not only the justifications for a parent licensing policy, but also the requirements for obtaining a license to parent.

Perusing the literature regarding child custody evaluations, psychiatrist Richard Gardner endorses several criteria. First, we should evaluate the "ability of the parents to properly and effectively raise the child, [including their] knowledge of child-rearing techniques and the utilization of humane and reasonable disciplinary measures [including their] knowledge of how to provide the child with guidance, instruction, and care."[19] One might wonder, however, how "properly" is defined. Second, Gardner suggests we should evaluate the parents' "honesty, sensitivity to the feelings of others, social commitment, lifestyle, and other personality qualities which would be useful for the child to emulate and identify with."[20] But which lifestyles would be considered unacceptable for emulation and identification? Third, the parents' "availability . . . for getting the child off to school, being available on their return, and being available to care for the child during illnesses and emergency situations" should be evaluated.[21] This one might lead to long overdue changes in other social policies, most especially workplace matters (if everyone who wants to parent must be available in that way, employers will have to be considerably more flexible about hours). Among Gardner's other criteria are several uncontroversial items: consideration of the parents' commitment to their child's education, health, and friends (commitment to the second might rule out parents who would refuse blood transfusions, for example), and the parents' physical and psychological health.

Psychotherapist and custody evaluator Diane Trombetta, also perusing the custody literature, questions the assumptions she finds therein: "Is there any evidence to show that parents who have more knowledge of child development, as measured by a paper-and-pencil test, are better parents? How valid and reliable are third-party reports submitted by friends, relatives, and school teachers?"[22] She concludes that "[p]arenting skills which are too vulnerable to individual or cultural bias, or which are too subtle to be measured easily, should probably not be evaluated at all."[23] And yet we do think teaching skills can be so measured.

Trombetta goes on to say that "[i]t may be that effective parenting is not attributable to a particular person but, rather, to a whole context which allows, fosters, and rewards good parenting."[24] While this is certainly true of teaching, which occurs in the context of a school, I think it might be less so of parenting—but just *less* so, not *not* so: after all, parenting does occur in the context of society. Or perhaps the difference is that a school is more defined, and therefore more constraining, than society. In any case, Trombetta's observation supports the suggestion that perhaps other changes (such as making toy guns illegal) should occur along with licensing parents.

Further, Trombetta suggests caution with custody evaluations that may be well-heeded for parent license evaluations as well: we must be aware of and take into account the many possible explanations for failing our licensing tests (especially if they include third-party observations as well as first-person pencil-and-paper tests) that may *not* indicate that the applicant is unsuitable: for example, examination-related stress, bias, and, perhaps most important of all, "unconscious resistance to the evaluation process itself."[25]

With regard to fostering, Robert Mnookin, author of "Foster Care—In Whose Best Interest?" notes that "[f]oster homes are usually licensed by the state, with regulations regarding aspects such as the size of the home, number of children. . . ."[26] Why shouldn't something similar be the case for nonfoster homes? Decisions about foster care are often made according to the "best interests of the child." Isn't a similar focus warranted for nonfoster care? Like Trombetta, however, Mnookin is critical of the standards in use: they are vague and open-ended, highly subjective, and "permit intervention not only when the child has been demonstrably harmed or is physically endangered but also when parental habits or attitudes are adverse to the inculcation of proper moral values."[27] What are "proper moral values"? One can imagine children being taken away if their parents are atheists. However, these problems should not lead us to abandon the policies; rather, they should lead us to improve them.

And with regard to adoption, McIntire pointedly asks what would occur "if adoption agencies offered their children on a first-come-first-served basis, with no screening process for applicants. . . . Imagine some drunk stumbling up and saying 'I'll take that cute little blond-haired girl over there.'"[28] And yet that's exactly what we currently allow with regard to nonadoptive parenting. Why do we cling to the irrational belief that biological parents are *necessarily* competent parents, given the overwhelming evidence to the contrary? We have, without justification, a double standard.

Glenn McGee, editor of *The Human Cloning Debate*, observes that "[p]arents who want to adopt must undergo a variety of pre-screens, including in most states a home visit and background check,"[29] and he proposes something similar for people who want to clone children: "The goal is to find some similar pre-screen procedure to ensure that parents who participate in new, highly complex, family-making technologies like egg and sperm donation, cloning, and nuclear transplantation meet a minimum test for providing flourishing opportunities to their children."[30] Unfortunately, he seems to think such screens are justified for adoption and access to NRTs but not for coital reproduction because the former are "unorthodox."[31]

Perhaps, however, the bar should be set *higher*, not lower, for those who want to raise their own offspring, in order to counteract the potential abuse that might arise when children are seen as ego extensions and/or private property. Indeed, Elizabeth Bartholet, professor of law and author of several books about adoption, notes that "the argument for parental screening [for adopting parents] rests largely on the assumption that children are subject to special risks when there is no biologic link between parent and child . . . [but] the fact that adoptive parents have *consciously chosen* parenthood would seem more than enough to compensate for any difficulties that might be inherent in adoptive parenting."[32] Pointing out that unwanted children are worse off than wanted children,[33] she asks, "Why would anyone think that those who consciously plan to adopt someone else's child pose *more* of a risk than those who fall unwittingly into pregnancy?"[34]

Benefits

It is this element of intention, of conscious choice, of deliberate willing, that would be one of the main benefits of a parent-licensing policy. "It is depressing, not comforting, to realize that most people are accidents,"[35] says philosopher Joseph Fletcher. Marjorie Schultz, professor of law, elaborates, arguing for intent as a determinant of legal parenthood (she restricts her proposal, however, to instances involving NRTs):

> Parenting relationships are among the most significant in life, both to the individuals involved and to the society whose future depends upon its children. While conception may occur quickly and without much deliberation, parenthood competently performed is an unusually important, substantial, and long-term activity. Parenting involves such large amounts of time, energy, and money that deep commitment to the task seems highly desirable. . . .[36]

> [D]eliberative, articulated, and acted-upon intentions regarding child rearing have great importance as indices of desirable parenting behavior. There is a correlation between choosing something and being motivated to do it consistently and well. Where the birth of children is not intended . . . biological connection will not guarantee love or adequate care.[37]

Licensing, by requiring intentional action prior to birth (e.g., making an application, at least, and perhaps also demonstrating certain capacities and competencies), could guarantee that intent (at least at the outset, for as Schultz points out, intentions can change), and insofar as intended children are more apt to be recipients of love and adequate care, it could increase the odds that children are indeed loved and cared for.

In a similar vein, the point of philosopher Margaret Battin's thought experiment wherein everyone uses "automatic reversible contraception" is that such a circumstance would "reverse the default mode, so to speak, in human reproduction, so that having a child would require a deliberate choice";[38] requiring people to obtain a license before they reproduce/parent would achieve the same effect. Referring to the effects of mandatory contraception, Battin's prediction is as applicable, I think, to mandatory licensing: "Our ways of thinking about pregnancy and childbearing would undergo radical change—from something one accepts or rejects when it happens to something one chooses to begin."[39]

There is a chance, however, that the more wanted a child is, the more it will be expected to fulfill the parents' egoistic wants; the more planned or controlled the child is, the less autonomy it will be allowed to develop. Philosopher Leon Kass suggests that "[t]hanks to our belief that all children should be *wanted* children . . . , sooner or later only those children who fulfill our wants will be fully acceptable."[40] However, "wanted" and "planned" need not mean "controlled."

Another benefit of licensing parents is that which philosopher Gregory Kavka identifies as a benefit of genetic engineering but that could apply to parenting as well as to parentage: "We might come to view parents as being more responsible for how their children turn out than we now view them."[41] No longer could parents say they can't be blamed, they didn't know . . . their license proves they did. Kavka goes on to describe "an awesome, possibly overwhelming, sense of responsibility"[42] akin to some existential dread; perhaps that response to parenthood is overdue. And indeed he goes on to suggest that "[i]t is possible . . . that a sense of awesome responsibility for our species' biological destiny might force us to become unusually careful and thoughtful as we develop responsive social policies"[43]—one of which might be parent licensing.

On the other hand, "Setting standards for parents . . . would protect people from assuming parenting burdens that restrict their own personal development and that cause stresses and failures in their own lives"[44]—competency need not mean self-sacrifice.

Yet another benefit, insofar as the licensing program would include an educational component, is described by philosopher Philip Kitcher (who proposes education *instead* of licensing, not *as part of* licensing): "People would make the right decisions because they would understand the consequences of their decisions, both for their offspring and for society."[45] Though we'd like to believe there is a connection between education and ethics, perhaps this would apply only some of the time to some of the people (others do wrong despite knowledge of consequences—for a number of reasons, including for no reason at all).

And certainly there are the many benefits of societal good, developed extensively by Westman, who connects incompetent parenting with criminality, welfare dependency, poor public health, and reduced national productivity.[46]

Licensing would also emphatically underscore the immorality of various kinds of parenting, and penalties for parenting without a license or for somehow "violating" the license might act to deter people from such parenting. However, perhaps the most obvious benefit is this: currently we assume that people are fit to parent unless or until proven otherwise, at which point we remove the children from their home—would it not be better to take a proactive, rather than a reactive, approach and make sure people are fit *before* they become parents?

BIOLOGICAL PARENTAGE

We are products, however, not only of our nurture but also of our nature. Biological parentage is, therefore, another aspect we might want to license in some way (just as parenting need not imply parentage, or vice versa, licensing one need not imply licensing the other). Not only could we license *whether* people can have children, we could license *what kinds* of children they can have. There are two components of biological parentage: the genetic material (that is, the DNA—whether from sperm, ova, or other cells) and the uterine environment.

Genetic Material

With regard to the first component, we could make genetic screening mandatory (along with other medical screening, such as that for AIDS and drug addiction); if the results indicate certain qualities (or lack thereof), then either a license would not be provided (conception should not occur or the conceptus should not develop) or the provision of a license would be conditional upon certain genetic engineering.

Philosopher Lawrence Ulrich argues that "[r]eproductive controls along much the same line as our current legislation regarding marriages of close kinship and venereal disease screening are the only approach . . . satisfactory in dealing with genetic disease of the high-risk early-appearance type within the context of species obligation."[47] He justifies "suspending" reproductive rights by appealing to both legal precedent and "species obligation," the latter deriving from his belief that "the survival of the human species is a good and that it is a good of such importance and value that it can be accredited as a right."[48] Bioethicist Ruth Macklin argues to the contrary, claiming that "attempts at government-based or scientist-directed eugenics programs —whether aimed at positive or negative eugenics—are bound to be misguided or dangerous or both."[49]

While not advocating legislative controls, philosopher Laura Purdy concludes, like Ulrich, that it's morally wrong to have children who are likely to have certain genetic diseases. Appealing to the individual rather than the species, she draws attention to the consequences of bringing disabled children into the world and argues that "people are better off without disease or special limitation, and that this interest is sufficiently compelling in some cases to justify the judgment that reproducing would be wrong."[50]

Some argue, however, that a policy restricting reproduction to the genetically "healthy" is harmful to the "differently abled." The nature of that harm, however, is unclear: such a policy does not imply that their lives are of less value, but only that given the choice between having the disease or not, it is better not,[51] because of the resultant suffering[52] and reduced opportunities.[53] Conceding the concern of disability activists that "narrow and rigid standards, and [the] utter lack of human empathy with those who fail to 'measure up' justifies wariness,"[54] Purdy responds by asking, "If health and well-being aren't valuable, what moral case is there for eradicating the social obstacles"[55] such activists seek to eradicate? Nevertheless, we are wise to heed Kitcher's attention to recognizing "where medicine ends and social prejudice takes over"[56] with regard to genetic engineering. And even though we may not know (now or ever) *exactly* where that line is, surely we know on which side of the line certain genes lie: not only are there clear cases of severe physical suffering due to genetic disease, there are clear cases of severe psychological suffering as well.

Commenting on the "societal good" that comes from genetic abortion, Kass observes that "[t]he societal standard is all too often reduced to its lowest common denominator: money."[57] This seems supported by the results of a survey conducted by Fenwick:

> The public resentment of reproductive choices by parents with known genetic risks at the time of conception is closely tied to the belief that the financial burden of caring for the children who inherit the disability will ultimately be shifted to the public. . . . Furthermore, [survey respondents] do not want to pay higher insurance premiums or taxes to cover the expenses of caring for the children born with genetic disabilities about which their parents had been forewarned.[58]

John Robertson, professor of law, counters this attitude by arguing that "[a]s long as persons who choose to ignore genetic information in reproducing are able and willing to rear affected offspring, the costs of their reproduction are unlikely to be sufficient to support a charge of reproductive irresponsibility,"[59] adding that "[e]ven if they did impose medical or other costs on taxpayers, those costs are ordinarily not sufficient to justify restricting a person's interest in procreation."[60] Indeed, Kass asks, "Who is a greater drain on society's precious resources, the average inmate of a home for the retarded or the average graduate of Harvard College?"[61] and replies that we don't and perhaps can't know. Clearly, as he points out, we need to define whose/which society we are talking about when we say "societal good." According to Kass, "Some use the term 'society' to mean their own particular political community, others to mean the whole human race. . . . Do we mean our 'society' as it is today? Or do we mean our 'society' as it ought to be?"[62]

As for violating the right of differently abled people to reproduce (that is, prohibiting reproduction rather than mandating genetic engineering when genetic disease is likely), surely one must wonder why genetic heritage is so important that a person will intentionally bring into the world a differently abled person just to perpetuate that heritage. Why wouldn't a disabled person choose to adopt or use surrogate genetic material instead (or, at the very least, if possible, try again until the genetic disability doesn't appear in the fertilized ovum)?

In addition to negative engineering (removing genetic traits), we could also regulate in some way positive engineering (adding or enhancing genetic traits). Should we approve (license) all additions and enhancements? As philosopher Thomas Beauchamp points out, "There are problems in regard to the wisdom of the choice of traits . . . and in regard to the alleged advantageousness of the traits. . . . Even if one were to select traits which virtually everyone admires . . . it would not follow that society would be improved if these traits were widely enhanced."[63] For example, suppose everyone wanted to increase their child's intelligence. If everyone became a genius, there wouldn't be any advantage in it. (At least there would be no *relative* advantage, but wouldn't there be an *intrinsic* value in such ability?) And, it might not be to society's overall advantage if everyone were a genius (unless we raised all our children to be happy being the proverbial "ditch-digger" for X number of hours per week). Furthermore, having the genes for genius is only part of the story; we'd need to be sure we have the nurturance (the competent parenting) in place to develop and actualize that genius.

The greater number of male than female babies born in China is a good example of this "collective imbalance," an imbalance that can occur "when a desirable distribution of characteristics in the general population is eliminated by the cumulative effects of individual decisions about the traits of offspring."[64] Licensing could prevent such occurrences if the regulatory body kept records of parenting decisions and intervened when necessary to maintain a balance. The nature of this "balance" would have to be clearly identified, of course, and this could get very complicated if we attended not only to biological diversity (because monocultures die) but also to social justice (see philosopher David Resnik). This particular example especially illuminates the need for enlightened social values, as Kitcher notes: "Individual choices are not made in a social vacuum, and unless changes in social attitudes keep pace with the proliferation of genetic tests, we can anticipate that many future prospective parents, acting to avoid misery for potential children, will have to bow to social attitudes they reject and resent."[65] State regulation might help to avoid that situation, if such regulation is guided by the forementioned enlightened values. On the other hand, perhaps imbuing state regulations with social values is dangerous; perhaps the negative element of past eugenics can be avoided by insisting that state regulations be guided only by medical/biological interests (which are value-free).

We should, however, consider not only the consequences to society, but also the consequences to the individual children. As philosopher Elizabeth Anderson points out, "A child who knew how anxious her parents were that she have the 'right' genetic makeup might fear that her parents' love was contingent upon her expression of these characteristics."[66] This echoes the concern expressed earlier about "wanted" children not necessarily being better off than "unwanted" children because of the increasing pressure to conform to their parents' "wants."

Uterine Environment

The second component of biological parentage, the uterine environment, may also be included within the scope of a parent licensing policy, for it also seriously affects one's nature and, therefore, one's quality of life. The uterine environment can be affected by drug use, diet, exercise, exposure to various substances, and fetal therapies. Detrimental effects can result in pain, injury, and illness.

For example, the use of drugs during pregnancy (illegal drugs such as crack cocaine and heroin, as well as legal drugs such as alcohol, nicotine, and prescribed drugs to treat conditions such as cancer and epilepsy) can cause in the newborn excruciating pain; vomiting; inability to sleep; reluctance to feed; diarrhea leading to shock and death; severe anemia; growth retardation; mental retardation; central nervous system abnormalities; and malformations of the kidneys, intestines, head, and spinal cord.[67] Exposure to tobacco, carbon monoxide, lead, alcohol, and infectious diseases can cause prenatal injury.[68] Refusal of fetal therapy techniques (such as surgery, blood infusions, and vitamin regimens) can result in respiratory distress as well as various genetic disorders and defects such as spina bifida and hydrocephalus.[69]

One is generally considered free to ingest whatever substances one wants as long as no harm to others is caused, but as attorney Lynn Paltrow points out, "The biological event of conception transforms the woman from drug user into a drug trafficker or child abuser";[70] drug-using men are also at fault to the extent the drugs affect the quality of their sperm.[71] (Furthermore, as psychiatrist Michelle Harrison points out, "men are not *required* to impregnate drug-addicted women"[72]—surely they are partly responsible, then, for such prenatal abuse.)

Indeed, given that there is a developmental continuum from embryo to fetus to infant to child, it is logically sound to extend policies about child abuse from postbirth to prebirth: "To begin legal protection and comprehensive obligations toward human beings only at birth is to assume that the most vulnerable period of all human life, the period during which the foundations of childhood and adulthood health are laid, is discontinuous with and of no influence on those later stages."[73] On this basis, the state may be justified in regulating the behavior of the (biological) parents.

Of course, the standard objection is that such regulation violates a woman's right to physical integrity/privacy and self-determination/autonomy. But rights are not absolute (as will be discussed later), and one can argue that the woman forfeits some of that privacy and autonomy when she becomes pregnant—when she begins to create another human being. Even if we grant that she owns the result of her body's resources and labor, there are limits to such property rights. Furthermore, her rights are not suppressed; they're just restricted, and then only temporarily, and only when she consents to become pregnant. If she doesn't want her physical privacy to be so restricted, she can choose to abort or adopt (if she wanted to parent). A licensing program could ensure these alternative courses of action, and drug addicts, for example, might not be allowed to gestate.

Philosopher George Schedler reaches the same conclusion, arguing that *society has a duty* to ensure that infants are born free of avoidable defects because of (1) the rights of the fetus as a future infant (he derives the infant's right to preventive action from the infant's [currently recognized by law of tort] right to compensation for prenatal injuries; also, if the state has a right to stop a third party from injuring the fetus, then, Schedler argues, surely the state has a right to stop the parents from doing so); (2) the rights of future persons (to be free from suffering); and (3) the economic and human costs of drug abuse during pregnancy (he appeals to both utilitarian and fairness arguments). Hence, Schedler concludes, society has the right to force pregnant drug addicts to abort. One can argue by extension that society has a right to prohibit conception by drug addicts in the first place and that this is achievable through licensing parents.

Lawyer Molly McNulty, however, claims that laws criminalizing women's acts or omissions during pregnancy (including "the failure to receive timely prenatal care, not complying with doctor's orders, and using drugs during pregnancy")[74] would be unfair (especially to members of low-income and minority groups who do not have economic access to prenatal services), ineffective (it does not lessen infant illness because pregnant drug-using women would simply avoid medical appointments), and unconstitutional. However, we could make prenatal care easily available, free of charge, to everyone (or at least to those licensed to parent); licensing could prevent drug-users from becoming pregnant in the first place; and the constitution could be changed.

Philosopher Bonnie Steinbock also argues against legislating behavior during pregnancy: "Coercing the mother to protect the not-yet-born child poses serious threats to women's privacy and bodily autonomy . . . [and] in most cases it is unlikely to do much to protect the health and lives of children."[75] For example, "If a woman is willing to risk criminal prosecution for [illegal] drug use, why should she be deterred by additional penalties for harming her unborn child?"[76] So again, legislating *prior* to pregnancy might be the sought-for solution. However, if the license requirements stipulate that certain behavior is to be avoided during pregnancy, then we are still legislating behavior during pregnancy.

Precedents

As in the case of parenting, there are contexts concerning parentage in which we already make decisions about who can and cannot parent: access to NRTs and prenatal abuse. These are worth examining again in order to clarify potential parent licensing policies and practices.

Insofar as cloning is merely reproducing, shouldn't anyone and everyone be allowed to clone if anyone and everyone is allowed to coitally reproduce? If not, what's the significant difference? A common answer is that cloning is unnatural. But certainly the biological material is natural. Why does it matter which cells are involved or how they get into the uterus? Furthermore, it's unclear why "unnatural" should imply "subject to greater regulation."

Nevertheless, the National Bioethics Advisory Commission (NBAC) has recommended "regulating" cloning to the point of outright prohibition. It is not the recommendation per se that is of interest here, but the reasons: "harms [physical and psychological] to the children who may be born [and] degradation of the quality of parenting."[77] Surely such harms and degradation are of concern with regard to coital reproduction as well. Surely pre- and postnatal abuse of coitally produced children can also result in the "severe developmental abnormalities"[78] mentioned by the NBAC, and while incompetent parenting may not affect the coitally produced child's sense of unique individuality in the way cloned children are imagined to be affected, incompetent parenting surely affects the child's self-worth and "experience of freedom and ability to create a life for oneself."[79]

The Canadian Royal Commission on New Reproductive Technologies has reached similar conclusions, recommending in its report titled *Proceed with Care* both that certain aspects of new reproductive technologies be illegal and that the provision of other technologies be licensed by the federal government because of "the potential for harm to individuals and the need to protect the vulnerable interests of individuals and society."[80] In particular, the following requirements are proposed as conditions for license:[81] "All potential donors should provide a signed, self-administered completed questionnaire providing information about their health and the health of their first-degree relatives . . . which should be reviewed by a clinical geneticist. Any indication of serious genetic anomalies or other high-risk factors should disqualify a potential donor from participating in the program" (item 88.a); tests for HIV and other infectious diseases must also be taken (items 88.f, h, i, and j). It is most perplexing that these requirements apply only when sperm is to be used by someone *other* than the sperm producer's "partner" (item 87). Furthermore, "a license is required to perform insemination at any site other than the vagina even if the recipient is the social partner."[82] Why, when the vagina is the site, is it "anything goes," but otherwise, we "proceed with care"?

The commission also recommends that the woman seeking to become impregnated through various assistive NRTs sign a statement indicating that she has "received, read, and understood" not only information materials outlining "the risks, responsibilities, and implications of donor insemination,"[83] but also the sperm screening and medical test results (item 99.f.iii). Why shouldn't women be required to provide such informed consent for "unassisted" reproduction as well?

Counseling should also to be provided, the commission recommends, addressing "information about alternatives . . . such as . . . living without children; avoidance of exposure to risk factors . . . ; some exploration of questions related to values and goals that patients may wish to take into account when making their decisions. . . ."[84] Again, why shouldn't we require this of coitally reproducing parents as well?

In short, why should children born as a result of assisted insemination or in vitro fertilization be privileged to a higher standard of care in their creation than children born as a result of coitus? This double standard is of concern not only because of the implications for quality of care, but also because of the implications for rights: why is state permission required by someone seeking assistance for reproduction but not by someone who doesn't need or want such assistance? We have the right to reproduce, but only if we can do it on our own? One could argue that the person seeking assistance is seeking societal resources, and that's why permission is required—not only to *use* those resources, but to ensure they're not *mis*used. But people reproducing without NRT assistance *also* use societal resources, most notably through the health care system for prenatal, natal, and postnatal care. Furthermore, in *both* cases, the resulting child certainly uses societal resources.

Regulations concerning "surrogacy" reveal a similar double standard, and provide further suggestions regarding parent license requirements. Susan Ince, author of "Inside the Surrogate Industry," describes the various tests one needs to pass before being accepted for a gestational contract, not all of which are relevant to being a "contract risk": a thorough medical exam, genetic screening if indicated, intelligence testing, and psychological evaluation. She also describes the "extensive behavioral controls over the surrogate," which include prohibitions against smoking, the consumption of alcohol, and the use of illegal drugs, and the insistence that all scheduled medical, psychological, and counseling appointments be kept.[85] "Any action that 'can be deemed to be dangerous to the well-being of the unborn child' constitutes a breach of contract."[86] Why do we not require this of *all* those who intend to gestate?

Granted, such controls have the potential to be excessive, and hopefully we can avoid crossing that line (certainly we should avoid the "plus any other [requirement] deemed necessary by the officer" clause). But suppose we don't: if a person isn't willing to make a nine-month commitment to sometimes unnecessary precautions and/or appointments, perhaps that person shouldn't become a parent. Perhaps we should consider even the tests that *are* contract-focused: to the extent they are motivated by the desire to secure intent and to minimize the changing of one's mind, are they not just as important in nonsurrogacy parenting arrangements? (And yet, as Westman often points out, the more simple the proposal, the more feasible.)

Similarly, Robertson suggests, with regard to surrogacy, that "regulation to minimize harm and assure knowing choices would be permissible."[87] He elaborates that "the state could . . . set age and health qualifications for surrogates, and structure the transaction to assure voluntary, knowing choices. The state could also define and allocate responsibilities among the parties to protect the best interests of the offspring. . . ."[88] Would these regulations not also be beneficial for nonsurrogacy parenting arrangements?

As Lori Andrews, professor of law, has pointed out, "Surrogacy contracts contain lengthy riders detailing the myriad risks of pregnancy, so potential surrogates are much better informed on that topic than are most women who get pregnant in a more traditional fashion."[89] At the very least, licensing might make *all* potential parents more informed.

Regulatory precedents regarding prenatal abuse are also worth examination. Criminal prosecution for prenatal abuse suggests a belief that children are entitled to be born healthy, of sound mind and body. However, such pros-ecution is by no means standard practice. The American Medical Association claims that "criminal sanctions not only fail to deter pregnant women from substance abuse, they will in fact prevent them from seeking prenatal care or medical help for their dependency."[90] Perhaps, therefore, as suggested ear-lier, preventing such people from becoming pregnant in the first place, which licensing might do, is preferable. The board also notes that such sanctions may encourage women to seek abortions, which may also be desirable.

Suzanne Scorsone, a commissioner for the Canadian Royal Commission on new Reproductive Technologies, has argued that judicial intervention in pregnancy is sometimes justifiable: "There can be no doubt that the incon-venience or loss of mobility or other effects experienced by a woman of mandatory but temporary care or treatment [confined to a prison or treat-ment facility] would be far less severe than the effects of an entire lifetime of mental and/or physical handicap on the child who is to be born."[91] Never-theless, she does not advocate "some sort of science-fictional infrastructure to enforce the compliance of every woman who did not seek adequate pre-natal care or who did not follow her doctor's advice."[92] And yet, there is already legislation in place, "some sort of infrastructure," to safeguard against prenatal harms that occur at the workplace. Why *not* also impose such safeguards elsewhere?

Population Concerns

The decision to prohibit biological reproduction, parentage, could be based not only on concerns for quality (through the genetic material and/or the uterine environment) but also on concerns for quantity. The two are, of course, related. Excessive quantity (society-wide or species-wide) decreases the quality of life for individuals (who are deprived of adequate resources) as well as the quality of the species (which is thus increasingly composed of low-quality individuals). A parent licensing policy might, therefore, also attend to population levels.

First, however, there is the question of whether or not there actually is a "population problem." This question need not be answered, however, because whether or not there is a problem at the moment, as long as our pop-ulation continues to increase, there will surely be a problem at some point in time if only because our planet is a closed system.

The second question, then, is whether or not a legislative response is required. There are some who argue that our numbers will be controlled naturally—through disease, famine, and so on. Others suggest that social policies, including education, are preferable. Still others suggest that indi-vidual choice, if voluntary and informed, will achieve the desired ends.

Chasteen argues that neither social policies nor individual choice has worked; he points to state regulation as the needed solution. Economist Amartya Sen; Betsy Hartmann, director of the Hampshire College Population and Development Program; and others, however, in examining countries such as Cuba, Sri Lanka, Korea, and Kerala, argue that it was not state regulation that effected reductions in reproduction, but changes in income and land distribution, employment opportunities, education, sex equality, accessibility to contraception, and so on.

A further question is whether the population controls are intended to be national or global. If one is proposing a national policy of limiting reproduction, then surely such a policy must be in tandem with other population control policies such as immigration/emigration controls and perhaps also euthanasia policies. For example, it may be objectionable for the state to limit people's right to reproduce when it continues to encourage or allow immigration; it may also be objectionable to prohibit the creation of new healthy people while keeping alive comatose people in irreversible vegetative states.

And if one is proposing a global policy, the following comments by Hartmann may make one reconsider: "It is the consumption explosion in the industrialized world rather than the population explosion in the Third World which is putting the most pressure on natural resources.... The average U.S. citizen uses almost 300 times as much energy as the average citizen of Bangladesh."[93] Perhaps we should regulate consumption in the First World before we regulate reproduction in the Third World.

RIGHTS ISSUES

Certainly proposals to license parents have not been without criticism. And perhaps the strongest objection to licensing parents is that it violates one or more of our rights—our right to reproduce/parent, our right to privacy, our right to physical integrity, our right to autonomy, and so on. Determining our rights in this case would first require a lengthy discussion of the nature and justification of rights in general. Such discussion, however, is complex and well beyond the scope of this overview.[94]

I am more concerned in this volume with moral rights than with legal,[95] political, social, or economic ones, but even so, one could distinguish between natural and acquired rights, positive and negative rights, inalienable rights and alienable rights (which are not necessarily the same as forfeitable rights), claim rights and liberty rights (freedoms), claims and entitlements, rights and privileges,[96] and rights and duties (obligations). As for justifications, philosopher Lawrence Becker groups them into four categories: (1) *utilitarian*—rights are useful in that they enable us to maximize well-being; (2) *contractarian*—rights are part of the consensual agreement we make when we live in a society (see the work of philosophers such as Hobbes, Burke, Bentham, Rawls, and many others); (3) *rationalist*—our rationality or ability to have a conception of good makes us moral agents, and we need rights in order to engage in moral action (see Alan Gewirth for this view as well as the various versions of human or natural rights debate, one of which proposes that we have a right to have our needs fulfilled insofar as that is possible [see H. J. McCloskey for opposition to this view], others of which refer to capabilities, interests, or desires instead of needs); and (4) *intuitionist*—no justification is required because we know intuitively that we have rights.

On what grounds could we claim a right to reproduce and/or parent? Merely *having* a capability does not entail the *right to exercise* that capability. Just because we can do something doesn't mean we should. Further, even having a right to do something may not be sufficient to justify action: sometimes, all things considered (such as other people's rights and consequences), one ought *not* exercise one's rights. As Purdy notes, "Seeking to satisfy the urge to reproduce may increase the suffering created by overpopulation, contribute to the failure to meet the needs of existing children, channel women into rigid and narrow social roles, promote technologies that harm women, and bring to existence children who are more likely than average to lead miserable lives."[97]

Some argue that the right to reproduce is a natural right (see S. L. Floyd and D. Pomerantz for a critique of this view). Others point to the need or desire to have a child as a basis for the right (see Chadwick for a critique of this view, among others, she offers the argument from desert, such that one might not deserve to be happy). Still others refer to its importance to personal well-being and identity (see Dan Brock and Robertson). Purdy criticizes this particular view, asking, "Is it really such a good idea to conceptualize the relationship between childbearing status and one's core self the way that Robertson does?"[98] She goes on to say that "it encourages people to care too much about their ability to have children . . . [and if] a person's whole self-concept depends on having them, they are set up for devastating disappointment";[99] this may be particularly true for women who "because of their socialization—as well as continuing sexist and pronatalist pressure—will more likely adopt this understanding of the meaning of life without seriously questioning it."[100]

And any of these grounds may be qualified by the capacity to appreciate the right (see Robertson and Robert Lee) or by the capacity to exercise that right (see Eike-Henner Kluge and Steinbock). As Steinbock points out, these arguments have been used to restrict the reproductive rights of those with diminished mental capacities:

> It is safe to say that severely retarded people cannot raise children, not even with help. If the right to procreate entails the ability to rear—and I argue that it does—then severely retarded people do not have a right to reproduce.

> ... [I]ndividuals who lack the capacity to be rearing parents do not have an interest in reproducing. Therefore, measures that preserve their ability to procreate in the future do not serve their interests or protect their rights.[101]

With respect to the objection that prohibiting the mentally challenged from parenting violates their rights, philosopher Alyce Vrolyk argues that "[a]n ethics that focuses on rights ... is a poorer guide than a consequentialist view that makes the goodness of the expected results the basic moral criterion."[102] Such arguments about capacities to appreciate and to exercise the right to parent could similarly be used in parent licensing policies. Certainly the definition of "exercise that right" would have to be carefully made. For example, to what extent would it refer to economic capacity?

Philosopher Onora O'Neill suggests another qualification: "I shall argue that the right to beget or bear is not unrestricted, but contingent upon begetters and bearers having or making some feasible plan for their child to be adequately reared by themselves or by willing others."[103] This, too, could be incorporated into the conditions under which licenses are granted. After all, as Ruth Chadwick comments (not in reference to licensing, however),

> It is essential to remember what is actually at issue. We are not simply talking about enabling adults to participate in an activity, like ice-skating, or to acquire certain possessions, like a new car. Speaking in terms of enabling people *to reproduce* or *to have children* sometimes disguises the reality of what is going on. We are talking about the circumstances in which new people should be born. In this context perhaps a concern for their welfare should take priority.[104]

Notwithstanding the previous discussion, whatever the nature of or justification for a right to be a parent, we will quickly get to "the bottom line": not all rights are absolute. So even if we did have a right to reproduce and/or a right to parent, that needn't imply that such a right always be respected. So the important question becomes not *whether* we have rights, but rather *when* our rights can be overridden. There are two instances that should be considered: the first is that of competing rights—the rights of another individual or the rights of society; the second is that of harm (or even risk of harm) to others (which, actually, could be conceptualized as the competing right to be free from harm).

The main contender for competing individual rights in this case would be the right to be born and raised with a healthy body and mind (insofar as these are separate): as Bartholet notes, "If we really care about children, we should question why there is so much talk of the adult's right to procreate, right to control his or her body, and right to parent, but so little talk of the child's right to anything."[105] In fact, wrongful life suits in which the parents of a child sue either the person, usually a physician, who "caused" the life (by failing to provide information that, if known, would have led the pregnant woman to abort) or the person who detrimentally affected the quality of the child's life (if it was damaged as an embryo/fetus), as well as wrongful life suits brought by a genetically defective infant against its mother, seem to indicate that we do think children have a right to be born healthy or at least free of avoidable defects. Further evidence of this belief is the view that it's not always morally right to give birth: some countries are developing policies and procedures supporting newborn euthanasia (in cases of severe and permanent deformity, perhaps also attendant with pain). Licensing parentage could go some way to protect that right, at least insofar as it is the parents themselves who cause the damage.

The United Nations Declaration of the Rights of the Child, focusing on the conditions of being raised rather than on the conditions of being born, lists the rights to "social security . . . , adequate nutrition, housing, recreation, and medical services" (Principle 4), the love and understanding needed for the full and harmonious development of his personality and an atmosphere of affection and of moral and material security (Principle 6), as well as the more obvious protection against "all forms of neglect, cruelty, and exploitation" (Principle 9). U.S. law is just as detailed, as Westman notes, drawing attention to children's rights to food, shelter, clothing, medical care, and freedom from abuse.[106]

The relevant competing rights of society may include the right to a certain quality of life, which can be attained only when a certain proportion of its individual members have a certain quality of life, or when the population density does not exceed a certain level. Stephen Isaacs, professor of public health, frames the issues of rights and population policies in terms of "balancing the common good, including that of future generations, against that of individuals."[107] He adds, referring to Sen, that "[r]elated questions include how to balance international human rights against national sovereignty and local custom or religion . . . [since] reproductive rights can . . . clash with national sovereignty or local custom and religion."[108] Certainly tribalistic people who want "more of us than them" would object to any restriction on reproduction; religionist people who subscribe to biblical commands such as "Be fruitful and multiply," the sanctity of life principle, or some sort of divine law with which licensing would interfere would also object.

With respect to the second basis for overriding a right to reproduce/parent, that of harm to others, one could consider both the potential injuries *incurred upon* the child as well as the potential injuries *caused by* the child (many argue that criminal behavior is at least in part due to poor parentage and/or poor parenting).

It is this limitation with respect to harm that provides a rebuttal to those who would argue that a policy of licensing parents violates individual rights to privacy: the right to privacy ends where harm to others begins. It also provides a rebuttal to the claim that such a policy fails to recognize people's autonomy. For example, McNulty contends that "[s]tate policing of pregnancy rests on the implicit assumption that women are less than fully moral beings who have no independent judgment."[109] Quite the contrary, a licensing policy may violate autonomy, but it does not fail to recognize such autonomy: it is precisely *because* women, and men, are autonomous and make independent decisions that we should legislate against those decisions that put others at nonconsensual risk of harm. It is precisely *because* women are autonomous that social policies will always be inadequate: despite them, some women will choose (that is, exercise their autonomy) to produce and raise a human being who will experience, and possibly cause, harm.

True, a license restricts rights *before* harm is done (that is, *in order to prevent* harm), rather than restricting rights *because* harm has been done. So to some extent the proposal presumes guilt rather than innocence. However, restricting one's rights need not be perceived as punishment for some as yet undemonstrated wrongdoing. Furthermore, the same preventive rationale is used for issuing other sorts of licenses, such as drivers' licenses. One might suggest, however, that driving is significantly different from parenting. Indeed it is, but in ways that make it *more*, not *less*, justifiable to prelicense parenting. Driving is a momentary activity, usually occurring once or twice a day for less than an hour; parenting, on the other hand, is continuous, twenty-four hours a day for about sixteen years. Driving has the potential mostly to incur physical harm, with derivative psychological injury; parenting has the potential to incur physical *and* psychological harm, separately or together, and the psychological injuries are many (not just the result of physical harm). While driving incurs harm more often on adults than children (if only because the driver must be an adult), parenting incurs harm on children, who are more vulnerable both to the physical and psychological injury. Driving incurs harm only on those who have consented to the risk; parenting incurs harm on those who are not only unable to consent, but also likely not to consent if the risks (of abusive parents, for example) were fully understood.

Another concern with licensing parents deals not with the violation of rights but with the repercussion for other rights. Specifically, if we restrict the right to reproduce, must we also restrict the right *not* to reproduce (that is, restrict the right to contraception and abortion)? How can we demand the reproductive freedom to abort but not also the reproductive freedom to conceive? Both the right to contraception and the right to abortion are anchored in the right to physical integrity, the right to control what happens to one's body. So, if that right is overridden with regard to parenting licenses, why shouldn't it also be overridden with regard to seeking contraception and abortion? One can respond that the difference is the harm principle: the right to bodily integrity can be overridden when it conflicts with the right to be free of harm, as it would, presumably, in the case of reproduction that is unlicensed. If an argument can be made that abortion and contraception similarly cause harm (all harms considered, including that to the woman should she be denied contraception and abortion), then the right to bodily integrity may be overridden in that case as well. The point of licensing parents is not that the state control parenting, but that the state be able to prohibit parenting when it's potentially harmful, and reproduction without a license (that is, without the relevant competencies that minimize the risk of harm) is potentially harmful, just as driving without a license (that is, similarly, without the relevant competencies that minimize the risk of harm) is potentially harmful; just as prohibiting incompetent people from driving does not entail forcing competent people to drive, prohibiting incompetent people from parenting does not entail forcing competent people to parent (that is, preventing access to contraception and abortion).

In any case, one might wonder about this emphasis on rights rather than on the flip side, responsibilities.[110] As Scorsone states, "All of us have . . . the right to make our own choices, but rights necessarily entail responsibilities; where our choices may or do harm others, our choices are, in fact, limited, and we are held accountable. . . ."[111] Laura Shanner, professor of public health and ethics, elaborates: "In reproducing I am not making decisions only for myself, but necessarily for another who not only cannot consent or refuse, but who would not even exist if not for my choices."[112] She goes on to say that "procreation therefore seems better described as an awesome responsibility rather than as a right."[113]

And perhaps it is not even just a *right*, but a *privilege*. Bartholet asks, "Why, for example, should biology be considered as determinative of parental rights as it now is? . . . Why should the privacy of the biologic family be so sacrosanct? . . . The notion that parenting is a privilege and not a right seems appropriate."[114] Chasteen agrees, claiming that "parenthood [is] a privilege extended by society, rather than a right inherent in the individual."[115] On this basis, he goes on to say that "[s]ociety has both the right and the duty to limit population when either its physical existence or its quality of life is threatened."[116]

As a conclusion to this section, whatever the basis for the right to reproduce, there is something very odd or at least very special about a right that involves *creating a person*. As for the right to parent, to have such a significant influence on a vulnerable person, surely it is as odd or special.

LEGISLATION ISSUES

Perhaps an equally strong objection to licensing parents is that it involves legislation or state regulation. To license parents is not just to say that some parenting is immoral; rather, it is to go one step further and say that some parenting should be illegal, presumably, but not necessarily, *because* it is immoral. There are many who would advise not taking that extra step: "Why would we want to resist legal enforcement of every moral conclusion? First, legal action has many costs, costs not necessarily worth paying in particular cases. Second, legal enforcement tends to take the matter out of the realm of debate and treat it as settled. . . . Third, legal enforcement would undermine individual freedom and decision-making capacity."[117] (Purdy goes on to say, however, that "[i]n some cases, the ends envisioned are important enough to warrant putting up with these disadvantages."[118])

One of the objections to licensing is that coercion in *any* case seldom works. At best, a grudging resentful compliance will result, which is certainly unhealthy and probably temporary. However, licensing parents doesn't coerce people to get licensed; it only says that if you want to parent, you must get licensed. This involves no more coercion than licensing drivers and physicians. Furthermore, insofar as the main part of the licensing program would be its educational component, it would be more like certification than license.

"It is certainly true," Scorsone says, "that a caring and nurturing relationship cannot be legislated."[119] She goes on to say that "[s]ociety does, however, quite routinely legislate the minimum fulfillment of the formal responsibilities and obligations of various social roles, including those, such as the parent-child or the marital role, which are best generated and supported by the informal and strong bonds of affect, caring, and commitment."[120]

Nevertheless, it is worth considering the various alternatives to coercion. Education is often advocated as preferable to legislative coercion (see Kitcher and Robertson). One has to wonder, however, whether such advocates aren't guilty of being patronizing: I would guess, for example, that most parents *already know* that cocaine isn't good for a fetus, that beating a baby isn't the best way to make it stop crying, and that screaming insults at an eight-year-old all the time will have some sort of negative effect. Furthermore, perhaps people are generally self-interested: as Chasteen points out, "It is unrealistic to expect individual parents to act in the best interest of society"[121]—they often must be legislated to do so.

Another alternative would be the provision of economic incentives. I don't think giving radios would work (see Isaacs, regarding the 1960s Indian government's incentive for sterilization),[122] but we might consider the policies in China: couples who agree to have only one child receive health and welfare subsidies, priority access to housing, and an additional old-age subsidy, while the child receives priority access to nurseries, schools, clinics, and employment; those couples who have more than one child must pay an "excess child" levy, which can amount to a 5–10 percent deduction from their total income for ten to sixteen years, in addition to all birth, medical, and educational expenses for the extra child, and they are not eligible for additional housing space or promotion.[123] Similar incentives might be offered to licensed parents.

Many claim that such incentives amount to coercion, but philosopher Michael Bayles would disagree: "Attempting to influence a person's decision by providing an incentive to choose one alternative rather than another does not limit a person's liberty to decide, or at least does not do so in a way which is *per se* morally objectionable."[124] Thus, with respect to limiting reproduction, he favors socioeconomic policies, and suggests providing incentives to have fewer children, removing current incentives for having children, and imposing penalties for having children, "if [such policies] will at least prevent a decrease in the quality of life."[125] However, he argues that stronger measures are also justified: "Policies limiting the liberty to procreate are justified to avoid the inability to provide a minimum standard of living."[126] He argues as follows:

> A limited population size or growth rate is a public good. But it is in the interest of an individual couple taken in isolation to have more children than will lead to a limited population size or growth rate. Thus, a public decision on family size is needed. Yet it is not in an individual couple's interest to comply with that decision unless they have assurance others will do so. Thus, a public policy on family size must assure general compliance.[127]

Hartmann's analysis supports Bayles's premise that individual couples will have more, not fewer, children. The factors motivating these couples include survival, security, infant/child mortality, and the subordination of women ("male dominance in the family, patriarchal social mores, the systematic exclusion of women from the development process, and the absence of decent birth control services . . .").[128] She points out, however, that "population control is substituted for social justice, and much needed reforms—such as land redistribution, employment creation, the provision of mass education and health care, and the emancipation of women—are conveniently ignored."[129] Certainly, solutions such as those should be attempted before the heavy hand of licensing. Robert Morison, working in public health, would agree, endorsing social policies rather than legislation to express society's "substantial interest in both the quantity and quality of the children to be born into its midst."[130]

Fenwick suggests a three-part legal test when considering government regulation of reproductive issues: Is a fundamental right involved? Is there a compelling need in the society at large that requires regulation of the rights of the individual to meet the overwhelming need of society? Is the regulation as narrow and limited as possible so that society's need is satisfied with as little infringement on the rights of the individual as there can be?[131] I have already discussed the first and second questions; the third must be kept in mind as the nature of the licensing policies and practices is discussed.

Further to the preceding comments about education as an alternative to coercion, there is concern about the success of the educational component of a parent licensing program. Martha Friendly, of the Child Care Resource and Research Unit of the Canadian Policy Research Network, suggests that "[p]eople inclined to take parenting courses are inclined to be good parents. . . . I've never seen anything to show that parenting courses actually do anything for the others."[132] Chasteen expresses similar doubt: "Those of us who teach are continually disheartened at the difficulties encountered in trying to teach what people do not want to learn."[133] However, these comments merely suggest that the education component of a parent licensing program may not increase competence; nevertheless, its screening component may decrease incompetence.

However, Frisch questions even this: he points out that licensing would not screen out those who abuse children willfully rather than out of ignorance, nor would it reduce abuse due to uncontrollable behavior; he therefore recommends family surveillance instead of licensing. LaFollette responds, however, maintaining that we do have reasonably reliable indicators of both willful abuse and uncontrollable behavior; Pap Mangel supports his claim.

Another objection to parent licensing is the potential for unjustified discrimination, suggested earlier. Certainly this will occur; we will have to vigilant. But the potential for abuse is an insufficient reason to refuse to adopt a policy. The Royal Commission on New Reproductive Technologies offers the following:

> To take the possibility of error as an argument for never acting upon expert advice under any circumstances whatever is an extreme which would paralyze all social action . . . [and] abdicate all active and governmental or custodial forms of human social responsibility.[134]

Again, one can refer to the many comparable licensing policies that are also open to abuse. As LaFollette points out, the harm done by *not* licensing at all is greater than the harm done by mistakenly denying licenses to some.

Another important objection to the proposal of licensing parents is the assumption that the government would be the licensing body. It may be, yes, a public rather than a private body, but it could also be a politically independent body. Criminal courts, child welfare agencies, and schools are all governmental bodies, but they are not, generally speaking, controlled by the political party of the day. Nevertheless, before embarking on a parent-licensing program, we would be wise to read the histories of eugenics; as

Elaine Tyler May, author of *Barren in the Promised Land*, claims, "Efforts to control fertility . . . are powerfully shaped by the political and social ideologies that surround parenthood."[135]

Even as an independent body, the decision-makers would be people—people deciding which other people can and cannot parent. However, the licensing body could be multidisciplinary (including specialists in ethics, social science, medicine, law, and so on), representing a broad range of experiences and perspectives. This would help protect against ideological single-mindedness. Certainly the body should also be multicultural, multiracial, multigendered, multigenerational, and so on. Consultation beyond the body is certainly possible, probably even advisable from time to time, and establishing the licensing criteria should involve wide public input. However, we should remember that the requirements for licensing need not be draconian: one can imagine all sorts of unreasonable and intrusive "shoulds" and "should nots," but the requirements for a license could be as simple as "eighteen years of age, freedom from substance abuse, and no prior convictions for child abuse."

Other objections concern enforcement. Some people may be horrified to think that somehow sexual intercourse would be monitored. But we don't have to do that—we merely have to monitor sexual reproduction.

And what about violators, the people without licenses who nevertheless have children? First, how would we know? Unless we had something like a mandatory contraception vaccination with a state-controlled antidote, we'd have to depend on the cooperation/collusion of educational and medical personnel. If the parents delivered at home without any prior prenatal care from the medical system and if they home-schooled their children, I suppose we'd never know. Second, what do we do? Force an abortion? Force an adoption?

Last, although one must usually pay a certain fee to obtain a license (whatever the other requirements), and although this may well be justified by administrative expenses, it might be advisable to avoid a fee in this case in order to completely avoid the interpretation that people are buying babies or the right to be a parent.

Certainly other changes must occur before parent licensing can be justified, let alone successfully implemented. For example, if we refuse to license people because of their genetic heritage, we'd better have free and easily accessible genetic screening. And if we refuse to license people because they are drug addicts, we'd better have enough treatment programs in place. If adequate prenatal and postnatal care is required for a license, it had also better be available. If we refuse to license people because they are too poor to raise a child, we'd better have employment or economic assistance available. And if we refuse to license people because they don't have the required knowledge, we'd better provide parent training courses. Certainly contraception and abortion must be available to avoid the problem of unlicensed people experiencing unintended pregnancies. Hopefully, a license would seldom have to be denied, and certainly in some instances, we should permit reapplication (if, for instance, the reason for failure is one that can in fact be remedied).

Like Shanner,

> I worry about the political context of controlling [procreative] decisions; the reluctance to judge others or unfairly limit their options is thus generally a good thing. We must exercise this reluctance to judge very carefully, however, and avoid turning such reluctance into an all or nothing acceptance of, and even promotion of, irresponsible procreation. . . . Despite my hesitation to identify people who might be qualified to make such judgments, and the specific grounds upon which such judgments might be made, I reject the claims that such judgments ought never to be made. . . .[136]

And like Battin discussing her proposal of automatic reversible contraception, I'm never sure how the proposal of licensing parents will be received: "as a recommendation, a prediction, a utopian fantasy, a totalitarian plot, a hypothetical conjecture, or a realistic solution."[137] It may be that only the irremediably "unfit" will object; those who are, or who genuinely want to become, competent parents will understand and accept the proposal. Certainly, no licensing arrangement is going to be perfect; the question is whether, all things considered, it will be more right than wrong.

A NOTE ABOUT THE READINGS

Some of the articles in this collection may be older than expected. This is simply because so few people, in any discipline, have written about the subject, especially recently. This silence cannot be attributed to the issue's lack of importance: to the extent that parenting involves more challenges today than in the past, competence, and hence the possibility of licensing, is more, not less, important. Rather, as is pointed out by a few authors, there seems to be a certain taboo about the subject; to even *mention* licensing parents is often to shock or outrage. But as is the case with most taboos on discussion, this one is irrational and dangerous—and hopefully this anthology will help break it.

NOTES

1. Laura Purdy, "Boundaries of Authority: Should Children Be Able to Divorce Their Parents?" in *Having and Raising Children: Unconventional Families,*

Hard Choices, and the Social Good, ed. Uma Narayan and Julia J. Bartkowiak (University Park: Pennsylvania State University Press, 1999), p. 157.

2. Hugh LaFollette, "Licensing Parents," *Philosophy and Public Affairs* 19, no. 2 (1980), rpt. in *Morality and Moral Controversies,* 5th ed., ed. John Arthur (Upper Saddle River, N.J.: Prentice-Hall, 1999), p. 522.

3. Roger McIntire, "Parenthood Training or Mandatory Birth Control: Take Your Choice," *Psychology Today* (October 1973): 133.

4. Jack C. Westman, *Licensing Parents: Can We Prevent Child Abuse and Neglect?* (New York: Plenum Press, 1994), p. 3.

5. Jeffrey Blustein, "Child Rearing and Family Interests," in *Having Children: Philosophical and Legal Reflections on Parenthood,* ed. Onora O'Neill and William Ruddick (New York: Oxford University Press, 1979), p. 119.

6. Katherine Covell and R. Brian Howe, "A Policy of Parent Licensing," *Policy Options* (September 1998): 34.

7. Westman, *Licensing Parents,* p. 25.

8. Covell and Howe, "A Policy of Parent Licensing," p. 34.

9. In a survey of 1,645 parents of children under six years of age, Invest in Kids discovered that "only 34% know that childhood experiences before the age of three will greatly influence a child's academic achievement; only half know that emotional closeness strongly affects a baby's intellect, and only 18% correctly said that an infant as young as six months cannot consciously manipulate its parents" (Celeste McGovern, "Little Do We Know: Parents Are Clueless about Raising Children, A Toronto Group Declares," *British Columbia Report* 10, no. 12 [April 1999]: 54).

10. Philip Montague, "The Myth of Parental Rights," *Social Theory and Practice* 26, no. 1 (spring 2000): 48.

11. Westman, *Licensing Parents,* p. 34.

12. Robert P. Hawkins, "It's Time We Taught the Young How to Be Good Parents (And Don't You Wish We'd Started a Long Time Ago?)," *Psychology Today* (November 1972): 30.

13. Ibid., p. 36.

14. Ibid., p. 37.

15. Edgar R. Chasteen, *The Case for Compulsory Birth Control* (Englewood Cliffs, N.J.: Prentice-Hall, 1971), p. 209.

16. See Carl Wood and Ann Westmore, *Test-Tube Conception* (London: George Allen & Unwin, 1984), pp. 3–4; see also Lynda Beck Fenwick, *Private Choices, Public Consequences* (New York: Penguin Putnam, 1998), p. 25.

17. Elizabeth S. Anderson, "Is Women's Labor a Commodity?" *Philosophy and Public Affairs* 19, no. 1 (winter 1990), rpt. in *Social and Personal Ethics,* 2d ed., ed. William H. Shaw (Belmont, Calif.: Wadsworth Publishing Company, 1996), p. 306.

18. Westman, *Licensing Parents,* pp. 31–32.

19. Richard A. Gardner, "Guidelines for Assessing Parental Preference in Child-Custody Disputes," *Journal of Divorce and Remarriage* 30, no. 1/2 (1999): 3.

20. Ibid.

21. Ibid.

22. Diane A. Trombetta, "Custody Evaluations: A Realistic View," *Family and Conciliation Courts Review* 29, no. 1 (January 1991): 49.

23. Ibid.

24. Ibid., p. 50.

25. Ibid., p. 51.

26. Robert Mnookin, "Foster Care—In Whose Best Interest?" *Harvard Educational Review* 43, no. 4 (November 1973): 599–638, rpt. in *Having Children: Philosophical and Legal Reflections on Parenthood,* ed. Onora O'Neill and William Ruddick (New York: Oxford University Press, 1979), p. 185.

27. Ibid., p. 182.

28. McIntire, "Parenthood Training or Mandatory Birth Control," pp. 133, 143.

29. Glenn McGee, "Cloning, the Family and Adoption," *Science and Engineering Ethics* 5, no. 1 (1999): 53.

30. Ibid., p. 54.

31. Ibid. The same traditionalism seems evident in Robertson's comment that "the question of a person's right to take on the rearing role becomes problematic if the procreator is unmarried or if someone beyond the family unit collaborates in the production of a child" (John A. Robertson, "Procreative Liberty and the Control of Conception, Pregnancy, and Childbirth," *Virginia Law Review* 69, no. 3 [April 1983]: 459).

32. Elizabeth Bartholet, *Family Bonds* (Boston: Houghton Mifflin, 1993), p. 81.

33. Ibid., p. 184.

34. Ibid., p. 69, my emphasis.

35. Joseph Fletcher, *The Ethics of Genetic Control: Ending Reproductive Roulette* (Amherst, N.Y.: Prometheus Books, 1988), p. 36.

36. Marjorie Maguire Schultz, "Reproductive Technology and Intent-Based Parenthood: An Opportunity for Gender Neutrality," *Wisconsin Law Review* (1990): 322–23.

37. Ibid., p. 343. Schultz also notes that "existing status-based parental responsibility has hardly been a model of success, particularly as regards divorced or unwed fathers' obligations to children. A narrow experiment with chosen rather than imposed responsibility could hardly come off worse than the dismal realities of abdication and non-compliance that now confront us" ("Reproductive Technology," p. 398).

38. Margaret P. Battin, "Sex and Consequences: World Population Growth vs. Reproductive Rights," *Philosophic Exchange* 27 (1997): 17.

39. Ibid., p. 30.

40. Leon Kass, "The Wisdom of Repugnance," in *Flesh of My Flesh: The Ethics of Human Cloning,* ed. Gregory E. Pence (Lanham, Md.: Rowman & Littlefield, 1998), p. 16.

41. Gregory S. Kavka, "Upside Risks: Social Consequences of Beneficial Biotechnology," in *Are Genes Us? The Social Consequences of the New Genetics,* ed. Carl F. Cranor (New Brunswick, N.J.: Rutgers University Press, 1994), pp. 172–73.

42. Ibid, p. 173.

43. Ibid.

44. Westman, *Licensing Parents,* p. 222.

45. Philip Kitcher, *The Lives to Come* (New York: Simon & Schuster, 1996), p. 202.

46. See Westman, *Licensing Parents,* chap. 4.

47. Lawrence P. Ulrich, "Reproductive Rights and Genetic Disease," in *Biomedical Ethics and the Law,* ed. James M. Humber and Robert F. Almeda (New York: Plenum Press, 1976), p. 358.

48. Ibid., p. 359.

49. Ruth Macklin, "Parents and Genetic Counselors: Moral Issues," in *Having Children: Philosophical and Legal Reflections on Parenthood*, ed. Onora O'Neill and William Ruddick. (New York: Oxford University Press, 1979), pp. 82–83.

50. Laura M. Purdy, "Loving Future People," in *Reproduction, Ethics, and the Law: Feminist Perspectives*, ed. Joan C. Callahan (Bloomington: Indiana University Press, 1995), p. 307.

51. Robertson argues, however, that it is better "to be created in a lesser form than not at all" (John A. Robertson, *Children of Choice* [Princeton, N.J.: Princeton University Press, 1996], p. 170). Others, however, say that the more accurate decision is between a child in that "lesser form" and one, possibly conceived the next month, not in such a form; as Andre, Fleck, and Tomlinson point out, "many genetic choices . . . amount to choices about which child will be conceived rather than harm to one who is" (Judith Andre, Leonard M. Fleck, and Tom Tomlinson, "On Being Genetically 'Irresponsible,'" *Kennedy Institute of Ethics Journal* 10, no. 2 [2000]: 137–38). Nevertheless, this doesn't change the claim that there is a moral decision involved; it merely changes the nature of the decision. And actually, it doesn't even change the nature of the decision, as genetic attribute choices are still involved; rather, it changes the focus of the decision—Child X with A or Child Y without A, rather than Child X with A or Not-Child X, or Child X with A or Child X without A).

52. Fenwick notes that "30 percent of all pediatric admissions are related to genetic conditions" (*Private Choices*, p. 100, citing *California Cryobank News* 1, no. 2 [spring 1992]: 1).

53. David Resnik supports genetic engineering on the grounds of social justice, arguing that "diseases place morally arbitrary restrictions on opportunity ranges and confer unfair disadvantages" (David B. Resnik, "Genetic Engineering and Social Justice: A Rawlsian Approach," *Social Theory and Practice* 23, no. 3 [fall 1997]: 435).

54. Purdy, "Loving Future People," p. 306.

55. Ibid., p. 305.

56. Kitcher, *The Lives to Come*, p. 214.

57. Leon R. Kass, "Implications of Prenatal Diagnosis for the Human Right to Life," in *Ethical Issues in Human Genetics*, ed. Bruce Hilton et al. (New York: Plenum Press, 1973), rpt. in *Biomedical Ethics and the Law*, ed. James M. Humber and Robert F. Almeda (New York: Plenum Press, 1976), p. 321.

58. Fenwick, *Private Choices*, pp. 100–101.

59. Robertson, *Children of Choice*, p. 152.

60. Ibid., p. 260, n. 4.

61. Kass, "Implications of Prenatal Diagnosis," p. 322.

62. Ibid., p. 323.

63. Thomas L. Beauchamp, "On Justifications for Coercive Genetic Control," in *Biomedical Ethics and the Law*, ed. James M. Humber and Robert F. Almeda (New York: Plenum Press, 1976), pp. 370, 371.

64. Kavka, "Upside Risks," p. 156.

65. Kitcher, *The Lives to Come*, p. 199.

66. Anderson, "Is Women's Labor a Commodity?" p. 308.

67. See Madam Justice Proudfoot, "Judgement Respecting Female Infant

'D.J.,'" in *Contemporary Moral Issues*, ed. Wesley Cragg (Toronto: McGraw-Hill Ryerson, 1992), p. 58; see also Deborah Mathieu, *Preventing Prenatal Harm: Should the State Intervene?* (Dordrecht: Kluwer, 1991), p. 5.

68. See Kathleen Nolan, "Protecting Fetuses from Prenatal Hazards: Whose Crimes? What Punishment?" *Criminal Justice Ethics* 9, no. 1 (1990): 14–15; see also Mathieu, *Preventing Prenatal Harm*, pp. 5–9.

69. Mathieu, *Preventing Prenatal Harm*, p. 7.

70. Lynn M. Paltrow, "When Becoming Pregnant Is a Crime," *Criminal Justice Ethics* 9, no. 1 (winter/spring 1990): 41.

71. See, for example, Bertin's "High Proof Paternity," *Health* 20 (June 1988).

72. Michelle Harrison, "Drug Addiction in Pregnancy: The Interface of Science, Emotion, and Social Policy," *Journal of Substance Abuse Treatment* 8 (1991): 267.

73. Edward W. Keyserlingk, *The Unborn Child's Right to Prenatal Care* (Montreal: Quebec Research Centre of Private and Comparative Law, 1984), p. 80.

74. Molly McNulty, "Pregnancy Police: The Health Policy and Legal Implications of Punishing Pregnant Women for Harm to Their Fetuses," *New York University Review of Law and Social Change* 16 (1988): 278.

75. Bonnie Steinbock, "The Relevance of Illegality," *Hastings Center Report* 22, no. 1 (January–February 1992): 19.

76. Ibid., p. 21.

77. National Bioethics Advisory Commission, "Cloning Human Beings," in *Flesh of My Flesh: The Ethics of Cloning Humans*, ed. Gregory E. Pence (Lanham, Md.: Rowman & Littlefield, 1998), p. 46.

78. Ibid., p. 48.

79. Ibid., p. 51.

80. Royal Commission on New Reproductive Technologies, *Proceed with Care* (Ottawa, Ont.: Minister of Government Services Canada, 1993), p. xxxvii.

81. Ibid., p. 476.

82. Ibid., p. 484.

83. Ibid., p. 481.

84. Ibid., p. 571.

85. Susan Ince, "Inside the Surrogate Industry," in *Test-Tube Women*, ed. Rita Arditti, Renate Duelli Klein, and Shelley Minden (London: Pandora Press, 1984), p. 105.

86. Ibid., p. 106.

87. Robertson, *Children of Choice*, p. 513.

88. Ibid.

89. Lori B. Andrews, *New Conceptions: A Consumer's Guide to the Newest Infertility Treatments* (New York: Ballantine Books, 1985), p. 172.

90. American Medical Association Board of Trustees, "Legal Interventions during Pregnancy," *Journal of the American Medical Association* 264, no. 20 (November 28, 1990): 2667.

91. Royal Commission, *Proceed with Care*, p. 1130.

92. Ibid.

93. Betsy Hartmann, *Reproductive Rights and Wrongs: The Global Politics of Population Control and Contraceptive Choice* (New York: Harper & Row, 1987), p. 21.

94. However, my focus is not on whether certain parenting is immoral but on whether certain parenting should be illegal.

95. With regard to legal rights in the United States, McNulty notes, for the record, that the constitutional "right to privacy includes the right to bodily integrity, the right of parental authority against the state, and the right to make childbearing decisions" ("Pregnancy Police," p. 314), so implementing a policy of licensing parents may require some constitutional change.

96. Interested readers are directed to Ronald Dworkin, *Taking Rights Seriously* (Cambridge: Harvard University Press, 1977); Joel Feinberg, "The Nature and Value of Rights," in *Rights, Justice, and the Boounds of Liberty* (Princeton, N.J.: Princeton University Press, 1980); David Lyons, ed., *Rights* (Belmont, Calif.: Wadsworth, 1979); L. W. Sumner, *The Moral Foundation of Rights* (New York: Oxford University Press, 1987); Judith Jarvis Thomson, *The Realm of Rights* (Cambridge: Harvard University Press, 1990) and *Rights, Restitution, and Risk: Essays in Moral Theory* (Cambridge: Harvard University Press, 1986); and Morton Winston, ed., *The Philosophy of Human Rights* (Belmont, Calif.: Wadsworth, 1989). For short introductions, I recommend the opening piece in Winston's book and Lawrence C. Becker's "Individual Rights," in *And Justice for All: New Introductory Essays in Ethics and Public Policy*, ed. Tom Regan and Donald VanDeVeer (Totowa, N.J.: Rowman & Littlefield, 1982).

97. Purdy, "Loving Future People," p. 302.

98. Laura M. Purdy, *Reproducing Persons: Issues in Feminist Bioethics* (Ithaca, N.Y.: Cornell University Press, 1996), p. 218.

99. Ibid., p. 219.

100. Ibid.

101. Bonnie Steinbock, "Reproductive Rights and Responsibilities," *Hastings Center Report* 24, no. 3 (May–June 1994): 15.

102. Alyce Vrolyk, "A Test Case for Rights: The Cognitively Handicapped Parent," *International Journal of Applied Philosophy* 3 (1987): 29.

103. Onora O'Neill, "Begetting, Bearing, and Rearing," in *Having Children: Philosophical and Legal Reflections on Parenthood*, ed. Onora O'Neill and William Ruddick (New York: Oxford University Press, 1979), p. 25.

104. Ruth F. Chadwick, "Having Children: An Introduction," in *Ethics, Reproduction and Genetic Control*, ed. Ruth F. Chadwick (London: Croom Helm, 1987), p. 31.

105. Bartholet, *Family Bonds*, p. 229.

106. Westman, *Licensing Parents*, p. 155.

107. Stephen L. Isaacs, "Incentives, Population Policy, and Reproductive Rights: Ethical Issues," *Studies in Family Planning* 26, no. 6 (November/December 1995): 364.

108. Ibid.

109. McNulty, "Pregnancy Police," p. 317.

110. Is this emphasis on the *right* to reproduce rather than on the *responsibility* of reproducing a result of our male-dominated attitudes, the male model emphasizing individuals and rights, the female model emphasizing communities and responsibilities? This precious right to have evidence of one's virility (narrowly and mistakenly measured by offspring) (and why is virility important anyway?), the need to have progeny, especially *male* progeny, to carry on one's (man's) name, one's ego . . . it is the right *not* to reproduce that has been historically been sought by *women*.

111. Royal Commission, *Proceed with Care*, p. 1131.

112. Laura Shanner, "The Right to Procreate: When Rights Claims Have Gone Wrong," *McGill Law Journal* 40, no. 4 (August 1995): 860.
113. Ibid.
114. Bartholet, *Family Bonds*, p. 46.
115. Chasteen, *The Case for Compulsory Birth Control*, p. 204.
116. Ibid.
117. Purdy, *Reproducing Persons*, p. 41.
118. Ibid.
119. Royal Commission, *Proceed with Care*, p. 1129.
120. Ibid.
121. Chasteen, *The Case for Compulsory Birth Control*, p. 87.
122. Isaacs, "Incentives," p. 363.
123. Hartmann, *Reproductive Rights and Wrongs*, p. 149.
124. Michael D. Bayles, "Limits to a Right to Procreate," in *Ethics and Population*, ed. Michael D. Bayles (Cambridge, Mass.: Schenkman, 1976), pp. 41–55, rpt. in *Having Children: Philosophical and Legal Reflections on Parenthood*, ed. Onora O'Neill and William Ruddick (New York: Oxford University Press, 1979), p. 14.
125. Ibid., p. 22.
126. Ibid.
127. Ibid., p. 17.
128. Hartmann, *Reproductive Rights and Wrongs*, p. 11.
129. Ibid., p. 31.
130. Robert S. Morison, "Implications of Prenatal Diagnosis for the Quality of, and the Right to, Human Life: Society as a Standard," in *Ethical Issues in Human Genetics*, ed. Bruce Hilton et al. (New York: Plenum Press, 1973), rpt. in *Biomedical Ethics and the Law*, ed. James M. Humber and Robert F. Almeda (New York: Plenum Press, 1976), p. 331.
131. Fenwick, *Private Choices*, pp. 22–23.
132. Quoted by Carla Yu in "Permission to Parent: Child-Rights Theorists Think That Family Licences Would Halt Child Abuse," *Alberta Report* 26, no. 11 (March 8, 1999): 33.
133. Chasteen, *The Case for Compulsory Birth Control*, p. 91.
134. Royal Commission, *Proceed with Care*, pp. 1135–36.
135. Quoted by Anne M. Boylan, "Neither Fruitful Nor Multiplying," review of *Barren in the Promised Land: Childless Americans and the Pursuit of Happiness*, by Elaine Tyler May, *Reviews in American History* 24, no. 2 (1996): 317.
136. Shanner, "The Right to Procreate," p. 865.
137. Battin, "Sex and Consequences," p. 27.

BIBLIOGRAPHY

American Medical Association Board of Trustees. "Legal Interventions during Pregnancy." *Journal of the American Medical Association* 264, no. 20 (November 28, 1990): 2663–70.
Anderson, Elizabeth S. "Is Women's Labor a Commodity?" *Philosophy and Public*

Affairs 19, no. 1 (winter 1990). Reprinted in *Social and Personal Ethics*, 2d ed., edited by William H. Shaw (Belmont, Calif.: Wadsworth Publishing Company, 1996).

Andre, Judith, Leonard M. Fleck, and Tom Tomlinson. "On Being Genetically 'Irresponsible.'" *Kennedy Institute of Ethics Journal* 10, no. 2 (2000): 129–46.

Andrews, Lori B. *New Conceptions: A Consumer's Guide to the Newest Infertility Treatments.* New York: Ballantine Books, 1985.

———. "Surrogate Motherhood: The Challenge for Feminists." In *Surrogate Motherhood: Politics and Privacy*, edited by Larry Gostin. Bloomington: Indiana University Press, 1990.

Bartholet, Elizabeth. *Family Bonds.* Boston: Houghton Mifflin, 1993.

Battin, Margaret P. "Sex and Consequences: World Population Growth vs. Reproductive Rights." *Philosophic Exchange* 27 (1997): 17–31.

Bayles, Michael D. "Limits to a Right to Procreate." In *Ethics and Population*, edited by Michael D. Bayles. Cambridge, Mass.: Schenkman, 1976. Reprinted in *Having Children: Philosophical and Legal Reflections on Parenthood*, edited by Onora O'Neill and William Ruddick (New York: Oxford University Press, 1979).

Beauchamp, Thomas L. "On Justifications for Coercive Genetic Control." In *Biomedical Ethics and the Law*, edited by James M. Humber and Robert F. Almeda. New York: Plenum Press, 1976.

Becker, Lawrence C. "Individual Rights." In *And Justice for All: New Introductory Essays in Ethics and Public Policy*, edited by Tom Regan and Donald VanDeVeer. Totowa, N.J.: Rowman and Allanheld, 1982.

Blustein, Jeffrey. "Child Rearing and Family Interests." In *Having Children: Philosophical and Legal Reflections on Parenthood*, edited by Onora O'Neill and William Ruddick. New York: Oxford University Press, 1979.

Boulding, Kenneth E. "Marketable Licenses for Babies." In *The Meaning of the 20th Century.* New York: Harper & Row, 1964. Reprinted in *Population Evolution and Birth Control: A Collage of Controversial Ideas*, edited by Garrett Hardin (San Francisco: W. H. Freeman, 1964).

Boylan, Anne M. "Neither Fruitful Nor Multiplying," review of *Barren in the Promised Land: Childless Americans and the Pursuit of Happiness*, by Elaine Tyler May, *Reviews in American History* 24, no. 2 (1996): 316–20.

Brock, Dan W. "Funding New Reproductive Technologies: Should They Be Included in Health Insurance Benefit Packages?" In *New Ways of Making Babies: The Case of Egg Donation*, edited by Cynthia B. Cohen. Bloomington: Indiana University Press, 1996.

Campbell, Tom, David Goldberg, Sheila McLean, and Tom Mullen, eds. *Human Rights.* Oxford: Basil Blackwell, 1986.

Chadwick, Ruth F. "Having Children: Introduction." In *Ethics, Reproduction and Genetic Control*, edited by Ruth F. Chadwick. London: Croom Helm, 1987.

Chasteen, Edgar R. *The Case for Compulsory Birth Control.* Englewood Cliffs, N.J.: Prentice-Hall, 1971.

Chavkin, Wendy. "Help, Don't Jail, Addicted Mothers." *New York Times*, July 18, 1989, p. A21.

Cohn, Anne H. "The Prevention of Child Abuse: What Do We Know about What

Works." In *Child Abuse and Neglect: Research and Innovation*, edited by Jerome E. Leavitt. The Hague: Martinus Nijhoff Publishers, 1983.

Covell, Katherine, and R. Brian Howe. "A Policy of Parent Licensing." *Policy Options* (September 1998): 32–35.

Fenwick, Lynda Beck. *Private Choices, Public Consequences*. New York: Penguin Putnam, 1998.

Firestone, Shulamith. *The Dialectic of Sex*. New York: William Morrow, 1970.

Fletcher, Joseph. *The Ethics of Genetic Control: Ending Reproductive Roulette*. Amherst, N.Y.: Prometheus Books, 1988.

Floyd, S. L., and D. Pomerantz. "Is There a Natural Right to Have Children?" In *Morality and Moral Controversies*, edited by J. Arthur. Englewood Cliffs, N.J.: Prentice-Hall, 1981.

Frisch, Lawrence E. "On Licentious Licensing: A Reply to Hugh LaFollette." *Philosophy and Public Affairs* 11, no. 2 (1981): 173–80.

Gardner, Richard A. "Guidelines for Assessing Parental Preference in Child-Custody Disputes." *Journal of Divorce and Remarriage* 30, no. 1/2 (1999): 1–9.

Gewirth, Alan. "The Basis and Content of Human Rights." *Nomos* 23 (1981): 119–47.

Harrison, Michelle. "Drug Addiction in Pregnancy: The Interface of Science, Emotion, and Social Policy." *Journal of Substance Abuse Treatment* 8 (1991): 261–68.

Hart, H. L. A. "Are There Any Natural Rights?" *Philosophical Review* 64 (April 1955): 175–91. Reprinted in *Rights*, edited by David Lyons (Belmont, Calif.: Wadsworth, 1979).

Hartmann, Betsy. *Reproductive Rights and Wrongs: The Global Politics of Population Control and Contraceptive Choice*. New York: Harper & Row, 1987.

Hawkins, Robert P. "It's Time We Taught the Young How to Be Good Parents (And Don't You Wish We'd Started a Long Time Ago?)." *Psychology Today* (November 1972): 28, 30, 36–38.

Hirschhorn, Kurt. "Practical and Ethical Problems in Human Genetics." In *Advances in Human Genetics and Their Impact on Society*, Birth Defects Original Article Series, vol. 8, no. 4, edited by D. Bergsma. White Plains, N.Y.: National Foundation, 1972. Reprinted in *Biomedical Ethics and the Law*, edited by James M. Humber and Robert F. Almeda (New York: Plenum Press, 1976).

Ince, Susan. "Inside the Surrogate Industry." In *Test-Tube Women*, edited by Rita Arditti, Renate Duelli Klein, and Shelley Minden. London: Pandora Press, 1984.

Isaacs, Stephen L. "Incentives, Population Policy, and Reproductive Rights: Ethical Issues." *Studies in Family Planning* 26, no. 6 (November/December 1995): 363–67.

Jones, Gary E., and Clifton Perry. "Can Claims for 'Wrongful Life' Be Justified?" *Journal of Medical Ethics* 9 (1983): 162–64.

Kass, Leon R. "Implications of Prenatal Diagnosis for the Human Right to Life." In *Ethical Issues in Human Genetics*, edited by Bruce Hilton et al. New York: Plenum Press, 1973. Reprinted in *Biomedical Ethics and the Law*, edited by James M. Humber and Robert F. Almeda (New York: Plenum Press, 1976).

———. "The Wisdom of Repugnance." In *Flesh of My Flesh: The Ethics of Human Cloning*, edited by Gregory E. Pence. Lanham, Md.: Rowman & Littlefield, 1998.

Kavka, Gregory S. "Upside Risks: Social Consequences of Beneficial Biotechnology." In *Are Genes Us? The Social Consequences of the New Genetics*, edited by Carl F. Cranor. New Brunswick, N.J.: Rutgers University Press, 1994.

Keyserlingk, Edward W. *The Unborn Child's Right to Prenatal Care*. Montreal, Que.: Quebec Research Centre of Private and Comparative Law, 1984.

Kitcher, Philip. *The Lives to Come*. New York: Simon & Schuster, 1996.

Kluge, Eike-Henner W. "Sterilisation of the Mentally Severely Handicapped: A Violation of the Right to Have Children?" *Ethical Problems in Reproductive Medicine* 1, no. 1 (1989): 12–15. Reprinted in *Readings in Biomedical Ethics: A Canadian Focus*, 2d ed., edited by Eike-Henner W. Kluge (Scarborough, Ont.: Prentice Hall Canada, 1999).

Krimmel, Herbert T. "The Case Against Surrogate Parenting." *Hastings Center Report* 13 (October 1983): 35–39.

LaFollette, Hugh. "A Reply to Frisch." *Philosophy and Public Affairs* 11, no. 2 (1981): 181–83.

———. "Licensing Parents." *Philosophy and Public Affairs* 9, no. 2 (1980): 182–97. Reprinted in *Morality and Moral Controversies*, 5th ed., edited by John Arthur (Upper Saddle River, N.J.: Prentice-Hall, 1999).

Lee, Robert, and Derek Morgan. "A Lesser Sacrifice? Sterilization and Mentally Handicapped Women." In *Birthrights: Law and Ethics at the Beginnings of Life*, edited by Robert Lee and Derek Morgan. London: Routledge, 1989.

Macklin, Ruth. "Parents and Genetic Counselors: Moral Issues." In *Having Children: Philosophical and Legal Reflections on Parenthood*, edited by Onora O'Neill and William Ruddick. New York: Oxford University Press, 1979. Originally appeared as "Moral Issues in Human Genetics: Counseling or Control?" *Dialogue* 14, no. 3 (1977): 375–96.

Malm, Heidi. "Paid Surrogacy: Arguments and Responses." *Public Affairs Quarterly* 3, no. 2 (April 1989). Reprinted in *Social and Personal Ethics*, 2d ed., edited by William H. Shaw. Belmont, Calif.: Wadsworth, 1996.

Mathieu, Deborah. *Preventing Prenatal Harm: Should the State Intervene?* Dordrecht: Kluwer, 1991.

McCloskey, H. J. "Human Needs, Rights and Political Values." *American Philosophical Quarterly* 13, no. 1 (January 1976): 1–11.

McGee, Glenn. "Cloning, the Family and Adoption." *Science and Engineering Ethics* 5, no. 1 (1999): 47–54.

McGovern, Celeste. "Little Do We Know: Parents Are Clueless about Raising Children, A Toronto Group Declares." *British Columbia Report* 10, no. 12 (April 1999): 54–55.

McIntire, Roger W. "Parenthood Training or Mandatory Birth Control: Take Your Choice." *Psychology Today* (October 1973): 34, 36, 38, 39, 132, 133, 143.

McNulty, Molly. "Pregnancy Police: The Health Policy and Legal Implications of Punishing Pregnant Women for Harm to Their Fetuses." *New York University Review of Law and Social Change* 16 (1988): 277–319.

Mnookin, Robert H. "Foster Care—In Whose Best Interest?" *Harvard Educational Review* 43, no. 4 (November 1973). Reprinted in *Having Children: Philosophical and Legal Reflections on Parenthood*, edited by Onora O'Neill and William Ruddick (New York: Oxford University Press, 1979).

Montague, Phillip. "The Myth of Parental Rights." *Social Theory and Practice* 26, no. 1 (spring 2000): 47–68.

Morison, Robert S. "Implications of Prenatal Diagnosis for the Quality of, and the Right to, Human Life: Society as a Standard." In *Ethical Issues in Human Genetics*, edited by Bruce Hilton et al. New York: Plenum Press, 1973. Reprinted in *Biomedical Ethics and the Law*, edited by James M. Humber and Robert F. Almeda (New York: Plenum Press, 1976).

National Bioethics Advisory Commission. "Cloning Human Beings." In *Flesh of My Flesh: The Ethics of Cloning Humans*, edited by Gregory E. Pence. Lanham, Md.: Rowman & Littlefield, 1998.

Nolan, Kathleen. "Protecting Fetuses from Prenatal Hazards: Whose Crimes? What Punishment?" *Criminal Justice Ethics* 9, no. 1 (1990): 13–23.

O'Donovan, Oliver. *Begotten or Made?* Oxford: Clarendon Press, 1984.

O'Neill, Onora. "Begetting, Bearing, and Rearing." In *Having Children: Philosophical and Legal Reflections on Parenthood*, edited by Onora O'Neill and William Ruddick. New York: Oxford University Press, 1979.

Overall, Christine. *Human Reproduction: Principles, Practices, Policies.* Toronto, Ont.: Oxford University Press, 1993.

Paltrow, Lynn M. "When Becoming Pregnant Is a Crime." *Criminal Justice Ethics* 9, no. 1 (winter/spring 1990): 41–47.

Pap Mangel, Claudia. "Licensing Parents: How Feasible?" *Family Law Quarterly* 22, no. 1 (spring 1988): 17–39.

Parfit, Derek. *Reasons and Persons.* New York: Oxford University Press, 1986.

Paul, Diane B. "Eugenic Anxieties, Social Realities, and Political Choices." *Social Research* 59, no. 3 (fall 1992): 663–84.

Proudfoot, Madam Justice. "Judgement Respecting Female Infant 'D.J.'" In *Contemporary Moral Issues*, edited by Wesley Cragg. Toronto, Ont.: McGraw-Hill Ryerson, 1992.

Purdy, Laura M. "Boundaries of Authority: Should Children Be Able to Divorce Their Parents?" In *Having and Raising Children: Unconventional Families, Hard Choices, and the Social Good*, edited by Uma Narayan and Julia J. Bartkowiak. University Park: Pennsylvania State University Press, 1999.

———. "Loving Future People." In *Reproduction, Ethics, and the Law: Feminist Perspectives*, edited by Joan C. Callahan. Bloomington: Indiana University Press, 1995.

———. *Reproducing Persons: Issues in Feminist Bioethics.* Ithaca, N.Y.: Cornell University Press, 1996.

Resnik, David. "Debunking the Slippery Slope Argument against Human Germ-Line Gene Therapy." *Journal of Medicine and Philosophy* 19 (1994): 23–40.

———. "Genetic Engineering and Social Justice: A Rawlsian Approach." *Social Theory and Practice* 23, no. 3 (fall 1997): 427–48.

Robertson, John A. *Children of Choice.* Princeton, N.J.: Princeton University Press, 1996.

———. "Procreative Liberty and the Control of Conception, Pregnancy, and Childbirth." *Virginia Law Review* 69, no. 3 (April 1983): 405–64.

———. "Surrogate Mothers: Not So Novel After All." *Hastings Center Report* 13 (October 1983): 28–34.

———. "Wrongful Life, Federalism, and Procreative Liberty: A Critique of the NBAC Cloning Report." In *Flesh of My Flesh: The Ethics of Cloning Humans*, edited by Gregory E. Pence. Lanham, Md.: Rowman & Littlefield, 1998.

Rodgers, Sanda. "Juridical Interference with Gestation and Birth." In *Legal and Ethical Issues in New Reproductive Technologies: Pregnancy and Parenthood*. Ottawa, Ont.: Royal Commission on New Reproductive Technologies, 1993.

Royal Commission on New Reproductive Technologies. *Proceed with Care*. Ottawa, Ont.: Minister of Government Services Canada, 1993.

Russell, Bertrand. *Marriage and Morals*. London: Allen and Unwin, 1929.

Schedler, George. "Does Society Have the Right to Force Pregnant Drug Addicts to Abort Their Fetuses?" *Social Theory and Practice* 17, no. 3 (fall 1991): 369–84.

Schultz, Marjorie Maguire. "Reproductive Technology and Intent-Based Parenthood: An Opportunity for Gender Neutrality." *Wisconsin Law Review* (1990): 297–398.

Sen, Amartya. "Freedom and Needs." *New Republic* 10, no. 17 (January 1994): 31–38.

Shanner, Laura. "The Right to Procreate: When Rights Claims Have Gone Wrong." *McGill Law Journal* 40, no. 4 (August 1995): 823–74.

Sherwin, Susan. "Feminist Ethics and *in Vitro* Fertilization." *Canadian Journal of Philosophy* suppl. vol. 13 (1987): 276–84.

Singer, Peter. "Creating Embryos." In *Biomedical Ethics*, 3d ed., edited by Thomas A. Mappes and Jane S. Zembaty. New York: McGraw-Hill, 1991.

———. "Making Laws on Making Babies." *Hastings Center Report* 15 (August 1985): 5–6.

Singer, Peter, and Deane Wells. *The Reproductive Revolution: New Ways of Making Babies*. Oxford: Oxford University Press, 1984.

Steinbock, Bonnie. "The Relevance of Illegality." *Hastings Center Report* 22, no. 1 (January–February 1992): 19–22.

———. "Reproductive Rights and Responsibilities." *Hastings Center Report* 24, no. 3 (May–June 1994): 15–16.

Stich, Stephen P. "Genetic Engineering: How Should Science Be Controlled?" In *And Justice for All: New Introductory Essays in Ethics and Public Policy*, edited by Tom Regan and Donald Van De Veer. Totowa, N.J.: Rowman and Allanheld, 1982.

Trombetta, Diane A. "Custody Evaluations: A Realistic View." *Family and Conciliation Courts Review* 29, no. 1 (January 1991): 45–55.

Ulrich, Lawrence P. "Reproductive Rights and Genetic Disease." In *Biomedical Ethics and the Law*, edited by James M. Humber and Robert F. Almeda. New York: Plenum Press, 1976.

Uniacke, Suzanne. "*In Vitro* Fertilization and the Right to Reproduce." *Bioethics* 1. no. 3 (1987): 241–54.

Verhey, Allen D. "Cloning: Revisiting an Old Debate." *Kennedy Institute of Ethics Journal* 4, no. 3 (1994): 227–34.

Vrolyk, Alyce. "A Test Case for Rights: The Cognitively Handicapped Parent." *International Journal of Applied Philosophy* 3 (1987): 29–36.

Westman, Jack C. *Licensing Parents: Can We Prevent Child Abuse and Neglect?* New York: Plenum Press, 1994.

Wood, Carl, and Ann Westmore. *Test-Tube Conception*. London: George Allen & Unwin, 1984.

I. PARENTING

*I*n this first part, the focus is on parenting (as opposed to parentage)—that is, the nurturing of children into adulthood.

1. Proposals

Each of the following authors proposes that we license parents, providing, together, an excellent discussion of rationales, precedents, and models, as well as objections and replies. They speak from the various disciplines of philosophy (LaFollette), psychiatry (Westman), psychology (Covell and McIntire), and political science (Howe).

LaFollette, in his classic "Licensing Parents," argues not only that is a licensing program a good idea in theory, but also that it can work in practice. Like driving, LaFollette argues, parenting is potentially harmful to others, good parenting requires a certain competence, and we have a moderately reliable procedure for determining such competence. Therefore, LaFollette claims, we should license parents just as we license drivers. Anticipating the main theoretical objection (see section III.1 of this book), LaFollette says that while it may be true that people have a right to have children, surely that right is not absolute—that is, surely it can be justifiably limited when, otherwise, innocent people will be harmed. Thus, LaFollette suggests, we can justifiably limit the right to parent to those people who demonstrate competence to parent. But can we determine such competence—efficiently and fairly? Yes, LaFollette responds, referring to the precedent of adoption and specifically addressing concerns such as abuse and enforcement of a parent licensing program.

Emphasizing the social consequences of good and bad parenting, and the justifiable societal interest in parenting competence that follows, Westman, like LaFollette, advocates limiting people's right to parent in order to prevent harm by licensing on the basis of competence. Westman extends LaFollette's discussion of precedents to include the licensing of marriage, day cares, and various professions, as well as other instances of state regulation. He also discusses in more detail how a licensing program might work in practice, addressing timing, criteria, administration, and testing.

Whereas Westman refers mostly to the legal and sociopolitical context of the United States, Covell and Howe write from the context of another country, Canada, and they refer to the obligations incurred by United Nations membership. Nevertheless, their arguments are the same: because of the individual and social costs of incompetent parenting, a license to parent should be mandatory. Further, like Westman, Covell and Howe address the contextual elements, in addition to the individual personal attributes and skills, that enable good parenting. However, unlike LaFollette and Westman, Covell and Howe emphasize that current policies and programs are largely reactive (addressing the harm *after* it has occurred); a parent licensing program would be, in contrast, proactive.

McIntire's article takes us back to LaFollette's focus on the individual, but his list of twelve topics with which people who parent should be familiar reveals attention to the practical more than to the theoretical. Nevertheless, like LaFollette and the others, McIntire recognizes and discusses theoretical objections, addressing, like Covell and Howe, the rights of the child as well as the rights of adults (his "Supermarket Scenario" is particularly memorable). Also, like the other authors presented in this section, McIntire discusses other licensing programs as precedents that provide rationales for licensing parents. Though written thirty years ago, McIntire's article continues to be not only important, but also relevant. In a deleted section of his original article, McIntire refers to "several scientists . . . currently conducting research on a contraceptive by which a man's sperm could be rendered inoperative" (36)—which apparently has *still* not made it to market (though, of course, Viagra has); it is sobering to see McIntire's expectations still unfulfilled. Of greater interest, perhaps, is his futuristic story, "Lock," set seven years into the future at 1980—it remains as visionary, and as obliquely cautionary, today, and his article is well worth the read for that alone.

LICENSING PARENTS

Hugh LaFollette

*I*n this essay I shall argue that the state should require all parents to be licensed. My main goal is to demonstrate that the licensing of parents is theoretically desirable, though I shall also argue that a workable and just licensing program actually could be established.

My strategy is simple. After developing the basic rationale for the licensing of parents, I shall consider several objections to the proposal and argue that these objections fail to undermine it. I shall then isolate some striking similarities between this licensing program and our present policies on the adoption of children. If we retain these adoption policies—as we surely should—then, I argue, a general licensing program should also be established. Finally, I shall briefly suggest that the reason many people object to licensing is that they think parents, particularly biological parents, own or have natural sovereignty over their children.

REGULATING POTENTIALLY HARMFUL ACTIVITIES

Our society normally regulates a certain range of activities; it is illegal to perform these activities unless one has received prior permission to do so. We require automobile operators to have licenses. We forbid people from practicing medicine, law, pharmacy, or psychiatry unless they have satisfied certain licensing requirements.

Society's decision to regulate just these activities is not ad hoc. The decision to restrict admission to certain vocations and to forbid some people from driving is based on an eminently plausible, though not often explicitly formulated, rationale.[1] We require drivers to be licensed because driving an auto is an activity which is potentially harmful to others, safe performance of the activity requires a certain competence, and we have a moderately reliable procedure for determining that competence. The potential harm is obvious: incompetent drivers can and do maim and kill people. The best way we have of limiting this harm without sacrificing the benefits of automobile travel is to require that all drivers demonstrate at least minimal competence. We likewise license doctors, lawyers, and psychologists because they perform activities which can harm others. Obviously they must be proficient if they are to perform these activities properly, and we have moderately reliable procedures for determining proficiency. Imagine a world in which everyone could legally drive a car, in which everyone could legally perform surgery, prescribe medications, dispense drugs, or offer legal advice. Such a world would hardly be desirable.

Consequently, any activity that is potentially harmful to others and requires certain demonstrated competence for its safe performance, is subject to regulation—that is, it is theoretically desirable that we regulate it. If we also have a reliable procedure for determining whether someone has the requisite competence, then the action is not only subject to regulation but ought, all things considered, to be regulated.

It is particularly significant that we license these hazardous activities, even though denying a license to someone can severely inconvenience and even harm that person. Furthermore, available competency tests are not 100 percent accurate. Denying someone a driver's license in our society, for example, would inconvenience that person acutely. In effect that person would be prohibited from working, shopping, or visiting in places reachable only by car. Similarly, people denied vocational licenses are inconvenienced, even devastated. We have all heard of individuals who had the "lifelong dream" of becoming physicians or lawyers, yet were denied that dream. However, the realization that some people are disappointed or inconvenienced does not diminish our conviction that we must regulate occupations or activities that are potentially dangerous to others. Innocent people must be protected even if it means that others cannot pursue activities they deem highly desirable.

Furthermore, we maintain licensing procedures even though our competency tests are sometimes inaccurate. Some people competent to perform the licensed activity (for example, driving a car) will be unable to demonstrate competence (they freeze up on the driver's test). Others may be incompetent, yet pass the test (they are lucky or certain aspects of competence—for example, the sense of responsibility—are not tested). We recognize clearly—or should recognize clearly—that no test will pick out all and only competent drivers, physicians, lawyers, and so on. Mistakes are inevitable. This does not mean we should forget that innocent people may be harmed by faulty regulatory procedures. In fact, if the procedures are sufficiently faulty, we should cease regulating that activity entirely until more reliable tests are available. I only want to emphasize here that tests need not be perfect. Where moderately reliable tests are available, licensing procedures should be used to protect innocent people from incompetents.[2]

These general criteria for regulatory licensing can certainly be applied to parents. First, parenting is an activity potentially very harmful to children. The potential for harm is apparent: each year more than half a million children are physically abused or neglected by their parents.[3] Many millions more are psychologically abused or neglected—not given love, respect, or a sense of self-worth. The results of this maltreatment are obvious. Abused children bear the physical and psychological scars of maltreatment throughout their lives. Far too often they turn to crime.[4] They are far more likely than others to abuse their own children.[5] Even if these maltreated children never harm anyone, they will probably never be well-adjusted, happy adults. Therefore, parenting clearly satisfies the first criterion of activities subject to regulation.

The second criterion is also incontestably satisfied. A parent must be competent if he is to avoid harming his children; even greater competence is required if he is to do the "job" well. But not everyone has this minimal competence. Many people lack the knowledge needed to rear children adequately. Many others lack the requisite energy, temperament, or stability. Therefore, child-rearing manifestly satisfies both criteria of activities subject to regulation. In fact, I dare say that parenting is a paradigm of such activities since the potential for harm is so great (both in the extent of harm any one person can suffer and in the number of people potentially harmed) and the need for competence is so evident. Consequently, there is good reason to believe that all parents should be licensed. The only ways to avoid this conclusion are to deny the need for licensing *any* potentially harmful activity; to deny that I have identified the standard criteria of activities which should be regulated; to deny that parenting satisfies the standard criteria; to show that even though parenting satisfies the standard criteria there are special reasons why licensing parents is not theoretically desirable; or to show that there is no reliable and just procedure for implementing this program.

While developing my argument for licensing I have already identified the standard criteria for activities that should be regulated, and I have shown that they can properly be applied to parenting. One could deny the legitimacy of regulation by licensing, but in doing so one would condemn not only the regulation of parenting, but also the regulation of drivers, physicians, druggists, and doctors. Furthermore, regulation of hazardous activities appears to be a fundamental task of any stable society.

Thus only two objections remain. In the next section I shall see if there are any special reasons why licensing parents is not theoretically desirable. Then, in the following section, I shall examine several practical objections designed to demonstrate that even if licensing were theoretically desirable, it could not be justly implemented.

Theoretical Objections to Licensing

Licensing is unacceptable, someone might say, since people have a right to have children, just as they have rights to free speech and free religious expression. They do not need a license to speak freely or to worship as they wish. Why? Because they have a right to engage in these activities. Similarly, since people have a right to have children, any attempt to license parents would be unjust.

This is an important objection since many people find it plausible, if not self-evident. However, it is not as convincing as it appears. The specific rights appealed to in this analogy are not without limitations. Both slander and human sacrifice are prohibited by law; both could result from the unrestricted exercise of freedom of speech and freedom of religion. Thus, even if people have these rights, they may sometimes be limited in order to protect innocent people. Consequently, even if people had a right to have children, that right might also be limited in order to protect innocent people, in this case children. Second, the phrase "right to have children" is ambiguous; hence, it is important to isolate its most plausible meaning in this context. Two possible interpretations are not credible and can be dismissed summarily. It is implausible to claim either that infertile people have rights to be *given* children or that people have rights to intentionally create children biologically without incurring any subsequent responsibility to them.

A third interpretation, however, is more plausible, particularly when coupled with observations about the degree of intrusion into one's life that the licensing scheme represents. On this interpretation people have a right to rear children if they make good-faith efforts to rear procreated children the best way they see fit. One might defend this claim on the ground that licensing would require too much intrusion into the lives of sincere applicants.

Undoubtedly one should be wary of unnecessary governmental intervention into individuals' lives. In this case, though, the intrusion would not often be substantial, and when it is, it would be warranted. Those granted licenses would face merely minor intervention; only those denied licenses would encounter marked intrusion. This encroachment, however, is a necessary side-effect of licensing parents—just as it is for automobile and vocational licensing. In addition, as I shall argue in more detail later, the degree of intrusion arising from a general licensing program would be no more than, and probably less than, the present (and presumably justifiable) encroachment into the lives of people who apply to adopt children. Furthermore, since some people hold unacceptable views about what is best for children (they think children should be abused regularly), people do not automatically have rights to rear children just because they will rear them in a way they deem appropriate.[6]

Consequently, we come to a somewhat weaker interpretation of this right claim: a person has a right to rear children if he meets certain minimal standards of child-rearing. Parents must not abuse or neglect their children and must also provide for the basic needs of the children. This claim of right is certainly more credible than the previously canvassed alternatives, though some people might still reject this claim in situations where exercise of the right would lead to negative consequences, for example, to overpopulation. More to the point, though, this conditional right is compatible with licensing. On this interpretation one has a right to have children only if one is not going to abuse or neglect them. Of course the very purpose if licensing is just to determine whether people *are* going to abuse or neglect their children. If the determination is made that someone will maltreat children, then that person is subject to the limitations of the right to have children and can legitimately be denied a parenting license.

In fact, this conditional way of formulating the right to have children provides a model for formulating all alleged rights to engage in hazardous activities. Consider, for example, the right to drive a car. People do not have an unconditional right to drive, although they do have a right to drive if they are competent. Similarly, people do not have an unconditional right to practice medicine; they have a right only if they are demonstrably competent. Hence, denying a driver's or physician's license to someone who has not demonstrated the requisite competence does not deny that person's rights. Likewise, on this model, denying a parenting license to someone who is not competent does not violate that person's rights.

Of course someone might object that the right is conditional on actually being a person who will abuse or neglect children, whereas my proposal only picks out those we can reasonably predict will abuse children. Hence, this conditional right *would* be incompatible with licensing.

There are two ways to interpret this objection and it is important to distinguish these divergent formulations. First, the objection could be a way of questioning our ability to predict reasonably and accurately whether people would maltreat their own children. This is an important practical objection, but I will defer discussion of it until the next section. Second, this objection could be a way of expressing doubt about the moral propriety of the prior restraint licensing requires. A parental licensing program would deny licenses to applicants judged to be incompetent even though they had never maltreated any children. This practice would be in tension with our normal skepticism about the propriety of prior restraint.

Despite this healthy skepticism, we do sometimes use prior restraint. In extreme circumstances we may hospitalize or imprison people judged insane, even though they are not legally guilty of any crime, simply because we predict they are likely to harm others. More typically, though, prior restraint is used only if the restriction is not terribly onerous and the restricted activity is one which could lead easily to serious harm. Most types of licensing (for example, those for doctors, drivers, and druggists) fall into this latter category. They require prior restraint to prevent serious harm, and generally the restraint is minor—though it is important to remember that some individuals will find it oppressive. The same is true of parental licensing. The purpose of licensing is to prevent serious harm to children. Moreover, the prior restraint required by licensing would not be terribly onerous for many people. Certainly the restraint would be far less extensive than the presumably justifiable prior restraint of, say, insane criminals. Criminals preventively detained and mentally ill people forcibly hospitalized are denied most basic liberties, while those denied parental licenses would be denied only that one specific opportunity. They could still vote, work for political candidates, speak on controversial topics, and so on. Doubtless some individuals would find the restraint onerous. But when compared to other types of restraint currently practiced, and when judged in light of the severity of harm maltreated children suffer, the restraint appears *relatively* minor.

Furthermore, we could make certain, as we do with most licensing programs, that individuals denied licenses are given the opportunity to reapply easily and repeatedly for a license. Thus, many people correctly denied licenses (because they are incompetent) would choose (perhaps it would be provided) to take counseling or therapy to improve their chances of passing the next test. On the other hand, most of those mistakenly denied licenses would probably be able to demonstrate in a later test that they would be competent parents.

Consequently, even though one needs to be wary of prior restraint, if the potential for harm is great and the restraint is minor relative to the harm we are trying to prevent—as it would be with parental licensing—then such restraint is justified. This objection, like all the theoretical objections reviewed, has failed.

PRACTICAL OBJECTIONS TO LICENSING

I shall now consider five practical objections to licensing. Each objection focuses on the problems or difficulties of implementing this proposal. According to these objections, licensing is (or may be) theoretically desirable; nevertheless, it cannot be efficiently and justly implemented.

The first objection is that there may not be, or we may not be able to discover, adequate criteria of "a good parent." We simply do not have the knowledge, and it is unlikely that we could ever obtain the knowledge, that would enable us to distinguish adequate from inadequate parents.

Clearly there is some force to this objection. It is highly improbable that we can formulate criteria that would distinguish precisely between good and less-than-good parents. There is too much we do not know about child development and adult psychology. My proposal, however, does not demand that we make these fine distinctions. It does not demand that we license only the best parents; rather it is designed to exclude only the very bad ones.[7] This is not just a semantic difference, but a substantive one. Although we do not have infallible criteria for picking out good parents, we undoubtedly can identify bad ones—those who will abuse or neglect their children. Even though we could have a lively debate about the range of freedom a child should be given or the appropriateness of corporal punishment, we do not wonder if a parent who severely beats or neglects a child is adequate. We know that person isn't. Consequently, we do have reliable and useable criteria for determining who is a bad parent; we have the criteria necessary to make a licensing program work.

The second practical objection to licensing is that there is no reliable way to predict who will maltreat their children. Without an accurate predictive test, licensing would be not only unjust, but also a waste of time. Now I recognize that as a philosopher (and not a psychologist, sociologist, or social worker), I am on shaky ground if I make sweeping claims about the present or future abilities of professionals to produce such predictive tests. Nevertheless, there are some relevant observations I can offer.

Initially, we need to be certain that the demands on predictive tests are not unreasonable. For example, it would be improper to require that tests be 100 percent accurate. Procedures for licensing drivers, physicians, lawyers, druggists, etc. plainly are not 100 percent (or anywhere near 100 percent) accurate. Presumably we recognize these deficiencies yet embrace the procedures anyway. Consequently, it would be imprudent to demand considerably more exacting standards for the tests used in licensing parents.

In addition, from what I can piece together, the practical possibilities for constructing a reliable predictive test are not all that gloomy. Since my proposal does not require that we make fine-line distinctions between good and less-than-good parents, but rather that we weed out those who are potentially very bad, we can use existing tests that claim to isolate relevant predictive characteristics—whether a person is violence-prone, easily frustrated, or unduly self-centered. In fact, researchers at Nashville General Hospital have developed a brief interview questionnaire which seems to have significant predictive value. Based on their data, the researchers identified 20 percent of the interviewees as a "risk group"—those having great potential for serious problems. After one year they found "the incidence of major breakdown in parent-child interaction in the risk group was approximately four to five times as great as in the low-risk group."[8] We also know that parents who maltreat children often have certain identifiable experiences, for example, most of them were themselves maltreated as children. Consequently, if we combined our information about these parents with certain psychological test results, we would probably be able to predict with reasonable accuracy which people will maltreat their children.

However, my point is not to argue about the precise reliability of present tests. I cannot say emphatically that we now have accurate predictive tests. Nevertheless, even if such tests are not available, we could undoubtedly develop them. For example, we could begin a longitudinal study in which all potential parents would be required to take a specified battery of tests. Then these parents could be "followed" to discover which ones abused or neglected their children. By correlating test scores with information on maltreatment, a usable, accurate test could be fashioned. Therefore, I do not think that the present unavailability of such tests (if they are unavailable) would count against the legitimacy of licensing parents.

The third practical objection is that even if a reliable test for ascertaining who would be an acceptable parent were available, administrators would unintentionally misuse that test. These unintentional mistakes would clearly harm innocent individuals. Therefore, so the argument goes, this proposal ought to be scrapped. This objection can be dispensed with fairly easily unless one assumes there is some special reason to believe that more mistakes will be made in administering parenting licenses than in other regulatory activities. No matter how reliable our proceedings are, there will always be mistakes. We may license a physician who, through incompetence, would cause the death of a patient; or we may mistakenly deny a physician's license to some one who would be competent. But the fact that mistakes are made does not and should not lead us to abandon attempts to determine competence. The harm done in these cases could be far worse than the harm of mistakenly denying a person a parenting license. As far as I can tell, there is no reason to believe that more mistakes will be made here than elsewhere.

The fourth proposed practical objection claims that any testing procedure will be intentionally abused. People administering the process will disqualify people they dislike, or people who espouse views they dislike, from rearing children.

The response to this objection is parallel to the response to the previous objection, namely, that there is no reason to believe that the licensing of parents is more likely to be abused than driver's license tests or other regulatory procedures. In addition, individuals can be protected from prejudicial treatment by pursuing appeals available to them. Since the licensing test can be taken on numerous occasions, the likelihood of the applicant's working with different administrative personnel increases and therefore the likelihood decreases that intentional abuse could ultimately stop a qualified person from rearing children. Consequently, since the probability of such abuse is not more than, and may even be less than, the intentional abuse of judicial and other regulatory authority, this objection does not give us any reason to reject the licensing of parents.

The fifth objection is that we could never adequately, reasonably, and fairly enforce such a program. That is, even if we could establish a reasonable and fair way of determining which people would be inadequate parents, it would be difficult, if not impossible, to enforce the program. How would one deal with violators and what could we do with babies so conceived? There are difficult problems here, no doubt, but they are not insurmountable. We might not punish parents at all—we might just remove the children and put them up for adoption. However, even if we are presently uncertain about the precise way to establish a just and effective form of enforcement, I do not see why this should undermine my licensing proposal. If it is important enough to protect children from being maltreated by parents, then surely a reasonable enforcement procedure can be secured. At least we should assume one can be unless someone shows that it cannot.

AN ANALOGY WITH ADOPTION

So far I have argued that parents should be licensed. Undoubtedly many readers find this claim extremely radical. It is revealing to notice, however, that this program is not as radical as it seems. Our moral and legal systems already recognize that not everyone is capable of rearing children well. In fact, well-entrenched laws require adoptive parents to be investigated—in much the same ways and for much the same reasons as in the general licensing program advocated here. For example, we do not allow just anyone to adopt a child; nor do we let someone adopt without first estimating the likelihood of the person's being a good parent. In fact, the adoptive process is far more rigorous than the general licensing procedures I envision. Prior to adoption the candidates must first formally apply to adopt a child. The applicants are then subjected to an exacting home study to determine whether they really want to have children and whether they are capable of caring for and rearing them adequately. No one is allowed to adopt a child until the administrators can reasonably predict that the person will be an adequate parent. The results of these procedures are impressive. Despite the trauma children often face before they are finally adopted, they are five times less likely to be abused than children reared by their biological parents.[9]

Nevertheless we recognize, or should recognize, that these demanding procedures exclude some people who would be adequate parents. The selection criteria may be inadequate; the testing procedures may be somewhat unreliable. We may make mistakes. Probably there is some intentional abuse of the system. Adoption procedures intrude directly in the applicants' lives. Yet we continue the present adoption policies because we think it better to mistakenly deny some people the opportunity to adopt than to let just anyone adopt.

Once these features of our adoption policies are clearly identified, it becomes quite apparent that there are striking parallels between the general licensing program I have advocated and our present adoption system. Both programs have the same aim—protecting children. Both have the same drawbacks and are subject to the same abuses. The only obvious dissimilarity is that the adoption requirements are *more* rigorous than those proposed for the general licensing program. Consequently, if we think it is so important to protect adopted children, even though people who want to adopt are less likely than biological parents to maltreat their children, then we should likewise afford the same protection to children reared by their biological parents.

I suspect, though, that many people will think the cases are not analogous. The cases are relevantly different, someone might retort, because biological parents have a natural affection for their children and the strength of this affection makes it unlikely that parents would maltreat their biologically produced children.

Even if it were generally true that parents have special natural affections for their biological offspring, that does not mean that all parents have enough affection to keep them from maltreating their children. This should be apparent given the number of children abused each year by their biological parents. Therefore, even if there is generally such a bond, that does not explain why we should not have licensing procedures to protect children of parents who do not have a sufficiently strong bond. Consequently, if we continue our practice of regulating the adoption of children, and certainly we should, we are rationally compelled to establish a licensing program for all parents.

However, I am not wedded to a strict form of licensing. It may well be that there are alternative ways of regulating parents which would achieve the desired results—the protection of children—without strictly prohibiting nonlicensed people from rearing children. For example, a system of tax incentives for licensed parents, and protective services scrutiny of nonlicensed parents, might adequately protect children. If it would, I would endorse the less drastic measure. My principal concern is to protect children from maltreatment by parents. I begin by advocating the more strict form of licensing since that is the standard method of regulating hazardous activities.

⑤   ⑤   ⑤

I have argued that all parents should be licensed by the state. This licensing program is attractive, not because state intrusion is inherently judicious and efficacious, but simply because it seems to be the best way to prevent children from being reared by incompetent parents. Nonetheless, even after considering the previous arguments, many people will find the proposal a useless academic exercise, probably silly, and possibly even morally perverse. But why? Why do most of us find this proposal unpalatable, particularly when the arguments supporting it are good and the objections to it are philosophically flimsy?

I suspect the answer is found in a long-held, deeply ingrained attitude toward children, repeatedly reaffirmed in recent court decisions, and present, at least to some degree, in almost all of us. The belief is that parents own, or at least have natural sovereignty over, their children.[10] It does not matter precisely how this belief is described, since on both views parents legitimately exercise extensive and virtually unlimited control over their children. Others can properly interfere with or criticize parental decisions only in unusual and tightly prescribed circumstances—for example, when parents severely and repeatedly abuse their children. In all other cases, the parents reign supreme.

This belief is abhorrent and needs to be supplanted with a more child-centered view. Why? Briefly put, this attitude has adverse effects on children and on the adults these children will become. Parents who hold this view may well maltreat their children. If these parents happen to treat their children well, it is only because they want to, not because they think their children deserve or have a right to good treatment. Moreover, this belief is manifestly at odds with the conviction that parents should prepare children for life as adults. Children subject to parents who perceive children in this way are unlikely to be adequately prepared for adulthood. Hence, to prepare children for life as adults and to protect them from maltreatment, this attitude toward children must be dislodged. As I have argued, licensing is a viable way to protect children. Furthermore, it would increase the likelihood that more children will be adequately prepared for life as adults than is now true.[11]

NOTES

1. "When practice of a profession or calling requires special knowledge or skill and intimately affects public health, morals, order or safety, or general welfare, legislature may prescribe reasonable qualifications for persons desiring to pursue such professions or calling and require them to demonstrate possession of such qualifications by examination on subjects with which such profession or calling has to deal as a condition precedent to right to follow that profession or calling." 50 S.E. 2nd 735 (1949). Also see 199 U.S. 306, 318 (1905) and 123 U.S. 623, 661 (1887).

2. What counts as a moderately reliable test for these purposes will vary from circumstance to circumstance. For example, if the activity could cause a relatively small amount of harm, yet regulating that activity would place extensive constraints on people regulated, then any tests should be extremely accurate. On the other hand, if the activity could be exceedingly harmful but the constraints on the regulated person are minor, then the test can be considerably less reliable.

3. The statistics on the incidence of child abuse vary. Probably the most recent detailed study (Saad Nagi, *Child Maltreatment in the United States* [New York: Columbia University Press, 1977]) suggests that between four hundred thousand and 1 millioin children are abused or neglected each year. Other experts claim the incidence is considerably higher.

4. According to the National Committee for the Prevention of Child Abuse, more than 80 percent of incarcerated criminals were, as children, abused by their parents. In addition, a study in the *Journal of the American Medical Association*, G. Duncan et al., "Etiological Factors of First Degree Murder," 168, no. 3 (1958): 1755–58, reported that first-degree murderers from middle-class homes and who have "no history of addiction to drugs, alcoholism, organic disease of the brain, or epilepsy" were frequently found to have been subject to "remorseless physical brutality at the hands of the parents."

5. "A review of the literature points out that abusive parents were raised in the same style that they have recreated in the pattern of rearing children. . . . An individual who was raised by parents who used physical force to train their children and who grew up in a violent household has had as a role model the use of force and violence as a means of family problem solving." R. J. Gelles, "Child Abuse as Psychopathology—A Sociological Critique and Reformulation," *American Journal of Orthopsychiatry* 43, no. 4 (1973): 618–19.

6. Some people might question if any parents actually believe they should beat their children. However, that does appear to be the sincere view of many abusing parents. See, for example, case descriptions in *A Silent Tragedy* by Peter and Judith DeCourcy (Sherman Oaks, Calif.: Alfred Publishing Co., 1973).

7. I suppose I might be for licensing only good parents if I knew there were reasonable criteria and some plausible way of deciding if a potential parent satisfied these criteria. However, since I don't think we have those criteria or that method, nor can I seriously envision that we will discover those criteria and that method, I haven't seriously entertained the stronger proposal.

8. The research gathered by Altemeir was reported by Ray Helfer in "Review of the Concepts and a Sampling of the Research Relating to Screening for the Poten-

tial to Abuse and/or Neglect One's Child." Helfer's paper was presented at a workshop sponsored by the National Committee for the Prevention of Child Abuse, December 3–6, 1978.

9. According to a study published by the Child Welfare League of America, at least 51 percent of the adopted children had suffered, prior to adoption, more than minimal emotional deprivation. See Elizabeth A. Lawder et al., *A Follow-up Study of Adoptions: Post Placement Functioning of Adoption Families* (New York: Child Welfare League of America, 1969).

According to a study by David Gil *(Violence against Children* [Cambridge: Harvard University Press, 1970]) only 0.4 percent of abused children were abused by adoptive parents. Since at least 2 percent of the children in the United States are adopted (John B. Turner, ed., *Encyclopedia of Social Work* [New York: National Association of Social Workers, 1977]), that means the rate of abuse by biological parents is five times that of adoptive parents.

10. We can see this belief in a court case chronicled by DeCourcy and DeCourcy in *A Silent Tragedy.* The judge ruled that three children, severely and regularly beaten, burned, and cut by their father, should be placed back with their father since he was only "trying to do what is right." If the court did not adopt this belief would it even be tempted to so excuse such abusive behavior? This attitude also emerges in the all-too-frequent court rulings (see S. Katz, *When Parents Fail* [Boston: Beacon Press, 1971]) giving custody of children back to their biological parents even though the parents had abandoned them for years, and even though the children expressed a strong desire to stay with foster parents.

In "The Child, the Law, and the State" (in *Children's Rights: Toward the Liberation of the Child*, Leila Berg et al. [New York: Praeger Publishers, 1971]), Nan Berger persuasively argues that our adoption and foster care laws are comprehensible only if children are regarded as the property of their parents.

11. For helpful comments and criticisms, I am indebted to Jeffrey Gold, Chris Hackler, James Rachels, and especially to William Aiken, George Graham, and the editors of the *Philosophy and Public Affairs.*

A NATIONAL PARENTING POLICY

Jack C. Westman

■

> . . . Causing the existence of a human being is one of the most responsible actions in the range of human life. To undertake this responsibility—to bestow a life which may be either a curse or a blessing—unless the being on whom it is to he bestowed will have at least the ordinary chances of a desirable existence, is a crime against that being.
>
> —John Stuart Mill, *On Liberty*, 1859[1]

*W*hen people talk about the right "to have children," they often do not take into account the fact that children are brought up, as well as brought into, the world. They assume that the right to procreate includes the right to rear a child as one wishes without special obligations to society. They are mistaken. In fact, "having a child" includes obligations that hinge on three separate rights.

First is the right to conceive a child. At one extreme is a desired conception consummated by the mutual assent of a female and a male. At the other extreme is forced conception through rape, which may be regarded as a reason for terminating a pregnancy. In between are accidental and unconsciously motivated conceptions. In each of these instances there are obligations that accompany the biological right to conceive a child, as illustrated by the duty of an unmarried father to financially support a child he conceives.

From *Licensing Parents: Can We Prevent Child Abuse and Neglect?* by Jack C. Westman. Copyright © 1994 by Jack C. Westman. Reprinted by permission of Perseus Books Publishers, a member of Perseus Books, L.L.C.

Second is the right to bear a child, but even this right includes obligations to protect the fetus on the part of the mother. There is a growing tendency to regard the rights of a mother and the rights of a fetus as respectively decreasing and increasing as a pregnancy progresses. In addition a host of questions about who has parental rights and obligations are being raised by the availability of artificial insemination and surrogate childbearing with different ways of uniting eggs and sperm. In each of those instances the obligations to the resulting offspring on the part of various parents have yet to be completely ascertained.

Third is the right to the custody and rearing of a child. The trend is away from assuming that a parent has a biological right to possess the child as property toward recognizing parenthood as the earned result of affectionate bonding with a child. Although the biological parent has a right to establish a relationship with a child by virtue of genetic and prenatal connections, the psychological, or "real," parent of a child is the person with whom the child actually forms an affectionate attachment bond after birth. Consequently, the parent-child relationship is defined by life experience, not by the event of birth. This redefinition of parenthood from simply being a question of biological conception and giving birth to a child to that of a lifestyle of child-rearing is an essential way of thinking if our society is to value the competent parenting of children.

The traditional mystique of biological parenthood needs to be placed in perspective, so that parenthood can be seen accurately, not as a state determined by conception and birth but as a relationship based upon a parent-child affectionate bond with reciprocal obligations between parents and children. As adoptive parents well know, parenthood really is a relationship and is not simply a status awarded by conceiving or giving birth to a child.

There are three models for parenthood as a relationship between parents and children. One that has been largely discredited in the United States is that children are the property of their parents. The second model is that parents are solely responsible for rearing their children, and society intervenes only when children are maltreated. The third model is that parents and society share responsibility for rearing children.

The third model is implicit in the United States because the education of children is generally regarded as a public responsibility. As it now stands, however, our society's interest in child-rearing is not explicitly defined. Many adults also are uncertain about their preparation for parenthood. . . .

. . . As it now stands, these people must be found to be unfit as parents after their abuse and neglect have damaged their children. Much of this damage to children could be prevented by expecting parents to be competent before damage from abuse and neglect takes place. . . .

THE CONCEPT OF PARENT LICENSURE

Although the desirability of setting expectations for parents has been suggested from time to time in the past, the idea of certifying the child-rearing competence of future parents was proposed in 1973 by the psychologist Harriet Rheingold.[2] The legal recognition of parenting through licensing to protect children from abuse and neglect was proposed in 1980 by the philosopher Hugh LaFollette.

In 1986, Senator Daniel Patrick Moynihan concluded that a credible family policy should insist that responsibility for a child begins with the individual parent, next the child's family, and then the child's community.[3] He called for public policies and practices that would provide status, encouragement, stability, and time for parenthood.

Since we have child abuse and neglect laws, you might reasonably ask why parent licensing is being raised as an issue now. You can say that we have managed without it. But we have not managed well without it. Children have no protection from damage by their parents before it occurs. As a result large numbers of damaged children have grown up to be unable to live successfully as adults, threatening the very fabric of our society.

Our society simply allows parents to rear their children as a private matter. At the present time any male and any female at any age are free to conceive a child and to assume complete parental rights to the custody and rearing of the child without any expectation that they should be competent to parent the child. They are free to conduct their lives and to do as they wish with the child, with public financial support if needed, until the child shows evidence of sufficient damage to warrant state intervention through child abuse and neglect statutes. Then the state both defends the parents and attempts to prove that they are unfit.

At no time before a child is damaged is it incumbent upon the male or the female to demonstrate that they possess minimal competencies, as they must do in order to obtain a motor vehicle operator's license, to marry, or to join the military forces.

Behind this situation is the general disengagement of our society from cultural values that emphasize the responsibilities of parents and children to each other. This has led to an intolerable level of incompetent parenting. This absence of societal support for competent parenting calls for developing social values that define and expect competent parenting. As is the case with any social value, the articulation of social values that support parenting will require persuasion, education, and legislation.

Although education and persuasion are important, the implementation of any societal value also requires regulation, because not everyone can be depended upon to be sufficiently influenced by knowledge. For those who do not respond to persuasion or education, a clear statement of each child's right to competent parenting with enforcement capacities is necessary in order to convey the value society places on parenting.

The idea of licensing parents may seem to be an outrageous intrusion into individual rights and the privacy of families. Yet in effect social agencies and courts already are licensing parents. Potential adoptive parents are screened intensively by social agencies, and laws mandate the assessment of parenting when children are alleged to have been maltreated by their parents. Furthermore, the family's absolute right to privacy is not guaranteed by the Constitution.

Child abuse and neglect laws are used now to prevent a mother from taking her newborn infant home from the hospital when her condition or home environment would place the child in jeopardy. In these instances the state seeks custody of the child under the applicable law, and a court decides whether or not the child will be endangered if placed in the parent's custody.

The concept of licensing parents applies to the stage of parenthood, not to the conception or birth stages of life. It would designate parenthood as a privilege for which one is qualified rather than as a right that accompanies the event of childbirth. It would define parenthood realistically as a relationship rather than as a biologically determined state. It would provide an opportunity to inform parents of available parenting resources. In addition, becoming and being licensed parents would provide a basis for eligibility for governmental financial aid and supportive services in order to ensure that public funding supports competent and not incompetent parenting.

At the societal level licensing would symbolically convey the message that parenting is at least as important as such things as marriage, military service, voting, access to alcohol and cigarettes, driving a motor vehicle, access to pornography, consent to health care, and all other age-graded activities. It also would be a concrete expression of a parenting policy based on a child's right to competent parenting and a parent's right to be competent. It would implement expectations of parents that already exist in child abuse and neglect statutes.

Most importantly, the process of licensing parents would focus attention on the importance of parenting in our society and would be the rallying call for a series of essential multilevel interventions to promote competent parenting. . . .

THE PRECEDENTS FOR LICENSING PARENTS

The law could be used much more effectively than it is in influencing parenting in the United States.

Laws are more than instruments for punishing behavior. In fact, society expresses its values and influences behavior through the simple existence of its laws more than through actual enforcement of them. Traffic laws determine which side of the road cars drive on and organize traffic flow with little actual need for enforcement. In the same way civil rights laws have created a consciousness of racism and sexism so that few people publicly advocate discrimination against adults today, and attitudes have changed without the actual need for enforcement of these laws. A similar outcome could be anticipated if there were legal expectations of parents.

The precedents for setting expectations for parents through the persuasive, educational, and enforcement aspects of laws are so plentiful that the fact that we do not have expectations of parents in our society is a clear-cut reflection of juvenile ageism. No one can deny that we really do not protect children from incompetent parenting, especially by their biological parents.

There is a long list of precedents for licensing parents that includes adoptive and foster parent licensing, marriage licensing, day care licensing, parental liability laws, child support enforcement laws, laws that mandate compulsory parental cooperation with schools, skill and professional licensing, competency procedures for executing contracts and wills, grandparent liability laws, termination of parental rights statutes, drug and pollutant regulations, and, ironically, pet owner requirements.

Adoptive and Foster Parent Licensing

Well-established adoption laws do recognize that not everyone is capable of rearing children, so that the investigation of the parenting abilities of adults who want to adopt children usually is required. In fact, stringent requirements for adoption are designed to protect children from being adopted by incompetent parents and from being casually transferred by their biological parents to the custody of others. The adoptive process is much more rigorous than any parent licensing procedures envisioned. In fact, it has been carried to unreasonable extremes at times.

Foster parents also are supposed to meet rigorous standards.[4] In most communities in order to obtain a foster parent license one must (1) be eighteen years old or over; (2) be in good health; (3) meet the state's home-safety standards; (4) have sufficient income for family needs; (5) be emotionally stable and have character references; (6) have no criminal record; (7) have sufficient bedrooms; (8) be willing to work with social workers; (9) agree to discipline without physical punishment; and (10) agree to attend foster parenting workshops.

There is an obvious double standard for adoptive and foster parents and for biological parents. No one is permitted to raise someone else's child without meeting standards in a screening process. Yet anyone can raise their own child without any questions being raised about their ability to do so.

If we think it is important to protect adopted and foster children, who are less likely to be maltreated than the children of biological parents, is it not reasonable to afford the same protection to children reared by their biological parents?

Marriage Licensing

Historically, marriage licensing has been a means of defining inheritance rights. It also has been a means of ensuring that adults are ready to handle the responsibilities of child-rearing.

The legal requirements for obtaining a marriage license and filing certification of the marriage are found in the marriage laws of each state.[5] Premarital physical examinations have been required by law in most states since 1913 and culminated in the Michigan Premarital Physical Examination Law of 1937. Although the actual effect of these laws has been to screen for sexually transmitted diseases, the Michigan statute also was described in legislative proceedings as creating a marriage counseling opportunity. Over the years, however, marriage licensing has become less of a statement of society's expectations of marriage and more of a registration process that establishes a legal contractual relationship between a married couple.

Most states impose conditions for marriage. There usually are waiting periods to reduce impulsive unions. There also are restrictions on kinship, on already being married, on perpetrating fraud in entering the marriage agreement, and on mental competence at the time of marriage. The local licensing authority receives marriage applications and informs the applicants of the waiting period, of the need for parental consent when appropriate, of premarital examinations, and of other legal requirements for obtaining a license. After both parties have completed the required documents, the license is issued. They are informed about the period of time and the geographic area for which the license is valid. The person performing the marriage ceremony receives the license and completes the marriage certificate, which is registered locally, in the state, and with the National Center for Health Statistics.

A reform in welfare eligibility related to marriage licensing is the "bridefare program" in which the disincentive to marriage in the Aid to the Families of Dependent Children regulations is removed by allowing fathers to be included in the AFDC grant if the parents marry.[6] In addition, the usual increases in AFDC grant levels are limited by half when a second baby is born and are frozen for subsequent children.

The progressive shift away from the expectation of commitment in adult relationships in our society has diluted the significance of marriage and its implied commitment to child-rearing, so that increasing numbers of children are being born into unmarried situations. This trend increases, rather than decreases, the need for parenting licenses as statements of the commitments of parents to their children.

Day Care Licensing

Although the licensing of day care has concentrated largely on the physical facilities and the ratios of children to adults, there is a growing emphasis on the qualifications of day care workers. In fact, an entire field of child development specialists has emerged with the setting of standards for their education and practice.

As the regulation of the quality of day care has become a public issue, regulating the quality of parent-child relationships logically follows, especially because even without day care worker certification requirements, there are parents who are rejected as supervised day care workers but who still have the unsupervised care and custody of their own children.

Legal Parental Liability

Strangely perhaps, common law has never imposed a duty on parents to provide financial support for their children, but it has penalized parents who neglect children to the point of death or physical injury and suffering.[7] For example, the 3rd District Court of Appeals in Wisconsin ruled that a man whose car accident led to the premature birth of his son and the baby's death two days later could be charged with vehicular homicide by driving while intoxicated.

Negligence occurring in the context of parenting generally has been protected by the principle of parental immunity. Consequently, successful proceedings by children for injuries caused by their parents have been infrequent and have been limited to gross negligence or intentional wrongdoing resulting in physical injury, such as the failure to lead a young child in crossing a street or the damage to a fetus due to an attempted abortion.

At the same time a body of law is developing in which parents can be held accountable more generally for their roles in harming children.[8] In a proceeding initiated by a minor, the Washington Supreme Court upheld a finding that she was incorrigible because of her parents' behavior. The court supported her refusal to return to her parents and affirmed the local court's decision to remove her from her parents' custody.

Traditionally, laws against contributing to the delinquency of minors have been enforced when adults contribute to the delinquency of someone else's child but not to the delinquency of their own child. Holding parents responsible for their behavior toward their own children can be seen as an extension of protecting children from the acts of adults in general.

State laws are beginning to assign specific responsibilities to parents. In California parents can be fined or jailed for allowing their children to participate in antisocial gangs. In Wisconsin and Hawaii they can be required to support the children of their own children. In Arkansas they can be fined when their children skip school. In Florida they can be jailed if their child hurts another person with a gun left accessible by the parent. In Wisconsin parents can lose welfare benefits if their children fail to attend school.

Across the nation parents are increasingly being held liable, sometimes even in a criminal sense, for the misbehavior of their children.[9] This has been the case particularly in tort law, in which parents have been successfully sued for injury and damage to others caused by their children. Adults abused as children also have been permitted to sue their parents or relatives for harm inflicted upon them during their formative years.

All of these developments reflect a trend toward holding parents accountable for their behavior with their children. The legal system is defining expectations of parents in a negative sense. Parent licensing would express positive expectations for parents.

Child Support Enforcement

The need for state interventions in some families is dramatically illustrated by the fact that left to their own devices, many unmarried and divorced parents would not meet their child support financial obligations through persuasion or education. Law enforcement procedures are necessary in those instances.

Without strict enforcement procedures most fathers have been found to neglect their child support obligations.[10] The threats of jail and the garnishing of wages have been necessary in order to obtain payment. This is a concrete example of how laws are required to effectively enforce society's expectations of parents and to prevent parents from avoiding their responsibilities to their children.

Compulsory Parental Cooperation with Schools

Further evidence of the fact that parenting responsibilities require societal support through legislation is illustrated by a 1989 California law based on the fact that compulsion is necessary to gain the cooperation of some parents with their children's schools and to induce employers to permit parents to do so during working hours.[11] The statute authorizes teachers to compel a parent or guardian to attend one of their child's classes following the child's suspension on the grounds of obscenity, habitual profanity, disruption of school activities, or defiance of school authorities. Employers are prohibited from using such school-required absences from work as reasons to discharge or otherwise to discriminate against affected employees.

In addition, in California the Quality Education Project, a federally funded program to gain parental participation in the education of their children, requires parents to pledge to provide the time, space, and materials for their children to do homework.[12]

Public health experts say that state laws that require that children be immunized against infectious diseases prior to school entry have been remarkably successful.[13] They suggest that similar requirements of parents for their preschool children by welfare and Medicaid programs would be effective, too.

These statutes and regulations illustrate the degree to which legal expectations beyond persuasion and education must be set to induce some parents to assume responsibilities for their children.

Skill and Professional Licensing

States do not hesitate to license and monitor activities that have far less potential for harm to others and society than does incompetent parenting. In fact, licensing or certification is expected for any person's activities that are potentially harmful to other people—except when those persons are parents and when other people are their children.

Any activities that are potentially harmful to others are regulated by requiring the demonstration of minimal levels of competence. We require automobile operators to qualify for licenses. We require professionals, such as real estate agents, physicians, lawyers, and pharmacists, to meet licensing requirements. All of these expectations require the demonstration of competence in activities that affect other people before damage has been caused to them.

Competence to Execute Contracts and Wills

The competence to make decisions is routinely required in the execution of legal contracts, most commonly in the legal status of wills. The decision-making power that parents hold over their children is far more important than any of these contractual matters.

Grandparent Liability Legislation

Legislative action has been taken to hold the parents of minors who conceive and give birth responsible for their grandchildren.

The grandparent liability provisions of Wisconsin's Family Responsibility Act of 1985 hold both sets of grandparents of a baby born to their unmarried minor offspring financially responsible for that baby's support.[14] One of the intents of the act was to promote communication between parents and teenagers, especially males, about the consequences of sexual behavior and about parental responsibilities.

Holding expectations for the parents of minors who become parents is a step toward setting expectations for all parents.

Termination of Parental Rights Statutes

The courts have held that before it may permanently terminate a parent's rights to a child, a state must show abandonment or harm to a child sufficient to support a compelling interest of the state in doing so.[15] Parents must be afforded procedural protections as well.

In order to establish grounds for the termination of parental rights in most jurisdictions, the following must be demonstrated:[16] (1) a repeated or continuous failure to meet the basic needs of a child; (2) evidence that this pattern has been damaging to the child; and (3) evidence that the parent-child interaction is not amenable to treatment or likely to change in the natural course of events soon enough to benefit the child. The first of these criteria corresponds to the definition of incompetent parenting used in this book.

When the termination of parental rights is being considered, the gross failure of the parent to meet the basic needs of a child usually is obvious to any fully informed, objective observer. The termination of parental rights is supposed to take into account the fact that the irreplaceable passage of time in children's lives limits the amount of time parents can be given to improve their parenting abilities. An adult may be incompetent for a limited period of time to parent a child, but that time may be critical from the point of view of that child's development. A parent's incompetence during the early years of a child's life precludes that parent from forming affectionate attachment bonds with that particular child and becoming that child's psychological, or "real," parent.

The existence of termination of parental rights statutes attests to the fact that there are parents who are unable or unwilling to become competent. As knowledge of the damaging effects of incompetent parenting on society accumulates, the compelling interest of society in identifying incompetent parents through a licensing process and preventing the abuse and neglect of children before they are damaged is evident.

Drug and Pollutant Regulation

Drugs and pollutants that threaten the lives of children, as well as adults, have been regulated through legislation.

In 1938 the U.S. Congress passed the Food, Drug, and Cosmetic Act as a result of the deaths of more than one hundred children from a liquid form of sulfanilamide.[17] The act requires firms to submit applications to the Food and Drug Administration before introducing pharmaceuticals into interstate commerce. Later, in 1962, following fetal deformities in Europe from the administration of thalidomide, the act was amended to require proof of a new drug's efficacy through regulated clinical testing as well.

In 1990 the federal government began a broad effort to eliminate lead poisoning of children based on the conclusion of the U.S. Centers for Disease Control that lead poisoning is the most important environmental problem facing children.[18] Twenty years before, Congress had declared lead-based paint a health hazard and ordered it stripped from federally subsidized housing. It banned the use of lead-based paint completely ten years ago.

These actions are illustrations of the willingness of the federal government to take regulatory action to protect children when dangers to them from material causes are demonstrated.

Pet Owner Requirements

The fact that the Society for the Prevention of Cruelty to Animals existed before the Society for the Prevention of Cruelty to Children is a revealing aspect of the history of juvenile ageism. Even today more attention is devoted to ascertaining the competence of those who care for pets than of those who rear children.

The San Francisco Society for the Prevention of Cruelty to Animals requires that persons adopting pets be adults and that they agree to: (1) give the animal proper and humane care, food, water, shelter, exercise, and all the other necessities; (2) provide it with veterinary care both on a regular basis and when the animal becomes ill or injured; (3) keep the animal as a pet and companion and never allow it to be used as a guard dog, fighting dog, or for experimentation; and (4) comply with all city, state, and federal laws relating to animals.[19] . . .

PROCEDURES FOR LICENSING PARENTS

Although possibly seeming like an onerous task, procedures for licensing parents actually would entail little more administrative effort than currently is involved in marriage licensing, birth registration, and protective services for children. The idea of licensing is to accord parenting appropriate status in society, not to create a new bureaucracy.

With a licensing process the question of parental fitness would be faced before rather than after damage to a child. Licensing would hold a parent responsible for being competent rather than forcing children to endure incompetent parenting until they themselves show publicly recognized signs of damage. The responsibility for demonstrating parental competence before a child is damaged would be with the parent, rather than the responsibility being with the state to demonstrate parental incompetence after a child has been damaged, as now is the case.

The practical aspects of licensing parents would include its timing, eligibility criteria, administration, the consequences of denial of licensure, and the question of testing for parental competence.

The Timing of Licensure Application

There are three circumstances under which the time for parent licensing would arise. The first time is prior to conception either at the time of marriage, on acceptance for adoption, or at the time of an unmarried person's decision to have a child. This could be handled through the existing marriage license procedures.

The second time is during the pregnancy. Unlike the marriage license, there is no existing point for providing a license under this circumstance. One would need to be established so that application for a license could be made, such as during prenatal care as an early extension of birth registration.

The third time is at the birth of a child. The already established procedure for registering births provides a structured point of contact at which the existence of a license could be ascertained; if necessary, a license could be obtained then.

Criteria for Licensure

The requirements for obtaining a parenting license would be simple and straightforward so that they could be easily met, as they are now for a marriage license. Unlike the marriage license, it would be obtained for each parent and validated for each child.

The first criterion would be the attainment of adulthood. Eighteen would be a reasonable age based on physical, social, and emotional maturity and the likelihood of completion of a high school education. For parents under the age of eighteen, as now with marriage, parental consent and parental assumption of responsibility for the minor and the child would be required so that the minor could obtain a provisional parenting license that would be fully validated when the minor becomes an adult.

The second criterion would be certification by the applicant that he or she agrees to care for and nurture the child and to refrain from abusing and neglecting the child. If this agreement was broken at a later time, the intervention upon a parent's rights then would be based upon the failure of that parent to fulfill a contractual commitment to the child with revocation of the license rather than on an adversarial quasi-criminal action, as is now the case.

The third, possibly optional, criterion would be completion of a parenting course or its equivalent. Family life education already is provided in many communities and public schools.[20] Every middle school and high school in the country could require courses that prepare young people for the responsibilities of parenthood. The laboratories for these courses could be in day care settings. This requirement would not be retroactive and would depend upon the availability of such courses.

In all likelihood, parent licensing would stimulate the development of family life education. Although the actual benefit of education in influencing parenting behavior is uncertain, the mass impact of such a program would be likely to discourage premature marriages and reinforce awareness of the gravity of child-rearing responsibilities. From the point of view of the educational curriculum, the importance of the subject matter to society is greater than any other academic subject. Moreover, the need for education in parenting is widely perceived today.

The Administration of Licensing

The administration of parent licenses would be at the level of state and local governments, although enabling federal legislation, such as requiring licensure for the receipt of federal funds, would be helpful in encouraging nationwide consistency. A new bureaucracy would not be needed, since licensing would involve revising the mandate of the existing marriage licensing, birth registration, and child protection systems.

First, the license application process could be handled through the framework of marriage licensing and birth registration, since it essentially would be a question of credentials. Second, questionable situations and the appeals-intervention process could be handled through currently existing protective services for children in county departments of human services guided by state statutes. The shift of protective services for children from an adversarial criminal focus after children have been damaged to a preventive focus would reduce the need for extensive interventions years later. Vulnerable parents and children would be identified at the outset of the children's lives and parent support services could be offered earlier than is now possible.

A general parenting license for each mother and father would be granted on meeting the criteria. It would then be validated for each child, clearly establishing a child-parent contract that includes financial responsibility and expectations of parental competence.

If protective services for a child were invoked by actual child abuse or neglect, the license could be placed on probationary status while treatment was ongoing, or it could be suspended during foster placement of the child and treatment of the parent. When a parent was unable or unwilling to remedy demonstrated incompetence, the license could be judicially revoked for that child through existing termination of parental rights procedures modified to correspond with revocation rather than the present quasi-criminal procedures.

If the parent of a child was ineligible for a parent license because of age or incapacity, that person could be issued a provisional license under the aegis of children's protective services with either concomitant parent training and supervision or foster placement and with a specified time during which that person could qualify for a regular license. If the person proved unable to acquire competency at the end of that time, that person's parental rights would be terminated, and the child would be adopted, as now takes place for parents who voluntarily place their children for adoption.

If a mother could not meet licensing standards, child protection laws would be invoked at the time of the child's birth. The custody of the child would be with an agency, and the child's placement would be determined by the circumstances of the situation, as it is now. Mothers who are minors could obtain provisional licenses underwritten by their own parents who agreed to do so and who met foster parent standards themselves.

The question of whether a child should be removed from an unlicensed mother at birth for adoption or whether the mother should care for the child under a provisional license with support and supervision would hinge on the most likely outcome. If the outlook was favorable and the risk to the child was low, therapeutic support of the mother with a provisional license would be preferable both from the mother's and the child's points of view. On the other hand, if the outlook for the child was poor, the alternatives of maternal or foster care would be less appealing from the child's point of view than adoption. Adoption also would meet the needs of the large pool of qualified adults who wish to adopt infants and young children.

The administration of protective services for children and the enforcement of child abuse and neglect statutes would be facilitated by parent licensing. From the legal point of view, the burden of proof would lie with parents to demonstrate evidence of minimal competence, or of their "parental fitness" in legal terms, rather than on the state, as is now the case, to prove "parental unfitness." If the state required all parents to become licensed before or upon the birth of their children, much later case-by-case adjudication under child protection laws after parents have damaged their children could be avoided, saving enormous amounts of time, financial expense, and other social costs.[21]

Parent licensing would remove protecting the welfare of children from the criminal arena of perpetrator and victim after children have been damaged to the prevention and treatment arena, in which expectations are held for parents and in which they can be assisted to be competent parents and helped to avoid damaging their children.

The Denial of Licensure

Parent licensing does not mean attempting to distinguish between "good" and "less good" parents.[22] It would exclude only the obviously incompetent ones. It would not be a birth control measure, although it probably would influence procreation by conveying the message that society values and holds expectations for child-rearing. The aim of licensing would be to elevate the status of parenting, not to prescribe parenting styles.

Parent licensing also would not be based upon the legal standard of the child's best interests. The practical problem with best-interest standards is that they tend to be idealistic and are used to remove children from their homes when less drastic and more effective remedies, such as training, assisting, and supervising foundering parents, can be used.

Individuals denied licensure would have opportunities for appeal through the usual legal channels. Those mistakenly denied licenses would be able to demonstrate their competence. Those whose parenting licenses were placed on probationary status or were suspended would be able to obtain treatment in order to qualify for reinstatement.

The denial or revocation of a parenting license would be expected to be a painful experience, particularly for mothers. Still, the fact that disappointment or inconvenience results for people who are denied licenses for other activities does not diminish the conviction that we must regulate activities or occupations that are potentially harmful to others. We also maintain licensing procedures and competency tests even though they sometimes are subject to error. The overall importance of protecting innocent children from incompetent parenting justifies the inconvenience to a few parents and the inevitable imperfections of a licensing system.

Parent-Competence Testing

At this time large-scale testing for signs of parental incompetence is premature. Thus far efforts to predict the parenting potential of pregnant women by testing have yielded inconsistent results.[23] There are apparently satisfactory ways of predicting parental behavior through intensive evaluations, such as the rigorous assessment procedures of those wanting to adopt children; however, those measures are not practical for large-scale use.

At the same time, attention should be focused on devising means for the early detection of parental incompetence. This ultimately would enhance the effectiveness of parent licensing and would alert incompetent individuals to their need to examine their motives for rearing children and encourage them to improve their parenting skills. . . .

THE RATIONALE FOR LICENSING PARENTS

A national parenting policy based on promoting competent parenting is urgently needed. The time has come to seriously consider protecting children from incompetent parenting by licensing parents for four straightforward reasons.

The first reason is the human rights principle that all individuals, including children, should be free from abuse and oppression. As it is now, millions of children are abused and oppressed by incompetent parents. Little is done before children are damaged by abuse.

The second reason is the civil rights principle that all individuals should have equal access to opportunities to develop their potentials in life, an especially important right for children who are beginning their lives. As it now stands, incompetent parents neglect their children and deprive them of opportunities to learn how to develop their potential.

The third reason is the common-good principle in which society has a right to regulate activities that are potentially harmful to others and to society. As it is now, incompetent parents not only harm their children; they gravely endanger the internal security and productivity of our society by disrupting the safety of our citizens and by creating financial burdens for our nation.

The fourth reason is the humanistic principle that the future success of children as citizens and as parents depends upon forming affectionate attachment bonds with their own parents. As it is now, incompetent parents do not form healthy affectionate attachment bonds with their children and thereby deprive their children of forming the capacity to respect others that underlies responsible adult citizenship and competent parenting.

Licensing parents would concretely articulate society's expectations of parents and provide an incentive for parents to be competent. It would accord parenting the status of a privilege rather than a right and would reduce the hazards of incompetent parenting for children. It would establish the existence of children as citizens with certain civil rights. Most importantly, it would demonstrate that society values and supports competent parenting.

Just as a marriage license signifies a contractual relationship between spouses, a parent license would establish a contractual relationship between parent and child. It would elevate child-rearing from the realm of caprice, accident, and ulterior motives by according parenting the dignity and legitimacy it deserves. It would require that parents complete their own growth and development before assuming child-rearing responsibilities. It would set the standard that parents be able to assume responsibilities for their own lives before assuming responsibility for the life of a child. If parents are unable to meet these criteria, society would help them. If that fails, society would arrange for adoption of the children by competent parents.

Parent licensing would be the symbolic basis for a multilevel approach to families that articulates society's respect for parenting as an important social role and society's expectation that parents will be competent. For those who are not, financial aid, educational programs, social services, and, when necessary, relief from the responsibilities of parenting are required. We know which educational programs and social services effectively help incompetent parents. We know that the success of these programs depends upon building safe, caring communities. What is lacking is an organizing theme to give these programs direction and to provide parenting-based criteria for evaluating their efficacy.

Parent licensing would place the responsibility on adults to be competent parents rather than on the state to financially support incompetent parenting and its consequences. It also would lay the foundation for dramatically reducing the need for costly and ineffective governmental welfare and correctional programs. Rather than only focusing our limited resources on trying to repair children and adults who have been damaged by incompetent parenting, as we do now, we would be able to increase the general level of competent parenting and positively affect generations to come. Tragically, many of our existing interventions perpetuate and aggravate the very social problems they are intended to alleviate.

The priority given to competent parenting now will determine the future of our nation. Because it does not now manifestly place a high priority on child-rearing, the United States faces an uncertain future. There now are few limits to what can be done to children. Instead the question should be what needs to be done for them. Our children depend upon us to ensure that they all will have a chance to become competent adults and to become competent parents themselves.

NOTES

1. John Stuart Mill, *On Liberty*, in *Great Books of the Western World*, vol. 43, ed. Robert Maynard Hutchins (Chicago: University of Chicago Press, 1952), p. 318.

2. Harriet L. Rheingold, "To Rear a Child," *American Psychologist* 28 (1973): 42–46; Hugh LaFollette, "Licensing Parents," *Philosophy and Public Affairs* 9 (1980): 182–97.

3. Daniel E. Moynihan, *Family and Nation* (San Diego, Calif.: Harcourt, Brace, Jovanovich, 1986), pp. 173, 192.

4. National Foster Parent Association, Information and Services Office, 226 Kilts Drive, Houston, TX, 77024.

5. National Center for Health Statistics, *Handbook on Marriage Registration* (Rockville, Md.: Department of Health, Education, and Welfare, 1972), publication no. (HSM) 72–111; Sylvester W. Trythall, "The Premarital Law: History and a Survey of Its Effectiveness in Michigan," *Journal of the American Medical Association* 187 (1964): 900–903.

6. Jeff Mayers, "Welfare Test Adds Counties," *Wisconsin State Journal*, September 12, 1992, p. 1D.

7. Helen Gamble, *The Law Relating to Parents and Children* (Sydney, Australia: Law Book Company, 1981), pp. 20, 52–55; Cary Segall, "Homicide Charge OK'd in Fatal Fetal Injuries," *Wisconsin State Journal*, September 13, 1989.

8. Leonard Karp and Cheryl L. Karp, *Domestic Torts: Family Violence, Conflict and Sexual Abuse* (Colorado Springs, Colo.: Shepard/McGraw-Hill, 1989); *In re Snyder*, 532 P. 2d 278, 85 Wash. 2d 182, 1985.

9. Thomas A. Nazario, *In Defense of Children: Understanding the Rights, Needs, and Interests of the Child* (New York: Scribner, 1985), p. 222.

10. David L. Chambers, *Making Fathers Pay: The Enforcement of Child Support* (Chicago: University of Chicago Press, 1979).

11. Pamela Holcomb, Demetra S. Nightingale, and Jennifer M. Pick, *Evaluation of the Western Interstate Child Support Clearinghouse Project* (Washington, D.C.: Urban Institute, 1989), California Education Code 48900.1 and California Labor Code 230.7.

12. Quality Education Project, *A System for Student Success Through Parental Involvement* (Quality Education Project, 2110 Scott Street, San Francisco, CA, 94115; [415] 921–8673).

13. Robert Pear, "Proposal Links Welfare Funds to Inoculations," *New York Times*, November 29 1990, p. A15.

14. Wisconsin Statutes—Grandparents' Liability Law; Public Assistance Act 49.90, 2–13.

15. Mark Hardin and Patricia Tazzara, *Termination of Parental Rights: A Summary and Comparison of Grounds from Nine Model Acts* (Washington, D.C.: National Legal Resource Center for Child Advocacy, and Protection, American Bar Association, 1981). For procedural protections for parents see *Alsager* v. *District Court of Polk County, Iowa* (1976). 545 F2d 1137 (8th cir.).

16. Jack C. Westman and David Kaye, "The Termination of Parental Rights as a Therapeutic Option," in *Who Speaks for the Children?* ed. Jack C. Westman (Sarasota, Fla.: Professional Resources Exchange, Inc., 1990).

17. Henry G. Grabowski and John M. Vernon, *The Regulation of Pharmaceuticals* (Washington, D.C.: American Enterprise Institute, 1983).

18. Philip J. Hilts, "U.S. Opens Drive on Lead Poisoning in Nation's Young," *New York Times*, December 20, 1990, pp. A1, A16.

19. San Francisco Society for the Prevention of Cruelty to Animals, Application for Pet Adoption, 1988.

20. Beth Creager Fallon, *Training Leaders for Family Life Education* (New York: Family Service Association of America, 1982); Carol Payne, ed., *Programs to Strengthen Families: A Resource Guide* (Chicago: Family Resource Coalition, 1983); Lynne Ann De Spelder and Nathalia Prettyman, *A Guidebook for Teaching Family Living* (Boston: Allyn & Bacon, 1980); Pearl Karal, *Parenting Education for the Young: A Literature Survey* (Toronto, Ont.: Ministry of Education, 1984); Dorothy Dolph Zeyen, *Educators' Challenge: Healthy Mothers, Healthy Babies: A Framework for Curriculum Development in Responsible Childbearing Preschool Through High School* (Alexandria, Va.: Association for Supervision and Curriculum Development, 1981); Patricia A. Gorzka et al., "Parenting: Categories for Anticipatory Guidance," *Journal of Child and Adolescent Psychiatric and Mental Health Nursing* 4 (1991): 16–19; Marilyn Clayton Felt, *Exploring Childhood* (Newton, Mass.: Education Development Center, 1994). For the three Rs of parent education see the Center for Population Options, *Life Planning Education* (Washington, D.C.: Center for Population Options, 1989).

21. Harold Leitenberg, "Primary Prevention of Delinquency," in *Prevention of Delinquent Behavior*, ed. John D. Burchard and Sara N. Burchard (Newbury Park, Calif.: Sage, 1987), p. 324.

22. Hugh LaFollette, "Licensing Parents," *Philosophy and Public Affairs* 9 (1980): 190.

23. D. P Sommerfeld and J. R. Hughes, "Do Health Professionals Agree on the Parenting Potential of Pregnant Women?" *Social Sciences and Medicine* 24 (1987): 285–88.

A POLICY OF PARENT LICENSING

Katherine Covell and R. Brian Howe

*T*he purpose of this article is to make the case for a new policy of parent licensing. We hold that such a policy is consistent with the principle of children's rights and with the United Nations Convention on the Rights of the Child, which Canada signed in 1990. Under the present system, Canada has a variety of laws and policies that deal with parenting, including ones in the areas of child abuse and neglect, custody and adoption, education, juvenile justice, and child labor. However, virtually all of the existing laws are reactive. Typically, intervention in child-parent relations occurs only after a child has experienced severe parental incompetence or abuse. It is our belief that what is needed to protect the child's best interests is a new policy that would involve a proactive approach to child protection and the promotion of healthy child development.

We argue here that a license to parent should be mandatory. Our rationale is based on: (1) the numbers of children whose development is compromised by incompetent parents, (2) the difficulties faced by child protection agencies in responding to the needs of incompetently parented children, and (3) the individual and social costs of incompetent parenting. In essence, incompetent parenting includes abuse and neglect, lack of appropriate responding through the first year, age-inappropriate expectations for self-control, lack of appropriate discipline strategies and teaching (e.g.. physical punishment instead of reasoning), and lack of modeling socially desirable behaviors.

Reproduced with the permission of the Institute for Research on Public Policy—*Policy Options* (September 1998), pp. 32–35.

INCOMPETENT PARENTING

Incompetent parenting is usually brought to our attention through high-profile abuse cases. Considerable media attention has been paid to such cases as twenty-two-month-old Shanay Johnson, an infant battered to death by her drug-addicted mother in Toronto in 1993; Sara Podniewicz dead at six months from a vicious beating from her parents in 1994 in Toronto; five-year-old Matthew Vaudreuil, beaten and tortured to death by his mother in Vancouver in 1992; the starvation death of three-year-old John Ryan Turner by his parents in Miramichi; and Jordan Desmond Heikamp, who died of starvation at thirty-seven days in Toronto in 1997. In fact, the murder rate of Canadian infants is more than double that of adult homicides (5.6 versus 2.7 per 100,000). But incompetent parenting is reflected not only in such obvious cases of death from abuse or neglect. Incompetent parenting is reflected also in the growing number of children manifesting conduct disorders, school failure, school dropout, justice offenses, early sexual activity, teen pregnancy, teen depression, and teen suicide. In addition, as stated recently by Frank Sampson, executive director of the Cape Breton Children's Aid Society, not only are the numbers of children with problems increasing, children are more seriously disturbed as a result of their early childhood experiences. It is not that Canadians are bad parents; it is that too many Canadians are attempting to parent under conditions that make competent parenting unlikely.

Characteristics of the parent such as age, education, addiction, emotional stability, health, and history of rearing make effective parenting difficult. Of particular concern over the past year is the significant increase in teen pregnancies, young single mothers, and the adoption of motherhood as a lifestyle choice by underprivileged teens. Contextual characteristics, economic and attitudinal factors, as well as societal supports for and value placed on child-rearing, also make effective parenting difficult.

CHILD PROTECTION AGENCIES

It is the mandate of child protection agencies (or children's aid societies) to protect children from abuse and neglect and to serve the best interests of the child. Whereas child protection legislation varies provincially, across the country agencies have little if any preventive role and face many constraints on intervention. The perspectives of parental rights and of the child as property undermine attempts by workers to act in the child's best interests. In deference to "parental rights," infants are returned to street kids to give them another chance (the Jordan Desmond Heikamp case), to parents with a history of incarceration for child abuse (the Sara Podniewicz case), and to known drug-abusing neglectful parents (the Shanay Johnson case). It is particularly noteworthy in the Shanay Johnson case that the infant's living conditions were not, under the law, a basis for removing her. She was described as frequently unfed, unwashed, and surrounded by addicts in a home strewn with excrement. Nonetheless, short of her mother being witnessed taking drugs, Shanay could not be removed.

There is no question that the public and professionals are trying to improve the situation of high-risk infants. There have been expressions of outrage at the failure of the protection system with regard to cases such as those mentioned above. Individual children's aid workers (e.g., Angie Martin in the Jordan Desmond Heikamp case) have been charged with criminal negligence. In Toronto, a special committee, called "Street Kids Having Kids," has been struck to deal with the rising number of street children, unable to care for themselves, having babies as a route to adult identity. Health Canada, in October of 1997, launched a major three-year study of child abuse. A committee, headed by retired lawyer Corrine Robertshaw, is working to repeal Section 43 of the Criminal Code—a statute that allows for the use of physical force in the discipline of infants as well as children. And at the time of writing, the Special Joint Committee on Custody and Access has just ended its cross-national meetings as its members attempt to find ways of reducing the hostilities over custody and access that are so traumatic for the sixty thousand children a year who are caught in their parents' divorce rancor. These are good initiatives. But a more radical approach is necessary. We believe that abuse and neglect in various forms will continue until we as a society value parenthood—until we regard parenting as a privilege, rather than as a by-product of sexual intercourse, a route to adult identity, or a route to social assistance.

COSTS OF INCOMPETENT PARENTING

The costs of incompetent parenting to the individual child and to Canadian society are indeed high. Perhaps for the individual the costs are highest in the psychological domain; with a poor start in life, the prognosis for satisfying adult interpersonal relationships or roles in society is poor. For Canadian society, the economic costs are staggering. The costs of two common outcomes of incompetent parenting illustrate the extent of the drain on the economy: school dropout and youthful offending. The National Crime Prevention Council of Canada in 1996 reported the cost of detaining one young offender for one year at $100,000. The National Council of Welfare found in 1993 that 58 percent of welfare recipients had not completed high school, and estimated that Canada stands to lose $4 billion over the lifetime of the 137,000 Canadian students who dropped out in 1987. Four billion dollars for one year's worth of dropouts! In the United States, Dr. Jack Westman of the University of Wisconsin Medical School estimated that competent parents contribute $1 million to the economy for each well-reared child. Incompetent parents, in sharp contrast, cost society $2 million for each child they damage. The figures are likely comparable here.

Criminality, abuse, early dropout, and related sequels of incompetent parenting, often attributed to widespread unemployment or poverty, are not a direct result of poverty or unemployment. Effective parenting is not due to socioeconomic status, nor is it gender specific. Effective parenting requires that the parent have knowledge of child development, be committed to child-rearing, and model expected behavior. Effective parenting also requires societal support.

A PARENTING LICENSE

The present policy clearly is inadequate. A better one would be to institute a system of parent licensing. Requiring a parenting license would be a policy consistent with the principle of children's rights, and it would be a societal validation of the importance of parenting.

In signing the UN Convention on the Rights of the Child, Canada is committed to the principle of children's rights and the implementation of the convention. At the core of the principle of children's rights is the belief that children are persons in their own right, with dignity and inherent rights. They are not the property or appendages of their parents. Children have basic rights, including ones related to parenting, and the state has the responsibility for ensuring that children are provided those rights. Under Article 19, for example, the state is required to protect children from abuse and neglect. Under Article 3, the state is required to ensure that the best interests of the child are to prevail in all legal and administrative decisions. And under Article 18, the state is obligated to assist parents or guardians in their responsibility for the upbringing of children. The convention, while standing firmly opposed to the traditional concept of the parental ownership of children, strongly endorses the importance of parenting. Good parenting is seen to be closely connected to children's rights.

A policy of parent licensing is desirable in that it would be supportive of both children's rights and the importance of parenting. While not officially endorsed, the traditional concept of children as parental property does persist. There remains a tendency among many parents to believe they have a right to have and to raise their children as they see fit. In their mind, the principle of parental rights comes before the one of children's rights. Intervention by the state in family life, beyond a reactive policy of taking action in severe cases of child abuse and neglect, is seen as intrusive. From such a perspective, instead of parenting being a privilege, parenting is a right. However, from a children's rights perspective, parenting is a privilege and not a right. Children have rights, parents have the privilege to parent, and parents have the responsibility to respect children's rights and to parent competently. This latter view would be affirmed by a system of parent licensing. The licensing of a parent would signify that a parent has been given the privilege to parent and the responsibility to provide for the rights of the child. It would signify a clear societal recognition of the importance of parenting and a commitment to children's rights. The system we propose here is based on a model first described by Jack Westman, who articulated the following three basic principles of licensure.

First, parents should have demonstrated ability to be responsible for their own lives before being allowed to assume responsibility for a child's life. Responsibility here is not defined in economic terms as much as some indicators of physical, social, and emotional maturity. Whereas Westman suggested the age of majority, we suggest completion of a high school education as a minimum indicator here. For younger adolescents who become pregnant, a provisional license could be obtained. In this case, another party, who is licensed, must agree to accept responsibility for child-rearing until the adolescent has completed high school and is able to apply for a full license. Those with physical or mental disabilities that preclude self-care will also be eligible for provisional licenses subject to a licensed other's acceptance of supervisory responsibility.

Second, prospective parents must sign a contract in which they agree to refrain from abusing or neglecting the child, or allowing others to abuse the child (e.g., in the case of incest). Abusive and neglectful behaviors would be defined clearly. In addition, parents must accept that their license will be revoked if they break the contract. We do not expect abused women to stay with their partners to "keep the family together." We do not hesitate to place a family pet for adoption when it is abused. We should no longer make children stay with, or be returned to, abusive parents while social workers attempt to teach their parents basic child-care skills. Children who come to the attention of child protection agencies generally do better when removed expeditiously and placed in foster care or an adoptive home. A recent analysis of Ontario judgments indicated it takes the courts and Children's Aid an average of forty-four months to "rescue" an abused child. A lot of irreversible damage is done to young children over a four-year period.

Third, to obtain a license, parents must have completed a certified parenting course on early infant development. Subsequent courses, appropriate to developmental stages (toddlerhood, preschool, school-aged child, early adolescence, later adolescence), would be required for license renewal. Further, parents would be required to update their license in accord with life changes, such as divorce, death of spouse or sibling, remarriage or step-parenting. In each of these cases, a course would be taken that focuses on the child's needs through the changes undergone.

Parent licenses would be required for all Canadian parents, fathers as well as mothers, biological and adoptive parents. Immigrants with children would be given provisional licenses for a limited time period during which they must apply and meet the conditions for a license.

ADMINISTRATION AND ENFORCEMENT

Given the nature of Canada's federal system and provincial jurisdiction over much of family policy and law, it would be most logical for the provinces to administer the licensing system. It also would be most logical for existing child protection agencies to assume responsibility for administration. This would avoid the costs of creating a new bureaucratic structure. Child protection agencies already provide family support services as part of their general functions of child protection and child care. Establishing a system of administration would be a question only of revising child protection legislation and extending existing support services of agencies. Whereas this may seem like adding an extra burden to already overworked child protection workers, it must be remembered that the licensing approach will lessen significantly the overall numbers of children coming into care.

The licensing process would begin with an application by prospective parents or guardians to the responsible agency. Birth parents would apply during the pregnancy or at the time of birth registration. Prospective adoptive parents would do so during the early stages of the adoption process. And immigrant parents would do so with entry into Canada. Applications would be forwarded to the agency for review. If the criteria are met—demonstrating responsibility, signing a contract to refrain from abuse or neglect, and completing a parenting course—the license would be granted.

A license would be revoked or suspended under conditions such as evidence of abuse or neglect, sexual or economic exploitation, or the denial of education or health care. Whereas we might allow for second chances for parents under conditions that clearly are temporary (e.g., the child is not well cared for during a parental illness), expectations for competent parenting would be much higher than at present. The best interests of the child would be the sole criterion of decisions concerning the placement of any child.

But where will it lead? Critics may argue, as they did in opposing voting rights for women or laws against discrimination, that such change will do more harm than good. Concerns will be expressed about intrusion into family life, about the impossibility of identifying "good parenting," and about freedom and the need to be sensitive to multiculturalism. It will mean, critics will insist, massive intrusion into family life and over-regulation of parents by meddling officials of the state. However, it must be kept in mind that family life and parental freedom already are regulated. But the current regulations are reactive. Parent licensing would be a more proactive approach, lessening the need for intervention and facilitating intervention when necessary.

The benefits to society from requiring a license to drive a motor vehicle are obvious. We do not simply assume competence. With no exceptions, every person must apply and qualify for a license before being allowed to drive. We do not see this licensing as intrusive and meddling; we acknowledge that the health and safety of society as a whole depends on driver licensing. The benefits to all individuals and to society as a whole must be expected to be at least as great if parents also are educated and licensed.

PARENTHOOD TRAINING OR MANDATORY BIRTH CONTROL

TAKE YOUR CHOICE

Roger W. McIntire

*F*ew parents like to be told how to raise their children, and even fewer will like the idea of someone telling them whether they can even have children in the first place. But that's exactly what I'm proposing—the licensing of parenthood. Of course, civil libertarians and other liberals will claim this would infringe the parents' rights to freedom of choice and equal opportunity. But what about the rights of children? Surely the parents' competence will influence their children's freedom and opportunity. Today, any couple has the right to try parenting, regardless of how incompetent they might be. No one seems to worry about the unfortunate subjects of their experimenting.

The idea of licensing parenthood is hardly new.[1] But until recently, our ignorance of environmental effects, our ignorance of contraception, and our selfish bias against the rights of children have inhibited public discussion of the topic. In recent years, however, psychologists have taught us just how crucial the effect of the home environment can be, and current research on contraception appears promising. . . .

THE CHILD VICTIM

Clearly, we will soon have the technology necessary [a contraceptive that remains in effect until it is removed or counteracted by the administration of a

---

second drug] to carry out a parenthood licensing program, and history tells us that whenever we develop a technology, we inevitably use it. We should now be concerned with developing the criteria for good parenthood. In some extreme cases we already have legal and social definitions. We obviously consider child abuse wrong, and look upon those who physically mistreat their children as bad parents. In some states the courts remove children from the custody of parents convicted of child abuse.

In a recent review of studies of child-abusing parents, John J. Spinetta and David Rigler concluded that such people are generally ignorant of proper child-rearing practices. They also noted that many child-abusing parents had been victims of abuse and neglect in their own youth. Thus our lack of control over who can be parents magnifies the problem with each generation.

In the case of child-abusing parents, the state attempts to prevent the most obvious physical mistreatment of children. At this extreme, our culture does demand that parents prove their ability to provide for the physical well-being of their children. But our culture makes almost no demands when it comes to the children's psychological well-being and development. Any fool can now raise a child any way he or she pleases, and it's none of our business. The child becomes the unprotected victim of whoever gives birth to him.

Ironically, the only institutions that do attempt to screen potential parents are the adoption agencies, although their screening can hardly be called scientific. Curiously enough, those who oppose a parent-licensing law usually do not oppose the discriminating policies practiced by the adoption agencies. It seems that our society cares more about the selection of a child's second set of parents than it does about his original parents. In other words, our culture insists on insuring a certain quality of parenthood for adopted children, but if you want to have one of your own, feel free.

Screening and selecting potential parents by no means guarantees that they will in fact be good parents. Yet today we have almost no means of insuring proper child-rearing methods. The indiscriminate "right to parent" enables everyone, however ill-equipped, to practice any parental behavior they please. Often their behavior would be illegal if applied to any group other than children. But because of our prejudice against the rights of children, we protect them only when the most savage and brutal parental behavior can be proved in court. Consider the following example:

Supermarket Scenario: A mother and daughter enter a supermarket. An accident occurs when the daughter pulls the wrong orange from the pile and thirty-seven oranges are given their freedom. The mother grabs the daughter, shakes her vigorously, and slaps her.

What is your reaction? Do you ignore the incident? Do you consider it a family squabble and none of your business? Or do you go over and advise the

mother not to hit her child? If the mother rejects your advice, do you physically restrain her? If she persists, do you call the police? Think about your
answers for a moment.

Now let me change one detail. *The girl was not that mother's daughter.* Do
you feel different? Would you act differently? Why? Do "real" parents have
the right to abuse their children because they "own" them? Now let me
change another detail. Suppose the daughter was twenty-five years old, and
yelled, "Help me! Help me!" Calling the police sounded silly when I first
suggested it. How does it sound with a mere change in the age of the victim?

Now let's go back to the original scene where we were dealing with a
small child. Were you about to advise the mother or insist? Were you going
to say she shouldn't or couldn't? It depends on whose rights you're going to
consider. If you think about the mother's right to mother as she sees fit, then
you advise; but if you think about the child's right as a human being to be
protected from the physical assault of this woman, then you insist. The
whole issue is obviously tangled in a web of beliefs about individual rights,
parental rights, and children's rights. We tend to think children deserve what
they get, or at least must suffer it. Assault and battery, verbal abuse, and even
forced imprisonment become legal if the victims are children.

When I think about the issue of children's rights, and the current development of new contraceptives, I see a change coming in this country. I'm tempted
to make the following prediction in the form of a science-fiction story:

Motherhood in the 1980s

"Lock" was developed as a kind of semi-permanent contraceptive in 1975. One
dose of Lock and a woman became incapable of ovulation until the antidote
"Unlock" was administered. As with most contraceptives, Lock required a prescription, with sales limited by the usual criteria of age and marital status.

Gradually, however, a subtle but significant distinction became apparent.
Other contraceptives merely allowed a woman to protect herself against
pregnancy at her own discretion. Once Lock was administered, however, the
prescription for Unlock required an active decision to allow the *possibility* of
pregnancy.

By 1978, the two drugs were being prescribed simultaneously, leaving
the Unlock decision in the hands of the potential mother. Of course, problems arose. Mothers smuggled Lock to their daughters and the daughters
later asked for Unlock. Women misplaced the Unlock and had to ask for
more. Faced with the threat of a black market, the state set up a network of
special dispensaries for the contraceptive and its antidote. When the first dispensaries opened in 1979, they dispensed Lock rather freely, since they could
always regulate the use of Unlock. But it soon became apparent that special

local committees would be necessary to screen applicants for Unlock. "After all," the dispensary officials asked themselves, "how would you like to be responsible for this person becoming a parent?"

. . . That same year, 1979, brought the school-population riots. Overcrowding had forced state education officials to take some action. Thanks to more efficient educational techniques, they were able to consider reducing the number of years of required schooling. This, however, would have thrown millions of teenagers out onto the already overcrowded job market, which would make the unions unhappy. Thus, rather than shortening the entire educational process, the officials decided to shorten the school day into two half-day shifts. That led to the trouble.

Until then, people had assumed that schools existed primarily for the purpose of education. But the decision to shorten the school day exposed the dependence of the nation's parents on the school as the great baby sitter of their offspring. Having won the long struggle for day care centers, and freedom from diapers and bottles, mothers were horrified at the prospect of a few more hours of responsibility every day until their children reached eighteen or twenty-one. They took to the streets.

In Richmond, Virginia, a neighborhood protest over the shortened school day turned into a riot. One of the demonstrators picked up a traffic sign near the school that cautioned drivers to "Protect Our Children," and found herself leading the march toward city hall. Within a week that sign became the national slogan for the protesters, as well as for the Lock movement. It came to mean not only protecting our children from overcrowding and lack of supervision, but also protecting them from pregnancy.

Because of the school-population riots, distribution of Lock took on the characteristics of an immunization program under the threat of an epidemic. With immunization completed, the state could control the birth rate like a water faucet by the distribution of Unlock. However, this did not solve the problem of deciding who should bear the nation's children.

. . . To settle the issue, Congress appointed a special blue-ribbon commission of psychologists, psychiatrists, educators, and clergymen to come up with acceptable criteria for parenthood, and a plan for a licensing program. The commission issued its report in 1984. Based upon its recommendations, Congress set up a federal regulatory agency to administer a national parenthood-licensing program similar to driver-training and licensing procedures.

The agency now issues study guides for the courses, and sets the required standards of child-rearing knowledge. Of course, the standards vary for parents, teachers, and child-care professionals, depending upon the degree of responsibility involved. The courses and exams are conducted by local community colleges, under the supervision of the federal agency. Only upon passing the exams can prospective parents receive a prescription for Unlock.

Distribution of Lock and Unlock is now strictly regulated by the federal agency's local commissions. Since the records of distribution are stored in federal computer banks, identification of illegitimate pregnancies (those made possible by the unauthorized use of Unlock) has become a simple matter. Parents convicted of this crime are fined, and required to begin an intensive parenthood-training program immediately. If they do not qualify by the time their child is born, the child goes to a community child-care program until they do.

As might be expected, the parent-licensing program has come under attack from those who complain about the loss of their freedom to create and raise children according to their own choice and beliefs. To such critics, the protect-our-children or Lock faction argues, "It's absurd to require education and a license to drive a car, but allow anybody to raise our most precious possession or to add to the burden of this possession without demonstrating an ability to parent."

"But the creation of life is in the hands of God," say the freedom-and-right-to-parent faction (referred to by their opposition as the "far-right people").

"Nonsense," say the Lock people. "Control over life creation was acquired with the first contraceptive. The question is whether we use it with intelligence or not."

"But that question is for each potential parent to answer as an individual," say the far-right people.

The Lock people answer, "Those parents ask the selfish question of whether they want a child or not. We want to know if the child will be adequately cared for—by them and by the culture."

The far-right respond, "God gave us bodies and all their functions. We have a right to the use of those functions. Unlock should be there for the asking. Why should the government have a say in whether I have a child?"

"Because the last century has shown that the government will be saddled with most of the burden of raising your child," say the Lock people. "The schools, the medical programs, the youth programs, the crime-prevention programs, the colleges, the park and planning commissions—they will be burdened with your child. That's why the government should have a say. The extent of the government's burden depends on your ability to raise your child. If you screw it up, the society *and* government will suffer. That's why they should screen potential parents."

From the right again, "The decision of my spouse and myself is sacred. It's none of their damn business."

But the Locks argue, "If you raised your child in the wilderness and the child's malfunctions punished no one but yourselves, it would be none of their damn business. But if your child is to live with us, be educated by us, suffered by us, add to the crowd of us, we should have a say."

FACE OF THE FUTURE

I can understand how some people might find this story either far-fetched or frightening, but I don't think any prediction in it is too far in the future. Carl Djerassi suggested the possibility of a semipermanent contraceptive such as "Lock" and "Unlock" (although he didn't use those brand names) as early as 1969, in an article in *Science*. . . .

Throughout history, as knowledge has eroded superstition about conception and birth, humans have taken increasing control over the birth of their offspring. Religious practices, arranged marriages, mechanical and biochemical contraception have all played a role in this regulation of procreation. Until now, however, such regulation has dealt only with the presence or absence of children, leaving their development to cultural superstitions. Anyone with normal biology may still produce another child, and, within the broadest limits, treat it any way he or she chooses.

We have taken a long time coming to grips with this problem because our society as a whole has had no demonstrably better ideas about child-rearing than any individual parent. And until now, people couldn't be stopped from having children because we haven't had the technology that would enable us to control individual fertility.

HOW TO REAR A CHILD

The times are changing. With the population problem now upon us, we can no longer afford the luxury of allowing any two fools to add to our numbers whenever they please. We do have, or soon will have, the technology to control individual procreation. And, most important, psychology and related sciences have by now established some child-rearing principles that should be part of every parent's knowledge.[2] An objective study of these principles need not involve the prying, subjective investigation now used by adoption agencies. It would merely ensure that potential parents would be familiar with the principles of sound child-rearing. Examinations and practical demonstrations would test their knowledge. Without having state agents check every home (and of course, we would never accept such "Big Brother" tactics), there could be no way to enforce the use of that knowledge. But insistence on the knowledge would itself save a great deal of suffering by the children.

The following list suggests a few of the topics with which every parent should be familiar:

1. Principles of sound nutrition and diet.
2. Changes in nutritional requirements with age.

3. Principles of general hygiene and health.

4. Principles of behavioral development: normal range of ages at which behavioral capabilities might be expected, etc.

5. Principles of learning and language acquisition.

6. Principles of immediacy and consistency that govern parents' reactions to children's behavior.

7. Principles of modeling and imitation: how children learn from and copy their parents' behavior.

8. Principles of reinforcement: how parent and peer reactions reward a child's behavior, and which rewards should be used.

9. Principles of punishment: how parents' reactions can be used to punish or discourage bad behavior.

10. Response-cost concept: how to "raise the cost" or create unpleasant consequences in order to make undesirable behavior more "expensive" or difficult.

11. Extinction procedures and adjunctive behavior: if rewards for good behavior cease, children may "act up" just to fill the time.

12. Stimulus-control generalization: children may act up in some situations, and not in others, because of different payoffs. For example, Mommy may give the child candy to stop a tantrum, whereas Daddy may ignore it or strike the child.

Most of us have some familiarity with the principles at the beginning of this list, but many parents have little knowledge of the other topics. Some psychologists would obviously find my list biased toward behavior modification, but their revisions or additions to the list only strengthen my argument that our science has a great deal to teach that would be relevant to a parenthood-licensing program.

MISPLACED PRIORITIES

Of course the word "licensing" suggests that the impersonal hand of government may control individual lives, and that more civil servants will be paid to meddle in our personal affairs. But consider for a moment that for our safety and well-being we already license pilots, salesmen, scuba divers, plumbers, electricians, teachers, veterinarians, cab drivers, soil testers, and television repairmen. To protect pedestrians, we accept restrictions on the speed with which we drive our cars. Why, then, do we encounter such commotion, chest thumping, and cries of oppression when we try to protect the well-being of children by controlling the most crucial determiner of that well-being, the competence of their parents? Are our TV sets and toilets more important to us than our children? Can you imagine the public outcry that would occur if adoption agencies offered their children on a first-come-first-served basis, with no screening process for applicants? Imagine some drunk stumbling up and saying, "I'll take that cute little blond-haired girl over there."

We require appropriate education for most trades and professions, yet stop short at parenthood because it would be an infringement on the individual freedom of the parent. The foolishness of this position will become increasingly apparent the more confident we become in our knowledge about child-rearing.

The first step toward a parenthood law will probably occur when child-abuse offenders will be asked or required to take "Lock" as an alternative to, or in addition to, being tried in court. Or the courts may also offer the child abuser the alternative of a remedial training program such as the traffic courts now use. The next step may be the broadening of the term "child abuse" to include ignorant mistreatment of a psychological nature. Some communities may add educational programs to marriage-license requirements, while others may add parenthood training to existing courses in baby care.

When the government gets around to setting criteria for proper child-rearing, these must be based upon a very specific set of principles of nutrition, hygiene, and behavior control. They cannot be based on bias and hearsay. Some of the criteria now used by adoption agencies, such as references from neighbors and friends, cannot be considered objective. We don't interview your neighbors when you apply for a driver's license, and it shouldn't be done for a parent's license either. But just as a citizen must now demonstrate knowledge and competence to drive a car, so ought he to demonstrate his ability to parent as well. Proof of exposure to education is not enough. We are not satisfied merely with driver-training courses, but demand a driver's test as well. We should require the same standards of parents.

We can hope that as progress occurs in the technology of contraception and the knowledge of child-rearing principles, the currently sacred "right to parent" will be reevaluated by our society. Perhaps we can construct a society that will also consider the rights that children have to be a humane and beneficial upbringing.

NOTES

1. Robert P. Hawkins, "It's Time We Taught the Young How to Be Good Parents (And Don't You Wish We'd Started a Long Time Ago?" *Psychology Today* (November 1972).

2. Roger W. McIntire, "Spare the Rod, Use Behavior Mod," *Psychology Today* (December 1970).

2. Assessment

*I*n this section, the focus is narrowed to the single issue of assessment, in particular to two questions: *Can* we accurately and reliably assess parent competence? *What* elements should be included in such an assessment?

Although concerned about the potential for administrative abuse (certain applicants may experience unjust discrimination, for example), and suggesting therefore that parent licensing programs have procedures in place to ensure confidentiality and impartiality, Mangel essentially endorses LaFollette's claim that we can indeed make the necessary assessments. She recommends a consideration of demographic factors (research has established a demographic profile of the abusive parent), *along with* individualized screening for personal and situational factors, and she describes two screening tools currently in use for this purpose. Mangel also points out in her article that the state already predicts parental competence and sometimes prevents a parent from taking her infant home from hospital, effectively denying custody before harm is done—so in this sense, a parent licensing program would be nothing new. It would, however, she says, be better in many ways to current practice—more objective, more expeditious, and less costly.

Trombetta, who has worked extensively as an evaluator for child custody decisions in divorce cases, would disagree with Mangel's conclusions. Since current tools rely on superficial and easily observable behavior, Trombetta says, assessments based on such tools will be equally superficial. Many parenting skills, however, are complex and value-laden. In order to properly assess such skills, time, energy, and money is required; otherwise, she suggests, they should not be evaluated at all.

Bartholet provides a firsthand account and critique of the screening system for parental fitness used by adoption agencies. It is, she concludes, "extremely crude" (page 120 in this volume) and rampant with discrimination on the bases of age, race, religion, disability, marital status, and sexual orientation. More aligned then with Trombetta than with Mangel, Bartholet advocates replacing the current system with a more minimalist system, one that might be used if we were to license biological parents. She does not advocate such licensing, but, also a biological parent, she offers some interesting comparative insights.

Overall adds to the discussion the context of new reproductive technologies (NRTs). As in the contexts of custody and adoption discussed by Trombetta and Bartholet, decisions about parental fitness—in this context, decisions about access to NRTs—are made on the basis of several factors. In the section of her article included here, Overall considers in detail the relevance of sexuality, exemplifying the kind of analysis that should accompany all discussions of assessment for parent competence. She concludes by conceding that a system of licensing parents, as suggested by LaFollette, may be appropriate given "a society such as ours" (p. 138), but it would be better to change the conditions and values of our society so that licensing wouldn't be necessary.

LICENSING PARENTS

HOW FEASIBLE?

Claudia Pap Mangel

Parents raise their children as a labor of love and not as a professional assignment. Unlike child development experts and other professional persons concerned with child care, parents are not specialists. Their responsibility is the whole child—his every need at all times.[1]

*A*s child advocates Joseph Goldstein, Anna Freud, Albert Solnit, and Sonja Goldstein point out above, raising a child is no easy task.[2] Recently, Hugh LaFollette has asserted that parenting is an activity potentially harmful to children and one requiring competence if harm is to be avoided.[3] Since child-rearing satisfies the general criteria for regulatory licensing, LaFollette argues that the state should require all parents to be licensed.

This essay presents an analysis of the feasibility of Hugh LaFollette's thesis that the state should require all parents to be licensed. It will first examine the rationale and justification for LaFollette's thesis, and then explore the present ability of screening methods to predict which parents are "at risk" of abusing their children. Next, it will consider the existing mechanism for state intervention and removal of children from their parents on grounds of "potential neglect."[4] Finally, the essay will conclude that compared to the existing "potential neglect" scheme for protecting children,

"Licensing Parents: How Feasible?" by Claudia Pap Mangel, *Family Law Quarterly* 12, no. 1 (spring 1988). Reprinted by permission.

Ed. note: Some notes have been deleted from the original for clarity and ease of reading.

licensing parents would be more objective, expeditious, and less costly. The present state framework for child protection should be changed to include a program in which parents would receive either regular or conditional parenting licenses and would not generally be denied licenses before they had an opportunity to care for their child.

HUGH LaFOLLETTE'S THESIS: LICENSING PARENTS

. . . Considering several theoretical and practical objections to licensing, LaFollette rejects the argument that it would be impossible to distinguish adequate parents from inadequate parents: "My proposal, however, does not demand that we make these fine distinctions. It does not demand that we license only the best parents; rather it is designed to exclude only the very bad ones."[5] The feasibility of LaFollette's thesis, that the state should require all parents to be licensed, thus hinges on the present ability of screening methods to predict which parents might abuse their children. The second part of this essay will focus on the identifiable characteristics of abusive parents and existing predictive screening instruments.

LaFollette dismisses the objections that any licensing procedure would be unintentionally misused by administrators or intentionally abused by those administering the predictive screening tests. He concludes that there is no reason to believe that more mistakes will be made, or more intentional abuse occur, in the administration of parenting licenses than in other regulatory or judicial activities. LaFollette's response to these objections is reasonable; however, it would most likely not dispel the fears of many parents.

There are many ways to rear a child and some, though they pose no threat to a child's well-being, may be inconsistent with community standards of child-rearing. Many parents would fear that a licensing scheme could be intentionally abused by those who administered it and used against parents whose ideas of child-rearing and family life are not in line with community standards. Therefore, where the values of a community are grounded in an identifiable cultural or ethnic background, parents in the community who are not members of the dominant cultural group would fear that a parent-licensing program would be used to pressure them into conforming to community standards of child-rearing. Other instances of intentional abuse of a licensing program can be easily imagined, such as frequent denial of licenses to parents who are poor or uneducated. The objection that a licensing program could be intentionally abused, by being used to impose the standards of the majority on the minority members in a community or otherwise misused, is not to be taken lightly. LaFollette's dismissal of such an objection, although rational, is neither comforting nor persuasive. To dispel fears of intentional abuse, a parent-licensing scheme would have to contain procedures designed to ensure confidentiality, impartiality, and prompt reviewability.

In response to the objection that a parent-licensing program could never be adequately or fairly enforced, in terms of dealing with "violators" and the children of unlicensed parents, LaFollette is unable to point to a ready enforcement mechanism. . . .

In the third part of this essay, an existing "potential neglect" mechanism for child protection will be discussed, in which "potentially" abusive or neglectful parents are denied custody of their infant before they have even had a chance to care for the child. While LaFollette's suggestion, that children of unlicensed parents or "violators" be removed from their parents, seems harsh and punitive, his later comments reveal that he considers measures short of rigid enforcement more realistic. . . . Parents would most likely be more receptive to a voluntary, tax-favored licensing scheme than a mandatory, state-enforced program.

LaFollette finds justification for his parent licensing program in the present regulatory system for adoption. . . . The comparison of a parent licensing program to the current adoption process is admittedly persuasive.

It is important to note that the first modern adoption law in U.S. history, a Massachusetts adoption statute enacted in 1851, was concerned primarily with "the welfare of the child and the parental qualifications of the adopters."[6] The Massachusetts Adoption of Children Act of 1851 became the model for adoption legislation in most of the common law states.[7] Between the 1850s and the 1950s, adoption became a legal process governed by state laws that usually required the consent of the biological parents, involvement of a child welfare agency, a probationary trial period in the adoptive home under agency supervision, issuance of a court decree, and secrecy concerning the identity of the natural parents.

The stringent requirements described were thought to protect children against being adopted by unsuitable parents or casually transferred by their natural parents into the custody of others. At the end of the 1960s and into the [next] decade, child welfare agencies were faced with a new challenge, "the need to safeguard and equitably balance the sometimes conflicting interests of members of the adoptive triad," that is, the child, his natural parents, and his adoptive parents.[8] It is appropriate to justify a parent licensing program by reference to the existing adoption system, as the adoption process attempts to distinguish adequate from inadequate parents, and protect children without detriment to the interests of the child, the natural parents, and the adoptive parents.

In a critique of LaFollette's thesis, Lawrence Frisch asserts that LaFollette's parent licensing scheme exceeds the forms of licensing which society has conventionally employed.[9] Frisch argues that LaFollette has shifted the focus of licensing from its traditional objective of assessing knowledge to the area of predicting future behavior and misconduct. LaFollette dismisses this claim in a response to Frisch (see note 13 and accompanying text).

Frisch's critique is largely unconvincing, primarily because he appears to attack LaFollette's choice of words rather than his thesis and supporting arguments. For example, while LaFollette notes that abused children "will probably never be well-adjusted, happy adults,"[10] Frisch dwells upon this language, asserting that "LaFollette's approach is that he bases his argument on an implicit human right to be 'well-adjusted and happy' as an adult, and he wants to give children claim on that right for their future."[11] Frisch concludes his critique by asserting that "family surveillance" would be more reasonable than licensing: "Such an approach would not focus on determining whether parents are fit to raise children in general, but only on whether a given child is being raised to a defined community standard in the family in which he or she is living."[12] It is difficult to conceive of a child protection scheme more subjective, intrusive, vulnerable to intentional abuse, and harder to implement than Frisch's suggestion that the state determine whether a child is being reared "to a defined community standard."

In response to Frisch, LaFollette argues that traditional licensing programs determine competence to perform the regulated activity by examining present abilities, but asserts that testing of current performance would be futile if present competencies were not considered realistic indicators of future behavior.[13] Referring to the procedures for screening parental behavior that are used in the adoption context, LaFollette observes that the strict "licensing procedures" imposed on adoptive parents are designed, in part, to predict abusive behavior and not merely to examine present skills. Considering the current adoption system, LaFollette concludes: "Nonetheless, we find the goal of protecting adopted children sufficiently worthy to justify such licensing procedures. Why should we protect other children any less?"[14] The second part of this essay will explore the feasibility of licensing biological parents by examining the predictive ability of available screening methods.

PREDICTIVE SCREENING: PRESENT ABILITY

Child abuse and neglect is a public health problem of epidemic proportions, both in the United States and throughout the world.[15] A discussion of the etiology, consequences, treatment, and prevention of child abuse is beyond the scope of this essay. In response to Hugh LaFollette's provocative argument that the state should require all parents to be licensed, the predictive ability of existing screening methods will be examined. It is appropriate at this point to recall LaFollette's qualifying statement:

My proposal, however, does not demand that we make these fine distinctions. It does not demand that we license only the best parents; rather it is designed to exclude only the very bad ones.[16]

Therefore, the real issue to be explored is whether existing screening methods can be used to predict which persons might be "very bad" parents. The following discussion will focus on the identifiable characteristics of abusive parents and the ability of existing tests to predict which parents might harm their children.

Recent research on the demographic characteristics of abusive parents shows that children are more likely to be mistreated by their mothers than their fathers; by younger, rather than older parents; by single, separated, or divorced, rather than married parents; and by parents of lower, rather than higher, socioeconomic status.[17] Additionally, women who do not experience nurturant and supportive environments, including positive emotional and affectional relationships, have difficulty providing such environments for their children.[18] Observation of the interactive patterns between abusive mothers and their children reveals that such mothers are insensitive to the moods and signals of their children.[19]

Known correlates of child maltreatment also include low income and other aspects of economic pressure, such as unemployment; values concerning the role of the child in the family; attitudes about the use of physical punishment; social isolation: poor coping and parenting skills; personal characteristics of parents and children, such as physical illness, poor ability to empathize (parents), unresponsiveness, aversive crying (children); history of maltreatment in a parent's family; contemporaneous spousal violence; and patterns of daily interaction in the home, school, or workplace characterized by low levels of social exchange, low responsiveness to positive behavior, and high responsiveness to negative behavior.[20] Parental mental illness appears to play a small overall role in child abuse and neglect, although many abusive parents exhibit inadequate personality characteristics.[21] A positive association has been found to exist between young maternal age and child abuse.[22] Adolescent parents appear to be faced with excessive stress, have inadequate social support systems, are developmentally immature, and lack both adequate knowledge of child development and appropriate child-rearing attitudes.[23]

Identification of parents at risk of abusing their children, through screening for the above characteristics, is useful in the development of prevention programs and allocation of limited resources. Child abuse prevention programs "depend on a predictive theory of child abuse," that is, a social psychological model of child abuse.[24] Identification of parents at risk, however, remains a controversial issue because incorrectly labeling parents as being at risk of abusing their children may bring about the behavior to be avoided.[25] Some investigators assert that screening programs cannot be de-

fended on ethical grounds because of the social cost incurred in falsely identifying families not at risk.[26]

It appears that screening of parents based on the discussed demographic
characteristics would not provide an adequate basis for the grant or denial of
parenting licenses. LaFollette's licensing scheme requires an instrument
capable of predicting which persons might be "very bad" parents. Demographic factors alone are not sufficiently predictive to reliably identify parents at risk of abusing their children.[27] It may even be difficult to separate
risk factors from reporting bias in some circumstances, such as where individuals with certain demographic characteristics are more likely to be suspected of child abuse than other parents, and consequently, reported to child
protection agencies more frequently.[28] Demographic risk factors supplemented by the use of an individualized screening method may, however, yield
a tool with the predictive reliability for which LaFollette is searching.

During the last six years, a sophisticated instrument for the prediction of
child abuse has been introduced, tested, and refined; this instrument is the
Child Abuse Potential Inventory.[29] The initial version of the Child Abuse
Potential Inventory was a 160-item, client-administered screening device
with a grade-three readability level, which required about twenty minutes to
complete.[30] The instrument was designed to assess an individual's child abuse
potential, and subjects were asked to "agree" or "disagree" with each of the
statements presented. The Child Abuse Potential Inventory was developed
on the basis of a comprehensive review of the literature and measured seven
factors descriptive of abusive parents: distress, rigidity, child with problems,
problems with family and others, unhappiness, loneliness, and negative concept of child and self.

In an early study, the Child Abuse Potential Inventory accurately and reliably distinguished child abusers from nonabusers in study populations.[31] A
later study was conducted to determine whether the Child Abuse Potential
Inventory could identify "at-risk" subjects who had been identified as "at risk"
by existing criteria, that is, subjects who had not been reported for abuse but
had one or more putative indicators of abuse, such as the demographic characteristics of abusive parents previously discussed. The results of the study
indicated that sufficient overlap existed between the results of the "at risk" criteria screening and elevated scores on the Child Abuse Potential Inventory, so
that either procedure could be used to distinguish a group of "at-risk" or
potentially abusive individuals from a group of nonabusive subjects. The
authors suggested that preliminary screening using the "at risk" criteria could
be conducted to identify an initial "at-risk" group, which could then be
administered the Child Abuse Potential Inventory to determine which individuals in the group were at the highest risk of abusing their children. In an
additional study, 77 of the 160 items in the Child Abuse Potential Inventory

were found to differ significantly between abusers and nonabuser control sub-jects who matched on various demographic characteristics.[32]

In a later study, using revised "at risk" criteria, the degree of concor-dance between an individual's potential parenting problems as determined by the "at risk" criteria and the same parent's abuse potential as determined by the Child Abuse Potential Inventory remained significant.[33] The revised "at risk" criteria screened for biological, psychological, social, and interactional risk factors, and the Child Abuse Potential Inventory employed in the study contained a lie scale.

Later studies using the 160-item Child Abuse Potential Inventory, de-signed to differentiate abusers from nonabusers, demonstrated the following correlations: emotional and personal problems, and ineffective coping and problem-solving skills, were related to elevated abuse scores; higher levels of apprehension, tension, and anxiety and lower levels of stability correlated with elevated abuse scores; and self-reported levels of life stress were signif-icantly related to abuse scores.[34] Additionally, the Child Abuse Potential Inventory has been shown to be effective in determining treatment effects in high-risk parents when given on a pretreatment, posttreatment, and follow-up basis, where the treatment consisted of a Family Life Education Program for High-Risk Parents.[35] Finally, recent data indicates a positive relationship between elevated abuse scores on the Child Abuse Potential Inventory and subsequent reports of abuse, a marginally significant relation between abuse scores and neglect, and no relation between abuse scores and failure to thrive. The investigators noted:

> These data support previous findings that the Inventory, which was designed to screen for abuse, more accurately detects abusive parents than neglectful parents or parents of [failure to thrive infants]. The lack of a relationship between abuse scores and confirmed FTT is consistent with observations [citation omitted] that abuse and FTT are two distinct pediatric illnesses.[36]

The Child Abuse Potential Inventory, therefore, is best able to predict which persons might be "very bad" parents, and less able to predict which individ-uals might be marginally inadequate parents.

The Child Abuse Potential Inventory has been refined through extensive research and has proven a reliable instrument for accurately discriminating between abusive and nonabusive parents.[37] Recent research provides support for the concurrent validity of the Child Abuse Potential Inventory.[38] Several reliability studies have been conducted on the psychometric qualities of the Child Abuse Potential Inventory,[39] as well as numerous construct validity studies.[40] It is important to note that in a study investigating the ability of the Child Abuse Potential Inventory to screen for child abuse in a group of spouse abusers, 36 percent of the spouse abusers had elevated child abuse scores, supporting an earlier finding that one-third of spouse abusers are also child abusers.[41]

The Child Abuse Potential Inventory appears to be a well-researched, reliable predictive instrument which would be appropriate for use in Hugh LaFollette's parent licensing program. Ideally, parents would be tested for future parenting problems by the use of both screening according to "at risk" criteria or demographic characteristics, and scoring on the Child Abuse Potential Inventory. Since the Child Abuse Potential Inventory has been shown to be an appropriate instrument for evaluating the effects of a treatment program on high-risk parents,[42] it could be used to retest unlicensed parents after they had received parenting-skills training or other supportive social services.

The Child Abuse Potential Inventory is not the only available predictive screening instrument. In a recent prospective study, accurate predictions of parenting ability were made prenatally, using a Family Stress Checklist.[43] The study focused on whether high-risk parents would, in fact, be more likely to abuse or neglect their children. The study screened the patient population of a large maternal and infant clinic, where women enrolled in a maternity care project between the third and sixth months of pregnancy. All women were interviewed by a social worker as part of the initial intake procedure, and the Family Stress Checklist was included in the interview. The Family Stress Checklist encompasses ten factors—each scored as no risk, moderate risk, or high risk—and is relatively easy to administer and use in collecting information.

Results of the study demonstrated that the Family Stress Checklist was an accurate predictor: 80 percent of the families identified as abusive or neglectful after the birth of their child (abuse or neglect had occurred in the family) had scored high (high-risk scores) on the prenatal Family Stress Checklist. . . . The Family Stress Checklist, therefore, constitutes a predictive screening instrument appropriate for use in LaFollette's parent licensing program.

The feasibility of LaFollette's licensing program hinges on the availability of reliable predictive screening methods. Three such procedures have been examined: identification of parents at risk of abusing their children through the use of demographic factors or "at risk" criteria, identification of potential child abusers through the use of the Child Abuse Potential Inventory, and prenatal identification of high-risk parents through the use of the Family Stress Checklist. However, if any or all of these screening methods were incorporated into a licensing program, opportunities for parent training and retesting would have to be provided for those parents denied licenses, or granted provisional licenses, on the ground that they were at risk of being "very bad" parents. A general discussion of treatment programs for abusive and neglectful parents is beyond the scope of this essay; however, options for providing high-risk parents support and training will be considered briefly. . . .

LICENSING PARENTS VERSUS EXISTING MECHANISMS

To many, Hugh LaFollette's parent licensing scheme may appear an outrageous intrusion by the state into family privacy. If LaFollette's suggested scheme were put into practice, then "unlicensed" parents would be prohibited from taking their child home from the hospital, or raising their child, if they could not become "licensed" parents. The fact of the matter is, however, that several jurisdictions use their "dependent child" or "deprived child" statutes to do exactly what LaFollette has suggested: prevent a parent from taking her infant home from the hospital where the parent's physical or mental condition or home environment would place the child in jeopardy. The issue usually arises in an adjudicatory context where the state seeks custody of the child under the applicable "dependent child" provisions. The parent is required to defend her condition or home environment, and the court must decide whether the child will be endangered if placed in the parent's custody.

Needless to say, such an adjudicatory proceeding is exceedingly costly in terms of time involved, financial expense, and detriment to the well-being of both the child and parent. The state incurs the financial cost of bringing the claim against the parent, and the parent must either pay her own legal fees or obtain counsel through a legal services agency. In addition, there is a serious social cost incurred: the parent is required to defend her condition or environment before a court of law, which is most likely a stressful and disturbing experience, and the newborn infant is placed in short-term foster care, essentially "limbo," until the case is decided. The effects of temporary foster care on infants and young children are varied, and discussion of the potentially damaging effects is beyond the scope of this essay. . . .

The cited cases show that, for the most part, courts are willing to intervene and deny parents custody of an infant where the facts indicate that an infant's health or safety may be jeopardized if placed in the parents' custody, even though the parents may have never had an opportunity to care for the child. What the courts are willing to do looks much like licensing parents on a case-by-case basis.

The conclusion to be drawn from consideration of the potential neglect scheme for protecting children is that courts are not reluctant to do what LaFollette has suggested: predict that an individual will be a bad parent, and then deny that parent custody of her infant before she has had a chance to care for the child. Compared to this rather arbitrary, judicial form of parent licensing, LaFollette's licensing program would be more objective, expeditious, and less costly.

If the state required all parents to become licensed before the birth of their child, much case-by-case adjudication under the "dependent child" provisions could be avoided, saving considerable time, financial expense, and other social costs, including detriment to the child and family. An established state framework for parent licensing would also be more objective than case-by-case review by different family courts of varied factual situations. In addition, a licensing program could provide parenting education and support services for those parents who did not become licensed on the first try. The program could even grant such parents a *provisional license* and thus allow them to care for their infant while requiring some supervision. The present state framework for child protection should be changed to include licensing of parents.

Most parents would cringe at the thought of a state framework for parent licensing, and rightfully so. What parent has never made an error in judgment that endangered his child's life, health, or safety? Most parents would fear that the licensing program would be abused by those who administered it, and used to take away their children for insubstantial reasons. However, two of LaFollette's arguments should be recalled: first, he does not propose that the state distinguish "between good and less-than-good parents," "make fine distinctions" in parenting skills, or "license only the best parents";[44] and, second, he does not state that mandatory licensing would be the only effective means of protecting children. LaFollette asserts that the licensing program he envisions would be "designed to exclude only the very bad [parents]."[45] In addition, he suggests that "a system of tax incentives for licensed parents, and protective services scrutiny of nonlicensed parents, might adequately protect children."[46]

It is therefore useful to think of parent licensing in terms of something other than mandatory state regulation of parents. LaFollette's "tax incentives" proposal is a good idea. A tax-favored licensing scheme could provide that parents who became "licensed" would be eligible for a tax credit, larger "dependent" deduction, special "licensed parent" deduction, or other tax benefit.

A similar financial incentive could be incorporated into the present welfare system, enabling "licensed" parents to receive additional funds or other benefits. Perhaps choosing a different term, such as parent "certification" instead of parent "licensing," would make the whole idea of state regulation of parenting more palatable. The word "license" evokes images of driving tests, medical boards, or bar exams, and similar involvement with law enforcement authorities.

LaFollette's suggestion of "protective services scrutiny of nonlicensed parents" is also a workable proposal. A framework for state regulation of parents in which no parent is actually denied a license can be envisioned. Parents would be required to become "licensed" or "certified" before the birth of their child in order to be able to take their infant home from the hospital. The availability of reliable predictive screening methods has been discussed, and it appears that instruments capable of predicting which persons might be "very bad [parents]" presently exist. Parents who did not become licensed before the birth of their child, whether due to test results indicating that they were at risk of abusing their child or failure to be tested, would be allowed to take their infant home from the hospital on a *provisional license*. The terms of the provisional license would require that the parents participate in some type of parent-support program, such as receiving counseling, cooperating with a "homemaker" or "public health nurse," enrolling in a parenting-skills "school" with their infant, or participating in activities at a community family support center designed to improve child-rearing skills.

Parents who were issued provisional licenses could be retested after they had received parent-support services, repeatedly if necessary, until they qualified for a regular parenting license or certificate. It should be noted that one of the predictive screening instruments examined, the Child Abuse Potential Inventory, has been successfully used to demonstrate "treatment" effects in parents initially identified as potential abusers and later provided parenting-skills education.[47]

More stringent enforcement measures might be needed to deal with parents who received provisional parenting licenses and then failed to satisfy the conditions of the provisional license. Temporary foster care placement of the children of such parents might be necessary to provide proper care for the children until their parents chose or became able to participate in the supportive social programs, required by the provisional license.

CONCLUSION

This paper has considered the rationale and justification for Hugh LaFollette's thesis that the state should require all parents to be licensed. The availability of reliable predictive screening procedures has been explored with focus on the identification of abusive parents through use of demographic factors or "at risk" criteria, screening for potential child abusers through use of the Child Abuse Potential Inventory, and prenatal identification of "high-risk" parents through use of a Family Stress Checklist. The existing state mechanism for removal of children from their parents on grounds of "potential neglect" is surprisingly similar to LaFollette's proposed licensing program. Compared to the existing "potential neglect" scheme for protecting children, a licensing program in which parents were granted either regular or provisional parenting licenses would be more objective, expeditious, and less costly in terms of both financial expenditure and individual burden for the state and family.

NOTES

1. J. Goldstein, A. Freud, A. Solnit, and S. Goldstein, *In the Best Interests of the Child: Professional Boundaries* (New York: Free Press, 1986).

2. Ibid., pp. 3–4.

3. Hugh LaFollette, "Licensing Parents," *Philosophy and Public Affairs* 9 (1980): 182, 184–85.

4. J. Areen, *Cases and Materials on Family Law* 1240 (2d ed. 1985).

5. LaFollette, "Licensing Parents," p. 190.

6. Zainaldin, *The Emergence of a Modern American Family Law: Child Custody, Adoption, and the Courts, 1796–1851,* 73 Nw. U.L. REV. 1038. 1042–43 (1979).

7. Howe, *Adoption Practice, Issues, and Laws 1958–1983,* 17 FAM. L.Q. 173, 176 (1983).

8. Ibid., p. 185.

9. Lawrence Frisch, "On Licentious Licensing: A Reply to Hugh LaFollette," *Philosophy and Public Affairs* 11 (1981): 173, 179.

10. Ibid., p. 185.

11. Ibid., p. 179.

12. Ibid., p. 180.

13. Hugh LaFollette, "A Reply to Frisch," *Philosophy and Public Affairs* 11 (1982): 181. LaFollette observes: "Licensing is supposed to decrease potential harm, not serve as an unnecessary cataloguing of people's skills." Frisch's first objection "seems misguided."

14. LaFollette, "Licensing Parents," p. 183.

15. Taylor and Newberger, "Child Abuse in the International Year of the Child," *New England Journal of Medicine* 301 (1979): 1205, 1206–12. [Ed. note: The author goes on to provide a lengthy list of references on child abuse to substantiate her claims; these references have been deleted partly because of space constraints and partly because most of the material has, no doubt, been updated and is easily accessible. Persons interested in these references can consult the original article by Pap Mangel.]

16. LaFollette, "Licensing Parents," p. 190.

17. Turner and Avison, "Assessing Risk Factors for Problem Parenting: The Significance of Social Support," *Journal of Marriage and Family* 47 (1985): 881. The authors note: "While these relationships are much too weak to be of any real predictive utility, they are of theoretical significance because such associations provide bases for the generation of causal hypotheses." See also Hergenroeder et al., "Neonatal Characteristics of Maltreated Infants and Children," *American Journal of Diseases of Children* 139 (1985): 295; Oates, Forrest, and Peacock, "Mothers of Abused Children: A Comparison Study," *Clinical Pediatrics* 24 (1985): 9. Statistically significant differences found between abuse and comparison group members in several areas, including family history and personality traits.

18. Turner and Avison, "Assessing Risk Factors for Problem Parenting," p. 889. See Altemeier et al., "Prospective Study of Antecedents for Nonorganic Failure to Thrive," *Journal of Pediatrics* 106 (1985): 360. Nonorganic failure to thrive correlates significantly with aberrant nurture during mother's childhood, conflict between parents and infant, and several perinatal events. Also see Altemeier et al., "Antecedents of Child Abuse," *Journal of Pediatrics* 100 (1982): 823; Groothuis et al., "Increased Child Abuse in Families with Twins," *Journal of Pediatrics* 70 (1982): 769.

19. Fontana and Robinson, "Observing Child Abuse," *Journal of Pediatrics* 105 (1984): 655, 656–60.

20. Garbarina, "What Have We Learned about Child Maltreatment?" in Children's Bureau, Office of Human Development Services Administration for Children, Youth, and Families, U.S. Department of Health and Human Services, publication no. 84-30338, *Perspectives on Child Maltreatment in the Mid 1980s* 6, no. 7 (1984).

21. See Garbarino and Crouter, "Defining the Community Context for Parent-Child Relationships: The Correlates of Child Mistreatment," *Child Development* 49 (1978): 604; Gargarino and Sherman, "High-Risk Neighborhoods and High-Risk Families: The Human Ecology of Child Mistreatment," *Child Development* 51 (1980): 188; J. Garbarino and S. Stocking, eds., *Protecting Children from Abuse and Neglect: Developing and Maintaining Effective Support Systems for Families* (San Francisco: Jossey-Bass, 1980).

22. Leventhal, Egerter, and Murphy, "Reassessment of the Relationship of Perinatal Risk Factors and Child Abuse," *American Journal of Diseases of Children* 138 (1984): 1037–38. The authors suggest that demographic factors are not sufficient to identify children at high risk of being abused and that such factors "need to be investigated in combination with other high-risk clinical characteristics, such as the mother's own nurturing (p. 1038).

23. Elster, McAnarney, and Lamb, "Parental Behavior of Adolescent Mothers," *Journal of Pediatrics* 71 (1983):494, 495–503. See also Marian Wright Edelman, "What Can We Do?" *Washington Post*, February 2, 1986, p. C8. Edelman, president of the Children's Defense Fund, suggests measures for preventing teenage pregnancy, with focus on the black community.

24. Gelles, "Child Abuse as Psychopathology: A Sociological Critique and Reformulation," *American Journal of Orthopsychiatry* 43 (1973): 621.

25. Shearman et al., "Maternal and Infant Characteristics in Abuse: A Case-Control Study," *Journal of Family Practice* 16 (1983): 289, 293.

26. Daniel et al., "Child Abuse Screening: Implications of the Limited Predictive Power of Abuse Discriminants from a Controlled Study of Pediatric Social Illness," *Child Abuse and Neglect* 2 (1978):247, 258.

27. Leventhal, Egerter, and Murphy, "Reassessment of the Relationship of Perinatal Risk Factors and Child Abuse," p. 1038. See also Turner and Avison, "Assessing Risk Factors for Problem Parenting: The Significance of Social Support," *Journal of Marriage and Family* 47 (1985): 881. See generally M. Farnell, *Screening Procedures for the Detection or Prediction of Child Abuse: An Annotated Bibliography* (Toronto, Ont.: Centre of Criminology, University of Toronto, 1980).

28. Jason et al., "Child Abuse in Georgia: A Method to Evaluate Risk Factors and Reporting Bias," *American Journal of Public Health* 72 (1982): 1353. See also Leventhal,

"Risk Factors for Child Abuse: Methodologic Standards in Case-Control Studies," *Journal of Pediatrics* 68 (1981): 684. Case-control studies of risk factors for child abuse should comply with seven methodologic standards to avoid bias or distortion of results.

29. Milner and Gold, "Screening Spouse Abusers for Child Abuse Potential," *Journal of Clinical Psychology* 42 (1986): 169. See also Milner and Wimberley, "An Inventory for the Identification of Child Abusers," *Journal of Clinical Psychology* 35 (1979): 95.

30. Milner and Ayoub, "Evaluation of 'At Risk' Parents Using the Child Abuse Potential Inventory," *Journal of Clinical Psychology* 36 (1980): 945.

31. Ibid.

32. Milner and Wimberly, "Prediction and Explanation of Child Abuse," *Journal of Clinical Psychology* 36 (1980): 875, 883.

33. Ayoub and Jacewitz, "Assessment of a Program's Effectiveness in Selecting Individuals 'At Risk' for Problems in Parenting," *Journal of Clinical Psychology* 39 (1983): 334, 338.

34. Milner et al., "Predictive Validity of the Child Abuse Potential Inventory," *Journal of Consulting and Clinical Psychology* 52 (1984): 879.

35. Thomasson et al., "Evaluation of a Family Life Education Program for Rural 'High Risk' Families," *Journal of Community Psychology* 9 (1981): 246.

36. Milner et al., "Predictive Validity of the Child Abuse Potential Inventory," pp. 882–83.

37. Pruitt and Erickson, "The Child Abuse Potential Inventory: A Study of Concurrent Validity," *Journal of Clinical Psychology* 41 (1985): 104.

38. Ibid.

39. Milner and Robertson, "Development of a Random Response Scale for the Child Abuse Potential Inventory," *Journal of Clinical Psychology* 41 (1985): 639.

40. Pobitaille et al., "Child Abuse Potential and Authoritarianism," *Journal of Clinical Psychology* 41 (1985): 839, 840–43. The authors report that the results of this study did not show the predicted general relationship between child abuse potential and authoritarianism (p. 842).

41. Milner and Gold, "Screening Spouse Abusers for Child Abuse Potential," p. 169.

42. See Thomasson et al., "Evaluation of a Family Life Education Program for Rural 'High Risk' Families."

43. Murphy, Orkow and Nicola, "Prenatal Prediction of Child Abuse and Neglect: A Prospective Study," *Child Abuse and Neglect* 9 (1985): 225, 233–34.

44. LaFollette, "Licensing Parents," p. 190.

45. Ibid.

46. Ibid., p. 195.

47. Thomasson et al., "Evaluation of a Family Life Education Program for Rural 'High Risk' Families."

CUSTODY EVALUATIONS
A REALISTIC VIEW
Diane A. Trombetta

*F*irst, the number and range of different psychological, social, and behavioral dimensions which have been suggested as relevant in custody determination is overwhelming. For example, under the general category of "parental functioning," one finds the following:

- Capacity to provide nurturance, to communicate, and to remain "in tune" with a child.[1]
- Mental health and possible psychopathology underlying observed parental deficits.[2]
- Parenting styles and child-rearing practices in the child's early development and currently, availability of the parent psychologically and physically, disciplinary techniques, receptivity and willingness to encourage healthy peer relations, and interests in recreational and social enrichment.[3]
- Parents' affection for the child.[4]
- Intelligence and personality of the parents.[5]

Clausen started with a list of parental tasks necessary to a child's proper and healthy development and generated a list of skills on which parents could be assessed for their ability to

Diane A. Trombetta, "Custody Evaluations: A Realistic View," *Family and Conciliation Courts Reviw* 29, no. 1 (January 1991): 45–55. Copyright © 1991 by Diane A. Trombetta. Reprinted by permission of Sage Publications, Inc.

- provide nurturance and physical care;
- train and channel physiological needs, such as toilet training and weaning;
- teach language, perceptual skills, and physical and self-care skills;
- orient the child to the immediate world of kin, community, and self-feelings;
- transmit cultural goals and values;
- promote interpersonal skills;
- guide and correct the child in formulating goals and activities.[6]

How would one go about assessing—fairly and reliably—these many attributes, skills, and sensitivities in a parent? Grisso made the task sound easy:

> Certain abilities referring to a parent's knowledge or awareness of various needs of children probably could be assessed adequately by developing content-relevant, structured interviews, or paper-and-pencil measures. Concepts referring to caretaking practices could be assessed by self-reports and third-party reports of a parent's past child-rearing behaviors, or by direct observation of parent-child interactions.[7]

One can imagine the ease with which such assessment methods could be attacked by an opposing counsel: Is there any evidence to show that parents who have more knowledge of child development, as measured by a paper-and-pencil test, are better parents? How valid and reliable are third-party reports submitted by friends, relatives, and school teachers? Does the fact that friends never saw Mom discipline the child mean that, indeed, she never did? If Dad was observed to be extremely competent with his six-year-old daughter, does that mean he will be equally competent when she reaches puberty? How do we know that the parents' performance on these various tests and during these observations is not profoundly influenced, for good or ill, by the custody battle itself? How can we explain the fact that two equally competent evaluators can observe the same set of parents and come to different conclusions regarding their relative strengths and weaknesses, not to mention the needs of the child?

Yes, evaluators are stuck with paper-and-pencil tests, interviews, and fleeting observations, for they do need to operationalize definitions of "knowledge" or "parenting skills" so that these can be measured in a fair and standardized way. What evaluators should not do is delude themselves into believing that the resulting report is anything more than a superficial look at extremely complex, culturally loaded questions and judgments. In fact, parenting skills which are too vulnerable to individual or cultural bias, or which are too subtle to be measured easily, should probably not be evaluated at all. For example, how would one properly evaluate the extent to which a parent "transmits cultural and subcultural goals and motivates the child to accept them for his own"?[8] The danger in telling themselves that they can measure such a skill in a few hours' time is that evaluators will inevitably rely on superficial and easily observed behavior, such as "church attendance," to rate a parent's ability to "transmit values." One cannot have it both ways: Either evaluators take on the assessment of complex, value-laden behaviors and spend the time, energy, and money necessary to do so, or they must ask more limited and realistic questions and gather information which, in fact, answers those questions.

Psychology's lack of valid, standardized assessment techniques is a serious problem; yet a more fundamental concern raised in recent years by family therapists is that any description of individual behavior which ignores the dynamics of the larger family system will be misguided and inaccurate, no matter how sophisticated the assessment techniques. Evaluations force us to assume a linear, cause-and-effect model of behavior because the judicial system for which they are designed assumes a need to choose between parents, compare parental attributes, and make either/or decisions. The court must be able to say "Parent A has characteristics x, y, and z." The court must presume that these are enduring attributes of the individual which exist apart from the dynamics of a particular family system, which is about to change drastically anyway. Even the standard of "best interests of the child" is applied by the courts and supported in the law as if a child's interest is separate from the parents'. A systems approach would suggest that a child's best interests will not be served within a family in which one parent is devastated by having lost custody or infuriated by having to share it. What McWhinney said about emotional disturbance would be equally true for parenting skills and behaviors: It may be that effective parenting is not attributable to a particular person but, rather, to a whole context which allows, fosters, and rewards good parenting. While this view may be closer to the truth, it is incompatible with the win/lose linear model of reality on which courtroom litigation is based.[9]

. . . Grisso provided an excellent list of possible explanations for a parent's "poor" performance during an evaluation: life-situational stress, examination-related stress, ambivalence, lack of information, and mental disorder or disability.[10] Other reasons for a poor rating by an evaluator include cultural, ethnic, and socioeconomic clashes or differences between parent and evaluator, misunderstanding or misinterpretation by the evaluator, poor communication skills of the parent, and unconscious resistance to the evaluation process itself.

NOTES

1. Seymour L. Halleck, *Law in the Practice of Psychiatry: A Handbook for Clinicians* (New York: Plenum Press, 1980).

2. T. Trunnell, "Johnnie and Suzie, Don't Cry: Mommy and Daddy Aren't That Way," *Bulletin of the American Academy of Psychiatry and the Law* 4 (1976): 120–26.

3. Richard A. Gardner, *Family Evaluation in Child Custody Litigation* (Cresskill, N.J.: Creative Therapeutics, 1982).

4. C. Lowery, "The Wisdom of Solomon: Criteria for Child Custody from the Legal and Clinical Points of View," *Law and Human Behavior* 8 (1984): 371–80.

5. T. Litwack, G. Gerber, and C. Fenster, "The Proper Role of Psychology in Child Custody Disputes," *Journal of Family Law* 18 (1979): 269–300.

6. John A. Clausen, "Perspectives in Childhood Socialization," in *Socialization and Society*, ed. John A. Clausen (Boston: Little, Brown, 1968).

7. Thomas Grisso, *Evaluating Competencies* (New York: Plenum Press, 1986), p. 202.

8. Clausen, "Perspectives in Childhood Socialization," p. 141.

9. R. McWhinney, "Issues in the Provision and Practice of Family Mediation," *Conciliation Courts Review* 26, no. 2 (1988): 33–41.

10. Grisso, *Evaluating Competencies*.

ADOPTION AND THE PARENTAL SCREENING SYSTEM

Elizabeth Bartholet

ON BEING SCREENED FOR FITNESS

*T*he rules of the parental screening game apply not just to such objective factors as age and marital status but to subjective assessments of my capacity to love and nurture an adopted child. I will be required to fill out a form inquiring into details about my childhood, my relationship with my parents, my former marriage and divorce, my current romantic and sexual life, and any other aspect of myself that is thought to be relevant to my parental fitness. The rest of the process involves interviews with the person I will call my social worker, who will explore the same issues. The home study is crucial to my prospects. At the conclusion a report will proclaim me fit or unfit, screen me in or out for the agency's purposes. Assuming that I am screened in, the home study will affect how the agency will treat me—how helpful it will be, for example, in finding a particular child for me to adopt. . . .

When I first became pregnant during my long-ago marriage, I was deemed to have a sacrosanct right to parent. Whatever struggles I may have had with my marriage, and whatever doubts I had about its future, were considered entirely my private business. During the years that I sought infertility treatment so that I could produce another child, no one asked me to demonstrate my fitness to parent. It was only when I sought to parent an already existing child produced by others that the government stepped in, asserting that I must understand that I had no rights whatsoever to engage in this form of parenting and that if I was even to be considered for the privilege, I must humble myself before the bureaucrats and demonstrate my fitness according to their rules. The theory is that the best interests of the child demand the screening of adoptive parents, but this makes sense only if you think that there is something deeply suspect about parenting a child born to another. Why would anyone think that those who consciously plan to adopt someone else's child pose more of a risk than those who fall unwittingly into pregnancy? What real threat do adoptive parents pose to children who cannot in any event be raised by their biologic parents—to children who are being raised by foster families or in institutions or on the streets? . . .

ASSESSING THE SYSTEM'S FITNESS

Screening for parental fitness is a basic part of the agency adoption process. Both public and private agencies conduct home studies designed to assess eligibility for adoptive parenthood. The process also determines the ranking of prospective parents for purposes of child assignment; that is, it determines which parents will be considered for which children within an agency's jurisdiction.[1] As discussed later, home studies are not part of the independent adoption process, in which birth parents place their children with adoptive parents either directly or through an intermediary.[2]

Defenders of the home study system claim that screening assesses such important qualities as the capacity to love and nurture an adopted child. They also claim that the child assignment, or "matching," process involves sophisticated judgments as to which particular parent-child combinations will work best. But the fact is that the screening and matching system is extremely crude and quite inconsistent with its alleged purposes.

The system ranks prospective parents from top to bottom in terms of relative desirability, which is assessed primarily on the basis of easily determined objective factors. These factors reflect the system's bias in favor of a biologic parenting model as well as a socially traditional family model. So heterosexual couples in their late twenties or early thirties with apparently stable marriages are at the top of the ladder. These are the kind of people who could, if not for infertility, produce children, and who should, in the system's view, be parents. Single and older adoptive applicants—those in their late thirties and forties—are placed lower on the ladder, along with people with disabilities. Gays, lesbians, and the seriously disabled are generally excluded altogether.[3]

Although social work practices reflect changing social realities, they tend to lag a generation or so behind. Bureaucratic rules take on a life of their own. Entrenched policies take time to reverse, and the bureaucratic mentality is averse to risk: the safe path for an adoption agency is to select parents on the basis of accepted models. Single adoptive parenting was essentially unheard of until the mid-1960s, when forty children were placed in single-parent homes by the Los Angeles Department of Adoptions.[4] Many adoption workers continued to treat single-parent adoption as highly suspect, and questioned whether singles should be found eligible to parent even those children who would not otherwise find adoptive homes. As late as 1969 a respected adoption expert found it necessary to defend single-parent adoption as "not inherently or necessarily pathogenic."[5] The fact that a large percentage of all children in our society were being raised by single parents took decades to sink into the bureaucratic mind and to have an impact on adoption practices.[6]

The adoption screening system ranks and categorizes children waiting for homes, as well as parents, in order to decide how to make particular parent-child matches. The children are placed on their own desirability list, with healthy infants at the top, somewhat older and less healthy children next, and the oldest and most seriously disabled children at the bottom. Children are also classified according to racial, ethnic, and religious heritage.

In matching children with parents, the system operates primarily on the basis of what looks roughly like a market system, one in which ranking produces buying power. The most "desirable" parents are matched with the most "desirable" children, and the less desirable with the less desirable, on down the list. The "marginally fit" parents are matched with the hardest-to-place children, which often means the children with the most extreme parenting needs and demands.

The matching system also demonstrates deference to a biologic model of parenting. As I have noted, in earlier times agencies made a significant effort to give prospective parents children as closely matched as possible in looks and temperament to the birth children they might have had. While this philosophy has been tempered in recent years by virtue of necessity, it still governs with respect to those attributes deemed most important. Older parents are often precluded from adopting children more than thirty-five or forty years younger than themselves on the ground that they would not have been likely to have produced such children themselves. Black parents are given black children, and Catholic parents are given the children surrendered by Catholic birth parents.

Discrimination is thus the name of the game in adoptive parenting. Those who procreate live in a world of near-absolute rights with respect to parenting. Those who would adopt have no rights. They must beg for the privilege of parenting, and do so in a state-administered realm that denies them both the right to privacy and the "civil rights" that we have come to think of as fundamental in the rest of our communal life. Differential treatment on the basis of age, race, religion, and disability has been outlawed in almost all areas of our lives. Increasingly, the law forbids discrimination on the basis of marital status and sexual orientation. It is only in the area of adoption that our system proudly proclaims not simply the right to discriminate but the importance of doing so.[7] It is not just the prospective parents who are treated shabbily but also the children, in whose best interests the system is supposedly designed. They are categorized in terms of their marketability, with the "undesirables" handed off to those deemed marginally fit to parent. . . .

LIMITS OF THE CURRENT REFORM DEBATE

The current debate about parental screening consists largely of a war between home study advocates, on the one hand, and independent adoption advocates, on the other. Adoption agency traditionalists promote the view that independent adoptions should be outlawed, or at a minimum regulated in ways that would make them look more like agency adoptions. In particular, they say, preplacement home studies should be required so that those who find their own children are at least screened for parental fitness before they take any child home to live. A number of recent reform proposals take this position,[8] and there seems to be popular support for calls to restrict the independent adoption "market." Any adoption scandal—a baby-selling ring, child abuse by an adoptive parent—is likely to trigger demands by public leaders and the media for laws and regulations that clamp down on independent adoption. However, this approach to reform is generally premised on the assumption that more regulation of the kind we already have is a good thing, that the current adoption agency model is a good model, and that parental screening systems function in a positive way.

Independent adoption advocates focus on the flaws in the agency model. They condemn some of the social biases inherent in the traditional screening process and note the absence of any evidence that screening actually succeeds in identifying superior parents. They also point to a variety of benefits associated with independent adoption: more services for the birth parents, more potential for communication between the birth and the adoptive parents and for other forms of openness in the adoptive arrangement, and earlier placement of children. But those who promote the advantages of independent adoption tend to ignore the question of whether it is *appropriate* to have a separate, "better" system, available only to parents with money, for the distribution of healthy white infants who have been siphoned off from the adoption agency system. If the agency system isn't working well, the appropriate solution involves restructuring that system rather than simply permitting those who are financially well off to bypass it.

Some voices have called for changes in the agency screening criteria, arguing, for example, that agencies should be barred from using such factors as age, marital status, religion, disability, and sexual orientation as the basis for categorically excluding certain groups from adoptive parenthood.[9] Some have proposed that agencies be required to screen in all applicants who satisfy a minimal fitness standard, excluding only those who are found demonstrably unfit.[10] But there is no consensus that this is the appropriate direction in which to move. In any event, these proposals would do little to change the essential nature of today's screening and matching system, which functions primarily not as a device to disqualify adoptive applicants but as a method to allocate available children to the parents deemed most desirable. Few groups are excluded as unfit, and a decision to include as minimally fit those who are now significantly excluded would mean little, since the system would place them at the bottom of its hierarchically ranked fitness lists. Reform proposals that have as their goal real changes in the system must take on not simply the eligibility cutoff determination but the entire ranking and matching setup.

AN ALTERNATIVE VISION

We now place an extremely high value on the right to procreate and the related right to hold on to our biologic product. We place no real value on the aspect of parenting that has to do solely with relationship. There is an essentially absolute right to produce a child, but there is no right to enter into a parenting relationship with a child who is not linked by blood—no right to adopt. Foster parents, stepparents, and others who develop nurturing relationships with children are deemed to have no right to maintain such relationships.[11] They and the children who may have come to depend on them are subject to the whim of the blood-linked parent. Such parents, in contrast, have enormous proprietary power over their children. Even in situations of serious abuse and neglect, the government is reluctant to interfere with parental rights. Children have essentially no rights and no entitlements, although the system is supposed to operate in their best interests. Everyone knows that their best interests require nurturing homes and parenting relationships, but it is painfully obvious that children have no enforceable rights to those things.

We could flip this rights picture, upend this hierarchical ranking of values. We could place the highest value on children and their interests in growing up in a nurturing relationship. We could place a higher value on nurturing than on procreation, and we might choose to do so in part because it seems to serve children's interests in being parented. A less radical step would be to accord at least more significant value than we now do to the nurturing aspect of parenting.

Any such revision of parenting rights and responsibilities would lead to a very different view of the role that adoption agencies should play. It would seem obvious that their primary function should be to create parent-child relationships—to find homes for children in need of nurturing parents, and to find children for adults who want to nurture. In this new world, agencies would become adoption advocates. They would commit themselves to finding a home for every child who cannot be cared for by his or her birth parents. They would reach out to find these children and the adults willing to parent them. They would encourage people dealing with infertility to consider adopting an existing child instead of undergoing treatment designed to produce another child. They would encourage those capable of procreation to consider adoptive or foster parenting instead. They might devote some resources to screening out those who are demonstrably unfit to parent, but they would be conscious of the importance of not creating barriers that would discourage people from providing homes to existing children in need. They would recognize the extensive evidence demonstrating that children are better off in permanent homes than in institutions or foster care. Their respect for adult interests in enjoying parenting relationships would make them reluctant to impose any screening requirements that do not seem necessary to protect children.

ELIMINATING THE CURRENT SCREEN

Quite obviously, this vision would mean abandoning the system of parental screening and matching that we know today. All who want to become adoptive parents would be presumed fit.

We could create a parental licensing system based on a minimalist screening principle to disqualify those found demonstrably unfit, for such reasons as a past history of serious and persistent drug or alcohol abuse, prior child abuse, apparent incapacity to provide for a child's most basic needs, serious ill heath, or advanced age. Such a licensing system might be politically essential, to assure people that adoption would not result in the kinds of abuses that occurred in the nineteenth century, when some children were turned over to families who saw them as a form of cheap labor. It might also be essential to assure foreign governments and agencies that children they send to the United States for adoption will receive adequate homes. But the standards for assessing minimal fitness should be adapted from those used to decide when children can be removed from blood-linked parents. They should be similar to the standards we would use if we were to impose a licensing requirement on those seeking to procreate.[12] Any such licensing scheme should be applied to all adoptive applicants. Money should not enable anyone to bypass the screening deemed essential to children's protection.

We would scrap the more extensive screening that goes on today. Adoption workers would get out of the business of ranking parental quality and lose their power to determine which kinds of children should be allocated to which kinds of parents. Prospective parents would make their own decisions as to which kinds of children to apply for and would be served on a first-come, first-served basis. Adoption workers would facilitate matches. They would seek to accommodate the interests of birth and adoptive parents as well as the interests of those children old enough to express their own preferences. They would offer all parties advice and counseling designed to further appropriate matches and to maximize the success of adoptive relationships. But they would not have the power to play God by deciding who should be allowed to parent or what kind of child they should be assigned.

Today's form of parental screening and matching would be understood as inconsistent with the new value accorded to the relational aspect of parenting. We would not dream of telling fertile people that they have no right whatsoever to produce a child—that childbirth is a privilege to be allowed or not at the entire discretion of the government. We would not dream of telling pregnant people that when they give birth, the government will decide whether they can keep the child on the basis of whether a social worker thinks that the child looks like a good match for their particular parenting profile. We would be horrified if the government tried to deny the right to procreate to those over forty, or to the physically handicapped, or to singles. Even the kind of minimalist licensing scheme I have suggested would strike most people as outrageous and presumptively unconstitutional if it were to be applied to biologic parenting.[13] Indeed, recent proposals to encourage welfare recipients to use contraceptive devices are condemned by many as interfering unduly with the right to procreate, as are proposals to force contraception on convicted child abusers.[14]

Parental screening in the adoption area has always been justified as necessary for the protection of children. But children have much to gain and little to lose from scrapping the system.

WHAT CHILDREN HAVE TO GAIN

One thing children have to gain is what they most need—homes. . . . Another thing children have to gain is parents who are prepared to parent and to deal with any special issues involved in adoptive parenting. The home study process is supposed to provide education, counseling, and preparation. Applicants are encouraged to explore issues that might interfere with good parenting and to discuss concerns about their infertility or anxieties about adoptive parenthood. They are supposed to consider honestly what they are looking for in a child and what kinds of children they would find it difficult to parent. They are told to think hard about how they should deal with issues involving their adopted child's birth family and racial or ethnic heritage.

These issues *should* be explored by those contemplating adoptive parenthood. The problem is that agencies cannot do a good job of education and counseling in the context of a process that simultaneously is functioning to screen and match. Most adoptive parents want to score well in the process in order to improve their chances of adopting and of being assigned the kind of child that they want to parent. Those with any game-playing abilities will know that to score well, they should *not* bring up any issues that might cause a social worker concern. Therefore, it is likely that the very issues that need serious exploration will get none, as the eager adoptive applicant strives to come up with the best possible version of a life story and a series of "right" answers to difficult questions.

WHAT CHILDREN HAVE TO LOSE

Many traditionalists claim that what children have to lose if we abandon the screening and matching process is appropriate parenting. The argument for parental screening rests largely on the assumption that children are subject to special risks when there is no biologic link between parent and child. But there is no reason to think that adoptive parents pose more of a risk than biologically linked parents do. Indeed, the fact that adoptive parents have *consciously chosen* parenthood would seem more than enough to compensate for any difficulties that might be inherent in adoptive parenting. Nor is there any evidence that the absence of a biologic link is relevant to the successful establishment of a parent-child relationship. Studies indicate that adoptive families function extremely well when compared with biologic families, and that adoptive parents are very successful in enabling their children to overcome the effects of unfortunate preadoptive histories. There is no evidence that adoptive parents are more likely to abuse their children than biologic parents are, or that they are otherwise problematic as a group. . . .

Beyond this, it is very likely that we do not know what we think we know about what makes for good parenting or happy families. Our views are necessarily shaped by a model of parenting sanctioned by biology and tradition. Single people and older people who push forward to ask for the opportunity to parent usually do not look much like the others in their categories in the general population. A large proportion of the people who are preferred because they fall into the married category will be divorced within a few years,[15] and their children will be subject to the trauma and change that divorce represents.[16] Generally, those children will effectively lose one parent, and their remaining parent will be less prepared to function as a single parent than the person who deliberately adopts on his or her own. People who choose to become parents in their late thirties and forties often testify that this is a particularly good stage of life in which to parent, because they feel less torn by the conflict between work and family and more capable of giving of themselves to a child than they did when they were younger. Some gays and lesbians maintain that for children with a same-sex or bisexual orientation, growing up with determinedly heterosexual parents can be oppressive.

The studies that exist provide no indication that the objective factors relied on by the current screening system function as useful predictors of good parenting. There is no evidence that these factors are correlated with success as an adoptive parent,[17] and there is no evidence that those who become adoptive parents by virtue of the agency screening process are more successful than those who use the independent adoption system and thereby avoid such screening.[18] Studies of some of the parents rated as marginal by the system, such as straight singles and gay singles and couples, reveal no significant disadvantages suffered by their children when compared to children raised in traditional two-parent households.[19]

Of course, these studies stop short of providing definitive proof of the current system's irrationality. They often rely on the adoptive parents' assessments of their children's adjustment—assessments that pose an obvious risk of bias. Moreover, it is extremely difficult to create adequate control groups and to define adoptive success. But these studies are all we have in the way of empirical evidence. At a minimum, they raise serious questions about the assumptions on which the agency screeners operate.

Parental screening has enormous costs from the perspective of those screened and categorized by the system. A declaration that a person is unfit, or marginally fit, to parent another human being is a serious condemnation. A denial of the opportunity to parent constitutes for many people a denial of what is most meaningful in life. The government should have to demonstrate a powerful interest in screening in order to justify such costs. . . .

NOTES

1. See Alfred Kadushin and Judith A. Martin, *Child Welfare Services*, 3d ed. (New York: Macmillan, 1980), and Cynthia Martin, *Beating the Adoption Game*, rev. ed. (New York: Harcourt Brace Jovanovich, 1988).

2. See Joan Hollinger, "Reflections on Independent Adoptions," in *Legal Advo-*

cacy for Children and Youth (Washington, D.C.: National Legal Resource Center, 1986), pp. 366–92; "Introduction to Adoption Law and Practice," in *Adoption Law and Practice*, sec. 1.05, ed. Joan Hollinger (New York: M. Bender, 1988); Jacqueline H. Plumez, *Successful Adoption: A Guide to Finding a Child and Raising a Family* (New York: Crown, 1982), pp. 69–79.

3. On issues involving gay and lesbian adoptive parenting, see Wendell Ricketts and Roberta Achtenberg, "The Adoptive and Foster Gay and Lesbian Parent," in *Gay and Lesbian Parents*, ed. Frederick W. Bozett (New York: Greenwood, 1987), pp. 89–111; Jonathan Crawford, "Agency Adoptions by Homosexuals in New York State," unpublished ms., Harvard Law School, 1990; Joseph Evall, "Sexual Orientation and Adoptive Matching," unpublished ms., Harvard Law School, 1990.

4. William Feigelman and Arnold R. Silverman, *Chosen Children: New Patterns of Adoptive Relationships* (New York: Greenwood, 1983), p. 177.

5. Alfred Kadushin, "Single-Parent Adoptions: An Overview and Some Relevant Research," *Social Service Review* 44 (1970): 263.

6. One study indicates that more than one-third of the children born between 1960 and 1980 spent part of their childhood in a single-parent family because of birth out of wedlock, divorce, or death; the figure went up to roughly half of those born in the 1970–1984 period. See Larry Bumpass and James Sweet, "Children's Experience in Single-Parent Families: Implications of Cohabitation and Marital Transitions," *Family Planning Perspectives* 21 (November/December 1989): 256.

7. Some recent court-made law prohibits use of such factors as race, age, religion, marital status, and sexual orientation to absolutely preclude an adoptive applicant from consideration or prevent a child's placement. But these rulings are of limited significance given the enormous discretion that adoption agencies have to consider these and other factors in arriving at a final determination of parental fitness.

8. See, e.g., National Conference of Commissioners on Uniform State Laws, "Proposed Uniform Adoption Act," draft of November 25, 1991, art. 3, sec. 21.

9. Ibid., art. 2 and comments.

10. Ibid., secs. 23(e) and (g), providing that adoptive applicants must be found suitable unless an investigator makes written findings as to the reasons that adoptive placement would pose a risk to the physical or psychological well-being of a child. See also Martin, *Beating the Adoption Game*, pp. 282–83, which advocates issuing parenting "licenses" to all adoptive applicants who are not demonstrably unfit.

11. The U.S. Supreme Court indicated significant respect for the foster parenting relationship but refused to establish any meaningful legal right to protect such a relationship, in *Smith* v. *Organization of Foster Families*, 431 U.S. 816 (1977).

12. For examples of proposals for licensing schemes in the area of biologic parenting, see Roger W. McIntire, "Parenthood Training or Mandatory Birth Control: Take Your Choice" *Psychology Today* 9, no. 5 (October 1973): 34–39, 132–33, 143, and Claudia Pap Mangel, "Licensing Parents: How Feasible?" *Family Law Quarterly* 22 (1988): 17.

13. The Supreme Court has accorded the right to procreate near-absolute protection against government intervention. See *Skinner* v. *Oklahoma*, 316 U.S. 535 (1942), and Lawrence H. Tribe, *American Constitutional Law*, 2d ed. (Westbury, N.Y.: Foundation Press, 1988), p. 1340.

14. See "A Plan to Pay Welfare Mothers for Birth Control," *New York Times,* February 9, 1991, p. A9, and "Judge Is Firm on Forced Contraception, But Welcomes an Appeal," *New York Times,* January 11, 1991, p. A17.

15. Reports indicate that roughly one-third of the children born to married parents experience the disruption of that marriage before the age of sixteen. See Bumpass and Sweet, "Children's Experience in Single-Parent Families."

16. See Judith Wallerstein and Sandra Blakeslee, *Second Chances: Men, Women, and Children a Decade after Divorce* (New York: Ticknor & Fields, 1989), which documents the ongoing pain and trauma suffered by the children of divorce.

17. See Alfred Kadushin, "Factors Associated with Adoptive Outcome," in Kadushin and Martin, *Child Welfare Services,* pp. 530–31.

18. See Hollinger, "Reflections on Independent Adoptions"; James B. Boskey, "Placing Children for Adoption," in *Adoption Law and Practice,* ed. Hollinger, sec. 3.04, pp. 3–36; W. Meezan, S. Katz, and A. M. Russo, *Adoptions without Agencies* (New York: Child Welfare League of America, 1978), p. 232.

19. On single-parent adoption, see Feigelman and Silverman, *Chosen Children,* pp. 173–92; Vie Groze, "Adoption and Single Parents: A Review," *Child Welfare* 50, no. 3 (May–June 1991): 321; Joan Shireman and Penny Johnson, "A Longitudinal Study of Black Adoptions: Single Parent, Transracial, and Traditional," *Social Work* (May–June 1986): 172, 175; and Joan Shireman, "Growing Up Adopted," *Chicago Child Care Society* (1988): 5, 36.

On gay and lesbian parenting, see Daniel Goleman, "Studies Find No Disadvantage in Growing Up in a Gay Home," *New York Times,* December 12, 1992, p. C14; *Opinion of the Justices,* 530 A.2nd 21, 28 (N.H. 1987) (Batcheldor, J., dissenting); D. Hutchens and M. Kirkpatrick, "Lesbian Mothers/Gay Fathers," in Diane H. Schetky and Elissa P. Benedek, *Emerging Issues in Child Psychiatry and the Law* (New York: Brunner-Mazel, 1985), pp. 115–26; David J. Kleber, Robert J. Howell, and Alta Lura Tibbits-Kleber, "The Impact of Parental Homosexuality in Child Custody Cases: A Review of the Literature," *Bulletin of the American Academy of Psychiatry and the Law* 14, no. 1 (1986): 81–87.

On age as a screening criterion, see H. Witmer, E. Herzog, E. Weinstein, and M. Sullivan, *Independent Adoptions: A Follow-up Study* (New York: Russell Sage Foundation, 1963), pp. 349–50.

REPRODUCTIVE RIGHTS AND ACCESS TO THE MEANS OF REPRODUCTION

Christine Overall

*U*ndoubtedly forms of screening for parenthood are occurring in many contexts in Western society. That is, one or more sets of criteria are employed to determine who will and who will not be permitted to become parents. This process of screening now occurs, most obviously, in the institution of adoption. But it is also a part of the determination of eligibility for access to reproductive technology such as in vitro fertilization, artificial insemination by donor, and surrogate parenting by means of embryo transfer. (Interestingly, criteria of eligibility for parenthood are apparently employed for some forms of reproductive technology and not for others. For example, "[s]urgical repair of a woman's fallopian tubes is now undertaken . . . without physicians or others asking whether she is married, is suited for motherhood or, for instance, has a history of child abuse.")[1]

In general, for most processes of artificial reproduction the criteria of eligibility include such characteristics as sexual orientation, marital status, and consent of the spouse. . . . Further criteria have also been used—for example, the number of existing offspring[2] and the absence of physical disabilities. . . .

According to those who are in the business of developing or providing reproductive technology, its preferred use is for women who demonstrate certain limited forms of sexual activity. Ordinarily they must be heterosexual, but only within a marriage or a "stable" union.[3] For example, a sociological study of AID [artificial insemination by donor] unequivocally recommends that "artificial reproduction should only take place where a couple responsible for nurturing the child are married."[4] Similarly, while not requiring that a couple be married, the Warnock Report explicitly assumes that a couple seeking access to reproductive technologies would inevitably be heterosexual.[5] Thus women who are independent of men as regards their living arrangements and/or their sexual activity are excluded from access to the technology, and this exclusion is held to be justified. This social use of reproductive technology both reinforces, at least indirectly, the connection of standard heterosexuality with reproduction and disengages other forms of sexual life expression from procreation.

The justification for the requirement that potential consumers of reproductive technology be heterosexual and married is usually couched in terms of concern for children or, more ambiguously, "the family."[6] Here is a representative example of such a justification, offered in some detail in a report by the British Council for Science and Society:

> In so far as the social norm clearly associates childbearing with family life and parents who are married, this practice [of providing AID for single women and lesbians] is abnormal. . . . AID to single women will increase the social problems of child care and welfare, and the encouragement of lesbian families can be seen as a threat to normal family life, to say nothing of both instances failing to provide a nurturing father figure. The imbalance of interests in these cases suggests that the practice should be discouraged.[7]

. . . [I]f . . . problems of "child care and welfare" were to arise, it is always open to the society in which they occur to provide better forms of socially assisted child care and medical care, and ultimately to change the social context that makes rearing children a severe economic problem for many women. It should not be assumed, on an a priori basis, that raising a child without a man must inevitably be a financial burden shouldered by the mother alone.

Second, the sincerity of the concern, in reports such as the one quoted, for a family for every child is called into question by their usually very negative evaluation of lesbian families. Although willing to refer to a lesbian couple as a family, the report quoted clearly does not regard it as a "normal" family. In a similar fashion, a case study of a lesbian couple seeking AID refers to lesbianism as a "problem" and a lesbian woman's desire for a child as a "dilemma." . . .

Such a family may of course not be statistically normal (what family now is?), but the study fails to adduce any evidence for its abnormality in any other sense likely to affect the child's well-being, which is the purported concern. The only explicitly alleged problem that is cited in the report I first quoted is the absence of a "nurturing father figure." It would be interesting to know what is meant here by nurturance and whether in this argument the kind of nurturance allegedly provided by "father figures" is thought to be different from that provided by mothers. Certainly it appears implausible to suppose that all intact "normal" heterosexual families include a "nurturing father figure." As a philosopher and not a social scientist I must be modest in the claims I make on this issue. But I would at least say that if by "nurturance" what is meant is concern and care for, involvement in, and cherishing of the developing life of the child, then the degree of nurturance provided by many fathers is not immediately evident. While it can scarcely be disputed that children need and deserve nurturance, it is not clear that "father figures" always provide it.

Therefore it is simply begging the question to claim, as some have, that "as a general rule it is better for children to be born into a two-parent family, with both father and mother."[8] The mere presence of a father in the home seems unlikely to protect a child from abuse, and in fact somewhat more fathers than mothers are responsible for physical violence directed against their children.[9] But in any case, even if it were conceded that most fathers are exceedingly nurturant, there is no a priori reason to suppose that such nurturance cannot also be provided by women, and it is unjust to rule out, in an a priori fashion, the possibility that individual women and female couples can provide it.

The reference in the report to "father figures" also suggests a concern about the importance to children of specifically male role models. In the case study cited earlier, one participant remarks,

> I do not think we can abandon the concept that a child normally develops out of an experience in which there is a male person, usually father, and a female person, usually mother, and that it is the interaction in that situation which does a great deal to fit him to eventual masculinity and her to feminity [sic].[10]

And the authors of a book on AID remark, "Once a stable marriage relationship is no longer a necessary precondition for AID, then the social and psychological implications of babies being born in households where no males are present have seriously to be considered."[11]

But the concern expressed in the examples just cited begs the question that feminists would raise: Is the type of modeling provided by most males essential in child-rearing? Is there some component of child-rearing that only males are capable of providing? One writer claims, "There are advantages to having both masculine and feminine influences on the child's development regardless of the child's sex."[12] But such a claim appears to assume without question both that models of traditional masculinity and traditional femininity are valuable in child-rearing, and that only parents of the "appropriate" sex can and do provide them. Those who point to the alleged necessity of male role models are taking for granted, without argument, that masculine behavior, attitudes, beliefs, and values ought to influence our children.

Yet another reason often cited for depriving women of access to reproductive technology on the basis of their sexuality is that the resultant offspring will suffer ostracism because of their mother's sexual orientation. For example, "Given the structure of our society, it is easier and more practical to bring children into the traditional two-parent family . . . [because] the child is less likely to be subjected to denigration by his peers."[13] One critic goes even further and suggests that lesbians who seek AID are "us[ing] the child as a catalyst to change society."[14] He argues that one should not deliberately put a child, who must in any case face the usual problems involved in growing up, in an environment in which extra problems, pertaining to the deviance of his parent, will be encountered.

Corea has pointed out that the notion that "every child should have a father" is an underlying value both in standard child custody proceedings and in the defense of the provision of artificial insemination.[15] This approach, of course, uses the sheer existence of the status quo to defend the status quo and then accuses those who wish to depart from the status quo of exploiting their children as a means to revolutionary change. This tactic is particularly unjust because it ignores the feminist criticism that the problems lesbian mothers face stem not from their inherent nature as women but from the heterosexist social context. A feminist analysis does not assume the moral validity and historical invariance of existing social arrangements.

One writer on artificial reproduction remarks that "it makes a difference whether artificial insemination [or IVF] is refused to a person simply because of that person's sexual orientation or because of the potential harm of that sexual orientation to the child who will be born. The latter is probably justifiable, the former may not be."[16] But what is also unjustifiable is to assume that there is inevitably a connection between the sexual orientation of the parent and potential harm to the offspring. If a woman changes her sexual orientation from heterosexual to lesbian, does she thereby become a worse parent? Would a child born to a lesbian parent be better off if it had never existed? Fitness to parent cannot and should not be evaluated on an a priori basis; at most it can be assessed only from individual case to individual case.

The Council for Science and Society sees the encouragement of lesbian families as "a threat to normal family life," but it has just been argued that the offspring themselves have not been shown to be endangered. Who or what, then, is threatened by providing access to reproductive technology to those who are not in suitable heterosexual relationships?

An answer is provided, perhaps inadvertently, by Michael D. Bayles. Although Bayles believes that the "ethical prohibition of AID for lesbians cannot be justified," he nevertheless cites a possible concern about providing AID for lesbians: "One might fear that their sexual preference would be transferred to their children. Female children might grow up hating males, and male children might grow up sexually confused."[17] Indeed, if one accepts the view that the family "provides the social milieu where children are brought up from infancy to *accept* the fundamental values of society,"[18] then one might well fear that lesbian and single heterosexual parents would fail to inculcate fundamental patriarchal values. For, as sociologists Snowden, Mitchell, and Snowden remark, a child born outside marriage is "at risk" in the sense that "there is no framework within which social control can be exercised over the responsibilities society has for the child."[19] As a result, one physician questions "very seriously whether it is ever psychologically advantageous to entrust the upbringing of a baby or toddler to any woman who is not currently loved by a man for her own sake."[20]

Bayles does not endorse this sort of concern, but merely to describe it is to lend it some dignity. It assumes that same-sex sexual orientation is like a contagious disease that can be transmitted to one's offspring. This fear of contagion appears also to animate an anonymous representative of the British Royal College of Obstetricians and Gynecologists, who has been quoted as observing, "[I]f donors knew their sperm was going to lesbians, one can't help wondering if they would think this was a good thing."[21] Hence it has also been suggested that one legal question about AID is whether it can be said "that the donor has donated his sperm for use for any purpose including inseminating a lesbian or single woman, or, even if there are not express and hence binding restrictions on use, would some usually be implied by the law and would these include a term that the sperm was only to be used to impregnate heterosexual and married women."[22]

Significantly, however, heterosexual orientation is not in a similar fashion typically regarded as contagious in the way that a disease is, since its transmission is not regarded as a threat. In any case, the notion of transmission at work here seems flawed, since it would fail to explain why so many homosexual individuals had heterosexual parents. Why did these parents fail to transmit their sexual orientation to their offspring?[23]

But the major concern here is more wide-ranging than just a concern about producing homosexual offspring: "Female children might grow up hating males, and male children might grow up sexually confused." This worry is echoed in the case study on providing AID to lesbian couples. One participant asks, "Could the demand for AID from lesbians arise from protest against hostile irrational attitudes against them as a group, to make up for a feeling that society is unjust to them, or as a basic hostility to men or to the traditional male pattern of society?"[24] The idea that the sexual orientation of lesbians is the result of, or is reducible to, hating men is not a new one. It is almost impossible for nonfeminists and antifeminists to see lesbianism as a positive choice for women.[25] But as one lesbian feminist explains, "I don't want to be a lesbian by default, the women I care for, I love because they are women, not because they are not men."[26]

The real threat, then, posed by lesbians and single heterosexual women who seek access to artificial reproduction is perceived as being directed against men, against the patriarchal control of women's sexual and reproductive capacities. One book, for example, while obliquely recognizing that some women may want "liberation from male dominance," describes the independent woman as wanting to "manage her own affairs single-mindedly without having to consider another's interests" and to "raise a child of her own in the way she wishes."[27] For such a woman, the book warns, "AID could become a means of dispensing with marriage and the inconvenience of a husband and, of course, with a father, too."[28] The perceived selfishness of this woman would also extend to her children: she is envisaged as entrusting her child to "nursemaids, nursery schools, housekeepers, and so forth."[29] The implication, surely, is that such a woman is too selfish to consider other individuals', particularly men's, interests because she regards such individuals as "inconvenient." Hence one writer asks, rhetorically, "Can the American social conscience accept a woman who feels she has no need of a husband or a father for her children?"[30]

As Mary O'Brien so wisely points out, paternity is not a natural relationship to a child but is rather a socially created right to appropriate a child.[31] Marilyn Frye suggests that "the progress of patriarchy *is* the progress toward male control of reproduction, starting with possession of wives and continuing through the invention of obstetrics and the technology of extrauterine gestation. Giving up that control would be giving up patriarchy."[32] A careful evaluation of their arguments shows that in the final analysis nonfeminists and antifeminists are troubled about giving lesbians and single heterosexual women access to reproductive technology because they fear that it would result in a partial disruption of patriarchal power, disruption brought about by the severance of marriage and motherhood and the separation from men of certain women and their reproductive capacities.[33] They therefore anticipate and seek to prevent this possibility by reinforcing the connection between heterosexuality and procreation and by condemning the forgoing of any links between artificial reproduction and other expressions of sexuality.

As I suggested earlier, feminists need not oppose this point of view by claiming a general right to reproduce; it is necessary instead to reveal the poor reasoning used in its defense and to expose its antifeminist and misogynist roots. A member of the Ontario Law Reform Commission claims, "To accept and encourage resort to the artificial reproduction technologies by persons outside a stable marital union under the existing legal regime, in my view, is to sow the seeds of injustice, hardship, and social disorder."[34] Perhaps what he vaguely recognizes is that the assumption of reproductive control by independent women could indeed have revolutionary implications. . . .

PARENTAL SCREENING

In the last two sections discussion was confined to the criteria for access to artificial reproduction, particularly artificial insemination by donor. Nevertheless it is not correct to assume that parental screening does not take place in other contexts; a covert form of parental screening occurs now and has always occurred in connection with reproduction. By means of the following practices the state helps to determine, both directly and indirectly, who will and who will not be parents[35]—that is, who will and who will not have access to the means of reproduction: (1) imposing social restrictions on sexual activity—for example, through the stigma of illegitimacy and regulations governing marriage;[36] (2) providing or failing to provide both contraceptive information and resources and abortion counseling and services; (3) instituting compulsory sterilization for those judged unfit to reproduce; and (4) providing or failing to provide parent support services such as paid maternity leave, child-care services, and family allowances. Regardless of what the expressed goal may be of a state's population policy, all of these devices serve to select who will and who will not become parents.

These observations show that the issue of parental screening must be situated within the larger context of the social regulation of reproduction and child-rearing. The reason for screening for parenthood is to legitimate some forms of procreation and parenting and proscribe others. The way in which the state screens potential parents implicitly says a lot about such things as what kinds of parents are desirable, what sort of parent-child relationships should be developed, and what kinds of people children should turn out to be. Ultimately, then, screening for parenthood is the unavoidable expression of the sorts of very fundamental concerns any society must have about the kinds of people its citizens will be.

Hence, existing practices of parental screening cannot be assessed on a piecemeal basis. The procedures by which it is decided who will adopt, who will have access to artificial reproduction, who will be permitted to conceive or abort or contracept, are part of a far-reaching system. To evaluate parental screening we must decide what is important. What value do we place upon fertility and upon children? What kinds of parenting do we want to encourage? Should procreation be a burden or a benefit for the women who engage in it? Is a biological connection of paramount importance in a family, so that to have one's "own" genetic child is essential? What is more important: the welfare of children, for their own sake, or the supposed "right" of a person to be a parent? . . .

LICENSING PARENTS

It may then appear that the relevant concerns in determining access to reproductive technology will be characteristics of prospective parents that promote competence in child-rearing: for example, such nebulous but significant characteristics as the capacity for nurturance, tolerance, and love; the ability to encourage, stimulate, and develop children; and the person's intentions and goals in seeking offspring.

Why not, then, follow Hugh LaFollette's recommendation that we "license" parents? LaFollette argues that "any activity that is potentially harmful to others and requires certain demonstrated competence for its safe performance" should be regulated,[37] and parenting clearly fulfills these criteria. He considers and replies carefully to a variety of objections to the proposal, including the claims that denial of a license could seriously harm a person, that competency tests might not be accurate, that tests for screening parents might intentionally or unintentionally be misused, and that a program of licensing parents could not be fairly enforced. He also recognizes that there might be skepticism as to whether most of the desiderata for parents can be effectively evaluated: Is it possible to devise tests that will accurately predict competence in child-rearing? LaFollette replies that the aim of licensing should not be to license only the best parents but merely to exclude the very bad ones—that is, those who would abuse their children.[38] Furthermore, he cites evidence suggesting that adoptive parents are less likely than biological parents to mistreat their children and argues that this suggests that we have already achieved a successful form of licensing.[39]

Many other practical objections to the licensing proposal have been raised,[40] but these are not the significant problem in assessing it. Given that screening of parents does and will occur, as I have argued, the question is whether the system of prior restraint proposed by LaFollette is appropriate.

At the very least it might be objected that licensing would contribute to the attitude that children are the property of their parents. LaFollette himself is highly critical of that attitude,[41] but it is arguable that successfully licensed parents might well think of children as a prize they have earned.

Even more important, such a system requires applicants to demonstrate (at least minimal) competence; hence such persons are assumed incompetent until proved competent. Such an assumption is quite legitimate for such skills as driving, and unfortunately it may not be unjustified for many prospective parents in a society such as ours with its lack of opportunities to practice caring for children, its allocation of responsibility for parenting almost exclusively to women and not to men, its high rate of child abuse, its dislike of children as individuals, its emphasis on acquiring one's "own" children, and its indifference to the fate of children not one's own. Such existing social conditions and values appear to create the need for a system of prior restraint.

These observations about the present social context for child-rearing indirectly suggest a more appropriate response to LaFollette's proposal: not to institute a system of licensing but rather to change the conditions and values that otherwise seem to make necessary the prior restraint of some potential parents. This would involve developing feelings of responsibility for all children, not just our "own"; rejecting the notion that a genetically related child is superior to one that is not; providing social supports for many varieties of families and contexts for parenting; respecting and appreciating children as the individuals they are and not for what they represent or will become; creating a climate in which adults and children have many opportunities to work and play together, so that adults will have the experience and practical education relevant to rearing children and children will benefit from not being ghettoized; and expecting as a matter of course that men as well as women will nurture children.

In other words, what is necessary is a child-positive society, a society governed by feminist rather than by patriarchal principles. Contrary to the claim of one infertility specialist, who said that legislation for artificial reproduction "must place the couple and donors first,"[42] and that of another, who claims, fetishistically, that we should "protect the integrity of artificial reproduction itself,"[43] I am suggesting that all of our policies and practices pertaining to reproduction must give top priority to the authentic experiences of women and the real needs of children.

NOTES

1. Ontario Law Reform Commission, *Report on Human Artificial Reproduction and Related Matters* I (Toronto, Ont.: Ministry of the Attorney General, 1985), p. 110.

2. Linda S. Williams, "Who Qualifies for in Vitro Fertilization? A Sociological Examination of the State Admittance Criteria of Three Ontario IVF Programs" (Paper delivered at the Conference of the Canadian Sociology and Anthropology Association, June 7, 1986), pp. 6–7.

3. Bartha Maria Knoppers, "Women and the Reproductive Technologies," in *Family Law in Canada: New Directions*, ed. Elizabeth Sloss (Ottawa, Ont.: Canadian Advisory Council on the Status of Women, 1985), p. 216; Gena Corea, *The Mother Machine: Reproductive Technologies from Artificial Insemination to Artificial Wombs* (New York: Harper & Row, 1985), p. 145; Somer Brodribb, "Reproductive Technologies, Masculine Dominance, and the Canadian State," Occasional Papers in Social Policy Analysis no. 5 (Toronto: Ontario Institute for Studies in Education, 1984), pp. 15–16;

Kathleen A. Lahey, "Alternative Insemination: Facing the Conceivable Options," *Broadside* 8, no. 1 (1986): 8–10; Anibal A. Acosta and Jairo E. Garcia, "Extra-corporeal Fertilization and Embryo Transfer," in *Infertility: Diagnosis and Management*, ed. James Aiman (New York: Springer-Verlag, 1984), p. 217.

4. R. Snowden, G. D. Mitchell, and E. M. Snowden, *Artificial Reproduction: A Social Investigation* (Boston: Allen & Unwin, 1983), p. 169.

5. Mary Warnock, *A Question of Life: The Warnock Report on Human Fertilisation and Embryology* (Oxford: Basil Blackwell, 1985), p. 10.

6. George J. Annas, "Redefining Parenthood and Protecting Embryos: Why We Need New Laws," *Hastings Center Report* 14 (October 1984): 50, 51.

7. Council for Science and Society, *Human Procreation: Ethical Aspects of the New Techniques* (Oxford: Oxford University Press, 1984), pp. 60–61. Compare H. Allan Leal, "Vice Chairman's Dissent," in *Report on Human Artificial Reproduction and Related Matters*, II, p. 288.

8. Warnock, *A Question of Life*, p. 11. Compare *Report on Human Artificial Reproduction and Related Matters* II, p. 158. Some questions might be raised here about what is meant by "mother" and "father": for example, are these terms intended in the sense of the social parents or in the sense of the genetic parents?

9. Alfred Kadushin and Judith A. Martin, *Child Abuse: An Interactional Event* (New York: Columbia University Press, 1981), pp. 10, 287.

10. "Case Conference—Lesbian Couples: Should Help Extend to AID?" *Journal of Medical Ethics* 4 (1978): 93.

11. Snowden, Mitchell, and Snowden, *Artificial Reproduction*, p. 13.

12. Margot Joan Fromer, *Ethical Issues in Health Care* (St. Louis: Mosby, 1981), p. 143.

13. Ibid.

14. "Case Conference—Lesbian Couples," p. 93.

15. Corea, *The Mother Machine*, p. 52.

16. Margaret A. Somerville, "Birth Technology, Parenting, and 'Deviance,'" *International Journal of Law and Psychiatry* 5 (1982): 133.

17. Michael D. Bayles, *Reproductive Ethics* (Englewood Cliffs, N.J.: Prentice-Hall, 1984), p. 18.

18. Snowden, Mitchell, and Snowden, *Artificial Reproduction*, pp. 168–69, my emphasis.

19. Ibid., p. 169.

20. Dr. Kenneth Shoddy, quoted in Jenny Teichman, *Illegitimacy: A Philosophical Examination* (Oxford: Basil Blackwell, 1982), p. 120.

21. Quoted in R. Snowden and G. D. Mitchell, *The Artificial Family: A Consideration of Artificial Insemination by Donor* (Boston: Allen & Unwin, 1981), p. 118.

22. Somerville, "Birth Technology," p. 135. Interestingly, the same assumption underlies questions raised by Somerville about homosexual sperm donors: "What if there is some inherited predisposition to homosexuality, should we exclude such donors or at least warn the female recipient of the sperm of this characteristic of the donor? Would it be acceptable to insist on married donors in order to reduce the chance that the donor is homosexual?" (p. 127).

23. See "Case Conference—Lesbian Couples," pp. 92–93.

24. Ibid., p. 95.

25. Marilyn Frye, *The Politics of Reality: Essays in Feminist Theory* (Trumansberg, N.Y.: Crossing Press, 1983), p. 98; and Adrienne Rich, "Compulsory Heterosexuality and Lesbian Existence," in *Women: Sex and Sexuality*, ed. Catharine R. Stimpson and Ethel Spector Person (Chicago: University of Chicago Press, 1980), p. 63.

26. Dianne Grimsditch, in *Love Your Enemy? The Debate Between Heterosexual Feminism and Political Lesbianism* (London: Onlywomen Press, 1981), p. 20.

27. Compare Fromer, *Ethical Issues in Health Care*, p. 156.

28. Snowden and Mitchell, *The Artificial Family*, pp. 118–19.

29. Ibid., p. 119.

30. Fromer, *Ethical Issues in Health Care*, p. 143.

31. Mary O'Brien, *The Politics of Reproduction* (Boston: Routledge & Kegan Paul, 1981), pp. 54–55.

32. Frye, *The Politics of Reality*, p. 102, Frye's emphasis.

33. Compare Jalna Hanmer, "Reproductive Technology: The Future for Women?" in *Machina Ex Dea: Feminist Perspectives on Technology*, ed. Joan Rothschild (New York: Pergamon Press, 1983), p. 183; and Brodribb, "Reproductive Technologies," p. 5.

34. Allan Leal, "Vice Chairman's Dissent," in *Report on Human Artificial Reproduction and Related Matters*, II (Toronto, Ont.: Ministry of the Attorney General, 1985), p. 288.

35. Elizabeth W. Moen, "What Does 'Control over Our Bodies' Really Mean?" *International Journal of Women's Studies* 2 (1979): 137–38.

36. Germaine Greer, *Sex and Destiny: The Politics of Human Fertility* (New York: Harper & Row, 1984), p. 80; Brodribb, "Reproductive Technologies," p. 20.

37. LaFollette, "Licensing Parents," p. 183.

38. Ibid., p. 190.

39. Hugh LaFollette, "A Reply to Frisch," *Philosophy and Public Affairs* 11 (1981): 183.

40. See Lawrence E. Frisch, "On Licentious Licensing: A Reply to Hugh LaFollette," *Philosophy and Public Affairs* 11 (1981): 173–80.

41. LaFollette, "Licensing Parents," p. 196.

42. J. Scott, quoted in Linda L. Long, "Artificially Assisted Conception," *Health Law in Canada* 5 (1985): 102.

43. Annas, "Redefining Parenthood and Protecting Embryos," p. 52.

II. PARENTAGE

*I*n this second part, the focus is on parentage (as opposed to parenting)—
that is, the creation of human beings.

1. Genetic Disease

While it is generally agreed that instances of child abuse, and even prenatal abuse, are indeed instances of abuse and therefore morally unacceptable behavior, there is less consensus about the morality of conceiving (or failing to abort) when there is a chance that the fetus will have a genetic disease. It is this issue that Purdy and Kass address, considering the child, the parents, the family, and the society. (Note, however, that arguments about the morality of reproducing genetic disease are independent of arguments about whether such reproduction should be, in any way, licensed or even prohibited.)

Most of the authors to this point have addressed, at some point and to some extent, the question of whether we have a moral right to parent; Purdy addresses head-on the question of whether we have a moral responsibility *not* to parent. And she argues that it is morally wrong to have a child when we know there's a good chance, or a high risk, that the child will have a serious disease (because of the consequences the child will experience—unnecessary happiness and unjust disadvantage). Purdy concedes that defining "serious" is difficult, but there are nevertheless, she claims, some clear cases. Defining "a high risk" is also difficult; she suggests that the worse the disease, the lower the level of acceptable risk. But isn't such a position—aborting fetuses because they are "defective"—saying that the lives of disabled people are less valuable than the lives of "normal" people? This is an important objection, and Purdy addresses it in the third excerpt included herein.

Kass continues the discussion of whether it is morally acceptable to abort fetuses with genetic defects. He considers as possible justifications, societal good, parental or familial good, and the natural standard—but he finds all three to be inadequate. While he mentions the justification that forms the basis of Purdy's view (loosely stated, that we have a moral obligation to see that children are born healthy), he does not discuss it; nor, unfortunately, does he discuss the consequence *to the child* of being born otherwise.

CAN HAVING CHILDREN
BE IMMORAL?

Laura M. Purdy

[Ed. note: This is a composite article—please see the notes preceding each section. This first section is excerpted from "Genetics and Reproductive Risk: Can Having Children Be Immoral?" chapter 1 of Purdy's *Reproducing Persons: Issues in Feminist Bioethics*.]

*I*s it morally permissible for me to have children? A decision to procreate is surely one of the most significant decisions a person can make. So it would seem that it ought not be made without some moral soul searching.

There are many reasons why one might hesitate to bring children into this world if one is concerned about their welfare. Some are rather general, such as the deteriorating environment or the prospect of poverty. Others have a narrower focus, such as continuing civil war in one's country or the lack of essential social support for child-rearing in the United States. Still others may be relevant only to individuals at risk of passing harmful diseases to their offspring. . . .

There is always some possibility that reproduction will result in a child with a serious disease or handicap. Genetic counselors can help individuals

From *Reproducing Persons: Issues in Feminist Bioethics*, by Laura M. Purdy. Copyright © 1996. Used by permission of the publisher, Cornell University Press; "Genetic Diseases: Can Having Children Be Immoral?" in *Genetics Now: Ethical Issues in Genetic Research*, ed. John J. Buckley Jr. (Washington, D.C.: University Press of America, 1978), reprinted with permission; and "Loving Future People," in *Reproduction, Ethics, and the Law: Feminist Perspectives*, ed. Joan C. Callahan (Bloomington: Indiana University Press, 1995), reprinted with permission.

determine whether they are at unusual risk and, as the Human Genome Project rolls on, their knowledge will increase by quantum leaps. As this knowledge becomes available, I believe we ought to use it to determine whether possible children are at risk *before* they are conceived.

... I want to defend the thesis that it is morally wrong to reproduce when we know there is a high risk of transmitting a serious disease or defect. This thesis holds that some reproductive acts are wrong, and my argument puts the burden of proof on those who disagree with it to show why its conclusions can be overridden. Hence it denies that people should be free to reproduce mindless of the consequences.[1] However, as moral argument, it should be taken as a proposal for further debate and discussion. It is not, by itself, an argument in favor of legal prohibitions of reproduction.[2]

There is a huge range of genetic diseases. Some are quickly lethal; others kill more slowly, if at all. Some are mainly physical, some mainly mental; others impair both kinds of function. Some interfere tremendously with normal functioning, others less. Some are painful, some are not. There seems to be considerable agreement that rapidly lethal diseases, especially those, such as Tay-Sachs, accompanied by painful deterioration, should be prevented even at the cost of abortion. Conversely, there seems to be substantial agreement that relatively trivial problems, especially cosmetic ones, would not be legitimate grounds for abortion.[3] In short, there are cases ranging from low risk of mild disease or disability to high risk of serious disease or disability. Although it is difficult to decide where the duty to refrain from procreation becomes compelling, I believe that there are some clear cases. I have chosen to focus on Huntington's disease to illustrate the kinds of concrete issues such decisions entail. However, the arguments are also relevant to many other genetic diseases.[4]

The symptoms of Huntington's disease usually begin between the ages of thirty and fifty:

> Onset is insidious. Personality changes (obstinacy, moodiness, lack of initiative) frequently antedate or accompany the involuntary choreic movements. These usually appear first in the face, neck, and arms, and are jerky, irregular, and stretching in character. Contradictions of the facial muscles result in grimaces; those of the respiratory muscles, lips, and tongue lead to hesitating, explosive speech. Irregular movements of the trunk are present; the gait is shuffling and dancing. Tendon reflexes are increased. ... Some patients display a fatuous euphoria; others are spiteful, irascible, destructive, and violent. Paranoid reactions are common. Poverty of thought and impairment of attention, memory, and judgment occur. As the disease progresses, walking becomes impossible, swallowing difficult, and dementia profound. Suicide is not uncommon.[5]

The illness lasts about fifteen years, terminating in death.

Huntington's disease is an autosomal dominant disease, meaning it is caused by a single defective gene located on a non-sex chromosome. It is passed from one generation to the next via affected individuals. Each child of such an affected person has a 50 percent risk of inheriting the gene and thus of eventually developing the disease, even if he or she was born before the parent's disease was evident.[6]

Until recently, Huntington's disease was especially problematic because most affected individuals did not know whether they had the gene for the disease until well into their childbearing years. So they had to decide about childbearing before knowing whether or not they could transmit the disease. If, in time, they did not develop symptoms of the disease, then their children could know they were not at risk for the disease. If unfortunately they did develop symptoms, then each of their children could know there was a 50 percent chance that they, too, had inherited the gene. In both cases, the children faced a period of prolonged anxiety as to whether they would develop the disease. Then, in the 1980s, thanks in part to an energetic campaign by Nancy Wexler, a genetic marker was found that, in certain circumstances, could tell people with a relatively high degree of probability whether or not they had the gene for the disease.[7] Finally, in March 1993, the defective gene itself was discovered.[8] Now individuals can find out whether they carry the gene for the disease, and prenatal screening can tell us whether a given fetus has inherited it. These technological developments change the moral scene substantially.

How serious are the risks involved in Huntington's disease? Geneticists often think a 10 percent risk is high.[9] But risk assessment also depends on what is at stake: the worse the possible outcome, the more undesirable an otherwise small risk seems. In medicine, as elsewhere, people may regard the same result quite differently. But for devastating diseases such as Huntington's this part of the judgment should be unproblematic: no one wants a loved one to suffer in this way.[10]

There may still be considerable disagreement about the acceptability of a given risk. So it would be difficult in many circumstances to say how we should respond to a particular risk. Nevertheless, there are good grounds for a conservative approach, for it is reasonable to take special precautions to avoid very bad consequences, even if the risk is small. But the possible consequences here *are* very bad: a child who may inherit Huntington's disease has a much greater than average chance of being subjected to severe and prolonged suffering. And it is one thing to risk one's own welfare but quite another to do so for others and without their consent. . . .

⑤　⑤　⑤

[Ed. note: This second section is excerpted from Purdy's earlier essay, "Genetic Diseases: Can Having Children Be Immoral?"]

. . . I think that these points indicate that the morality of procreation in situations like these demands further study. I propose to do this by looking first at the position of the possible child, then at that of the potential parent.

The first task in treating the problem from the child's point of view is to find a way of referring to possible future offspring without seeming to confer some sort of morally significant existence upon them. I will call children who might be born in the future but who are not now conceived "possible" children, offspring, individuals, or persons. I stipulate that this term implies nothing about their moral standing.

The second task is to decide what claims about children or possible children are relevant to the morality of childbearing in the circumstances being considered. There are, I think, two such claims. One is that we ought to provide every child with at least a normal opportunity for a good life. The other is that we do not harm possible children if we prevent them from existing. Let us consider both these matters in turn.

Accepting the claim that we ought to try to provide for every child a normal opportunity for a good life involves two basic problems: justification and practical application.

Justification of the claim could be derived fairly straightforwardly from either utilitarian or contractarian theories of justice, I think, although a proper discussion would be too lengthy to include here. Of prime importance in any such discussion would be the judgment that to neglect this duty would be to create unnecessary unhappiness or unfair disadvantage for some persons.

The attempt to apply the claim that we should try to provide a normal opportunity for a good life leads to a couple of difficulties. One is knowing what it requires of us. Another is defining "normal opportunity." Let us tackle the second problem first.

Conceptions of "normal opportunity" vary among societies and also within them; de rigueur in some circles are private music lessons and trips to Europe, while in others providing eight years of schooling is a major sacrifice. But there is no need to consider this complication since we are concerned here only with health as a prerequisite for normal opportunity. Thus we can retreat to the more limited claim that every parent should try to ensure normal health for his child. It might be thought that even this moderate claim is unsatisfactory since in some places debilitating conditions are the norm. One could circumvent this objection by saying that parents ought to try to provide for their children health normal for that culture, even though it may be inadequate if measured by some outside standard. This conservative position would still justify efforts to avoid the birth of children at risk for Huntington's chorea and other serious genetic diseases.

But then what does this stand require of us: is sacrifice entailed by the duty to try to provide normal health for our children? The most plausible answer seems to be that as the danger of serious disability increases, the greater the sacrifice demanded of the potential parent. This means it would be more justifiable to recommend that an individual refrain from childbearing if he risks passing on spina bifida than if he risks passing on webbed feet. Working out all the details of such a schema would clearly be a difficult matter; I do not think it would be impossible to set up workable guidelines, though.

Assuming a rough theoretical framework of this sort, the next question we must ask is whether Huntington's chorea substantially impairs an individual's opportunity for a good life.

People appear to have different opinions about the plight of such persons. Optimists argue that a child born into a family afflicted with Huntington's chorea has a reasonable chance of living a satisfactory life. After all, there is a 50 percent chance the child will escape the disease if a parent has already manifested it, and a still greater chance if this is not so. Even if the child does have the illness, he or she will probably enjoy thirty years of healthy life before symptoms appear and, perhaps, may not find the disease destructive. Optimists can list diseased or handicapped persons who have lived fruitful lives. They can also find individuals who seem genuinely glad to be alive. One is Rick Donohue, a sufferer of the Joseph family disease: "You know, if my mom hadn't had me, I wouldn't be here for the life I have had. So there is a good possibility I will have children."[11] Optimists therefore conclude that it would be a shame if these persons had not lived.

Pessimists concede these truths, but they take a less sanguine view of them. They think a 50 percent risk of serious disease such as Huntington's is appallingly high. They suspect that a child born into an afflicted family is liable to spend his or her youth in dreadful anticipation and fear of the disease. They expect that the disease, if it appears, will be perceived as a tragic and painful end to a blighted life. They point out that Rick Donohue is still young and has not experienced the full horror of his sickness.

Empirical research is clearly needed to resolve this dispute: we need much more information about the psychology and life history of sufferers and potential sufferers. Until we have it we cannot know whether the optimist or the pessimist has a better case; definitive judgment must therefore be suspended. In the meantime, however, common sense suggests that the pessimist has the edge.

If some diseased persons do turn out to have a worse than average life, there appears to be a case against further childbearing in afflicted families. To support this claim two more judgments are necessary, however. The first is that it is not wrong to refrain from childbearing. The second is that asking individuals to so refrain is less of a sacrifice than might be thought.[12] I will examine each of these judgments.

Before going on to look at reasons why it would not be wrong to prevent the birth of possible persons, let me try to clarify the picture a bit. To understand the claim it must be kept in mind that we are considering a prospective situation here, not a retrospective one; we are trying to rank the desirability of various alternative future states of affairs. One possible future state is this: a world where nobody is at risk for Huntington's chorea except as a result of random mutation. This state has been achieved by sons and daughters of persons afflicted with Huntington's chorea ceasing to reproduce. This means that an indeterminate number of children who ought to have been born were not born. These possible children can be divided into two categories: those who would have been miserable and those who would have lived good lives. To prevent the existence of members of the first category it was necessary to prevent the existence of all. Whether or not this is a good state of affairs depends on the morality of the means and the end. The end, preventing the existence of miserable beings, is surely good; I will argue that preventing the birth of possible persons is not intrinsically wrong. Hence this state of affairs is a morally good one.

Why then is it not in itself wrong to prevent the birth of possible persons? It is not wrong because there seems to be no reason to believe that possible individuals are either deprived or injured if they do not exist. They are not deprived because to be deprived in a morally significant sense one must be able to have experiences. But possible persons do not exist. Since they do not exist, they cannot have experiences. Another way to make this point is to say that each of us might not have been born, although most of us are glad we were. But this does not mean that it makes sense to say that we would have been deprived of something had we not been born. For if we had not been born, we would not exist, and there would be nobody to be deprived of anything. To assert the contrary is to imagine that we are looking at a world in which we do not exist. But this is not the way it would be: there would be nobody to look.

The contention that it is wrong to prevent possible persons from existing because they have a right to exist appears to be equally baseless. The most fundamental objection to this view is that there is no reason to ascribe rights to entities that do not exist. It is one thing to say that as-yet-nonexistent persons will have certain rights if and when they exist: this claim is plausible if made with an eye toward preserving social and environmental goods.[13] But what justification could there be for the claim that nonexistent beings have a right to exist?

Even if one conceded that there was a presumption in favor of letting some nonexistent beings exist, stronger claims could surely override it.[14] For one thing, it would be unfair not to recognize the prior claim of already existing children who are not being properly cared for. One might also argue that it is simply wrong to prevent persons who might have existed from doing so. But this implies that contraception and population control are also wrong.

It is therefore reasonable to maintain that because possible persons have no right to exist, they are not injured if not created. Even if they had that right, it could rather easily be overridden by counterclaims. Hence, since possible persons are neither deprived nor injured if not conceived, it is not wrong to prevent their existence.

. . . I said that two claims are relevant to the morality of childbearing in the circumstances being considered. The first is that we ought to provide every child with at least a normal opportunity for a good life. The second is that we do not deprive or injure possible persons if we prevent their existence.

I suggested that the first claim could be derived from currently accepted theories of justice: a healthy body is generally necessary for happiness and it is also a prerequisite for a fair chance at a good life in our competitive world. Thus it is right to try to ensure that each child is healthy.

I argued, with regard to the second claim, that we do not deprive or injure possible persons if we fail to create them. They cannot be deprived of anything because they do not exist and hence cannot have experiences. They cannot be injured because only an entity with a right to exist could be injured if prevented from existing; but there are no good grounds for believing that they are such entities.

From the conjunction of these two claims I conclude that it is right to try to ensure that a child is healthy even if by doing so we preclude the existence of certain possible persons. Thus it is right for individuals to prevent the birth of children at risk for Huntington's chorea by avoiding parenthood. The next question is whether it is seriously wrong *not* to avoid parenthood.

I have so far argued that if choreics live substantially worse lives than average, then it is right for afflicted families to cease reproduction. But this conflicts with the generally recognized freedom to procreate and so it does not automatically follow that family members ought not to have children. How can we decide whether the duty to try to provide normal health for one's child should take precedence over the right to reproduce?

This is essentially the same question I asked earlier: how much must one sacrifice to try to ensure that one's offspring is healthy? In answer to this I suggested that the greater the danger of serious disability, the more justifiable considerable sacrifice is.

Now asking someone who wants a child to refrain from procreation seems to be asking for a large sacrifice. It may, in fact, appear to be too large to demand of anyone. Yet I think it can be shown that it is not as great as it initially seems.

Why do people want children? There are probably many reasons, but I suspect that the following include some of the most common. One set of reasons has to do with the gratification to be derived from a happy family life—love, companionship, watching a child grow, helping mold it into a good person, sharing its pains and triumphs. Another set of reasons centers around the parents as individuals—validation of their place within a genetically continuous family line, the conception of children as a source of immortality, being surrounded by replicas of themselves.

Are there alternative ways of satisfying these desires? Adoption or technological means provide ways to satisfy most of the desires pertaining to family life without passing on specific genetic defects. Artificial insemination by donor is already available; implantation of donor ova is likely within a few years. Still another option will exist if cloning becomes a reality. In the meantime, we might permit women to conceive and bear babies for those who do not want to do so themselves.[15] But the desire to extend the genetic line, the desire for immortality, and the desire for children that physically resemble one cannot be met by these methods.

Many individuals probably feel these latter desires strongly. This creates a genuine conflict for persons at risk for transmitting serious genetic diseases like Huntington's chorea. The situation seems especially unfair because, unlike unafflicted people, through no fault of their own, doing something they badly want to do may greatly harm others.

But if my common sense assumption that they are in grave danger of harming others is true, then it is imperative to scrutinize their options carefully. On the one hand, they can have children; they satisfy their desires but risk eventual crippling illness and death for their offspring. On the other hand, they can remain childless or seek nonstandard ways of creating a family: they have some unfulfilled desires, but they avoid risking harm to their children.

I think it is clear which of these two alternatives is best, for the desires that must remain unsatisfied if they forgo normal procreation are less than admirable. To see the genetic line continued entails a sinister legacy of illness and death; the desire for immortality cannot really be satisfied by reproduction anyway; and the desire for children that physically resemble one is narcissistic and its fulfillment cannot be guaranteed even by normal reproduction. Hence the only defense of these desires is that people do in fact feel them.

Now, I am inclined to accept William James's dictum regarding desires: "Take any demand, however slight, which any creature, however weak, may make. Ought it not, for its own sole sake be satisfied? If not, prove why not."[16] Thus I judge a world where more desires are satisfied to be better than one in which fewer are. But not all desires should be regarded as legitimate, since, as James suggests, there may be good reasons why these ought to be disregarded. The fact that their fulfillment will seriously harm others is surely such a reason. And I believe that the circumstances I have described are a clear example of the sort of case where a desire must be judged illegitimate, at least until it can be shown that sufferers from serious genetic diseases like Huntington's chorea do not live considerably worse than average lives. Therefore, I think it is wrong for individuals in this predicament to reproduce.

Let me recapitulate. At the beginning of this essay I asked whether it is wrong for those who risk transmitting severe genetic disease like Huntington's chorea to have "blood" children. Some despair of reaching an answer to this question.[17] But I think such pessimism is not wholly warranted and that if generally accepted would lead to much unnecessary harm. It is true that in many cases it is difficult to know what ought to be done. But this does not mean that we should throw up our hands and espouse a completely laissez-faire approach; philosophers can help by probing the central issues and trying to find guidelines for action.

Naturally there is no way to derive an answer to this kind of problem by deductive argument from self-evident premises, for it must depend on a complicated interplay of facts and moral judgments. My preliminary exploration of Huntington's chorea is of this nature. In the course of the discussion I suggested that, if it is true that sufferers live substantially worse lives than do normal persons, those who might transmit it should not have any children. This conclusion is supported by the judgments that we ought to try to provide for every child a normal opportunity for a good life, that possible individuals are not harmed if not conceived, and that it is sometimes less justifiable for persons to exercise their right to procreate than one might think.

I want to stress, in conclusion, that my argument is incomplete. To investigate fully even a single disease, like Huntington's chorea, empirical research on the lives of members of afflicted families is necessary. Then, after developing further the themes touched upon here, evaluation of the probable consequences of different policies on society and on future generations is needed. Until the results of a complete study are available, my argument could serve best as a reason for persons at risk for transmitting Huntington's chorea and similar diseases to put off having children. Perhaps this essay will stimulate such inquiry.

⑤　⑤　⑤

[Ed. note: This third section is excerpted from Purdy's essay "Loving Future People" in *Reproduction, Ethics, and the Law: Feminist Perspectives,* ed. Joan C. Callahan.]

. . . [One of the objections that] have emerged against the position that procreation is sometimes irresponsible. . . . The other comes from disability rights activists who hold that it is, among other things, bias against disabled people, not well-grounded moral argument. . . .

One of the clearest and most powerful messages to come from both Adrienne Asch and Marsha Saxton[18] is that much suffering of disabled persons arises not from their disabilities but from the social response to their disabilities. . . .

Asch and Saxton are certainly right here: it is clear that the plight of disabled persons would be much improved if each had all the help possible. And, such help should be available: we waste billions on the military and other boondoggles, whereas a fraction of that amount would enable us to create a society that would meet people's needs far better.

Quite apart from our evaluation of disabilities themselves, however, this nasty state of affairs raises the question of the extent to which we ought to take into account socially imposed obstacles to satisfying lives when we try to judge whether it is morally right to bring a particular child into the world. As a dyed-in-the-wool consequentialist, I cannot ignore the probable difficulties that await children with special problems. It seems to me that only the truly rich can secure the well-being of those with the most serious problems. Given the costs and other difficulties of guaranteeing good care, even very well-to-do individuals might well wonder whether their offspring will get the care they need after their own deaths. This question is still more acute for those who aren't so well off—the vast majority of the U.S. population. Furthermore, it would be unwise to forget that many women are at risk for divorce and its financial aftermath.[19] Although the solution is obvious—more social responsibility for individual needs—it's beginning to look as though none of us will see that come about in our lifetimes. It seems to me that this consideration should be, in the case of some decisions about future children, decisive.

Other facets of the inadequacy of the social response to disabled people involve common habits, attitudes, and values. Ignorance leads even basically nice people to behave in hurtful ways; less good-hearted ones may be thoughtless or cruelly unsympathetic. In addition, apparently innocent values we hold make life difficult. "[W]e, especially in the United States, live in a culture obsessed with health and well-being. We value rugged self-reliance, athletic prowess, and rigid standards of beauty. We incessantly pursue eternal youth," writes Saxton.[20] Certainly, excessive admiration for independence, along with athleticism and narrow conceptions of beauty, make life more painful than it need be for many; they are especially problematic for some disabled people. They constrict the range of prized achievement and characteristics in unjustifiable and harmful ways, and could often be traced, I suspect, to unexamined gender-, race-, or class-based prejudice. It would therefore be desirable to see much of the energy now directed toward promoting these values channeled instead toward others, such as intellectual or artistic achievement, creating warm and supportive emotional networks, and opening our eyes to the beauty of a wide variety of body types. Unfortunately, our culture doesn't seem to be moving in that direction. It's all very well to believe that such social values shouldn't count, but that doesn't do much to lessen their impact on our children.[21]

Furthermore, there are serious objections to lumping health and well-being together with these other suspect values. Good health and the feeling of well-being it helps engender are significant factors in a happy life. They enable people to engage in a wide variety of satisfying activities, and to feel good while they are doing them. When they are absent, our suffering is caused not by our consciousness of having failed to live up to some artificial social value but by the intrinsic pain or limitation caused by that absence.

Denigrating these values is doubly mistaken. First, denying the worth of goals that can be achieved only partially (if at all) by some people would seem to require us to exclude from the arena of desirable traits many otherwise plausible candidates.[22] Perhaps more importantly, it also denies the value of less-than-maximal achievement of such values, and hence undermines the primary argument in favor of allocating social resources to help people cope with special problems. If health and well-being aren't valuable, what moral case is there for eradicating the social obstacles Asch and Saxton complain of so bitterly? Surely it is just their importance that obligates us to provide the opportunity to help people reach the highest levels of which they are capable. If health and well-being are of no special value, what is wrong with letting people languish in pain, or sit in the street with a tin cup when a prosthetic leg or seeing-eye dog could make them independent?

Second, it is important to resist the temptation to identify with our every characteristic. Members of oppressed groups quite rightly want to change society's perception of the features that oppressors latch onto as the mark of their alleged inferiority.[23] Such is the source of such slogans as "Black is beautiful!" of the emphasis on gay pride, and of the valorizing of women's nurturing capacity. However fitting this approach may be in some cases, its appropriateness for every characteristic does not follow. Moral failings are one obvious example.

More generally, we need to think through more carefully any leap from qualities to persons. First, qualities must be evaluated on independent grounds, not on the basis of their connection with us. Then, it is important to keep in mind that to value some characteristic isn't necessarily to look with contempt upon those who lack it. Such an equation would suggest, among other things, that teachers always (ought to) have contempt for their pupils. And, on the one hand, we may admire diametrically opposed characteristics that could not, by their very nature, be found in a single individual. Consider your widely read couch potato friend: do you really have contempt for her because she isn't Mikhail Baryshnikov? Or the converse? On the other hand, our assessment of and liking for individuals is not determined in any obvious way by whether they exemplify our favorite traits. Don't we all know people who, given their characteristics, ought to be our dearest friends—yet we just don't click? And don't we all have friends who don't meet our "standards" at all?

None of this is to deny that it might be appropriate in some contexts for disability rights activists to downplay the effects of certain impairments. It might be helpful, for example, to forcefully remind able-bodied individuals that people with physical problems are people first and foremost. That would help reinforce the point that, like other citizens with special difficulties, their needs should be secured as unobtrusively and respectfully as possible, and that they ought not to be viewed as mere objects of pity. . . .

NOTES

1. This is, of course, a very broad thesis. I defend an even broader version in "Loving Future People."

2. Why would we want to resist legal enforcement of every moral conclusion? First, legal action has many costs, costs not necessarily worth paying in particular cases. Second, legal enforcement tends to take the matter out of the realm of debate and treat it as settled. But in many cases, especially where mores or technology are rapidly evolving, we don't want that to happen. Third, legal enforcement would undermine individual freedom and decision-making capacity. In some cases, the ends envisioned are important enough to warrant putting up with these disadvantages.

3. Those who do not see fetuses as moral persons with a right to life may nonetheless hold that abortion is justifiable in these cases. I argue at some length elsewhere that lesser defects can cause great suffering. Once we are clear that there is nothing discriminatory about failing to conceive particular possible individuals, it makes sense, other things being equal, to avoid the prospect of such pain if we can. Naturally, other things rarely are equal. In the first place, many problems go undiscovered until a baby is born. Second, there are often substantial costs associated with screening programs. Third, although women should be encouraged to consider the moral dimensions of routine pregnancy, we do not want it to be so fraught with tension that it becomes a miserable experience. See "Loving Future People."

4. It should be noted that failing to conceive a single individual can affect many lives: in 1916, 962 cases could be traced from six seventeenth-century arrivals in America. See Gordon Rattray Taylor, *The Biological Time Bomb* (New York: Penguin, 1968), p. 176.

5. *The Merck Manual* (Rahway, N.J.: Merck, 1972), pp. 1363, 1346. We now know that the age of onset and severity of the disease are related to the umber of abnormal replications of the glutamine code on the abnormal gene. See Andrew Revkin, "Hunting Down Huntington's," *Discover* (December 1993): 108.

6. Hymie Gordon, "Genetic Counseling," *Journal of the American Medical Association* 217, no. 9 (August 30, 1971): 1346.

7. See Revkin, "Hunting Down Huntington's," 99–108.

8. "Gene for Huntington's Disease Discovered," *Human Genome News* 5, no. 1 (May 1993): 5.

9. Charles Smith, Susan Holloway, and Alan E. H. Emery, "Individuals at Risk in Families—Genetic Disease," *Journal of Medical Genetics* 8 (1971): 453.

10. To try to separate the issue of the gravity of the disease from the existence of a given individual, compare this situation with how we would assess a parent who neglected to vaccinate an existing child against a hypothetical viral version of Huntington's.

11. *New York Times*, September 30, 1975, p. 1. The Joseph family disease is similar to Huntington's disease except that symptoms start appearing in the twenties. Rick Donohue was in his early twenties at the time he made this statement.

12. There may be a price for the individuals who refrain from having children. We will be looking at the situation from their point of view shortly.

13. This is in fact the basis for certain parental duties. An example is the maternal duty to obtain proper nutrition before and during pregnancy, for this is necessary if the child is to have normal health when it is born.

14. One might argue that as many persons as possible should exist so that they may enjoy life.

15. Some thinkers have qualms about the use of some or all of these methods. They have so far failed to show why they are immoral, although, naturally, much careful study will be required before they could be unqualifiedly recommended. See, for example, Richard Hull, "Genetic Engineering: Comment on Headings," *Humanist* 32 (September/October 1972): 13.

16. A. Castell, ed., *Essays in Pragmatism* (New York: Hafner Publishing, 1948), p. 73.

17. For example, see Gerald Leach, *The Biocrats* (Middlesex, England: Penguin Books, 1972), p. 138. One of the ways the dilemma described by Leach could be lessened would be if society emphasized those aspects of family life not dependent on "blood" relationships and downplayed those that are.

18. Marsha Saxton, "Born and Unborn: The Implications of Reproductive Technologies for People with Disabilities," in *Test-Tube Women: What Future for Motherhood?* ed. Rita Arditti, Renate Duelli-Klein, and Shelley Minden (London: Pandora, 1984); Adrienne Asch, "Can Aborting 'Imperfect' Children Be Immoral?" in *Ethical Issues in Modern Medicine*, ed. John Arras and Nancy Rhoden (Mountain View, Calif.: Mayfield Press, 1989).

19. The recent (1991–92) recession, which included widespread unemployment, cuts in federal and state welfare programs, and the increasingly serious health insurance crisis, should give pause to those of modest means who assume that they will be able to make sure their children's needs will be met. Furthermore, it is by now generally known that women usually fare poorly after divorce, especially if they have stayed at home to take care of children. Alimony is now rare, and women must now earn a living (with nonexistent or rusty job skills). Since they are usually granted custody of the children, and are given only the inadequate child support offered by most fathers, they must somehow cover childcare expenses, too. With a divorce rate of 50 percent, no married woman can be sure that she will not find herself trapped in such difficult circumstances.

156 · PART 2: PARENTAGE

20. Saxton, "Born and Unborn," p. 301.

21. Anybody who has tried to raise thoughtful and caring children knows how difficult it is to teach them these values, as well as the hostility they face if they accept them. It does not follow that we should give up on such projects, but we need to be realistic about their toll. Therefore, we should think twice about imposing such burdens on children.

22. This approach to grading values might lead to a reductio ad absurdum rejection of any value, even that of life itself, since, after all, not everybody can live.

23. Thanks to Dianne Romain for helping me think more clearly about this issue.

IMPLICATIONS OF PRENATAL DIAGNOSIS FOR THE HUMAN RIGHT TO LIFE

Leon R. Kass

*W*hat would constitute an adequate justification of the decision to abort a genetically defective fetus? Let me suggest the following formal characteristics, each of which still begs many questions. (1) The reasons given should be logically consistent, and should lead to relatively unambiguous guidelines—note that I do not say "rules"—for action in most cases. (2) The justification should make evident to a reasonable person that the interest or need or right being served by abortion is sufficient to override the otherwise presumptive claim on us to protect and preserve the life of the fetus. (3) Hopefully, the justification would be such as to help provide intellectual support for drawing distinctions between acceptable and unacceptable kinds of genetic abortion and between genetic abortion itself and the further practices we would all find abhorrent. (4) The justification ought to be capable of generalization to all persons in identical circumstances. (5) The justification should not lead to different actions from month to month or from year to year. (6) The justification should be grounded on standards that can, both in principle and in fact, sustain and support our actions in the case of genetic abortion and our notions of human rights in general.

Though I would ask the reader to consider all these criteria, I shall focus primarily on the last. According to what standards can and should we judge a fetus with genetic abnormalities unfit to live, i.e., abortable? It

From *Ethical Issues in Human Genetics*, ed. Bruce Hilton et al. (New York: Plenum Press, 1973), reprinted in *Biomedical Ethics and the Law*, ed. James M. Humber and Robert F. Almeda (New York: Plenum Press, 1976), pp. 313–27.

seems to me that there are at least three dominant standards to which we are likely to repair.

The first is societal good. The needs and interests of society are often invoked to justify the practices of prenatal diagnosis and abortion of the genetically abnormal. The argument, full-blown, runs something like this. Society has an interest in the genetic fitness of its members. It is foolish for society to squander its precious resources ministering to and caring for the unfit, especially those who will never become "productive," or who will never in any way "benefit" society. Therefore, the interests of society are best served by the elimination of the genetically defective prior to their birth.

The societal standard is all too often reduced to its lower common denominator: money. Thus one physician, claiming that he has "made a cost-benefit analysis of Tay-Sachs disease," notes that "the total cost of carrier detection, prenatal diagnosis, and termination of at-risk pregnancies for all Jewish individuals in the United States under 30 who will marry is $5,730,281. If the program is set up to screen only one married partner, the cost is $3,122,695. The hospital costs for the 990 cases of Tay-Sachs disease these individuals would produce over a thirty-year period in the United States is $34,650,000."[1] Another physician, apparently less interested or able to make such a precise audit has written: "Cost-benefit analyses have been made for the total prospective detection and monitoring of Tay-Sachs disease, cystic fibrosis (when prenatal detection becomes available for cystic fibrosis), and other disorders, and in most cases, the expenditures for hospitalization and medical care far exceed the cost of prenatal detection in properly selected risk populations, followed by selective abortion."* Yet a third physician has calculated that the costs to the state of caring for children with Down's syndrome is more than three times that of detecting and aborting them. (These authors all acknowledge the additional nonsocietal "costs" of personal suffering, but insofar as they consider society, the costs are purely economic.)

There are many questions that can be raised about this approach. First, there are questions about the accuracy of the calculations. Not all the costs have been reckoned. The aborted defective child will be "replaced" by a "normal" child. In keeping the ledger, the "costs" to society of his care and maintenance cannot be ignored—costs of educating him, and removing his wastes and pollutions, not to mention the "costs" in nonreplaceable natural resources that he consumes. Who is a greater drain on society's precious resources, the average inmate of a home for the retarded or the average graduate of Harvard College? I am not sure we know or can even find out. Then there are the costs of training the physician and genetic counselors, equipping their laboratories, supporting their research, and sending them and us to conferences to worry about what they are doing. An accurate economic

---

*Ed. Note: Source citation unavailable.

analysis seems to me to be impossible, even in principle. And even if it were possible, one could fall back on the words of that ordinary language philosopher, Andy Capp [a comic-strip character], who, when his wife said that she was getting really worried about the cost of living, replied: "Sweet 'eart, name me one person who wants t'stop livin' on account of the cost."

A second defect of the economic analysis is that there are matters of social importance that are not reducible to financial costs, and others that may not be quantifiable at all. How does one quantitate the costs of real and potential social conflict, either between children and parents, or between the community and the "deviants" who refuse amniocentesis and continue to bear abnormal children? Can one measure the effect of racial tensions of attempting to screen for and prevent the birth of children homozygous (or heterozygous) for sickle-cell anemia? What numbers does one attach to any decreased willingness or ability to take care of the less fortunate, or to cope with difficult problems? And what about the "costs" of rising expectations? Will we become increasingly dissatisfied with anything short of the "optimum baby"? How does one quantify anxiety? humiliation? guilt? Finally, might not the medical profession pay an unmeasurable price if genetic abortion and other revolutionary activities bring about changes in medical ethics and medical practice that lead to the further erosion of trust in the physician?

An appeal to social worthiness or usefulness is a less vulgar form of the standard of societal good. It is true that great social contributions are unlikely to be forthcoming from persons who suffer from most serious genetic diseases, especially since many of them die in childhood. Yet consider the following remarks of author Pearl Buck on the subject of being a mother of a child afflicted with phenylketonuria:

> My child's life has not been meaningless. She has indeed brought comfort and practical help to many people who are parents of retarded children or are themselves handicapped. True, she has done it through me, yet without her I would not have had the means of learning how to accept the inevitable sorrow, and how to make that acceptance useful to others. Would I be so heartless as to say that it has been worthwhile for my child to be born retarded? Certainly not, but I am saying that even though gravely retarded it has been worthwhile for her to have lived.
>
> It can be summed up, perhaps, by saying that in this world, where cruelty prevails so many aspects of our life, I would not add the weight of choice to kill rather than to let live. A retarded child, a handicapped person, brings its own gift to life, even to the life of normal human beings. That gift is comprehended in the lessons of patience, understanding, and mercy, lessons which we all need to receive and to practice with one another, whatever we are.[2]

The standard of potential social worthiness is little better in deciding about abortion in particular cases than is the standard of economic cost. To drive the point home, each of us might consider retrospectively whether he would have been willing to stand trial for his life as a fetus, pleading only his worth to society as he now can evaluate it. How many of us are not socially "defective" and with none of the excuses possible for a child with phenylke-tonuria? If there is to be human life at all, potential social worthiness cannot be its entitlement.

Finally, we should take note of the ambiguities in the very notion of soci-etal good. Some use the term "society" to mean their own particular political community, others to mean the whole human race, and still others speak as if they mean both simultaneously, following that all-too-human belief that what is good for me and mine is good for humankind. Who knows what is genetically best for humankind, even with respect to Down's syndrome? I would submit that the genetic heritage of the human species is largely in the care of persons who do not live along the amniocentesis frontier. If we in the industrialized West wish to be really serious about the genetic future of the species, we would concentrate our attack on mutagenesis, and especially on our large contribution to the pool of environmental mutagens.

But even the more narrow use of "society" is ambiguous. Do we mean our "society" as it is today? Or do we mean our "society" as it ought to be? If the former, our standards will be ephemeral, for ours is a faddish "society." (By far the most worrisome feature of the changing attitudes on abortion is the suddenness with which they change.) Any such socially determined stan-dards are likely to provide too precarious a foundation for decisions about genetic abortion, let alone for our notions of human rights. If we mean the latter, then we have transcended the societal standard, since the "good society" is not to be found in "society" itself, nor is it likely to be discovered by taking a vote. In sum, societal good as a standard for justifying genetic abortion seems to be unsatisfactory. It is hard to define in general, difficult to apply clearly to particular cases, susceptible to overreaching and abuse (hence, very dangerous), and not sufficient unto itself if considerations of the good community are held to be automatically implied.

A second major alternative is the standard of parental or familial good. Here the argument of justification might run as follows. Parents have a right to determine, according to their own wishes and based upon their own notions of what is good for them, the qualitative as well as the quantitative character of their families. If they believe that the birth of a seriously deformed child will be the cause of great sorrow and suffering to themselves and to their other children and a drain on their time and resources, then they may ethically decide to prevent the birth of such a child, even by abortion.

This argument I would expect to be more attractive to most people than the argument appealing to the good of society. For one thing, we are more likely to trust a person's conception of what is good for him than his notion of what is good for society. Also, the number of persons involved is small, making it seem less impossible to weigh all the relevant factors in determining the good of the family. Most powerfully, one can see and appreciate the possible harm done to healthy children if the parents are obliged to devote most of their energies to caring for the afflicted child.

Yet there are ambiguities and difficulties perhaps as great as with the standard of societal good. In the first place, it is not entirely clear what would be good for the other children. In a strong family, the experience with a suffering and dying child might help the healthy siblings learn to face and cope with adversity. Some people have even speculated that the lack of experience with death and serious illness in our affluent young people is an important element in their difficulty in trying to find a way of life and in responding patiently yet steadily to the serious problems of our society.[3] I suspect that one cannot generalize. In some children and in some families, experience with suffering may be strengthening, and in others, disabling. My point here is that the matter is uncertain, and that parents deciding on this basis are as likely as not to be mistaken.

The family or parental standard, like the societal standard, is unavoidably elastic because "suffering" does not come in discontinuous units, and because parental wishes and desires know no limits. Both are utterly subjective, relative, and notoriously subject to change. Some parents claim that they could not tolerate having to raise a child of the undesired sex. I know of one case where the woman in the delivery room, on being informed that her child was a boy, told the physician that she did not even wish to see it and that he should get rid of it. We may judge her attitude to be pathological, but even pathological suffering is suffering. Would such suffering justify aborting her normal male fetus?

Or take the converse case of two parents, who for their own very peculiar reasons, wish to have an abnormal child, say, a child who will suffer from the same disease as his grandfather, or a child whose arrested development would preclude the threat of adolescent rebellion and separation. Are these acceptable grounds for the abortion of "normals"?

Granted, such cases will be rare. But they serve to show the dangers inherent in talking about the parental right to determine, according to their wishes, the quality of their children. Indeed, the whole idea of parental rights with respect to children strikes me as problematic. It suggests that children are like property, that they exist for the parents. One need only look around to see some of the results of this notion of parenthood. The language of duties to children would be more in keeping with the heavy responsibility we bear in affirming the continuity of life with life and in trying to transmit what wisdom we have acquired to the next generation. Our children are not our children. Hopefully, reflection on these matters could lead to a greater appreciation of why it is people do and should have children. No better consequence can be hoped for from the advent of amniocentesis and other technologies for controlling human reproduction.

If one speaks of familial good in terms of parental duty, one could argue that parents have an obligation to do what they can to ensure that their children are born healthy and sound. But this formulation transcends the limitation of parental wishes and desires. As in the case of the good society, the idea of "healthy and sound" requires an objective standard, a standard in reality. Hard as it may be to uncover it, this is what we are seeking. Nature as a standard is the third alternative.

The justification according to the natural standard might run like this. As a result of our knowledge of genetic diseases, we know that persons afflicted with certain diseases will never be capable of living the full life of a human being. Just as a nonnecked giraffe could never live a giraffe's life, or a needle-less porcupine would not attain true "porcupine-hood," so a child or fetus with Tay-Sachs disease or Down's syndrome, for example, will never be truly human. They will never be able to care for themselves, nor have they even the potential for developing the distinctively human capacities for thought or self-consciousness. Nature herself has aborted many similar cases, and has provided for the early death of many who happen to get born. There is no reason to keep them alive; instead, we should prevent their birth by contraception or sterilization if possible, and abortion if necessary.

The advantages of this approach are clear. The standards are objective and in the fetus itself, thus avoiding the relativity and ambiguity in societal and parental good. The standard can be easily generalized to cover all such cases and will be resistant to the shifting sands of public opinion.

This standard, I would suggest, is the one that most physicians and genetic counselors appeal to in their heart of hearts, no matter what they say or do about letting the parents choose. Why else would they have developed genetic counseling and amniocentesis? Indeed, the notions of "disease," of "abnormal," of "defective," make no sense at all in the absence of a natural norm of health. This norm is the foundation of the art of the physician and of the inquiry of the health scientist. Yet, as Motulsky and others have pointed out, the standard is elusive. Ironically, we are gaining increasing power to manipulate and control our own nature at a time in which we are increasingly confused about what is normal, healthy, and fit.

Although possibly acceptable in principle, the natural standard runs into problems in application when attempts are made to fix the boundary between potentially human and potentially not human. Professor Lejeune has clearly demonstrated the difficulty, if not the impossibility, of setting clear molecular, cytological, or developmental signposts for this boundary.[4] Attempts to induce signposts by considering the phenotypes of the worst cases is equally difficult. Which features would we take to be the most relevant in, say, Tay-Sachs disease, Lesch-Nyhan syndrome, Cri du chat, Down's syndrome? Certainly, severe mental retardation. But how "severe" is "severe"? As . . . I have argued, mental retardation admits of degree. It too is relative. Moreover it is not clear that certain other defects and deformities might not equally foreclose the possibility of a truly or fully human life. What about blindness or deafness? Quadriplegia? Asphasia? Several of these in combination? Not only does each kind of defect admit of a continuous scale of severity, but it also merges with other defects on a continuous scale of defectiveness. Where on this scale is the line to be drawn: after mental retardation? blindness? muscular dystrophy? cystic fibrosis? hemophilia diabetes? galactosemia? Turner's syndrome? XYY? club foot? Moreover, the identical two continuous scales—kind and severity—are found also among the living. In fact, it is the natural standard that may be the most dangerous one in that it leads most directly to the idea that there are second-class human beings and subhuman beings.

But the story is not complete. The very idea of nature is ambiguous. According to one view, the one I have been using, nature points to or implies a peak, a perfection. According to this view, human rights depend upon attaining the status of humanness. The fetus is only potential; it has no rights, according to this view. But all kinds of people fall short of the norm: children, the mentally impaired, some adults. This understanding of nature has been used to justify not only abortion and infanticide, but also slavery.

There is another notion of nature, less splendid, more humane and, though less able to sustain a notion of health, more acceptable to the findings of modern science. Animal nature is characterized by impulses of self-preservation and by the capacity to feel pleasure and to suffer pain. Man and other animals are alike on this understanding of nature. And the right to life is ascribed to all such self-preserving and suffering creatures. Yet on this understanding of nature, the fetus—even a defective fetus—is not potential, but actual. The right to life belongs to him. But for this reason, this understanding of nature does not provide and may even deny what it is we are seeking, namely, a justification for genetic abortion, adequate unto itself, which does not simultaneously justify infanticide, homicide, and enslavement of the genetically abnormal.

There is a third understanding of nature, akin to the second, nature as sacrosanct, nature as created by a Creator. Indeed, to speak about this reminds us that there is a fourth possible standard of judgments about genetic abortion: the religious standard. I shall leave the discussion of this standard to those who are able to speak of it in better faith.

Now that I am at the end, the reader can better share my sense of frustration. I have failed to provide myself with a satisfactory intellectual and moral justification for the practice of genetic abortion. Perhaps others more able than I can supply one. Perhaps the pragmatists can persuade me that we should abandon the search for principled justification, that if we just trust people's situational decisions or their gut reactions, everything will turn out fine. Maybe they are right. But we should not forget the sage observation of Bertrand Russell: "Pragmatism is like a warm bath that heats up so imperceptibly that you don't know when to scream." I would add that before we submerge ourselves irrevocably in amniotic fluid, we take note of the connection to our own baths, into which we have started the hot water running.

NOTES

1. I assume this calculation ignores the possibilities of inflation, devaluation, and revolution.

2. Pearl S. Buck, foreword to *The Terrible Choice: The Abortion Dilemma* (New York: Bantam Books, 1968), pp. ix–xi.

3. Eric Cassell, "Death and the Physician," *Commentary* (June 1969): 73–79.

4. J. Lejeune, "On the Nature of Man," *American Journal of Human Genetics* 22 (1970): 121.

2. Genetic Control

*I*n this section, the focus is broadened to include not only genetic disease but also genetic enhancement. Further, the focus is on controlling the genetic component of parentage.

Fletcher considers in the excerpt herein the moral responsibility of the individual to control genetics. Like Purdy, he considers it morally irresponsible not to make controlling decisions about the genetic makeup of our children. However, he extends his discussion to consider the responsibility of the state as well, pointing out that our laissez-faire policy hasn't been "altogether just"—"there are too many who do not control their lives out of moral concern" (p. 171). Conceding the tension between rights and regulation, Fletcher argues for the latter, citing other "invasions of privacy" our society wisely accepts.

Unlike Purdy, Kass, and Fletcher, Resnik discusses in detail providing genetic enhancement, as opposed to eliminating genetic defect. If parents have the right to promote the health of their children and provide them with benefits, then, Resnik argues, they have the right to genetic enhancement technologies. He anticipates several objections, addressing primarily the concern that "legitimate" eugenics will lead to "illegitimate" eugenics. Resnik concludes that in order to prevent the potential harms and social injustices that may occur, genetic enhancement technologies should be

165

accompanied by education and subject to state regulation (such as might occur—though Resnik doesn't actually suggest this—as part of a licensing parents program).

Ulrich also argues in favor of state control, but whereas Resnik looks mostly to our society as his context, Ulrich turns to our species. He argues that our species has a right to survive and this right entails certain obligations, one of which is to refrain from passing on genetic diseases. It is this obligation, along with legal precedent (he cites existing restrictions of the right to reproduce, such as the prohibition of marriage between closely related people), that justifies premarital screening followed by, if there's a high risk of transmitting genetic disease, a suspension of reproductive rights.

Macklin presents an opposing view, arguing against programs of genetic control, whether additive or subtractive and whether government based or scientist directed. Developing four separate arguments, she concludes that such programs would be "misguided or dangerous or both" (p. 197). Instead, she claims, the individual parents-to-be should be the ones to make the decisions required; she believes that with counseling and education, most such decisions will actually be beneficial not only to the parents, but also to society.

THE ETHICS OF
GENETIC CONTROL

SOME ANSWERS

Joseph Fletcher

O ur moral obligation is to control the quality as well as the quantity of the children we bring into the world. We owe it to a prospective child, to ourselves as parents of integrity, to our families that have only so much in the way of human and economic resources, and to society. Ethically it is in the discretion of a woman to prevent or end any pregnancy she does not want, unless she has promised the child to a husband or lover who justifiably insists on it, or unless a clear case can be made that society has a supervening interest in its birth. (Rarely indeed would either of these limitations cut into her personal freedom.) . . .

The looming moral issue has to do with *compulsory* birth control. Up to the present we have relied upon a voluntary policy, and everything else being equal it is better to be responsible for our reproduction of our own free will than to be compelled. But the two control goals, quality and quantity, cannot rightly be ignored by individuals to the common hurt. Birth control is not merely a private matter. We may have to face compulsory controls of fertility and dysgenic inheritances, however regrettably, as we have had to face compulsory vaccination for communicable diseases.

A contemporary and morally responsible ethics of reproduction calls for whatever policy works. An English clergyman, typifying a not uncommon and truly nihilistic irresponsibility, said recently that without a free private

Reprinted from *The Ethics of Genetic Control: Ending Reproductive Roulette*, by Joseph Fletcher (Amherst, N.Y.: Prometheus Books, 1988).

option to reproduce we lose our humanity, and that if therefore population reaches disastrous proportions, "well, then we die."[1]

Laissez-faire has not proved to be altogether a just policy in the production of economic goods and services, Adam Smith to the contrary notwithstanding, and the same can be said of human reproduction. Fortunately, birth control is spreading through all the world, including Asia and Africa, in spite of various religions and customs. We ought not to forget that the original Latin for population, *populare*, means to devastate or lay waste; it can come exactly to that. . . .

⑤   ⑤   ⑤

An editorial by Dr. Malcolm Watts in the journal of the California Medical Association in 1970 remarked that "man exercises ever more certain and effective control" over the quality of human life. "It will become necessary and acceptable to place relative rather than absolute values on such things as human lives, the use of scarce resources, and the various elements which are to make up the quality of life or of living which is to be sought." All of this, he said, requires "a new ethic" in "a rational development" of "what is almost certain to be a biologically oriented world society."

Physicians in the past, the editorial points out, have tried "to preserve, protect, repair, prolong, and enhance every human life which comes under their surveillance."[2] This was the old vitalistic, undiscriminating sanctity-or-quantity-of-life ethics, now giving way to a responsible, decisional quality-of-life ethics. To repair and prolong lives, indiscriminately, may be a kind of technical virtuosity but it is not *control*. To control means to choose, and therefore any absolute morality about always keeping life going, before or after birth, regardless of quality considerations, is the very opposite of control and a denial of quality.

If we choose family size, we should choose family health. This is what the controls of reproductive medicine make possible. Public health and sanitation have greatly reduced human ills; now the major ills have become genetic and congenital. They can be reduced by medical controls. We ought to protect our families from the emotional and material burden of such diseased individuals, and from the misery of their simply "existing" (not *living*) in a nearby "warehouse" or public institution.

We have an example in hemophilia. If a man has a recessive gene for it, even though he himself is all right, he passes it on—not to his sons but to his daughters. They won't have the disease (it is sex-linked) but they will pass it on to their children. By controlling his reproduction through sex selection or preemptive abortion, keeping only male embryos, this man would stop the scourge once and for all in his family line. That is his moral responsibility.

If the state is morally justified in repelling an unwelcome invader, why should not a woman do so when burdened or invaded by an unwelcome pregnancy? And why shouldn't the family be protected from an idiot or terribly diseased sibling? Control is human and rational; submission, the opposite of control, is subhuman. Suffering and misfortune cannot be utterly escaped, it is true, and human beings can grow tremendously in pain and disappointment. But a basic ethical principle of medicine and health care is nonetheless the minimization of human suffering, by deliberate control.

Producing our children by "sexual roulette" without preconceptive and uterine control, simply taking "pot luck" from random sexual combinations, is irresponsible—now that we can be genetically selective and know how to monitor against congenital infirmities. As we learn to direct mutations medically, we should do so. Not to control when we can is immoral. This way it will be much easier to assure our children that they really are here because they were *wanted*, that they were born "on purpose."

Controlling the quality of life is not negative; it just rejects what fails to come up to a positive standard. The new biology equips us to save and improve the defective, as well as to maintain a sensible standard. For example, it was once prohibitively expensive to correct dwarfism when human growth hormone (HGH) had to be extracted from human pituitaries at autopsy, but biochemistry has synthesized HGH and one day soon it will be available economically. (Such achievements are undesirable only if we allow the dwarfs we treat to pass their genetic defect along to innocent progeny.)

We began our human history by learning to control the physical environment (and still make serious mistakes). We have made some progress in controlling our social life, and we are learning to control our behavior. It is time, then, that we accepted control of our heredity.

⑤　　⑤　　⑤

The essence of tragedy is the conflict of one good with another. The conflict of good with evil is only melodrama. We often have to calculate the relative desirability of things. We pay for what we get, always. Choosing high-quality fetuses and rejecting low-quality ones is not tragedy; it is sad, but not agonizing.

A heavier trial of the spirit and a real test of responsible judgment, if we want to exert serious control, would be a problem like deciding whether to induce abortion when only one of a pair of nonidentical twins has an untreatable metabolic disorder. It would mean losing a good baby to prevent a bad one. But even here compassionate control should not hesitate: the good one is still only potential, and pregnancy could—at least ordinarily—be restarted. It is far more callous not to prevent the fate of a foreseeably diseased baby than it is disappointing to postpone a good one for a matter of only months.

To be responsible, to take control and reject low-quality life, only seems cruel or callous to the morally superficial. Actually, it is practical compassion. Robert Louis Stevenson was shocked at first when he found the Polynesians practicing "infanticide." Their ignorance of contraception and obstetrics meant they had to resort to "abortion at birth" when a newborn turned out to be defective, or when the small atolls they lived on simply could not yield food and shelter for any more people. It was loving concern for *actual* children in their radically finite world that led them to abortion and population control; it was a matter of costs and benefits.

Stevenson said, somewhat bemused, that never had he seen people anywhere who loved their children as much as those coral reef dwellers did. Of course. The world's finiteness is harder to hide on a Pacific coral reef.

Not to control, and not to weigh one thing against another, would be subhuman. A mature ethics is social, not egocentric. Call it what you will—mathematical morality, ethical arithmetic, moral calculus—we are obliged in conscience to think of benefits relative to costs.

Trying to be responsible we have to calculate. We issue drivers' licenses, for example, even though the cars of some will become lethal weapons; it is the price we pay for motor transport. If we could tell which applicants for a license will be killers, we would not license them. It used to be that we had no way of knowing which couples were carrying a common gene defect or which pregnancies were positive for it. But now we *can* know; we have lost that excuse for taking genetic risks. To go right ahead with coital reproduction in many couples' cases is like walking down a line of children blindfolded and deliberately maiming every fourth child. It is cruel and insane to deprive normal but disadvantaged children of the care we could give them with the $1,500,000,000 we spend in public costs for preventable retardates.

Ethics is not loftily independent of economics and utilitarian or distributive justice. Economics deals with preferences among competing choices, and utility aims at spreading expectable benefits. What we need morally is a telescope, not just a microscope. . . .

Mothers and fathers are of several different kinds now. Take mothers: some are genetic (they provide the egg), some are natal (they carry the fetus), some are social (they rear or "'bring up" the child). All of them can play a part in a child's creation—yet no one of them needs to fill more than one of these roles. All of them, or any combination, would be ethical as far as the functions themselves are concerned.

Parental (and kin) relationships need to be reconceptualized. They cannot any more be based on blood or wombs or even genes. Parenthood will have to be understood nonbiologically or, to be specific, *morally*. Its own achievements have forced biology out of court in validating parental relations. The mere fact of conceiving a child or donating the elements of its conception or gestating it does not establish anybody as a father or a mother. Parental love has by this time become truly interpersonal; no longer can it be merely germinal, somatic, or physiological—and certainly not merely genital. An authentic parental bond is established morally, by care and concern, not by some simple physicalist doctrine. . . .

All alleged human rights cease to be right, become unjust, when their exercise would victimize innocent third parties and bystanders. All rights are "imperfect," not absolute or uncontingent. We might say this particularly of the so-called right to privacy as it bears on propagating at will and inordinately. The social welfare and protection of third parties has a prior claim. The "right" to reproduce, like all others, is—morally weighed—really only a privilege.

A worrisome side to the practice of control is whether it should ever be imposed or must always be voluntary. If people could be relied upon to be compassionate, we would have no reason to even consider mandatory controls. But there are too many who do not control their lives out of moral concern; they are self-centered about what they do or neglect to do, even though they may be "cagey" about it. Large families and a pious disregard of genetic counseling, like refusing to undergo vaccinations until it is made a matter of police enforcement, show how the common welfare often has to be safeguarded by compulsory control or what Garrett Hardin calls "mutual coercion mutually agreed upon."[3]

Coercion is a dirty word to liberals, but all social controls—e.g., the government's tax powers—are really what the majority agree upon, however reluctantly, out of enlightened self-interest and a quid pro quo willingness to give up something to get something better. It might be protection from overpopulation, for instance. Ideally it is better to do the moral thing freely, but sometimes it is more compassionate to force it to be done than to sacrifice the well-being of the many to the egocentric "rights" of the few. This obviously is the ethics of a sane society. Compulsory controls on reproduction would not, of course, fit present interpretations of due process in the Fifth and Fourteenth Amendments to the Constitution.[4] Here, as in so many other ways, the law lags behind the ethics of modern medicine and public health knowledge.

A good illustration of the tension between rights and regulation takes shape in trying to control hereditary disease. Each of us carries from five to ten genetic faults. If they match up in sexual roulette, tragedy results. How can we avoid or curtail the danger? Denmark prohibits marriages of certain couples unless they are sterilized. But if this or any other method of control and prevention is used, how do we find out *who* are the ones who should not marry or, if they do, should not have babies by the natural or coital mode? Screening by one means or another is the obvious way to fulfill our obligation to potential children, as well as to the community that has to suffer when defectives are born.

The law in most countries is far behind our emerging medical information. People are not required to make their bad genes known to their mates, nor are physicians required to reveal the facts. A man with polycystic kidney disease is not required to let it be known—even though it is highly immoral (unjust) to keep knowledge of such a hereditary disaster (renal failure in middle age) from his children and those they marry. Medical genetics will continue to isolate more and more such diseases, so that as our ability to prevent disease and tragedy increases so does the moral guilt of secrecy, indifference to the consequences for others, and fatalistic inaction.

Conquering infectious diseases reduces the cause of the trouble, but to conquer genetic diseases *increases* the cause or source of the trouble. This dysgenic effect is the first big-scale moral dilemma for medicine—truly a dilemma. Infections come from the environment around us but genetic faults come from within us, and therefore any line of genetic sufferers allowed to propagate will spread their disease through more and more carriers. As we cut down on the infectious diseases we are threatened with a relative rise in deaths and debility due to genetic disorders. We are now approaching a situation in which genetic causes account for as many or *more* deaths than "disease" in the popular sense.

Our moral obligation to undergo voluntary screening, if it is indicated, is too obvious to underline. The squeeze here, ethically, is that the social good often requires *mass* screening. When it is voluntary it is "nicer," as we see in the popular acceptance of tests for cervical cancer. But let it be compulsory if need be, for the common good—Hardin's "mutual coercion mutually agreed upon." Francis Crick has said that "if we can get across to people the idea that their children are not entirely their own business and that it is not a private matter, it would be an enormous step forward."[5] The biophysicist Leroy Augenstein estimated in 1972 that a total of 6 percent of births, or one out of seventeen, are defective. Of these, he said, forty thousand to fifty thousand children every year "are so defective that they don't know that they are human beings."[6] His figures are more impressive than his formulation, however; if an individual cannot "know" he is a human being, he is not a human being.

Parents of adopted children and those who donate sperm for artificial insemination are much more carefully screened and selected than "natural" parents—which is logically ridiculous even though we can understand how it came about. A socially conscientious system would be a national registry: blood and skin tests done routinely at birth and fed into a computer-gene scanner would pick up all anomalies, and they would be printed out on data cards and filed; then when marriage licenses are applied for, the cards would be read in comparison machines to find incompatibilities and homozygous conditions.

The objection is, predictably, that it would "violate" a "right"—the right to privacy. It is even said, in a brazen attack on reason itself, that we have a "right to *not* know." Which is more important, the alleged "privacy" or the good of the couple as well as of their progeny and society? (The couple could unite anyway, of course, but on the condition Denmark makes—that sterilization is done for one or both of them. And they could even still have children by medical and donor assistance, bypassing their own faulty fertility.)

Screening is no more an invasion of privacy than "contact tracing" in the treatment of venereal disease, or income tax and public health records, or compulsory fluoridation of the water, or the age-old codes of consanguinity (which were based on nonsense). A good education for those who balk would be a week's stay in the wards of a state institution for the "retarded"—a term used to cover a host of terrible distortions of humanity. Just let them *see* the nature and extent of it; that would convince them.

🌀   🌀   🌀

The ethical issues raised about preselection of children's sex are mainly two: whether it is wrong to exercise that much control over our progeny, and whether it is right to throw the sex ratio out of balance. The second "issue" is based on an assumption that most people would prefer boys to girls.

By way of answering, we would say that control as such is good, not evil, and the more the better, but that it should not be used for immoral purposes. Throwing the sex ratio out of near balance might be undesirable if it denied some people their aliquot share of sexual partnership. This could be the case in a strictly monogamous culture, even though single persons and celibates (to say nothing of group-marriage members) could have children asexually. With fewer progeny needed or wanted, and sexual intercourse freer in part because of that fact, there is now much less need for a near balance of the sexes. And in the last resort, reproduction no longer will have to depend on marital-coital-gestational reproduction.

The assumption that the male gender is better and more desirable is a bare-faced piece of male chauvinism and androcentric psychology. To suppose that fetal sex choice and freedom of abortion would mean throwing out "worthless females" is both hilarious and foolish. If men were stupid enough to do it (they aren't), the women would soon set things straight.

There is also the related issue, the assertion that embryos are human beings and that superfetation and selection is "mass murder." This strident protest is not ethically tenable. Even its metaphysical validity is dubious, to say nothing of its unethical and antimedical consequences if it were followed out logically. . . .

⑤　⑤　⑤

Human acts and things are both like poker chips: they have whatever value or worth we—human beings—choose to assign to them. A red one is worth so much, a blue one so much, a white one so much. Put negatively, nothing has intrinsic value—things have no value apart from how human beings feel about them. As in games where chips are used, so in real affairs we agree about the relative values of what we do and what we want in terms of humanly desirable and exchangeable needs and aspirations.

For example, would we on principle "bump" a suicide from an intensive care unit to save an auto accident victim, if it had to be one or the other? The answer, surely, is No. We cannot say that all suicides want to die, nor that all auto accident casualties want to live. It depends. Every case has to be looked at on its own merits.

How we judge or weigh our decisions in real-life situations will depend on what we know or suppose we know about the alternatives. One thing we can be sure of: it is immoral in the extreme to say, as one member of the British Parliament did in the debate on the Abortion Act of 1967, "We are not here to listen to professional opinion, we are here to legislate." That posture, Don't Bother Me with the Facts, My Mind Is Made Up, is the last word in irresponsibility.

As we have seen in nearly all of our ethical problems, the pressure comes when the social interest fails to phase with the personal. The conviction throughout this book, perhaps because we believe that without survival of the species all talk about ethics is academic, is that the general welfare comes first. Look at Robert Louis Stevenson's turnaround experience. He went to Polynesia *sure* that "infanticide" is wrong. What happened to him?

Stevenson already knew "in the back of his mind" that we exist in a finite world inescapably. But he never really understood what he "knew" until he stood on a small atoll in the vast surrounding sea, trying to identify with the outlook of the inhabitants. Then he could grasp the fact that these tiny atolls are true paradigms of the finite "spaceship Earth." When too many babies were born (because the atoll dwellers did not yet know how to prevent it), they accepted the moral responsibility of "aborting at birth" *because they loved their children* and knew that there is a point of too much. He finally saw the ethical error of his simplistic prohibition of infanticide.

This may appear to be a remote example or ultima ratio of the relativity of values. But before we dismiss it too lightly, we should hold it long enough in mind to test the ethical validity of the concepts of species survival and social conscience.

⑤   ⑤   ⑤

We have already reached the conclusion that sometimes it is wrong to procreate a life, but let it be nailed down again. In the law they speak of wrongful death—deaths due, for example, to criminal negligence. Now the new biology and reproductive medicine are confronting us ethically with the reality of wrongful *life*, too.

A wrongful death is one that results from a "tort" or injurious, blameworthy act for which the victim or his agents and beneficiaries should be indemnified or somehow compensated. In any case, the tort is by definition blameworthy, wrong. People who know a child will be defective, or could have known if they had cared but nonetheless allowed it to be born, are as guilty of wrongdoing as those who culpably contribute to a wrongful death.

The ethical principle, as distinct from (but not unrelated to) the legal category of wrongful death, is that there is indeed such a thing as wrongful life. Already the courts have accepted two or three suits by the victims of misconception and misgestation, or by others involved; the principle is taking form, inevitably. We are as morally responsible for what we do at the start of a life as we are for what we do at the end of it. And the test, at both the alpha and the omega on the continuum, is loving concern.

NOTES

1. G. Dunstan, *Morals and Medicine*, ed. Joseph Fletcher (Boston: Beacon, 1960), p. 67.

2. M. Watts, "A New Ethic for Medicine and Society," *California Medicine* 113 (September 1970): 67–68.

3. G. Hardin, *Exploring New Ethics for Survival* (New York: Viking Press, 1972), pp. 260–62.

4. F. Grad, "Legislative Responses to the New Biology: Limits and Possibilities," *UCLA Law Review* 15 (February 1968): 486.

5. Quoted by A. Rosenfeld, *The Second Genesis* (Englewood Cliffs, N.J.: Prentice-Hall, 1969), p. 161.

6. Leroy Augenstein, "Birth Defects," in *Humanistic Perspectives in Medical Ethics*, ed. M. Visscher (London: Pemberton, 1972), p. 207.

DEBUNKING THE SLIPPERY SLOPE ARGUMENT AGAINST HUMAN GERM-LINE GENE THERAPY

David Resnik

O ne of the more influential arguments against human germ-line gene therapy (HGLGT) is that it would lead us down a slippery slope toward genetic enhancement.[1] HGLGT might begin as merely an attempt to eradicate genetic diseases (negative eugenics) and eventually lead to the alteration of human beings for various purposes (positive eugenics). Since the prospect of genetically altered humans brings to mind the eugenics programs of the Nazis, Aldous Huxley's *Brave New World*, and other horrifying scenarios, many writers argue that we must never attempt human germ-line gene therapy. . . .

. . . What is wrong with genetic enhancement? Is genetic enhancement unjust or unfair? Does it rob enhanced and unenhanced individuals of their dignity or create social stigmas and prejudices?

. . . I will argue that genetic enhancement need not be unjust or immoral as long as it is governed by proper regulations and is accompanied by adequate education. . . .

THE ROAD TO GENETIC ENHANCEMENT

. . . [F]or the purposes of this essay, HGLGT shall refer to the genetic modification of early-stage embryos [a process that involves inserting genes, repairing defective genes, or deleting genes]. . . .

Reprinted from the *Journal of Medicine and Philosophy* 19 (1994): 23–40. Copyright © 1994 Kluwer Academic Publishers.

Before turning to arguments against HGLGT,[2] we need to ask the question "Who would conduct human germ-line gene therapy?" Here we have two different answers: governments (or other social institutions) and parents. Governments could practice HGLGT for various purposes, e.g., in order to eradicate genetic diseases, produce superior athletes and scientists, and so on. Individual couples might pursue HGLGT in order to benefit their children or prevent them from having genetic diseases. Whether institutions or parents conduct HGLGT, questions of parental autonomy and parental rights would be paramount, since it would be clearly unjust for a government (or any social institution) to perform HGLGT without the consent of the parents, since this procedure would violate their autonomy. And of course parents should not be allowed to seek HGLGT unless they have a right to do so.

Thus, in addressing HGLGT, we need to focus on the question "Do parents have a right to pursue HGLGT for their children?" Prima facie, this question can be answered in the affirmative, provided that we assume a generally accepted principle of parental autonomy: parents have a right to bear children, to raise children, and to make decisions concerning their health, education, and welfare. If we assume this principle, and it turns out that some forms of HGLGT promote health, then parents have the right to pursue forms of HGLGT that promote health.[3] That is, they have a right to conduct HGLGT in order to prevent genetic diseases.

The same kind of argument extends from negative eugenics to positive eugenics. Parents not only have the right to promote the health of their children, they also have a right to benefit them, i.e., to provide them with education, opportunities, wealth, and the like. Genetic enhancement is not fundamentally different from these other benefits. Giving a child enhanced genes, one might argue, is analogous to giving a child a Harvard education, a trip to Europe, piano lessons, a personal computer, a nose job, or a new car. If parents have the right to give their children these other benefits, then they have the right to give them enhanced genes.

It also follows that if parents have rights relating to HGLGT, then institutions should be allowed to help parents exercise these rights. An analogy with health care is useful here: if I have a right to take care of my child's health, then a state agency, hospital, or clinic should be allowed to help me exercise this right.

ARGUMENTS AGAINST HUMAN GERM-LINE GENE THERAPY

Although parents have at least prima facie rights to pursue HGLGT, these rights can be overridden. Parental rights might be overridden in order to prevent harm to future generations or to prevent grave social, political, and economic injustices. Five of the arguments against HGLGT, including the slippery slope argument, address these reasons for overriding parental rights. The other argument, the theological argument, focuses on a different aspect of HGLGT.

These arguments against HGLGT are as follows:

(1) *The risk argument.* HGLGT would involve too many long-term and short-term risks to subjects and their offspring.[4]

(2) *The consent argument.* HGLGT would be experimentation on subjects who cannot, in principle, give informed consent.[5]

(3) *The cost argument.* HGLGT will always be so costly that it will never merit a high priority in the allocation of resources.[6]

(4) *The integrity argument.* HGLGT would violate the rights of future generations who would like to inherit genetic material whose integrity has not been violated through intentional modification.[7]

(5) *The theological argument.* HGLGT is "playing God." It tampers with material that is sacred, should not be altered by humans, and so on.[8]

(6) *The slippery slope argument.* HGLGT will start us down a slippery slope toward genetic enhancement, a horrible prospect.[9]

The first five arguments against HGLGT have been criticized by other writers, including Fowler, Zimmerman, Berger and Gert, and Munson and Davis.[10] Since my aim is to focus on the slippery slope argument, I will refer readers to these papers and take up my main task. . . .

THE SLIPPERY SLOPE ARGUMENT

The slippery slope argument, more than any other, has captured our imagination and aroused our worst fears. The argument, as I shall interpret it, actually contains two slopes: a slope from negative eugenics to positive eugenics, and one from (possibly) legitimate positive eugenics to illegitimate (unjust, immoral) positive eugenics. The argument goes as follows:

1. We should not engage in an otherwise justifiable activity if engaging in that activity will probably lead us to engage in another activity that is not justifiable.

2. HGLGT to prevent genetic diseases (negative eugenics) is an otherwise justifiable activity that will probably lead to a completely unjustified activity, that is, illegitimate or immoral attempts at genetic enhancement (positive eugenics).

3. Hence, we should not conduct HGLGT even to prevent genetic diseases.

This version of the slippery slope argument is an empirical one because its plausibility hinges on the truth or falsity of premise 2, an empirical claim.[11] Although premise 2 is empirical, it is still highly speculative in that we lack enough evidence to affirm or deny it. Some writers (e.g., Berger and Gert) argue that we can prevent the slippery slope by adopting adequate regulations and safeguards.[12] Others (e.g., Lappe) take the opposite view, claiming that we cannot stop the slide once it starts.[13]

It will become clear later on in this essay that I believe that we cannot stop the slide from negative to positive eugenics. But I believe that we can stop the slide from justified positive eugenics to immoral and unjust positive eugenics. That is, I think it is possible to practice genetic enhancement without violating commonly accepted principles of ethics or social justice. In thinking about these issues, we need to distinguish between two distinct kinds of worries addressed by the slippery slope argument:

(A) Genetic enhancement will cause significant harm to future generations.
(B) Genetic enhancement will violate important principles of social justice, that is, the equality of liberty and opportunity.

The concerns expressed in (A) and (B) are related but conceptually distinct. Harms can cause social injustice. For example, a factory could pollute a city in such a way that people living in the poorer sections of town would receive more pollution than people living in the richer part of the city. Not only would the poorer people be harmed, but they would also suffer an injustice in that they would bear an unfair burden of the effects of pollution. Conversely, injustices can cause harms. People who are discriminated against may suffer from prejudice, stigmatization, feelings of inferiority, and so on. However, concerns about harm and justice are conceptually distinct: it is possible to inflict harm without threatening principles of social justice and vice versa. The factory could pollute in such a way that everyone received a fair share of pollution and a person could be discriminated against without suffering from significant psychosocial harm. Thus I will discuss the concerns expressed by (A) and (B) separately.

HARM TO FUTURE GENERATIONS

Before considering possible harms to future generations, we need to answer a preliminary question: is it wrong to harm future generations? There are some significant conceptual difficulties in granting future generations rights.[14] One difficulty is that it seems counterintuitive to grant nonexistent beings rights. A second difficulty is that it seems problematic to grant rights to beings if we cannot know what they will need or want or how our conduct will affect their needs and wants. Nevertheless, most people would agree that we should avoid intentionally harming future generations. And if we assume that this obligation not to harm—the duty of nonmaleficence—entails rights, then we can say that future generations at least have a right not to be harmed even if they do not have other rights.[15]

Assuming that we should avoid intentionally harming future generations, we need to answer another question: how might HGLGT harm future generations? Since we are assuming a scenario in which HGLGT is safe, the possible harms we need to address are psychological harms or psychosocial harms, not medical ones. To aid our analysis, we can look at two different groups of people who might be harmed, genetically engineered people and people who are not genetically engineered.

One might argue that genetically engineered individuals could suffer from psychological harms in that they would come to regard themselves as mere "artifacts" of their parents' (or designers') desires.[16] HGLGT would threaten their conceptions of themselves as independent beings and destroy their sense of dignity or worth. If we can design people like we design houses or cars, then won't those people who are designed regard themselves as having no more dignity or worth than houses or cars?

Although many might find this argument compelling, on closer examination we can see that it rests on a dubious assumption: it assumes that our conceptions of ourselves as independent persons and our human dignity depend on not having our genomes intentionally manipulated. This would seem to be true only if we assume a strong principle of genetic determinism, namely that our genes completely determine all of our physiological, psychological, and social characteristics. But according to modern biology, this principle is false in human beings: most of our traits result from a combination of genetic and environmental factors. Although some traits, such as skin color and height, are strongly genetically determined, many others, such as intelligence and personality, are not. The fact that we are not genetically determined gives us the ability to develop conceptions of ourselves as independent persons and a sense of self-worth even when we know that our genome has been designed by someone. To see why this is so, consider the following case.

Identical twins have the exact same genetic material yet they develop conceptions of themselves as independent persons with their own self-worth. This is due to the fact that each twin has different experiences and a different interpretation of these experiences. They also have different relationships, and develop different values, beliefs, habits, hobbies, personality traits, and so forth. For nearly all identical twins, their conceptions of themselves as independent persons and their self-worth do not depend on having separate genetic identities.[17]

We can extend this point a bit further and make it more relevant to HGLGT by considering a thought experiment. Imagine that you are snooping around your parents' house one day and you find your genetic blueprints. You find your height, weight, eye color, and many other qualities specified in the blueprints. Would you believe that your conception of yourself as an independent person had been severely violated and that you lack dignity or self-worth? Would you come to view yourself as an artifact of your parents' wishes? Although some people might feel violated, I believe most people would be able to absorb the shock. Some might even find the knowledge enlightening and use it to develop a fuller self-conception. As long as we are not completely determined by our genetic programming, knowing that someone designed that programming should not threaten our conceptions of ourselves as independent people. As long as we think of ourselves as more than our genes—and most people do—this knowledge should not threaten us.

Of course, some engineered people may mistakenly believe that they are genetically determined and they may suffer from psychological harms as a result of their ignorance. But we also find the same concern in other areas of biomedicine, especially in diagnosis. A person who is diagnosed with a mild form of skin cancer may hear the word "cancer" and succumb to irrational fears or panic. The solution to this problem is to educate people about their condition, to tell them about it. The same point applies to genetic engineering. We need to make sure that genetically engineered people know the truth about themselves, know that they are not genetically determined, and so forth. Thus, the worry that genetically engineered individuals will suffer from great psychological harm is a genetic boogeyman that can exorcised by careful reflection and education.

The possible harms to individuals who are not genetically engineered are not so easily dismissed, however. One might argue that these people would suffer from a variety of psychological and psychosocial harms.[18] First, people with genetic defects or abnormalities would be treated as "defectives" or "damaged goods" who slipped through the genetic screen. Second, "normal" but unenhanced people would also be viewed as less than perfect or subpar. In both cases, the people could suffer from social stigmas and prejudices, and they would feel inferior. Further, the whole idea of engineering people to meet technically achievable goals would contribute to existing problems of discrimination and prejudice.

Regarding the psychosocial harm to unenhanced or genetically disabled people, we should compare HGLGT to other practices that we already accept. Most of us agree that people have a right to obtain a wide variety of luxuries and benefits even though some people who do not obtain these goods may suffer from prejudice, stigmatization, or feelings of inferiority because they lack these goods. Suppose I graduated from high school but never had the opportunity to obtain a higher education. As an educationally unenhanced person I might suffer from prejudice, stigmatization, or feelings of inferiority. Even so, my suffering does not justify denying other people a higher education. Or suppose I am born with very poor eyesight (a genetic disability) yet do not have enough money for a decent pair of glasses. Again, I may suffer from prejudice, stigmatization, and feelings of inferiority. Nevertheless, we should not deny other people glasses because I suffer.

In both of these cases, the psychosocial harms experienced as a result of someone else's benefits do not justify denying goods to the benefited persons. The same point applies to HGLGT. HGLGT, whether in the form of positive or negative eugenics, is not radically different from higher education, luxuries, medical treatment, or other social goods. Some people who lack HGLGT may suffer from prejudice, stigmatization, or feelings of inferiority, but these psychosocial harms do not justify denying HGLGT to others.

Regarding the claim that HGLGT will only contribute to existing problems of prejudice and discrimination, this may indeed be true. But we already accept many things that contribute to existing problems of discrimination, such as higher education, private social clubs, differences in dialects, computers, fancy cars and clothes, and so forth. Even if we eliminated all of these contributing factors, people would still find ways to discriminate against each other. Rather than focus on these contributing factors, we should focus on the underlying problem, i.e., people's attitudes and stereotypes. This underlying problem is best solved through education, not by suppressing technological developments that may contribute to it.

Thus, although HGLGT may create some psychological and psychosocial harms, the prospect of these possible harms does not justify banning HGLGT. Moreover, some of these harms may be abated through education. Of course, there is more to this issue than questions about harm. A person who suffers from harms because of some social injustice has a much stronger case than a person who simply suffers from harms. This brings us to the another possible bad consequence of HGLGT, social injustice.

GENES AND JUSTICE

HGLGT, whether practiced by parents or institutions, could create enormous social injustices.[19] It could exacerbate existing social and economic inequalities and eventually lead to an elite class of superhumans. This concern has even more force when we consider that a genetic advantage may be at least as important as a socioeconomic one. Being born into a rich family does not guarantee success, since many rich children squander their opportunities and wealth. But being born with superior intelligence, athletic ability, or musical or artistic talent, and a socioeconomic advantage may be a sure-fire ticket to success. I do not mean to imply or assume any kind of genetic determinism here; "optimal" genes do not always cause "optimal" results. My point is that since success in any area of life depends on genetic and environmental factors, one's chances of success are significantly increased by having the best genes and the best environment.

If we assume that HGLGT would further exacerbate social and economic inequalities, we need to ask whether this new distribution would be unjust. If the distribution would be unjust, then we might have an argument for limiting parental autonomy for the good of society. However, since most of us would claim that parental autonomy is a very important right, it should not be limited for trivial reasons. We would be justified in restricting parental autonomy when and only when parental rights pose a serious threat to social justice. The question we need to ask, then, is "Would HGLGT pose a serious threat to social justice?"

There seem to be at least three principles of justice that could be threatened by HGLGT:

(E) Equality: all persons in society should have equal moral, political, and legal rights and freedoms.

(EO) All persons in society should have the same opportunities to education, wealth, power, and other economic and social goods.

(D) Distributions of economic and social goods should not be so unequal that they undermine (E) or (EO).

Although I will not offer a thorough defense of these principles, they (or ones like them) have been defended by many different writers.[20] John Rawls, for instance, explicitly defends (E) and (EO).[21] Anyone who accepts (E) and (EO)—and many writers do—should also accept (D), since (D) merely requires that some conditions necessary for (E) and (EO) are met.

In discussing issues of social justice, I shall employ a roughly Rawlsian framework. The approach is only roughly Rawlsian because it treats natural goods as primary goods. Rawls's theory is by no means the only one available, but it is highly influential and quite useful for discussing questions of genetic justice.[22] In fact, as we shall soon see, Rawls even anticipates the very questions I am raising here.

The concept of justice, according to Rawls, is a virtue of social systems and institutions. Principles of social justice are rules for deciding upon various social arrangements that, in turn, determine distributions of benefits.[23] These benefits, or primary goods, are things that any rational person would want. The seven chief ones are rights and liberties, powers and opportunities, income and wealth, and self-respect.

Rawls also notes that other goods—he calls them natural goods (or assets)—are not directly under the control of social institutions, and hence, are not part of traditional concerns of social justice. Natural goods include health and vigor, intelligence, and imagination.[24] In general, this list of natural goods could be extended to all genetically based traits, including height, weight, athletic ability, resistance to cancer, personality, and so on. We should also note, however, that Rawls's assumption that the distribution of natural goods is beyond social control is questionable, given futuristic genetic science and technology. In the scenario I am asking us to consider, society may have as much control over the intelligence or health of its members as it does over their income or wealth. Hence, the distribution of natural goods should be a question answered by the theory of social justice.

Rawls defends two principles for distributing primary goods. The first one requires that all people in a society have equal moral and political rights and some basic freedoms. That is, the primary goods "rights" and "liberties" should be distributed equally. This principle is a version of the principle of equality (E) stated above. However, not all primary goods need be distributed equally. The second principle holds that other primary goods may be distributed unequally as long as (a) social and economic differences among people benefit everyone in a society (especially the least advantaged members), and (b) these inequalities are attached to positions open to all.[25] Part (a) of this second principle is known as the difference principle; part (b) is a maxim similar to the principle of equality of opportunity (EO) stated above.

It is interesting to see that as early as 1971 Rawls anticipated some of the social and political questions raised by HGLGT. However, as we saw earlier, he considered these questions to be outside the bounds of the traditional concerns of social justice, since they would involve natural goods. Nevertheless, Rawls develops a position that can be applied to HGLGT:

> I have assumed so far that the distribution of natural assets is a fact of nature and that no attempt is made to change it, or even take it into account. . . . I shall not consider questions of eugenics, confining myself throughout to the traditional concerns of social justice. We should note, though, that it is not to the advantage of the less fortunate to propose policies which reduce the talents of others. Instead, by accepting the difference principle, they view the greater abilities as a social asset to be used for the common advantage. But it is also in the interest of each to have greater natural assets. . . . In the original position, then, the parties want to insure for their descendents the best genetic endowment (assuming their own to be fixed). The pursuit of reasonable policies in this regard is something that earlier generations owe to later ones, this being a question that arises between generations. Thus over time a society is to take steps at least to preserve the general level of natural abilities and to prevent the diffusion of serious defects.[26]

Although Rawls claims that he does not take up questions of eugenics, he does. It seems clear from this passage that Rawls simply extends his theory of justice to eugenics and that he endorses both positive and negative eugenics, as long as these policies conform to his principles of justice. Likewise, I will also extend the principles of justice discussed earlier to eugenics.

If we assume that HGLGT would not be limited to negative eugenics but would include attempts at positive eugenics, it is an open and interesting question whether it would violate any principles of justice. We can certainly imagine a scenario in which genetic enhancement would not violate either (E) or (EO). We could suppose that genetically enhanced humans are given the same moral and political rights and liberties and that everyone has an equal opportunity to bestow genetic benefits on their children. Genetically enhanced individuals would most likely benefit all members of society through their increased natural talents. They could use their intelligence in making scientific discoveries, in creating new technologies, in music, art, athletics, and so on. Their other enhanced abilities could also benefit society. Given the potentially tremendous social benefits of HGLGT used to enhance people, why would anyone ever think that it would be unjust?

Our concerns about justice arise, I think, when we ponder more troubling scenarios. There are several ways in which HGLGT could lead to grave injustices. Suppose that genetically enhanced individuals came to be regarded (and regarded themselves) as morally and politically superior. Suppose they were given more rights and liberties than other members of society and were regarded as a "master race." Or suppose that rights and liberties varied in accordance with the level of one's enhancement: the more enhanced would have more rights; the less enhanced would have fewer rights. The human race might eventually consist of different social castes based on different levels of genetic enhancement. These ugly scenarios might not arise immediately, but they might occur over many generations of human germ-line gene therapy. It would clearly violate principle (E) and would be unjust.

We can also see how HGLGT might violate (EO). If HGLGT were available only to rich people or to people in positions of power, then it would be unjust, since it would prevent many members of society from gaining access to genetic technology. Indeed, distinct social, economic, or genetic classes could emerge if the genetically enhanced people continued to occupy positions that were not open to all or if the genetically disadvantaged people were confined to lower socioeconomic positions. We could end up with a situation in which rich, powerful people conduct genetic enhancement, produce genetically enhanced, rich, powerful offspring, who reproduce and so on and so forth.

It seems clear from the preceding discussion that HGLGT could lead to social injustices. But parental autonomy concerning the genetic make-up of offspring should not be restricted on the grounds that it could lead to social injustices, since we accept many practices that could have this effect, such as private education, European vacations, fraternities, and so on. Parental autonomy with regard to HGLGT should be restricted only if we have good reasons to believe that it *probably* would lead to grave social injustices.

So is genetic enhancement likely to generate grave social injustices? Although pessimists will argue that once we start conducting genetic enhancement, we can only advance down a path that leads to genetic castes, aristocracies, and "master races," I think we have good reasons to side with the optimists. If we take a careful look at some of our other social and biomedical practices that can (and sometimes do) generate grave social injustices, we will get a more optimistic (and realistic) view of HGLGT.

We allow parents to give their children all kinds of benefits that could create grave injustices but that do not violate principles (E) or (EO). Parents can give their children new cars, fancy clothes, private tutors, trips to Europe, money, and other significant benefits. We avoid the grave injustices by (1) ensuring that these benefits do not confer greater political, legal, or moral rights and liberties and (2) by ensuring that the benefits are (in principle at least) available to even the worst-off members of society. In other words, one does not need to have a new car or a trip to Europe in order to have freedom of speech or the right to life. And we like to believe that it is possible for a disadvantaged person to obtain wealth and give his or her children a new car or a trip to Europe.

The lesson we can draw from other social and medical practices is that if we practice HGLGT, then it should be treated no differently from private education, plastic surgery, wealth, or other benefits. No political or moral rights or liberties should be attached to HGLGT, and this privilege should be available (in principle at least) to even the worst-off members of society. These two conditions may not be obtained unless we adopt proper safeguards and regulations to ensure that they do. For instance, it may be useful to enact legislation forbidding genetic discrimination, genetic favoritism, and so forth.[27] It may also be useful to make HGLGT available to poorer people through governmental programs, such as Medicaid. At this point in time, it is difficult to foresee the exact regulations and safeguards we would need to adopt, but it is not unreasonable to suppose that we would be prepared to propose and adopt them as we learn more about HGLGT's impact on social justice.

CONCLUSION

I have tried to undermine the slippery slope argument against human germline gene therapy on the grounds that the downside of this slope, genetic enhancement, need not be as immoral or unjust as many people think. Regarding questions of morality, HGLGT's harms to future generations probably will not be as severe as some people imagine, and we can use education to counteract these harms. Human germ-line gene therapy need not rob genetically engineered individuals of their dignity or self-worth. While it may cause harm to unengineered people by contributing to existing prejudices and social stigmas or by creating new ones, these potential harms do not justify banning HGLGT. The most serious problem I see with HGLGT concerns questions of social justice. HGLGT could lead to grave social injustices, and we must take appropriate steps to prevent these consequences if we are to permit its use.

Although I have tried to defuse some myths about genetic enhancement, I by no means view genetic enhancement as the main reason for conducting HGLGT. The main reason for conducting human germ-line gene therapy is to prevent genetic diseases. Since this rationale has been well defended by Zimmerman, Berger and Gert, as well as by many other writers, I chose not to explore it in depth here.[28] My essay should thus be viewed as an attempt to help clear the way for the use of HGLGT to treat genetic pathologies, not as an unabashed endorsement of genetic enhancement. Further, I have not argued that we should conduct HGLGT at the present time or in the near future, since we lack the scientific and technological know-how to make this process safe, feasible, and effective. Indeed, I find the risk and cost arguments against HGLGT highly compelling and would not even consider HGLGT until genetic technology has made considerable advances.

In closing, I will consider a potentially damaging objection to my argument. Someone might object that adopting safeguards and regulations and educating people would be too much trouble and that it would be easier (and safer) if we simply nip HGLGT in the bud. If we ban all forms of human germ-line gene therapy, then we'll never have to worry about regulation and education. Or we could save ourselves a lot of trouble by simply banning genetic enhancement.

This objection seems quite simple and attractive, but it is unrealistic. It assumes that we can successfully control the course of scientific and technological development and human nature. It has us believe that we can prevent people from practicing HGLGT once it becomes feasible. But if history teaches us anything, it teaches us that these are idealistic assumptions.[29] We cannot control the course of science and technology: we have opened the Pandora's box of human genetics by sequencing the human genome and starting somatic gene therapy in humans. Once genetic HGLGT becomes available, some people will inevitably try it. At first, we may use it simply to eradicate diseases, but eventually we'll also use it to enhance people. As human beings, we succumb to temptations, and we have good reasons to believe that HGLGT would be a very powerful temptation. The most realistic policy is one that accepts these possibilities and ensures that HGLGT is conducted in a safe, just, and proper way, not a policy that tries to close Pandora's box. Thus, I agree that we are sliding down a slippery slope from somatic gene therapy to germ-line gene therapy to genetic enhancement. However, it is my belief (and hope) that we can avoid the slide from justified genetic enhancement to immoral and unjust genetic enhancement.

NOTES

I thank Ed Sherline and anonymous referees from the *Journal of Medicine and Philosophy* for helpful comments and criticism.

1. E. Juengst, "Germ-Line Gene Therapy: Back to Basics," *Journal of Medicine and Philosophy* 16 (1991): 587–92; E. Berger and B. Gert, "Genetic Disorders and the Ethical Status of Germ-Line Gene Therapy," *Journal of Medicine and Philosophy* 16 (1991): 667–83.
2. I will not explore arguments for HGLGT in any depth; B. Zimmerman, "Human Germ-Line Therapy: The Case for Its Development and Use," *Journal of Medicine and Philosophy* 16 (1991): 593–612, provides a fine explication of them.
3. Zimmerman, "Human Germ-Line Therapy," pp. 593–612.
4. M. Lappe, "Ethical Issues in Manipulating the Human Germ-Line," *Journal of Medicine and Philosophy* 16 (1991): 621–40; D. Suzuki and P. Knudson, *Genethics: The Clash Between the New Genetics and Human Values* (Cambridge: Harvard University Press, 1989).
5. Lappe, "Ethical Issues"; K. Nolan, "How Do We Think About the Ethics of Human Germ-Line Genetic Therapy?" *Journal of Medicine and Philosophy* 16 (1991): 613–19.
6. Lappe, "Ethical Issues."
7. Nolan, "How Do We Think About the Ethics?"; D. Heyd, *Genethics: Moral Issues in the Creation of People* (Berkeley and Los Angeles: University of California Press, 1992).
8. P. Ramsey, "Genetic Therapy: A Theologian's Response," in *The New Genetics and the Future of Man*, ed. M. Hamilton (Grand Rapids, Mich.: Eerdmanns, 1971).
9. L. Kass, *Toward a More Natural Science: Biology and Human Affairs* (New York: Free Press, 1985); W. Anderson, "Human Gene Therapy: Why Draw a Line?" *Journal of Medicine and Philosophy* 14 (1989): 81–93; E. Berger and B. Gert, "Genetic Disorders."
10. C. Fowler et al., "Germ-Line Gene Therapy and the Clinical Ethos of Medical Genetics," *Theoretical Medicine* 19 (1989): 151–57; Zimmerman, "Human Gene-Line Therapy"; Berger and Gert, "Genetic Disorders"; R. Munson and L. Davis, "Germ-Line Gene Therapy and the Medical Imperative," *Kennedy Institute of Ethics Journal* 2 (1992): 137–58.
11. There is also a conceptual version of the slippery slope argument that I will

not discuss here, since the empirical version has played a more important role in debates about the morality of HGLGT. For more on slippery slope arguments in biomedical ethics, see B. Williams, "Which Slopes Are Slippery," in *Moral Dilemmas in Medicine*, ed. M. Lockwood (Oxford: Oxford University Press, 1985), pp. 126–37.

12. Berger and Gert, "Genetic Disorders."

13. Lappe, "Ethical Issues."

14. M. Golding, "Obligations to Future Generations," *Monist* 56 (1972): 85–99.

15. D. Richards, "Contractarian Theory, Intergenerational Justice, and Energy Policy," in *Right Conduct*, 2d ed., ed. M. Bayles and K. Henley (Cambridge: Harvard University Press, 1983), pp. 358–66.

16. Heyd, *Genethics.*

17. R. Smith, *Lives of Twins* (New York: Simon & Schuster, 1987).

18. W. Anderson, "Human Gene Therapy"; President's Commission for the Study of Ethical Problems in Medicine and Biomedical Research, "Splicing Life: A Report on the Social and Ethical Issues of Genetic Engineering with Human Beings" (Washington, D.C.: U.S. Government Printing Office, 1982); Kass, *Toward a More Natural Science.*

19. President's Commission, "Splicing Life."

20. B. Barry, *Theories of Justice* (Berkeley and Los Angeles: University of California Press, 1989).

21. J. Rawls, *A Theory of Justice* (Cambridge: Harvard University Press, 1971).

22. Norman Daniels, *Just Health Care* (Cambridge: Harvard University Press, 1985), also applies Rawls's principles of justice to biomedical problems and provides a convincing rationale for employing a Rawlsian approach. For more on the justification of Rawls's principles of justice, see Norman Daniels, "Wide Reflective Equilibrium and Theory Acceptance in Ethics," *Journal of Philosophy* 76 (1979): 256–82.

23. Rawls, *A Theory of Justice.*

24. Ibid.

25. Ibid.

26. Ibid., pp. 107–108

27. L. Gostin, "Genetic Discrimination: The Use of Genetically Based Diagnostic and Prognostic Tests by Employers and Insurers," *Journal of Law and Medicine* 17 (1991): 109–44; L. Andrews and A. Jaeger, "Confidentiality of Genetic Information in the Workplace," *Journal of Law and Medicine* 17 (1991): 75–108.

28. Zimmerman, "Human Gene-Line Therapy"; Berger and Gert, "Genetic Disorders."

29. R. Westrum, *Technologies and Society* (Belmont, Calif.: Wadsworth Publishing Co., 1991).

REPRODUCTIVE RIGHTS
AND GENETIC DISEASE

Lawrence P. Ulrich

T his essay attempts to examine each of the four issues contained in the title: (1) rights; (2) rights with regard to the reproductive function of human organisms; (3) disease in general; (4) disease that has a currently identifiable genetic etiology. The thesis I wish to adopt is this: Reproductive rights are not absolute and those who are at high risk for passing on clearly identifiable, severely deleterious genes and debilitating genetic disease should not be allowed to exercise their reproductive prerogative. . . .

. . . In conclusion, there is indeed a class of rights that can be called "human" but these are to be understood as unwritten claims acknowledged by society rather than as intrinsic properties of "human nature."

I would now like to turn to the matter of the rights of individual humans in the reproductive process. The right to conceive and bear offspring is seemingly implied in the right to life, liberty, and the pursuit of happiness articulated, for example, in the Declaration of Independence of the United States. And the implied claim is that such activity is a natural human right. However, the legal codes, in the United States at least, do not respect this right to reproduce as absolute. We can cite two cases: (1) marriages of close kinship and (2) marriages of parties who have not passed the venereal disease screening test. (Marriage in these cases is considered the normal vehicle for reproduction.) Society imposes this abridgment of reproductive rights for the promotion of the public good in the area of public health. . . .

Reprinted from *Biomedical Ethics and the Law*, ed. James M. Humber and Robert F. Almeda (New York: Plenum Press, 1976), pp. 351–60.

We can now turn to the question of species survival. In the past hundred years, we have come to know that the actions of a species and the interactions of a species with other species or with its environment frequently lead to extinction. The species always "attempts" to survive and is frequently temporarily successful. Its actions, then, are survival oriented, but the end result of those actions over time is generally extinction. If rights were directly deducible from actions, then the answer to the question "Does a species have the right to survive?" would be both yes and no and we would get nowhere. A reasonable case could be made for the affirmative position in view of some natural selective tendencies that select for the survival of the fit. A reasonable case could be made for the negative position because of the general end result of natural selective tendencies toward extinction. But if survival, as opposed to extinction, is accredited as a good then we might be in a position to claim survival as a right and attempt to gain acknowledgment of that right. We humans are egocentric enough to think that our continued presence on the planet is important and that it is to be construed as a good to be pursued. Moreover, we humans seem to be the only species on this planet, that we know of, that can pursue its own survival as a *good*. While other animals survive instinctively, we engage in long-range actions to ensure (somewhat) our survival as a good. (Many conservation groups accredit the survival of other species in the same way.) I suggest that in the past few generations, we humans have at least tacitly accepted our survival as a species as a good and even laid claim to it as a right. If we have tacitly accepted our species survival as a good and indirectly claimed it as a right, it seems appropriate to articulate the right more strongly, attempt to gain explicit acknowledgment of it, and examine the obligations that this right entails. The area of species survival and thus of species obligation with which I am particularly concerned is that of reproductive practices. . . .

There are several ways we could deal with the problem of genetic disease in the area to which I have confined myself.

1. The classical libertarian would leave the choice to the parents, even in high-risk situations, and medical resources would be available to those who can pay the price.
2. An amniocentesis could be performed in each pregnancy where the parents are at risk and parents could have the option of aborting identifiable abnormalities or laws could be passed requiring that identifiable abnormalities be aborted. The former would be an outgrowth of the libertarian position, the latter would be part of a social control package. There are some risks involved in amniocentesis and some errors in extraction of samples can occur. In the case of more than one fetus in the uterus, one of which is diseased and the other not, the

appropriate action is unclear. This alternative, of course, involves a positive resolution to the abortion argument.

3. The classical libertarian might suggest genetic counseling so that parents could make an informed decision concerning their reproductive practices. I suggest that genetic counseling with the libertarian attitude is most appropriate in cases (a) where the risk of disease is not exceptionally high, (b) where the disease is easily treatable but nevertheless incurable, and (c) where the disease does not manifest itself until well into the growth process. Parents in such cases can be given all the genetic information, the options can be laid open to them, and support and aid given in the decision-making process.

4. Reproductive controls along much the same line as our current legislation regarding marriages of close kinship and venereal disease screening are the only approach that I find satisfactory in dealing with genetic disease of the high-risk, early-appearance type within the context of species obligation. Research should be directed to clearly and economically identifying carriers of severely debilitating diseases of the kind to which I have narrowed my remarks. This is no simple task because a variety of tests may be necessary, chemical analysis; karyotyping, pedigree analysis, and so on. Premarital screening should take place to compare disease-producing genetic conditions. For those couples identified as high risk, reproductive rights should be suspended. By "high risk" I mean a chance of one in four that the offspring would be affected and a chance of two in four that the offspring would be a carrier. In other words, if parents can produce a genetically healthy noncarrier for the clearly identifiable trait in only one chance in four, then the risk is too great. I suggest that there is both legal precedent and a species obligation to suspend reproductive rights under these conditions. . . .

To summarize my argument briefly: My fundamental commitment is that the survival of the human species is a good and that it is a good of such importance and value that it can be accredited as a right. From this I deduce that individuals and social units have the concomitant obligation to pursue courses of action that will foster and protect the right of species survival. Among these acknowledged and traditional courses of action is general health care. One segment of that health care involves the protection of the population from the transmission of identifiable, seriously deleterious genes and from debilitating and costly (in terms of natural, economic, and human resources) genetic disease that can neither be cured nor treated with any preservation of the quality of life and relative independence of the afflicted. Because individual human rights are negotiable according to their historical context and because there is legal precedent for restricting the exercise of reproductive rights, those who are at high risk for passing on clearly identifiable and severely deleterious genes and debilitating genetic disease should not be allowed to exercise their reproductive prerogative.

BIBLIOGRAPHY

Brown, Stuart. "Inalienable Rights." *Philosophical Review* 64, no. 2 (April 1955): 192–211.

Callahan, Daniel, and Robert Murray. "Genetic Disease and Human Health." *Hastings Center Report* 4, no. 4 (September 1974): 4–7.

Feinberg, Joel. *Social Philosophy*. Englewood Cliffs, N.J.: Prentice-Hall, 1973.

Frankena, William. "Natural and Inalienable Rights." *Philosophical Review* 64, no. 2 (April 1955): 212–32.

Harris, Maureen, ed. *Early Diagnosis of Human Genetic Defects*. Fogarty Symposium, 1970. International Center for Advanced Study in the Health Sciences. National Institutes of Health, Bethesda, Maryland. Washington, D.C.: U.S. Government Printing Office, 1971.

Hart, H. L. A. "Are There Any Natural Rights?" *Philosophical Review* 64, no. 2 (April 1955): 175–91.

———. *The Concept of Law*. Oxford: Clarendon Press, 1961.

Hilton, Bruce, et al., eds. *Ethical Issues in Human Genetics: Genetic Counseling and the Use of Genetic Knowledge*. Fogarty Symposium, 1971. International Center for Advanced Study in the Health Sciences and the Institute of Society, Ethics and the Life Sciences. New York: Plenum Press, 1973.

Lappe, Marc. "Allegiances of Human Geneticists." *Hastings Center Studies* 1, no. 2 (1973): 63–78.

———. "Moral Obligations and the Fallacies of Genetic Control." *Theological Studies* 33 (September 1972): 411–27.

Melden, A. I. *Human Rights*. Belmont, Calif.: Wadsworth, 1973.

Rawls, John. *A Theory of Justice*. Cambridge: Harvard University Press, 1971.

Rensch, Bernhard. *Biophilosophy*. Translated by C. A. M. Sym. New York: Columbia University Press, 1971.

Watson, J. D. *Molecular Biology of the Gene*. 2d ed. Menlo Park, Calif.: Benjamin, 1970.

PARENTS AND
GENETIC COUNSELORS
MORAL ISSUES
Ruth Macklin

[T]he question "valuable to what end?" is one of extraordinary complexity. For example, something obviously valuable in terms of the longest possible survival of a race (or of its best possible adaptation to a given climate, or of the preservation of its greatest numbers) would by no means have the same value if it were a question of developing a more powerful type. The welfare of the many and the welfare of the few are radically opposite ends.
—Friedrich Nietzsche, *The Genealogy of Morals*

There is no question that genetic engineering in many forms . . . will come about. It is a general rule that whatever is scientifically feasible will be attempted. The application of these techniques must, however, be examined from the point of view of ethics, individual freedom and coercion. Both the scientists directly involved and, perhaps more important, the political and social leaders of our civilization must exercise utmost caution in order to prevent genetic, evolutionary, and social tragedies.
—Kurt Hirschhorn, M.D.[1]

*I*n the field of human genetics, the last several decades have witnessed a great increase in both theoretical knowledge and technological power. Like so many other areas in biomedical ethics, the attainment of new knowledge and the development of new technology have given rise to moral problems that never had to be faced before. But while the biomedical contexts are

From "Moral Issues in Human Genetics: Counseling or Control?" *Dialogue* 14, no. 3 (1977): 375–96. Copyright © 1977 Canadian Philosophical Association. Reprinted by permission.

new, the moral problems are ancient. Such problems arise at the level both of the individual and of society, where decisions must be made about such matters as whether compulsory genetic screening programs constitute a violation of individual privacy; whether enforced sterilization of genetically unhealthy individuals is ever justifiable in the interest of socially desirable outcomes; whether genetic counselors are obligated to tell the truth, the whole truth, and nothing but the truth to their clients even in cases where learning the truth is likely to be harmful. Ethical dilemmas about such matters as the rights of individuals when these conflict with anticipated social benefits, the morality of withholding the truth, the acceptability of paternalistic coercion of persons "for their own good"—these age-old moral problems are found in new settings created by advances in human genetics, as is the case in other biomedical areas.

A catalog of representative moral issues in this domain would include at least the following concerns.

1. *The ethics of screening for incurable heritable disease.* Should tests such as the L-dopa test for presymptomatic Huntington's chorea—a fatal, degenerative neurological disease—be made available to patients even in the absence of any treatment or cure? Should persons known to be at risk for such incurable hereditary conditions be informed of such tests and urged to undergo them? Or should testing be withheld until there is something tangible to offer those who show a positive result? Ought information gained through genetic screening be made available to others besides the patient, when such knowledge may affect the decision of other family members to bear children or undergo screening themselves?

2. *Responsibilities of genetic counselors.* To whom is the genetic counselor responsible? The patient or married couple alone? Their unborn child? Other family members? Future generations who may suffer increasing numbers of persons with genetic defects? Should genetic counselors merely present the "facts" to those who come for counseling? Or does the greater theoretical knowledge and practical experience of the genetic counselor warrant his giving advice or urging a specific course of action? It is often noted that even in cases where a counselor believes himself to be simply imparting information, he nonetheless betrays his attitude in a way that is likely to influence a patient's decision. If this is so, does it suggest a reason for the counselor to render his own view explicit instead of trying (unsuccessfully) to remain neutral?

3. *Moral limits in the use of amniocentesis and abortion.* Are there good reasons for remaining selective in the use of amniocentesis—the technique by which a small amount of amniotic fluid is taken from a woman early in pregnancy and fetal cells are cultured to ascertain the presence of genetic disorders? Do risks to the fetus—however slight—indicate that the procedure should be used selectively? Is the use of amniocentesis and subsequent abor-

tion justifiable for reasons such as sex determination of the fetus? Should amniocentesis be ruled out in cases where the parents indicate that they are opposed to abortion in all circumstances?

4. *The morality of positive and negative eugenics.* Do we have a moral obligation to refrain from "polluting the human" gene pool? How far into the future does our obligation to future generations lie? If there is such an obligation, ought it be mandated by government legislation and enforcement? What are the moral limits of developing and using radically new techniques such as high-precision surgery on genetic material, when there are significant risks in the form of accidental creation of hapless monsters, or abuse on the part of unethical investigators? Is some form of eugenics justifiable on the grounds that presently existing society must bear the enormous costs of maintaining defective infants and even adults who survive because of the capabilities of modern medicine?

In all of these questions and others we shall explore shortly, the moral categories include a number of alleged rights of the individual: the "right to know" (or *not* to know); the right to make autonomous decisions; the "right to bear children," even when a high probability exists that these children will either suffer from or be carriers of genetic disease. These moral issues need not be couched in the language of rights, but may instead (perhaps more profitably) be viewed as ethical dilemmas where cogent reasons can be offered for two or more alternative courses of action. It is the existence of just such alternatives that gives rise to the need for moral decision-making on the part of individual physicians, their patients, and the larger society.

Before we can begin to answer the question "Who shall make the decisions?" we must first be clear about what decisions there are to be made. Since the issues in human genetics are so complex and multilayered, I shall spend a bit of time sorting them out and try to show how the practices of genetic screening, genetic counseling, and genetic engineering pose interconnected moral problems. In the course of this essay, I shall argue for two separate but related theses. The first is that the individual (meaning also the individual couple, where appropriate) should have final decision-making authority in matters of his or her own reproductive acts and capacities, as well as continuation or termination of pregnancy, where the reasons for these decisions refer to genetic factors. The second thesis is that attempts at government-based or scientist-directed eugenic programs—whether aimed at positive or negative eugenics—are bound to be misguided or dangerous or both. Having asserted these theses, let me now go back and lay the groundwork. I shall try, first, to identify the chief moral issues in human genetics, showing just where and in what ways the need for decision-making arises. Then I shall have the way paved for arguing the two theses just stated.

As the terms imply, "genetic screening" denotes a process of detection and diagnosis of heritable conditions; "genetic counseling" refers to the activity of informing or advising those who are afflicted with such conditions or are carriers; and "genetic engineering" involves manipulation of either genetic material itself or else the reproductive acts or capacities of persons. About each of these activities, the following questions must be posed: What purpose is the practice designed to serve? Who stands to benefit from the practice? What individual rights or liberties stand to be abridged? What other values are involved in decision-making in these areas?

Beginning with genetic screening, let's look briefly at each of these activities to see where the need for decision-making arises and what sorts of decisions are involved. The range of diagnostic procedures known as genetic screening can be grouped roughly into the following five categories, of which I shall discuss the first four: (1) newborn metabolic screening; (2) chromosome screening; (3) carrier screening; (4) prenatal diagnosis; and (5) susceptibility screening.[2]

1. The most prevalent example of newborn metabolic screening is that of the relatively simple and inexpensive test for phenylketonuria (PKU), a rare autosomal recessive condition in which the afflicted infant has inherited one defective gene from each parent. Those suffering from phenylketonuria lack a critical enzyme for metabolizing phenylalanine, an essential amino acid. If left untreated, PKU leads to irreversible mental retardation; when treated by introducing a synthetic diet virtually free of phenylalanine and begun shortly after birth, children with PKU do not suffer the consequence of severe retardation, but there is now some evidence that the special diet does not restore intelligence totally.[3] While PKU screening is an example of genetic screening where some treatment or cure exists for afflicted individuals, its use is not free of difficulties. For one thing, there have been significant instances of false positives—a source of difficulty because the synthetic diet can be harmful to a normal child. Moreover, a serious reproduction problem has arisen, since PKU women give birth to children who are retarded, no matter what their genotype, because of a toxic uterine environment. A different sort of problem stems from the fact that most states in the United States have adopted a program of mandatory PKU screening—a practice that some believe will serve as a model for increasing numbers of medical procedures compelled by law.[4] So while PKU screening has the virtue of being a diagnostic procedure for a condition having a treatment or cure that now exists, it may, for that very reason, be an unwelcome paradigm of legally compelled medical procedures, which will make inroads into the privacy of individuals in our society.

2. The most notorious example of chromosome screening of newborns is that of the XYY chromosomal anomaly. The extra Y chromosome is thought by some to result in an unusual degree of antisocial, aggressive behavior on the part of the so-called super-males who possess this abnormality. Unlike the case of PKU, there is no known "cure" or even a scientifically well-confirmed treatment program for males who have this chromosomal abnormality, nor has it been fully ascertained that this special population is significantly different in behavior patterns from "normal" XY males who come from similar backgrounds. But XYY screening has drawn sharp criticism for reasons other than those pertaining to theoretical and diagnostic uncertainties of this sort. Severe criticism has been leveled at a study in Boston, which has offered therapy to young boys found through screening to have the extra Y chromosome. One argument runs as follows:

> Either the researcher must withhold from the parents the information that the child being studied is XYY (which is probably immoral and perhaps also illegal), or that information must be disclosed, which will alter the way the parents feel about the child (probably for the worse). It will also render the study scientifically worthless, since for the study to demonstrate whether there are behavioral problems with the XYY male it is necessary that his upbringing be as "normal" as possible, so he can be compared with an XY boy.[5]

This argument is persuasive, especially given the circumstance that the therapy for aggressive or antisocial behavior is, at best, uncertain, and at worst, coercive. But even if it is morally permissible or even desirable to seek to alter the deviant behavior of XYY male children, the other points in the argument remain. The moral conflict surrounding how much and what specific information should be transmitted to whom arises directly in many cases of genetic counseling, as we shall see shortly. The problem of informing parents that they have an XYY child is wider than that raised by the Boston study. Even if no therapy were offered, there would remain the problem of adverse effects on the parents' expectations about and treatment of their sons whom they knew to possess an extra Y chromosome. While many screening programs for XYY seem to have been dropped, controversy still rages over whether it is morally permissible to employ screening techniques of this kind at all.

3. Carrier screening is different from the two varieties just discussed in that it is aimed not at those afflicted with a genetic disease but rather at a carrier—one

> who is clinically well himself, but risks having a child with a disease. These programs do not involve case-finding and treatment in the conventional sense, but rather represent an attempt to identify the person at risk and to intervene in his or her reproductive life, an approach not taken by any previous screening program.[6]

The two diseases for which carriers have been screened are Tay-Sachs disease—a rare metabolic disorder that leads to blindness, paralysis, and death, usually before the age of four—and sickle-cell anemia, a painful and often life-shortening disease found largely among blacks. Tay-Sachs disease, found mostly among Jews of Eastern European descent, can be diagnosed in utero by means of amniocentesis, so afflicted fetuses can be aborted. While the condition itself has no cure, the purpose served by screening programs is to supply information for those parents who would choose abortion rather than bear an afflicted child who will certainly suffer and die within a few years after birth. The purpose served by screening for sickle-cell carriers is not so clear, however. The disease cannot be detected in utero, so screening for carriers does not present many options. Sickle-cell anemia is autosomal recessive, which means that both parents must be carriers before it is possible to give birth to a child with the disease, and there is a one-in-four chance with each pregnancy of having an afflicted child. So parents found to be carriers can either take their chances of bearing a child who will have the disease, or choose artificial insemination with a noncarrier donor, or seek to adopt a child. Screening programs for sickle-cell have come under fire on the grounds that they are potentially dangerous as weapons that might be used for racist purposes by whites against blacks. It is difficult to see what sorts of persuasive arguments could be offered for compulsory sickle-cell screening programs, in the absence of intrauterine detection of diseased fetuses or a cure for the disease. Optional screening programs can be justified on the grounds that they enable couples to make a more informed choice about whether or not to have children; while some couples may well choose to take the one-in-four chance with each pregnancy, others will not. There seem to be no clear social benefits that accrue to mandatory programs, and their drawbacks lie largely in raising fear and suspicion about the possible repressive uses such programs might serve.

4. Prenatal diagnosis as a form of genetic screening overlaps with the category of chromosomal screening discussed earlier. In one form of prenatal diagnosis, fetal cells from the amniotic fluid are cultured and subjected to chromosomal analysis. In this way, XYY males can be detected in utero and aborted; the moral permissibility of abortion on these grounds is another issue currently under debate. A more significant use of prenatal diagnosis is found in the case of Down's syndrome. Women over forty—or even over thirty-five—are known to be at greatly elevated risk for having a child with Down's syndrome—the type of retardation formerly known as mongolism. Again, controversy exists over whether prenatal diagnosis ought to be routinely offered to women of any age, or particularly to those over thirty-five. While there seem to be sound reasons for having such programs available on a voluntary basis, there appear to be no good grounds for imposing prenatal

diagnosis on women unwilling to undergo the slight physical risk or to receive genetic information about their child. There is, further, the consideration that a chromosomal analysis will turn up other genetic information, which even parents who are eager to learn about Down's syndrome may not wish to know. Here is where the moral dilemmas raised by genetic screening intersect with those of genetic counseling. . . .

⑨   ⑨   ⑨

The notion of genetic engineering appears to have both a narrower and a broader definition. The narrow conception refers to approaches involving laboratory manipulation of genes or cells: somatic cell alteration and germ cell alteration.[7] When this meaning is assigned to genetic engineering, the term "eugenics" is used to refer to selection of parents or of their germ cells.[8] But sometimes the term "genetic engineering" is used in a fully general sense, to refer to any manipulation of the reproductive acts or capacities of persons or their parts. It is this latter sense that will be used in the remainder of this account.

At least the idea behind eugenics—if not the practice itself in some form—is ancient. Positive eugenics was promoted in Plato's *Republic* long before the science of genetics provided the theoretical basis and systematic data that today's proponents of genetic engineering have to work with. The lack of personal freedoms allowed the citizens in the *Republic* is well known to those familiar with Plato's work, and is evident in the following passage discussing regulation of unions between the sexes:

> It is for you, then, as their lawgiver, who have already selected the men, to select for association with them women who are so far as possible of the same natural capacity. . . . [A]nything like unregulated unions would be a profanation in a state whose citizens lead the good life. The Rulers will not allow such a thing. . . . [I]f we are to keep our flock at the highest pitch of excellence, there should be as many unions of the best of both sexes, and as few of the inferior, as possible, and . . . only the offspring of the better unions should be kept. . . . Moreover, young men who acquit themselves well in war and other duties, should be given, among other rewards and privileges, more liberal opportunities to sleep with a wife, for the further purpose that, with good excuse, as many as possible of the children may be begotten of such fathers.[9]

But lest we conclude that a eugenics movement can only be promoted or gain adherents in a rigidly controlled society like Plato's *Republic* or a totalitarian regime such as Nazi Germany, let us consider the view of a twentieth-century Nobel Prize–winning geneticist. The late Hermann Müller was an arch proponent of positive eugenics, based on his belief that the human gene pool is deteriorating. Müller argued for voluntary programs of positive eugenics, rejecting any form of state-imposed regulations. He claimed that "democratic control . . . implies an upgrading of the people in general in both their intellectual and social faculties, together with a maintenance or, preferably, an improvement in their bodily condition."[10] Müller was one of a number of contemporary geneticists who have made gloomy prophecies about the increasing load of mutations in the human gene pool. The particular brand of positive eugenics that he advocated was a voluntary artificial insemination program using donor semen (AID). He envisaged preserving the semen of outstanding men for future use in artificial insemination, choosing such greats as Einstein, Pasteur, Descartes, Leonardo, and Lincoln as men whose child no woman would refuse to bear.[11]

Müller's method of freezing the semen of intellectual and creative men is only one of several proposals favoring some form of *positive* eugenics—a program for improving the species, breeding a better race, or trying to prevent further deterioration by taking active countermeasures. Greater attention has been directed to the question of whether *negative* eugenics should be practiced on carriers or those afflicted with heritable diseases, in the form of enforced or encouraged abortions, sterilization, or less repressive but nonetheless coercive measures. The dilemma of choosing between preserving the individual freedom to marry and procreate as one chooses, and preventing further pollution of the gene pool would, indeed, pose an agonizing moral choice if the facts were as clear-cut as the eugenicists take them to be. There seems, however, to be enough uncertainty about the possible and probable outcomes of any attempts at eugenics to warrant extreme caution in mounting such grandiose schemes for genetic improvement. Many scientists agree that trying to reduce the load of mutations in the human gene pool through negative eugenics would be ineffective, at best. And the arguments against positive eugenics point to a number of potentially infelicitous outcomes. There are at least five separate arguments against the feasibility or desirability of any large-scale attempt at genetic engineering for eugenic purposes—arguments that, if taken together, give strong support to my conclusion that genetic engineering with this aim is misguided or dangerous or both. A sixth argument is the religious one that creating or modifying the human species is a task not for man, but for God.[12] For those to whom this sort of argument is compelling, it may lend added strength to the other five. I shall confine my discussion to four of the five considerations that do not require belief in a supernatural deity. Each of the following arguments against a systematic effort to mount any sort of eugenics program will be discussed in turn below:

1. We're too ignorant to do it right;
2. In any case, we are likely to alter the gene pool for ill;

3. Negative eugenics can't possibly work unless carriers are eliminated, but this would soon eliminate the entire species;

4. Some methods of genetic engineering carry grave moral risks of mishap.

The fifth argument is essentially that most—if not all—methods of genetic engineering are dehumanizing in basic ways.[13] While I think this attack contains some interesting points and raises questions of value that generally deserve important consideration, it is a gratuitous argument in this context. If the first four arguments are sound, they obviate the necessity for the fifth, since the scientific and practical objections to eugenic programs would rule them out before the value issues need be brought into consideration. So I shall treat only the first four arguments in what follows.

1. The claim that we are too ignorant to do the job right has several variants, each with significant implications. The first consideration points to our general ignorance about the value of a gene to a given race or to the species. As one prominent geneticist notes:

> We know only about its value to the individual carrying it and then only in instances where the effect is severe. In the light of such ignorance, it seems to me that the best procedure is to avoid all changes in the environment which are likely to change the mutation rate. . . . The quality of a gene or genotype may be determined only by the reaction or the associated phenotype in the environment in which it exists. A phenotype may be disadvantageous in some environments, essentially neutral in others, and advantageous in others. In the face of a rapidly changing and entirely new environment (new in an evolutionary sense), I do not believe that we can determine the value of specific genotypes to the species.[14]

This brand of ignorance constitutes our lack of knowledge of what to select for—a form of ignorance that some may argue is confined to the present state of development of the science of genetics. But a second variant of the "we're too ignorant" argument notes that "if we alter the gene pool, independent of environment, we are acting on the basis of present environmental criteria to select a gene pool for the future. Since the environment is changing a thousandfold times faster than our gene pool, it would be a disastrous approach."[15] But the difficulty here is not simply one of our inability to predict accurately what the future will be like. Questions of value enter in—questions that invariably resurrect the memory of attempts at positive eugenics among the Nazis. One writer asks:

> Who will be the judges and where will be the separation between good and bad? The most difficult decisions will come in defining the borderline cases. Will we breed against tallness because space requirements become more critical? Will we breed against nearsightedness because people with glasses

may not make good astronauts? Will we forbid intellectually inferior individuals from procreating despite their proved ability to produce a number of superior individuals?[16]

The last variant on the "we're too ignorant" theme that we shall consider here requires us to recall Hermann Müller's proposal for positive eugenics. Müller would not be alone in including Abraham Lincoln on a list of men whose child no woman would refuse to bear. Yet there is now considerable evidence that Lincoln was afflicted with Marfan's syndrome, an inheritable disease of the connective tissue that is transmitted by a dominant gene. The evidence is based on a number of factors. Lincoln's bodily characteristics and facial features—the very qualities we term "Lincolnesque"—are typical features of bone deformities common to Marfan's syndrome. The disease was first named in 1896, some thirty years after Lincoln's death. It was believed for some time that Lincoln had Marfan's disease, on the basis of physical defects he was known to have had, as well as the early death of one of his children. One sign of the disease was Lincoln's abnormally long limbs. Also, casts made of Lincoln's body in the year of his inauguration reveal that his left hand was much longer than his right hand, and his left middle finger was elongated. He is also known to have suffered from severe farsightedness, in addition to having difficulty with his eyesight that stemmed from distortions in his facial bone structure. These bodily asymmetries are common to Marfan's syndrome, as is cardiac disease. It is believed that Lincoln inherited the disease from his father's side. His father was blind in one eye, his son Robert had difficulties with his eyes, and his son Tad had a speech defect and died at the age of eighteen, probably from cardiac trouble. The likelihood that Lincoln himself suffered from Marfan's syndrome was further confirmed in 1959, when a California physician named Harold Schwartz recognized the disease in a boy of seven who was known to share an ancestor with Lincoln.[17] Since the gene for Marfan's disease is dominant, those who have it and reach childbearing age stand a 50 percent chance of having an afflicted child.

Now consider the consequences for the gene pool if Lincoln's frozen sperm were to be disseminated widely in the population. At least until the facts became evident, the result would be exactly the opposite of what Müller intended by his proposal. And if the mistake went beyond the case of Lincoln and Marfan's syndrome, including other individuals who, despite their outstanding achievements, might be afflicted with or be carriers of other little known or as yet undiagnosed genetic diseases, the results would be dysgenic in the extreme. This last consideration leads directly to the second argument against eugenics programs, to which we turn next.

2. This argument holds that in any event, we are likely to alter the gene pool for ill. Leaving aside the less likely incidence of this occurrence as exem-

plified just now in the Abraham Lincoln story, we may look at another prominent consideration noted by some geneticists.

This consideration is often referred to as "heterozygote advantage." One geneticist explains the situation as follows:

> There is . . . good evidence that individuals who carry two different forms of the same gene, that is, are heterozygous, appear to have an advantage. This is true even if that gene in double dose, that is, in the homozygous state, produces a severe disease. For example, individuals homozygous for the gene coding for sickle-cell hemoglobin invariably develop sickle-cell anemia, which is generally fatal before the reproductive years. Heterozygotes for the gene are, however, protected more than normals from the effects of the most malignant form of malaria. It has been shown that women who carry the gene in single dose have a higher fertility in malarial areas than do normals.[18]

Here again, it is not only in the cases where there is known heterozygote advantage that the likelihood exists of altering the gene pool for ill by trying to eliminate genes for heritable diseases. There are, in addition, all of the cases where heterozygote advantage may exist but is at present unknown. If one uses risk-benefit ratios or something like a utilitarian schema for deciding moral issues in biomedical contexts, the evidence seems clearly to indicate a greater risk of dysgenic consequences than a possibility of beneficial results from attempts to alter the human gene pool by means of negative eugenics. A successful effort to eliminate carriers for heritable diseases would result at the same time in eliminating heterozygote advantage, which is believed to be beneficial to the species or to subpopulations within the species. While little is known at the present stage of inquiry in genetics about all of the particular advantages that exist, it is an inference made by many experts in the field on the basis of present data and well-confirmed genetic theory. One biologist asks us to

> Consider the gene leading to cystic fibrosis (C.F.). Until quite recently homozygotes for this gene died in infancy. Yet the gene causing C.F. is very common among all Caucasoid populations thus far studied. . . . It is too widespread in the race to be accounted for by genetic drift. The gene is also too frequent for it to be likely to be maintained by mutation pressure. Hence, we are driven to assume heterozygote advantage.[19]

It would seem, then, that what is gained by the elimination of homozygotes may well be lost by the elimination of heterozygotes, resulting in no clear benefits and possibly some significant disadvantages in populations that suffer from genetic diseases. But the argument just given assumes that it would in fact be possible to eliminate genes for heritable diseases by preventing carriers from reproducing and thereby passing on such genes to future generations. The next argument against genetic engineering questions such a possibility.

3. This argument maintains, in sum, that negative eugenics can't possibly work unless carriers are eliminated as well as diseased individuals; but a successful attempt to prevent all carriers or potentially lethal genes from reproducing would effectively eliminate the entire species. The effects of negative eugenics on the general population are assessed by one geneticist as follows:

> With a few exceptions, dominant diseases are rare and interfere severely with reproductive ability. They are generally maintained in the population by new mutations. Therefore, there is either no need or essentially no need for discouraging these individuals from reproduction. . . . The story is quite different for recessive conditions. . . . [A]ny attempt to decrease the gene frequency of these common genetic disorders in the population by prevention of fertility of all carriers would be doomed to failure. First, we all carry between three and eight of these genes in a single dose. Secondly, for many of these conditions, the frequency of carriers in the population is about 1 in 50 or even greater. Prevention of fertility for even one of these disorders would stop a sizable proportion of the population from reproducing. . . .[20]

If this assessment is sound, it has significant implications for the prospects of favorably altering the human gene pool by negative eugenics. Such an argument is persuasive if the purpose of negative eugenics is viewed as that of improving the human gene pool for the sake of future generations. But if the purpose of negative eugenics is seen as improving the quality of life for those in the present and next generation, then the argument just given is beside the point. We should recall the dual purpose for which proposals for genetic engineering are put forth. The one we have been discussing here is the proposed improvement or prevention of deterioration of the gene pool for the sake of future generations of humans. The other purpose, tied to voluntary genetic screening programs and the activity of genetic counseling, is to present options to individuals or couples that will help them avoid the birth of a defective child whose quality of life will be poor and who will most likely be a burden on both parents and society. For this latter purpose, the practice of negative eugenics through voluntary screening and sensitive genetic counseling can serve to improve the quality of life of persons in this and the next generation. But when transformed into a program designed to control the reproductive acts or capacities of people for the sake of future generations, then the practice of negative eugenics seems to be scientifically and practically misguided. Indeed, taking this argument and the previous one together, the conclusion may be put succinctly in the words of one writer:

> Neither positive nor negative eugenics can ever significantly improve the gene pool of the population and simultaneously allow for adequate evolu-

tionary improvement of the human race. The only useful aspect of negative eugenics is in individual counseling of specific families in order to prevent some of the births of abnormal individuals.[21]

4. The fourth argument against genetic engineering focuses specifically on those practices involving manipulation of genetic material itself. This argument raises questions about the grave risks involved in any such manipulation, especially since mishaps that may arise are likely to be far worse than what happens when nature takes its course. One geneticist sees the prospects as follows:

> The problem of altering an individual's genes by direct chemical change of his DNA presents technically an enormously difficult task. Even if it became possible to do this, the chance of error would be high. Such an error, of course, would have the diametrically opposite effect to that desired and would be irreversible; in other words, the individual would become even more abnormal.[22]

Some observers fear the creation of hapless monsters as a result of various manipulations on genetic material. Whether or not the laboratory techniques are sufficiently refined at present to enable researchers to develop procedures for widespread use, it is likely that these techniques will be available soon enough to deserve careful reflection now. We need to ask, once again, whether the purpose served by laboratory methods of genetic engineering is helping those who are at risk for bearing defective children to prevent such occurrences, or instead, breeding a genetically improved species for the future. If such techniques are perfected and become available for use in spite of the attendant risks of mishap, they would then be offered to couples on a voluntary basis in the same way that current methods of genetic intervention are employed. Where a practice is aimed at the genetic improvement of a couple's own progeny, there are no grounds for methods that involve coercion. What is needed in such cases is counseling and education, not coercion and control.

At the outset, I said I would argue for two separate but related theses. First, the individual or couple should have final decision-making authority in matters of his or her own reproductive acts and capacities, as well as in continuation or termination of pregnancy where the reasons for these decisions refer to genetic factors. Second, attempts at government-based or scientist-directed eugenics programs are bound to be misguided or dangerous or both. The four arguments at the end were offered in support of the second thesis. If those arguments are sound, they demonstrate that there is no warrant for those in power to take final decision-making authority away from the individual where the reasons for such actions refer to eugenic considerations. Recall also our earlier conclusion that final decision-making should be left to the individual or couple in the context of genetic counseling, except in cases where the decision requires medical expertise that a patient is unlikely to have. Now if genetic screening should be practiced on a voluntary basis; and if decisions arising out of counseling should be left to the individual; and if, in addition, positive and negative eugenics aimed at future generations are basically misguided; then there seems to be only one consideration remaining that might argue in favor of limiting individual rights for the sake of social benefits. That consideration points to the burden placed on society for treating and maintaining defective infants and others who might have been aborted or never even conceived by dint of state policy.

Time does not permit an examination of this last issue, but it is worth making a final observation in closing. If the notion of social benefit is understood largely in terms of increased financial resources that would otherwise be allocated to caring for those afflicted with heritable diseases, then something crucial is being left out of the balance between individual rights and social benefits. What is socially beneficial must be viewed not only in terms of increases in financial and other tangible resources but also in terms of a range of freedom and autonomy that members of a society can reasonably expect to enjoy. It is important to preserve that freedom and autonomy through ensuring the individual's right to decide about his or her own reproductive acts and capacities. With increased availability of voluntary genetic screening programs and widespread education of the public, it is hard to imagine that most people will choose to burden themselves and society with defective children when other options are open to them. Even if there are some who refuse screening or abortion, society as a whole would be better off to accommodate their freely chosen reproductive acts than to impose compulsory genetic screening, abortion, or sterilization on its members.

NOTES

1. Kurt Hirschorn, "Practical and Ethical Problems in Human Genetics," *Birth Defects* 8, no. 4 (July 1972): 29–30.
2. Tabitha Powledge, "Genetic Screening," in *Encyclopedia of Bioethics*, ed. Warren T. Reich (New York: Free Press, 1978).
3. Ibid.
4. Ibid.
5. Tabitha Powledge, "The XYY Man: Do Criminals Really Have Abnormal Genes?" *Science Digest* (January 1976): 37.
6. Powledge, "Genetic Screening."
7. Bernard D. Davis, "Threat and Promise in Genetic Engineering," in *Ethical Issues in Biology and Medicine*, ed. Preston Williams (Cambridge, Mass.: Schenkman, 1973), pp. 17–24.
8. Ibid.

9. Francis MacDonald Cornford, trans., *The Republic of Plato* (New York: Oxford University Press, 1945), pp. 157–60.

10. Hermann J. Müller, "Genetic Progress by Voluntarily Conducted Germinal Choice," in *Man and His Future*, ed. Gordon Wolstenholme (Boston: Little, Brown, 1963), p. 256.

11. Theodosius Dobzhansky, *Mankind Evolving* (New Haven: Yale University Press, 1962), p. 328.

12. Such arguments are offered by Paul Ramsey in *Fabricated Man* (New Haven: Yale University Press, 1970).

13. This argument is given by Ramsey in *Fabricated Man* and also by Leon R. Kass, "Making Babies—The New Biology and the 'Old' Morality," *Public Interest* 26 (winter 1972): 18–56.

14. Arthur Steinberg, "The Genetic Pool. Its Evolution and Significance—'Desirable' and 'Undesirable' Genetic Traits," in *Recent Progress in Biology and Medicine: Its Social and Ethical Implications*, ed. Simon Btesh (Geneva: Council for International Organizations of Medical Sciences, 1972), pp. 83–93.

15. Kurt Hirschhorn, "Symposium: Ethics of Genetics Counseling," *Contemporary OB/GYN* 2, no. 4: 128.

16. Kurt Hirschhorn, "Practical and Ethical Problems in Human Genetics," p. 28.

17. Ibid., p. 23.

18. Arthur Steinberg, "The Genetic Pool."

19. René Dubos and Maya Pines. *Health and Disease* (New York: Time, 1965), pp. 123–24.

20. Kurt Hirschhorn, "Practical and Ethical Problems in Human Genetics," 22–23.

21. Ibid., p. 25.

22. Ibid., p. 27.

III. OBJECTIONS AND REPLIES

*I*n this third part, the focus is on objections to parent licensing proposals and replies to those objections.

1. Do We Have a Right to "Have Children"?

That licensing parents violates our right to have children (whether that is understood to refer to parenting or parentage) is perhaps the strongest objection to such a proposal. If we don't have such a right, or if such a right may be justifiably restricted, then licensing parents may be morally permissible.

Both Robertson and Brock argue that we do indeed have such a right. Robertson appeals to personal identity, meaning, and dignity (and though he concedes that the desire to reproduce is in part socially constructed, he also argues that it is a strong instinct); Brock appeals to self-determination and individual well-being (and though he argues from the context of access to NRTs, his arguments can apply beyond that context). However, neither Robertson nor Brock claim that the right to have children is absolute; in particular, Robertson suggests as limiting factors the incapacity to appreciate the meaning of parenthood (such as in the case of severely mentally handicapped people), "manifest unfitness" ("Procreative Liberty" p. 459), and harm to the child (but he suggests the latter limit only parenting, not parentage).

After examining the implications of having a right to something (for example, it suggests that others shouldn't interfere in one's pursuit of that something) and the meaning of "natural right" (for example, we have it simply because we are persons), Pomeroy and Floyd provide a critique to two arguments put forth to support the view that we have a natural right to reproduce: the self-determination argument (put forth by Brock and others) and the bodily autonomy argument. They find both inadequate, for several reasons, and conclude that we do not have a natural right to have children.

Like Brock, Chadwick frames her discussion in the narrow context of access to NRTs, but, again, her comments can be applied to the general case. She focuses, in the excerpt herein, on yet another argument put forth in support of the right to have children: the desire argument. It too fails to survive critical examination, and she concludes (like Pomeroy and Floyd, but unlike Robertson and Brock) that we do not have a right to have children.

Kluge develops further the suggestion made by Robertson that severely mentally handicapped people be restricted from parenting; whereas Robertson focuses on their incapacity to find significance in reproduction, Kluge focuses on their inability to fulfil the requirements of the parenting role and the violation that such a right would entail of the rights of others, the children, and the proxy-parents involved. Kluge also considers, albeit briefly, four arguments put forth to support the general right to reproduce: the species argument, considered in the previous section by Ulrich; the desire argument, considered in this section by Chadwick; the human potential argument, similar to the identity and self-determination arguments offered in this section by Robertson and Brock; and the social policy argument, not elsewhere considered. Kluge finds none of these sufficient grounds for a right to parent.

Lastly, the very brief excerpt from Shanner's article questions the value of even using a rights framework when discussing having children. Procreation involves producing a person—it is thus, says Shanner, better described as a responsibility than as a right.

PROCREATIVE LIBERTY

John A. Robertson

[Ed. note: This is a composite article—please see the note preceding the second section. This first section is from "Procreative Liberty and the Control of Conception, Pregnancy, and Childbirth."]

*P*rocreation is a complex activity that develops over time and involves many disparate behaviors. The importance of procreation as a whole derives from the genetic, biological, and social experiences that comprise it. Reproduction is a basic instinct that supplies societies with the members who maintain and perpetuate the social order and who provide services for others. Reproduction also satisfies an individual's natural drive for sex and his or her continuity with nature and future generations. It fulfills cultural norms and individual goals about a good or fulfilled life, and many consider it the most important thing a person does with his or her life.

Claims of procreative freedom logically extend to every aspect of reproduction: conception, gestation and labor, and child-rearing. Although these three components combine to create a powerful experience, each of them has personal value and meaning independent of the others. For example, it is meaningful to say that one has reproduced when one has merely passed on genes and neither gestated nor reared the resulting child.[1] A gene contributor may find genetic transfer a vital source of feelings connecting him or her

---

Reprinted from "Procreative Liberty and the Control of Conception, Pregnancy, and Childbirth," *Virginia Law Review* 69, no. 3 (April 1983): 405–64, and *Children of Choice*, copyright © 1994 by Princeton University Press. Reprinted by permission of Princton University Press.

with nature and future generations.[2] These feelings persist even if gestation and rearing, the biological and social aspects of reproduction, do not accompany the genetic transfer. Indeed, genetic and social parenting are often separated in our society—as, for example, when natural parents give their child up for adoption—yet the progenitor is recognized as having an important interest at stake.

Similarly, the biological experience of bearing and giving birth is so important for women that it should be recognized as an independent exercise of procreative freedom. Some women find enormous satisfaction and significance in pregnancy and childbirth, even if they never see or rear the child.[3] The importance to them of the gestational experience goes beyond gene transfer, for they have literally brought the child into the world.

By the same token, we recognize parenting as an essential aspect of reproduction. Child-rearing is a rewarding and fulfilling experience, deserving respect whether or not the person who rears also provided the genes or bore the child. To deny someone who is capable of parenting the opportunity to rear a child is to deny him an experience that may be central to his personal identity and his concept of a meaningful life. Although child-rearing is not, strictly speaking, reproduction, it is such an essential part of the reproductive experience that freedom to enter or leave the rearing role should be considered part of the freedom to procreate.[4]

Each aspect of reproduction can thus be a separate source of fulfillment and significance closely related to that provided by the other aspects. One thinks of oneself as procreating whether one conceives without gestating or rearing, gestates without rearing or conceiving, or rears without conceiving or gestating. Procreative freedom includes the right to separate the genetic, gestational, or social components of reproduction and to recombine them in collaboration with others.[5] . . .

Not everyone is capable of exercising every element of procreative choice. Many people are capable of begetting children, yet only some of them have the mental capacity to understand the meaning of procreation, and still fewer are capable of rearing. On the other hand, some people are capable of rearing and willing to rear, yet because of sterility are unable to conceive or bear. Finally, even those who have the physical capacity to conceive and rear a child and the mental capacity to understand the meaning of these acts may be subject to social or financial limitations on their right to procreate.

To decide who qualifies for procreative rights, one must first determine the minimum physical and mental capacity needed to participate in reproduction. Lack of physical capacity alone should not disqualify a person from exercising procreative choice. Sterility bars one from conceiving or bearing only to the extent that medicine or society cannot overcome the particular cause of infertility, and sterility never bars one from rearing a child. A sterile individual will have an interest in his or her partner's decisions to conceive or bear and in rearing any child that results.

Mental capacity, however, is an essential condition to exercising reproductive choice. Some people have argued that a minimum mental capacity is required because of the responsibility that procreation entails. For example, Onora O'Neill, in a cogent philosophical analysis of reproductive rights, asserts as a minimum condition for a right to procreate the ability to take care of the child or to transfer the obligation to one who can fulfill it.[6] She states that a person who is unable to fulfill parental obligations

> might reasonably be held to have no right to procreate under those conditions. If decisions to procreate create parental obligations, then those who realize (or should realize, given the information available to them) that they can neither discharge nor transfer such obligations have no right to procreate at that time.[7]

According to this view, interfering with a person's begetting and bearing capacity would not interfere with any right to procreate if that person were incapable of carrying out parental obligations or of transferring them to another.

O'Neill's view is clearly defensible if the core of the right to procreate is exclusively child-rearing, and it may be defensible even if the essence of the right also includes gene transferring and childbearing. Although mental capacity to rear is not essential to exercise the physical *capacity* to conceive or bear, a person who conceives and bears and who is not able to fulfill parental obligations for the well-being of the child (or to transfer them to one who can) will harm the child. Such a person's interest in conceiving and bearing does not create a right to procreate because it can be justifiably overridden by the need to prevent harm to the child.

Although O'Neill's argument is cogent, it is sufficiently qualified to make little difference in practice. Under her formulation, a person utterly incapable of fulfilling rearing responsibilities would still have a right to bear and beget as long as there were a reasonable likelihood that he or she could transfer parental obligations to one who was fit to rear the child. Social mechanisms exist to assure the well-being of a child by determining when the child is neglected and transferring parental responsibilities. The existence of this social arrangement fulfills O'Neill's alternate condition—that the person begetting and bearing the child be able to transfer parental obligations to one who can carry them out—and thus preserves the right of persons utterly incapable of child-rearing to bear and beget children. Mandatory contraception, abortion, or sterilization would interfere with the right of these people to procreate.

A more restrictive reason for requiring a minimum level of mental capacity to qualify as a rightsholder is that minimum mental capacity is essential to give bearing and begetting meaning for the participant. Reproduction—whether genetic, gestational, or parental—is significant because of the biological and psychosocial meaning it has for individuals. A person needs a minimum mental capacity to experience this meaning. Reproduction for a severely retarded person is a meaningless act. It amounts to a transfer of genes alone, or a transfer of genes in combination with gestation, without any sense of the meaning that begetting and bearing have. Mandatory contraception, sterilization, or abortion cannot violate such a person's right to procreate because the person lacks the mental capacity to be the subject of such a right.[8] Having no procreative interests at all, discussion of such a person's right to procreate is meaningless.[9]

A mildly retarded person, who may understand the significance of procreation but be unfit to parent, presents a different case. Because genetic transfer and gestation are themselves significant sources of meaning, capacity for performing and appreciating those functions should qualify one as a holder of a right to procreate for those purposes. Practically speaking, this means that mentally ill and moderately or mildly retarded persons with the capacity to appreciate procreation have a right to procreate and that compulsory sterilization, abortion, or contraception would infringe this right. The right may be overridden in certain cases, but only when the heavy burden is met for justifying limitations on the right to procreate and whatever other rights are infringed in the process. . . .[10]

Procreative autonomy is rooted in the notion that individuals have a right to choose and live out the kind of life that they find meaningful and fulfilling. Reproduction occupies a central position in the lives of many people who consider reproduction meaninful only if the child they produce has certain characteristics such as good health. Some couples may also consider reproduction burdensome unless the mother is able to avoid the physical or social burdens of pregnancy and childbirth by delegating these tasks to another. The right to choose one's mate and to avoid conception recognizes that people are free not to add a child to the family if the characteristics and traits that make having a child meaningful are missing. By the same token, the procreative autonomy of couples must include the right to take positive steps to enhance the possibility that offspring will have desired characteristics—subject, of course, to limitations to protect the child from harm.

ⓢ   ⓢ   ⓢ

The freedom to take on or leave the rearing role, with its characteristic rights and duties, should be considered a fundamental right. Decisions to rear should be left to the individual's discretion except where a compelling state interest, such as the welfare of the child or the valid interests of another person, justify limitation.[11]

The principle that a married couple should be free to take on the rearing role is ordinarily unproblematic. Except in the case of manifest unfitness, the idea of stopping married couples from rearing a child they conceived and bore is shocking. Yet the question of a person's right to take on the rearing role becomes problematic if the procreator is unmarried or if someone beyond the family unit collaborates in the production of a child. . . .

In sum, the positive freedom to procreate includes the right to take on the rearing role through complete or partial reproduction with one's partner, or with the partial or complete collaboration of others beyond oneself or one's partner. Moral concerns about the nature of the family or how the rearing role should be entered would not justify state interference, though regulation to protect the interest of the offspring would. For example, the child's interest in fit parents could justify advance screening to make sure that the designated rearers are fit for the role. . . .[12]

⑤ ⑤ ⑤

[Ed. Note: The following excerpts are from "The Presumptive Primacy of Procreative Liberty," chapter 2 of Robertson's more recent work, *Children of Choice*.]

Procreative liberty should enjoy presumptive primacy when conflicts about its exercise arise because control over whether one reproduces or not is central to personal identity, to dignity, and to the meaning of one's life. For example, deprivation of the ability to avoid reproduction determines one's self-definition in the most basic sense. It affects women's bodies in a direct and substantial way. It also centrally affects one's psychological and social identity and one's social and moral responsibilities. The resulting burdens are especially onerous for women, but they affect men in significant ways as well.

On the other hand, being deprived of the ability to reproduce prevents one from an experience that is central to individual identity and meaning in life. Although the desire to reproduce is in part socially constructed, at the most basic level transmission of one's genes through reproduction is an animal or species urge closely linked to the sex drive. In connecting us with nature and future generations, reproduction gives solace in the face of death. As Shakespeare noted, "nothing 'gainst Time's scythe can make defense/save breed."[13] For many people, "breed"—reproduction and the parenting that usually accompanies it—is a central part of their life plan, and the most satisfying and meaningful experience they have. It also has primary importance as an expression of a couple's love or unity. For many persons, reproduction also has religious significance and is experienced as a "gift from God." Its denial—through infertility or governmental restriction—is experienced as a great loss, even if one has already had children or will have little or no rearing role with them.

Decisions to have or to avoid having children are thus personal decisions of great import that determine the shape and meaning of one's life. The person directly involved is best situated to determine whether that meaning should or should not occur. An ethic of personal autonomy as well as ethics of community or family should then recognize a presumption in favor of most personal reproductive choices. Such a presumption does not mean that reproductive choices are without consequence to others, nor that they should never be limited. Rather, it means that those who would limit procreative choice have the burden of showing that the reproductive actions at issue would create such substantial harm that they could justifiably be limited. Of course, what counts as the "substantial harm" that justifies interference with procreative choice may often be contested. . . .

A closely related reason for protecting reproductive choice is to avoid the highly intrusive measures that governmental control of reproduction usually entails. State interference with reproductive choice may extend beyond exhortation and penalties to gestapo and police state tactics. Margaret Atwood's powerful futuristic novel *The Handmaid's Tale* expresses this danger by creating a world where fertile women are forcibly impregnated by the ruling powers and their pregnancies monitored to replenish a decimated population.[14]

Equally frightening scenarios have occurred in recent years when repressive governments have interfered with reproductive choice. In Romania and China, men and women have had their most private activities scrutinized in the service of state reproductive goals. In Ceauşescu's Romania, where contraception and abortion were strictly forbidden, women's menstrual cycles were routinely monitored to see if they were pregnant.[15] Women who did not become pregnant or who had abortions were severely punished. Many women nevertheless sought illegal abortions and died, leaving their children orphaned and subject to sale to Westerners seeking children for adoption.[16]

In China, forcible abortion and sterilization have occurred in the service or a one-child-per-family population policy. Village cadres have seized pregnant women in their homes and forced them to have abortions.[17] A campaign of forcible sterilization in India in 1977 was seen as an "attack on women and children" and brought Indira Gandhi's government down.[18] In the United States, state-imposed sterilization of "mental defectives," sanctioned in 1927 by the United States Supreme Court in *Buck* v. *Bell*, resulted in sixty thousand sterilizations over a forty-year period.[19] Many mentally normal people were sterilized by mistake, and mentally retarded persons who posed little risk of harm to others were subjected to surgery.[20] It is no surprise that current proposals for compulsory use of contraceptives such as Norplant are viewed with great suspicion. . . .

In addition to freedom to avoid procreation, procreative liberty also includes the freedom to procreate—the freedom to beget and bear children if one chooses. As with avoiding reproduction, the right to reproduce is a negative right against public or private interference, not a positive right to the services or the resources needed to reproduce. It is an important freedom that is widely accepted as a basic, human right.[21] But its various components and dimensions have never been fully analyzed, as technologies of conception and selection now force us to do.

As with avoiding reproduction, the freedom to procreate involves the freedom to engage in a series of actions that eventuate in reproduction and usually in child-rearing. One must be free to marry or find a willing partner, engage in sexual intercourse, achieve conception and pregnancy, carry a pregnancy to term, and rear offspring. Social and natural barriers to reproduction would involve the unavailability of willing or suitable partners, impotence or infertility, and lack of medical and child-care resources. State barriers to marriage, to sexual intercourse, to conception, to infertility treatment, to carrying pregnancies to term, and to certain child-rearing arrangements would also limit the freedom to procreate. The most commonly asserted reasons for limiting coital reproduction are overpopulation, unfitness of parents, harm to offspring, and costs to the state or others. . . .

The moral right to reproduce is respected because of the centrality of reproduction to personal identity, meaning, and dignity. This importance makes the liberty to procreate an important moral right, both for an ethic of individual autonomy and for ethics of community or family that view the purpose of marriage and sexual union as the reproduction and rearing of offspring. Because of this importance, the right to reproduce is widely recognized as a prima facie moral right that cannot be limited except for very good reason.

Recognition of the primacy of procreation does not mean that all reproduction is morally blameless, much less that reproduction is always responsible and praiseworthy and can never be limited. However, the presumptive primacy of procreative liberty sets a very high standard for limiting those rights, tilting the balance in favor of reproducing but not totally determining its acceptability. A two-step process of analysis is envisaged here. The first question is whether a distinctively procreative interest is involved. If so, the question then is whether the harm threatened by reproduction satisfies the strict standard for overriding this liberty interest. . . .

What kinds of interests or harms make reproduction unduly selfish or irresponsible and thus could justifiably limit the presumptive right to procreate? To answer this question, we must distinguish between coital and noncoital reproduction. Surprisingly, there is a widespread reluctance to speak of coital reproduction as irresponsible, much less to urge public action to prevent irresponsible coital reproduction from occurring. If such a conversation did occur, reasons for limiting coital reproduction would involve the heavy costs that it imposed on others—costs that outweighed whatever personal meaning or satisfaction the person(s) reproducing experienced. With coital reproduction, such costs might arise if there were severe overpopulation, if the persons reproducing were unfit parents, if reproduction would harm offspring, or if significant medical or social costs were imposed on others.

Because the United States does not face the severe overpopulation of some countries, the main grounds for claiming that reproduction is irresponsible is where the person(s) reproducing lack the financial means to raise offspring or will otherwise harm their children. Both grounds are seriously inadequate as justifications for interfering with procreative choice. Imposing rearing costs on others may not rise to the level of harm that justifies depriving a person of a fundamental moral right. Moreover, protection of offspring from unfit parenting requires that unfit parents not rear, not that they not reproduce. Offspring could be protected by having others rear them without interfering with parental reproduction.

A further problem, if coital reproduction were found to be unjustified, concerns what action should then be taken. Exhortation or moral condemnation might be acceptable, but more stringent or coercive measures would act on the body of the person deemed irresponsible. Past experience with forced sterilization of retarded persons and the inevitable focus on the poor and minorities as targets of coercive policies make such proposals highly unappealing. Because of these doubts, there have been surprisingly few attempts to restrict coital reproduction in the United States since the era of eugenic sterilization, even though some instances of reproduction—for example, teenage pregnancy, and inability to care for offspring—appear to be socially irresponsible. . . .

[Ed. note: The following excerpts are from "Class, Feminist, and Communitarian Critiques of Procreative Liberty," Chapter 10 of Robertson's more recent work, *Children of Choice*.]

My approach has been explicitly and unswervingly rights based. Taking procreative liberty as a fundamental moral and legal right, it has assumed that the individual's procreative liberty should rule unless there are compelling reasons to the contrary.

While such an approach characterizes many social issues in the United States, a rights-based approach has been strongly criticized in recent years as overly individualistic and insufficiently sensitive to the needs of the community. In a recent book, for example, Prof. Mary Ann Glendon has argued that rights talk is limiting because it is absolutist, individualist, and inimical to a sense of social responsibility.[22] Others have argued that rights talk is too private and individualistic, ignoring how public claims interpenetrate the private sphere.[23] It also exposes a social blindness to the claims of interdependence and mutual responsibility that are at the heart of social living.[24]

These criticisms of rights talk are especially applicable to reproduction. A rights-based perspective tends to view reproduction as an isolated, individual act without effects on others. The determinative consideration is whether an individual thinks that a particular technology will serve his or her personal reproductive goals. Except for the rare case of compelling harm, the effects or reproductive choices on offspring, on women, on family, on society, and on the general tone and fabric of life are treated as irrelevant to moral analysis or public policy.[25]

Yet reproduction is the act that most clearly implicates community and other persons. Reproduction is never solipsistic. It always occurs with a partner, even if that partner is an anonymous egg or sperm donor, and usually requires the collaboration of physicians and nurses. Its occurrence also directly affects others by creating a new person who in turn affects them and society in various ways. Reproduction is never exclusively a private matter and cannot be completely accounted for in the language of individual rights. Emphasizing procreative rights thus risks denying the central, social dimensions of reproduction.

Critics of rights talk point particularly to the abortion debate, where the prochoice claim ignores both the interests of fetuses and the interests of fathers and potential grandparents.[26] This criticism might also be leveled against other reproductive technologies, from in vitro fertilization (IVF) and collaborative reproduction to genetic screening and fetal tissue transplants. Emphasizing procreative rights necessarily deemphasizes the effects of these technologies on prenatal life, offspring, handicapped children, the family, women, and collaborators.

Although powerful and important, however, this critique of rights does not defeat the priority assigned to procreative rights any more than it defeats the priority of free speech, due process, travel, and other important rights. To begin with, the critique does not always prove the ill effects that it claims. Glendon, for example, overlooks the fact that many rights "encourage precisely the forms of deliberation and communal interaction" that Glendon herself favors.[27] This is true of political and social rights, which make communal deliberation and democracy possible.[28] It is also true of rights to use procreative technologies. Thus IVF encourages the formation of families and the cooperative, dependent relationships that inhere therein. The use of donors and surrogates requires a special kind of cooperation, often among strangers, that leads to new forms of community. Even aborting to get fetal tissue for a loved one can be a sacrifice that binds rather than divides.

Second, rights-based approaches to reproduction or other issues do not ignore other interests so much as judge them, after careful scrutiny, as inadequate to sustain interference with individual choice. If harmful effects are clearly established or the action in question does not implicate central features of fundamental liberty, public concerns may take priority over private choice. In many cases, however, the state is relegated to exhortation and non-coercive sanctions to protect communal interests because it cannot satisfy the burden of serious harm necessary to justify overriding fundamental rights.

A third problem with the critique of rights is that the alternative it offers is weak and thin, even less desirable than whatever excesses rights might breed. Without the protection of rights, important aspects of individual dignity and integrity have no protection from legislative majorities or policymakers. Elizabeth Kingdom's hope that getting beyond rights will enable public policy to make "a wider calculation of the proper distribution of social benefits" overlooks the need for rights to protect us from the policy calculations of zealous administrators.[29] Indeed, the emergence of rights is due to the failure of the community and public officials to give due regard to the needs of affected individuals.

This is especially clear in the case of abortion, which Glendon and Elizabeth Fox-Genovese claim shows the divisive, individualistic vices of a rights approach. The claim for a right to abortion comes out of a failed collective responsibility toward motherhood, which makes abortion an essential option. If prolife groups were truly concerned with the weak and vulnerable, as their concern with the fetus claims, they would make greater efforts to rectify the social and economic conditions that make abortion a necessary option for women. Their failure in this regard suggests rather an interest in controlling "women's reproductive capacities . . . (in order) . . . to continue a system of discrimination that is based on sex."[30] Rights are essential precisely to guard against discriminatory agendas that deny dignity and integrity to women and men. They are responses to failures of social responsibility, not the causes of them.[31]

To be convincing, however, a rights-based approach must acknowledge its defects even while proclaiming its strengths. It cannot ignore the social dimension, even if social claims are seldom sufficient to limit procreative choice. To assure that full credence is given to these dimensions, three specific criticisms of a rights-based approach are discussed. In each case we will see that procreative liberty, despite some qualifications, emerges alive and well. . . .

NOTES

1. Michael Bayles argues, however, that genetic transfer for its own sake, without bearing and rearing, is irrational. Michael D. Bayles, *Reproductive Ethics* (Englewood Cliffs, N.J.: Prentice-Hall, 1982), pp. 27–28.

2. For an account of reproduction as a kind of symbolic immortality, see Robert Lifton, *The Life of the Self: Toward a New Psychology* (New York: Simon & Schuster, 1976).

Arthur Dyck, a noted writer on the ethics of population control, has eloquently articulated the importance of procreation to individuals:

Children . . . provide a deeply gratifying link to the human community and to the future. Decisions about how we will use our reproductive powers are decisions about our own future and about our own contribution to the future of the human community, about how one's life is to count, and how far its influence is to extend. . . .

If these are the values guiding our reproductive decisions, the very dignity and identity of the person as a moral being is at stake in any decision to use compulsion in controlling reproductive behavior. . . .

. . . Choosing to have a child of one's own is a choice as to one's own genetic continuity. One should be free to express one's gratitude to one's parents and to honor their desire for continuity in the human community; one should be free to seek a place in the memory of future generations. If our lives are to be deprived of any choices in establishing these links to the past and the future, we have lost a great deal of what life is all about and, indeed, we have lost the most predictable way known to us of extending our lives on this earth.

Arthur Dyck, "Population Policies and Ethical Acceptability," National Academy of Sciences 2, *Rapid Population Growth: Consequences and Policy Implications* 618 (1971): 625–26, 628–29.

3. This explains in part why some women are willing to serve as surrogates who conceive and bear children for infertile couples.

4. One reason for the regard we give to the genetic and biological aspects of reproduction is that they provide the participants with a child to rear. Although child-rearing alone does not involve genetic reproduction, the child-rearer has the opportunity to transmit cultural, social, and psychological aspects of the child-rearer's self. In this sense, a nongenetically related rearer may be said to reproduce himself.

5. Though all three components are reproductive, the importance that individuals attach to each can vary. For example, some persons may be more concerned about social or gestational than about genetic parentage.

6. Onora O'Neill, "Begetting, Bearing and Rearing," in *Having Children: Philosophical and Legal Reflections on Parenthood*, ed. Onora O'Neill and William Ruddick (New York: Oxford University Press, 1979), p. 26.

7. Ibid., p. 29.

8. These procedures may violate other rights, however, such as a right of bodily integrity, that do not depend on some minimum level of intelligence.

9. The persons described here are not just temporarily without the requisite mental capacity, but are permanently disabled. Of course, there are problems in assessing a person's mental capacity to determine whether procreation means anything to him or her; but if one reasonably determines that procreation is meaningless to a person, then subjecting that person to involuntary sterilization, contraception, or abortion would not violate his or her right to procreate.

10. Justifiable cases would include those situations in which sterilization or abortion serves the person's best interest because, as judged from the person's own perspective, it provides medical or social benefits that outweigh the procreative inter-

ests. Under the substituted judgment test used by some courts in these cases, medical procedure that meets this requirement is reasonably likely to have been chosen by the person herself if she were competent and able to communicate her preference. . . .

11. These two situations arguably could, however, justify limiting the couple's right to reproduce, and thus could prevent them from rearing. Preventing transmission of genetic disease would not justify interference with procreative freedom to avoid harm to offspring for, in most instances, giving birth to a child with a genetic defect would wrong it.

12. Fitness screening should be conducted to assure parental fitness and not to allocate a limited supply of babies or reproductive opportunities among fit parents, as adoption agencies now do.

13. Sonnet 12 ("When I do count the clock that tells the time/And see the brave day sunk in hideous night"). . . .

14. Margaret Atwood, *The Handmaid's Tale* (Boston: Houghton Mifflin, 1986).

15. "Where Death and Fear Went Forth and Multiplied," *New York Times*, January 14, 1990.

16. B. Meredith Burke, "Ceauşescu's Main Victims: Women and Children," *New York Times*, January 25, 1990.

17. Sheryl WuDunn, "China, with Ever More to Feed, Pushes Anew for Small Families," *New York Times*, June 2, 1991.

18. The 1977 sterilization campaign plays a key role in the denouement of Salmon Rushdie's *Midnight's Children: A Novel* (New York: Knopf, 1981). . . .

19. Phillip Reilly, *The Surgical Solution* (Baltimore: Johns Hopkins University Press, 1991).

20. Paul A. Lombardo, "Three Generations, No Imbeciles: New Light on *Buck v. Bell*," *New York University Law Review* 60 (1985): 30.

21. This right has received explicit recognition in the United Nations' 1978 Universal Declaration of Human Rights ("men and women of full age . . . [have the right] to marry and found a family"), the International Covenant of Civil and Political Rights (art. 23, 1976), and the European Convention on Human Rights (art. 12, 1953).

22. Mary Ann Glendon, *Rights Talk: The Impoverishment of Political Discourse* (New York: Free Press, 1991).

23. Elizabeth Fox-Genovese, "Society's Child," review of *Life Itself: Abortion in the American Mind*, by Roger Rosenblatt, *New Republic* 18 (May 1992): 40–41.

24. This is one of Elizabeth Kingdom's criticisms of rights in *What's Wrong with Rights: Problems for Feminist Politics of Law* (Edinburgh, Scotland: Edinburgh University Press, 1991), pp. 79–84.

25. I am grateful to Daniel and Sidney Callahan for first making me aware of this aspect of reproductive rights.

26. See Fox-Genovese, "Society's Child"; Daniel Callahan, "Bioethics and Fatherhood," *Utah Law Review* 3 (1992): 735.

27. Cass Sunstein, "Righttalk," *New Republic*, September 2, 1991, p. 34.

28. As Sunstein notes, rights of speech and association, jury trial and antidiscrimination, are basic preconditions for social involvement, thus enhancing rather than dividing community. In addition, rights and duties are correlative, thereby creating an implicit sense of social responsibility. Ibid., p. 35.

29. Kingdom, *What's Wrong with Rights*, p. 83.

30. Sunstein, "Righttalk," p. 36. Sunstein further notes: "If one looks at the context in which restrictions on abortion take place, at their real purposes and real effects, then the abortion right is most plausibly rooted not in privacy but in the right to equality on the basis of sex. Current law nowhere compels men to devote their bodies to the protection of other people, even if life is at stake, and even if men are responsible for the very existence of those people. . . . Such restrictions are an important means of reasserting traditional gender roles."

31. If the social vision of reproduction is to claim our allegiance, then society's commitment to the sanctity of life must be reflected in a social commitment to support it at all stages, including in those pregnant women who desire an abortion because they lack the resources to care for a child.

THE MORAL BASES
OF A RIGHT TO
REPRODUCTIVE FREEDOM

Dan W. Brock

*W*hat moral arguments serve as the defense or basis of a right to reproductive freedom that includes access to New Reproductive Technologies [NRTs]? I will sketch three alternative accounts or bases for securing
that right. These three accounts can also be understood as addressing the relative moral importance of the benefits of NRTs. Is that moral importance sufficient that NRTs should be included within basic health care benefit packages
in either public or private health insurance? I shall not note the differences in
detail needed to apply these arguments to one or the other purpose when
those differences do not affect the principal substance of the arguments.

Probably the most common argument for access to NRTs grounds that
access in an individual right to, or interest in, self-determination. The second
argument, most natural within, though not exclusive to, utilitarian or general
consequentialist moral views, derives access to NRTs from the important
contribution they typically make to individuals' good or well-being. The
third argument grounds access to NRTs in a principle of equality; in the version I sketch here, specifically equality of expectations and opportunity. I
emphasize that these three different moral arguments for access to NRTs are
not mutually exclusive. Instead, I believe each captures something morally
important about access to NRTs, so that a full account of the moral basis of
that access must incorporate all three lines of argument.

Reprinted from "Funding New Reproductive Technologies," by Dan W. Brock, in *New Ways of
Making Babies: The Case of Egg Donation*, ed. Cynthia B. Cohen (Bloomington: Indiana University Press, 1996), pp. 213–30. Reprinted with permission.

SELF-DETERMINATION

By people's interest in self-determination, I mean their interest in making significant decisions about their own lives for themselves, according to their own values or conception of a good life, and having those decisions respected by others. John Rawls has characterized this as a highest-order interest, based on people's capacity to form, revise over time, and pursue a plan of life.[1] The idea is that because people have conceptions of themselves as beings who persist over time, they have the capacity to form more or less long-term plans, goals, and intentions for their lives. Other things being equal, the further into the future, the less detailed and fixed these plans will typically be.

In addition, persons have the capacity to form what Harry Frankfurt has called second-order desires, desires that take other desires, not first-order activities and experiences, as their object.[2] I prefer to put this point in terms of our capacity to value having particular desires or motivations. It is this capacity that makes it sensible to say that, unlike other animals, people have a conception of the good that is more than simply having desires and motivations, the feature we share with other animals.

By this second-order reflection about what we value doing, having, and being, we form and then act on a conception of our good, rather than simply being guided by instinct and environmental stimulus. Of course, none of this is to deny that people's social and natural environment deeply affects their values and conception of the good. But by having our choices respected by others, at least in the sense that they do not interfere within limits with those choices, even though they may disagree with them, we take control over and responsibility for our lives and for the kinds of persons we become.

In characterizing our autonomy or self-determination interest as a highest-order interest, Rawls meant in part that it is of a higher order of importance than the particular aims and values that give content to our conception of the good or plan of life at any point in time.[3] We know from our own and others' experience that these specific aims and values can and will change over time in both predictable and unpredictable ways. Our interest in self-determination is our interest in being valuing agents, able to guide our own lives in this way. Self-determination is a central condition of moral personhood, part of a moral ideal of the person, whose value does not lie only in maximizing the satisfaction of our other desires. Applied to decisions about reproduction, self-determination is not simply of instrumental value, resting only on individuals making the best or wisest decisions, but is also of intrinsic value, as part of an attractive moral ideal of the person.

The exercise of self-determination is also of more or less importance or value on different occasions and for different decisions. Perhaps the most important factor determining this differential importance or value is the nature of the decision in question. Other things being equal, the more central and far-reaching the impact a particular decision will have on an individual's life, the more substantial the individual's self-determination interest in making it. This is why self-determination is typically so important in most of the decisions or choices that compose reproductive freedom—specifically, choices about whether, with whom, when, how often, by what means, and in what circumstances to procreate. Few decisions that people make are more personal than these, in the sense that what is the best choice depends on people's own personal aims and values, or more far-reaching in their impact on people's lives.

The moral case for access to NRTs can thus be based on individuals' self-determination interest being of sufficient moral importance that decision-making authority regarding their use should in nearly all cases be left with those individuals (I say "in nearly all cases" because I do not believe such a right is plausibly taken to be absolute or unlimited and never overridden by other moral considerations, although I cannot pursue these limits here). Our moral right to or interest in self-determination is often interpreted as requiring only noninterference by others with relevant areas of behavior, that is, as only a negative right. The ideal of the person that self-determination suggests can often ground moral claims on others to provide at least some necessary means to enable us to take control and responsibility for our lives. The importance of individual self-determination can ground at least some moral claim on others or the society at large to make NRTs available.

INDIVIDUAL GOOD OR WELL-BEING

A second line of argument in defense of access to NRTs appeals to the contribution they typically make to individuals' well-being or good. (Hereafter, I shall usually use only the notion of individual "good," though these concepts are not interchangeable in all contexts.) The precise form this argument takes will depend in part on the account of individual good employed. In the philosophical literature three main theories of the good for persons are commonly distinguished. Each is a theory of what is intrinsically good or valuable, that is, roughly, good independent of its consequences and relations to other things; many other things, of course, are instrumentally good because they lead to what is intrinsically good.

Conscious experience theories of the good hold that people's good is composed of certain kinds of positive conscious experiences, often characterized as pleasure or happiness (although on many theories of happiness, it is not fully reducible to any kind of conscious experience) and the absence of pain or unhappiness. Preference or desire satisfaction theories of the good hold that people's good consists of the satisfaction of their desires or preferences. Satisfying people's desires is different from, and should not be confused with, the satisfaction people normally experience when their desires are satisfied. A desire is satisfied when the object of that desire is obtained; for example, my desire to be in Boston tomorrow is satisfied if I am in Boston tomorrow, independent of any conscious experience of satisfaction or enjoyment I may or may not experience when I am there. Finally, what I will call "objective good theories" deny that people's good consists only of positive conscious experiences or the satisfaction of their desires, but hold that some things are good for people even if they do not want them and will not obtain pleasure or happiness from them.[4] Different versions of objective good theories differ about what is objectively good for persons, but they typically appeal to the possession of certain virtues, for example, courage or trustworthiness, or ideals of the person, such as having deep personal relations like that between parent and child.

Many difficult and complex issues are involved in developing full and precise accounts of these alternative theories of the good for persons, and some of those issues have important implications for a defense of access to NRTs based on their promotion of individuals' good. Just to illustrate this point, for both NRTs and reproductive freedom more generally, desire satisfaction theories of the good for persons do not equate people's good simply with the satisfaction of their actual desires at any point in time. Rather, it is only the satisfaction of those desires that have been suitably corrected or "laundered" that can plausibly be held to be good for people.[5] People sometimes desire what will be bad for them due to misinformation about the objects of their desires, due to socialization that has shaped their desires in irrational ways, and due to the many other ways in which people's desires can be defective and not a reliable measure of their good.

When access to NRTs is defended as promoting people's good, what specific services, choices, and conditions should be provided will depend importantly on the details of the account of the good for persons employed. Nevertheless, it is clear that there is at least a broad connection between people's good and securing access to NRTs for them, as well as reproductive freedom more generally, on each of the three main accounts of that good. Securing access to NRTs for infertile individuals, like respecting other components of reproductive freedom, will generally contribute to people's happiness, satisfy people's desires concerning reproduction, and promote some typical objective components of the good such as the deep personal relations between parent and child. But it is important to this line of defense of access to NRTs, as well as of reproductive freedom more broadly, that each of these empirical claims is plausible only with the qualification "generally" that I have given it.

Securing access to NRTs for infertile individuals typically, but not always, provides them with a very substantial benefit, good, or contribution to their well-being. The claim is not that overcoming infertility is essential to human well-being, in the sense that it is necessary for mere survival or for a decent life. Infertile individuals can and often do compensate for this disability with other aims or pursuits, and so have a good life despite their infertility, just as people are able to do with other disabilities. The point is instead that for infertile individuals who want to overcome their infertility with the use of NRTs, being able to do so typically makes a substantial positive impact on their good or well-being. But in the case in which a person becomes resigned to being infertile and achieves a level of well-being from other pursuits comparable to what he or she would have obtained from parenting, there may still be a moral claim to access to NRTs to overcome infertility. The ground of that claim is likely the self-determination and/or the equality-of-opportunity argument, not the appeal to well-being.

Defending a moral right to access to NRTs, or to broader reproductive freedom, by their promotion of people's good comes up against the general problems of defending moral rights by appeal to the good consequences of respecting them—sometimes we believe that rights should be respected even when better consequences would be produced by violating them.[6] A distinctive feature of rights claims generally, and of a moral right to reproductive freedom in particular, is that the rights' possessor is morally entitled to make her own reproductive choices even when those choices may not produce the most good for all affected, or will not best promote her own good when others are not significantly affected. It is notoriously difficult to defend moral rights that have this nonutilitarian or nonconsequentialist character, as opposed to social or legal rights, within a general utilitarian or consequentialist moral framework of maximizing the good. The point is not that a consequentialist moral framework fails to make a moral right to reproductive freedom absolute, in the sense that it can never be overridden by other conflicting moral considerations. I do not believe that any moral rights to reproductive freedom in general, or to access to NRTs in particular, are absolute in that sense. Instead, my point is that a moral right to reproductive freedom including access to NRTs that is nonabsolute, but nevertheless nonconsequentialist in its strength, is difficult or impossible to defend by appeal to the good consequences of having and respecting that right. However, this is only a problem for the formulation of the argument in terms of a moral right to reproductive freedom. It remains true that access to NRTs for infertile individuals does usually contribute substantially to their good.

NOTES

1. John Rawls, *A Theory of Justice* (Cambridge: Harvard University Press, 1971).
2. Harry Frankfurt, "Freedom of the Will and the Concept of a Person," *Journal of Philosophy* 68 (1971): 5–20.

3. John Rawls, "Kantian Constructivism in Moral Theory," *Journal of Philosophy* 77 (1980): 515–72.

4. I have discussed all three of these theories at much greater length in "Quality of Life Measures in Health Care and Medical Ethics," in *The Quality of Life*, ed. A. Sen and M. Nussbaum (Oxford: Oxford University Press, 1993). There I called objective good theories "ideal theories" because they typically posit some ideal of the person as what is objectively good. One of the best recent treatments of these alternative theories is James Griffin, *Well-Being* (Oxford: Oxford University Press, 1986).

5. See Robert Goodin, "Laundering Preferences," in *Foundations of Social Choice Theory*, ed. J. Elster and A. Hylland (Cambridge: Cambridge University Press, 1986).

6. Much of the very large literature on this problem is within the framework of giving a utilitarian or general consequentialist account of moral rights. See, for example, Thomas Scanlon, "Rights, Goals, and Fairness," in *Public and Private Morality*, ed. S. Hampshire (Cambridge: Cambridge University Press, 1978) and Raymond Frey, ed., *Utility and Rights* (Minneapolis: University of Minnesota Press, 1984).

IS THERE A NATURAL RIGHT TO HAVE CHILDREN?

S. L. Floyd and D. Pomerantz

*I*n attempting to establish the existence of such a right, we note that a right to have children appears to reflect our autonomy. It seems that to deny me the liberty to have children is to not respect me as an autonomous agent. Perhaps, it is on this basis that there is a natural right to have children. Now, we ask, why does the liberty to have children seem to be connected with autonomy? There are two answers. First, to recognize my liberty to have children, it may be argued, is to recognize my right to do with my body what I will. But it may not be simply autonomy with respect to body that is at issue here. Being a parent is often an important part of one's self-conception; in this respect, the liberty to have children may be a part of one's right to self-determination. We will explore these suggestions in this section. There are intriguing consequences for the right to have children if it is based on our right to be respected as autonomous. But our most startling conclusion is that there is no sound moral argument that can show that the right to have children follows from the right to autonomy.

One way to understand bodily autonomy is to think of the body as an owned object. This body belongs to me, and thus it is up to me to decide how it shall be used and what shall be done to it. If I want my appendix or the hair under my arms removed, others ought to recognize my liberty to so decide. Of course, this right does not grant me permission to use my body in ways that violate others' rights. The right to do with my body as I will no more

Reprinted from "Is There a Natural Right to Have Children?" by S. L. Floyd and D. Pomerantz, in *Morality and Moral Controversies*, ed. John Arthur (Englewood Cliffs, N.J.: Prentice-Hall, 1981).

permits me to strangle you than the right to use my baseball bat as I will permits me to bop you over the head.

What does this mean for the right to have children? The matter appears quite straightforward. The right to do with our bodies as we will yields a right to make love and bear the consequences. Bodily autonomy implies a right to have children. To deny the right to have children seems to require one to interfere with the right to have sex or to prevent the consequences by means of more direct intrusion on the bodies of participants. . . .

[T]he problem with subsuming the right to have children under bodily autonomy [is that a] child is not merely the physical product or extension of my body in the way that my hair is. Although it is convenient to speak of the baby as the product of a woman's labor, it is a misleading metaphor if we fail to recognize that the baby is a distinct being. Children become (or can become) full persons, our moral equals. A right to have children based on the potential parent's bodily autonomy neglects this other locus of moral rights insofar as it treats the child as a mere appendage.

Can the right to self-determination fare any better as the basis for the right to have children? There is some reason for hope. The right to self-determination is the right to develop a self-conception and act on it. One determines for oneself what are the goals worth seeking and the vocational or cultural interests worth pursuing. After well-informed deliberation, one leads the kind of life one thinks one should. To think about oneself in certain ways or to lead a certain sort of life is beyond the scope of bodily autonomy. Another important feature is this: Some self-conceptions can be pursued in isolation and others cannot. If I wish to develop my muscles, for example, this does not require me to relate to others in any special ways. However, if I seek to share a long-term commitment with another, this essentially involves being related to another. It is a necessary condition for acting on some of my self-conceptions that I relate to others in special ways. The right to have children would fall under this rubric. . . .

But, does self-determination generate an analogous right to have children? The right to be married is similar to the supposed right to have children in an important respect. Bearing and raising a child can be as significant to being the sort of person I wish to be as being married is. But there are some respects in which the right to be married and the presumed right to have children are disanalogous. These are both rights that require being related to another person in special ways. But, while one can agree to be married, no one can consent to being born. There is no being to speak for itself on the matter. So, our argument is this: since one can have a relational right based on self-determination only if all parties to the relation consent, and no one consents to be introduced into the world by someone else, it follows there is no relational right to be a parent. . . .

Let us clarify two points about hypothetical consent. First, such consent entails that I consider, in the present, what it would have been like had I not chosen to be born. That is certainly an odd consideration. In any event, hypothetical consent to being born is saying that I am content to have been born. But saying this is possible only as a result of being born and raised in this manner by my parents. And it is these parents who bear and raise me that need my consent in order to have the right to be parents. Consider this example: a spiritual leader brings me to believe I want to be a disciple. It is analogous in that my present consent to the relationship results from my having been in the relationship. The way in which I came to be content with the relationship is not specified. I might be brainwashed or, in some other way, deviously influenced. Insofar as my present consent to having been brought into this relationship can arise in these unacceptable ways, this sort of hypothetical consent should not have justificatory force. So the right to be a parent should not be based on hypothetical consent. For these reasons, there is no relational right to have children based on self-determination.

We have analyzed the right to have children based on the right to autonomy, specifically in terms of the right over one's body and the right to self-determination. My right to do with my body what I will cannot found a right to create and raise another autonomous being. If the right to have children were based on the right to self-determination it would be unlike all other relational rights insofar as it does not respect the autonomy of all the people engaged in the relationship. It does not take into account the impossibility of a being's actual or hypothetical consent to becoming a child. Thus, we conclude that the right to have children cannot be derived from respect for the autonomy of potential parents. . . .

HAVING CHILDREN

INTRODUCTION

Ruth F. Chadwick

*T*he phrase "having children" is deceptively simple. On the face of it, it describes an activity that is practiced universally and always has been. But the process is surrounded by an ever-increasing number of problems. Childbirth itself is a subject of controversy, as to how it should best be managed. To what extent the state should interfere between parents and children is another live issue. . . .

IS THERE A RIGHT TO REPRODUCE?

. . . The function of a right to reproduce was traditionally to prevent interference in individuals' lives by such methods as compulsory sterilization. In other words, it was seen as a negative right with a corresponding duty of non-interference.

A distinction is commonly drawn between such negative rights and positive rights, which suggests that right-holders are entitled to have positive steps taken to enable them to exercise their rights. So a positive right to reproduce could indicate the provision of reproductive technology. . . .

An alternative view [to the natural rights view put forth by Floyd and Pomeroy] is that a right to reproduce can be seen as an aspect of the right to privacy.

Reprinted from *Ethics, Reproduction, and Genetic Control*, ed. Ruth F. Chadwick (London: Croom Helm, 1987), pp. 3–43.

In the U.S. case of *Eisenstadt* v. *Baird*, Justice Brennan said:

> If the right of privacy means anything, it is the right of the individual, married or single, to be free from unwarranted governmental intrusion into matters so fundamentally affecting a person as the decision whether to bear or beget a child.[1]

To discuss whether there is a right to privacy is not our concern. The important question is whether or not reproduction is a private matter. There may be something in the suggestion that reproduction should be something for which society as a whole assumes responsibility, even at the begetting stage. This need not involve Plato's mating festivals or the type of ticket system for sexual intercourse envisaged in Zamyatin's *We*. It *might* involve public decision-making about resources, e.g., whether society can afford to waste the resource of large numbers of aborted fetuses on the one hand while on the other hand spending large amounts of money on providing in vitro fertilization.

The most familiar arguments for social responsibility take place concerning the *rearing* of children. One advocate of shared responsibility is Penny Perrick, writing in the *Times*:

> Far from urging less government interference I would like to see the appointment of a Minister for Children. And please let it be . . . somebody who insists that the basic rudiments of parenthood are taught as part of the school curriculum.[2]

Similarly, a case can be made for public concern with rearing by the argument that if society wants children then there should be public provision, in the form of funding out of the public purse for such facilities as day nurseries. Should public concern apply only to rearing and not to begetting? . . .

Justice Brennan's statement quoted above has special relevance where an invasion such as compulsory sterilization is envisaged, but it is difficult to see the right to privacy as providing a basis for a positive right to reproduce.

Perhaps the right to reproduce could be seen as the *conclusion* of an argument. The right in this sort of case would function very differently than in the former case. For what is argued is that there are moral arguments supporting the view that it is desirable for people to have children, which outweigh any arguments suggesting that they ought not to be allowed to do so. In other words, having looked at the moral arguments, the conclusion is that the persons concerned ought to have the freedom to have a child. Thus a right, negative or positive, could be *assigned* on the basis of a utilitarian argument. This is totally different from saying that the right is natural or self-evident. . . .

An argument that is very frequently encountered in the literature is based on the desire for a child. . . .

THE DESIRE FOR A CHILD

The first question to be borne in mind is: what is the content of this desire? It is helpful, when speaking of reproduction issues, to keep in mind the distinction between the concepts of begetting, rearing, and bearing. In some discussions there is talk simply of "the desire for a child" without specifying what exactly is desired. At other times it is assumed that one or another of the above is meant, without showing good reasons for such an assumption. For example, Mary Warnock says: "In addition to social pressures to have children, there is, for many, a powerful urge to perpetuate their genes through a new generation. This desire cannot be assuaged by adoption."[3] But it is not justifiable to make this assumption about the content of the desire without investigation, and the particular desire that is in question can make a very large difference to the conclusions that may be reached. For example, however important we may feel it is to enable people to satisfy a desire to pass on their genes, this could not, *without more*, provide an argument for male pregnancies (one of the latest suggestions for the application of medical expertise).[4]

Let us look more closely at the differences involved.

The Desire to Rear

In principle it is possible for this desire to be satisfied for everyone without recourse to artificial reproductive technology. For if individuals are unable for some reason to have their own children, they may rear those of other people. It may of course be impossible in practice owing to a shortage of babies for adoption.

Given such a shortage, this desire may be important in the surrogacy debate. In the type of case where the carrying mother provides not only her womb but also her egg, the commissioning mother is enabled only to rear a child but not to beget or to bear.

It is beyond question that the desire to rear a child can be and often is a very strong one. It is this that is at issue in custody disputes.

The Desire to Bear

Traditionally this has been a desire that only (but not all) women could satisfy. Even reproductive technology however, as presently envisaged, cannot make this possible for every woman. For some it may involve a serious risk to their health to bear a child.

Recently there has been a suggestion that there are some males who would like to become pregnant. The demand is said to come partly from transsexuals and partly from men who would like to bear children for their wives. Whatever the reason (they may simply want to have a new experience), it is important to consider this desire as another aspect of wanting to have a child.

To some it may seem that in any case a man cannot bear a child in the same sense that a woman can. We need to distinguish between carrying and giving birth. It is clear from the recent Wendy Savage case that it is important for some *women* not only to carry but also to give birth. But for others the birth experience has been so technologized that it has come to seem a terrifying and alien experience. As Germaine Greer points out:

> Yet women continue to want to bear children. They may say that they want to experience childbirth. What they can mean by that when there is no telling whether they will be allowed to experience it, given the aggressiveness of childbirth management, is not at all clear. Far too many women have no experience of birth at all, but simply of anesthesia. . . . Women who want the experience of childbirth are in the curious position of desiring the unknown.[5]

The Desire to Beget

The term "beget" is used more commonly of men than of women. But understanding this term in the sense of passing on genes, it can be used sensibly for both parents.

This is the desire that Warnock saw as the significant one. But as we have already seen, we cannot assume that this is the only desire in question, otherwise all methods that involve a donor would not be satisfying the desires of at least one party of a donee couple (assuming a case where there is a couple both of whom have a desire for a child).

One interesting result of seeing this as the central desire, however, is that in principle, if it is thought to provide an argument for enabling a person to reproduce, it seems also to provide an argument for cloning.[6] Is there a significant difference between wanting to pass on *half* my genes in sexual reproduction, and wanting to pass on *all* my genes, as in cloning? It is not clear what the difference is.

In addition to these possible aspects of the desire to reproduce, there are other factors that might be involved.

The Desire to Have a Child with Someone

It might be argued that the above distinctions are missing the point. Surely the central case (the argument might go) of having a child is wanting to have a child with a particular person, as an expression of that relationship. The excitement comes from seeing the result as a mixture of the two of you. This seems to have been completely overlooked in the debate on reproductive technology. Of the new methods, in vitro fertilization provides a way to satisfy this particular desire, in the sort of case where technology is used simply in order to assist a man's sperm in the fertilization of his partner's egg. But any method that involves gamete donation does not.

But much of the discussion of these issues in the literature sees the desire for a child as a desire for something for *oneself*. Much is made of enabling a person to have a child of his or her own. Thus one argument in the Warnock Report supported surrogacy as it provided the only way for some men to have a child of their own.[7] Perhaps the child is seen as an extension of the self. In wanting to pass on one's own genes, maybe one is making a bid for a kind of immortality. Similarly one might want to bear a child for oneself, as an experience one wants to have, like wanting to have the experience of looking at the Grand Canyon.

Socially Induced Desires

It is envisaged by some that the desire for a child may be an aspect of a desire to appear as a "normal" family. Thus a letter in *NACK*, the *Quarterly Journal of the National Association for the Childless*, points to the problems caused by "the lack of sons-in-law and daughters-in-law, no grandchildren, the silver wedding with no family, the passing round of photos and stories of grandchildren."[8] The social pressure is recognized by Warnock:

> Family and friends often expect a couple to start a family, and express their expectations, either openly or by implication. . . . Parents likewise feel their identity in society enhanced and confirmed by their role in the family unit.[9]

The Desire for an Heir

In societies where property and inheritance are valued, the desire for an heir plays a large part in the desire for a child. This provides a perfect example of the extent to which social factors influence the desire to reproduce. Women have been divorced for failing to provide an heir.

The history of the concept of legitimacy is important here. The desire for an heir has traditionally involved a desire not only for a child but for a legitimate child. This brings out the point that in societies where legitimacy is an important factor, the desire for a child is not nearly so central as the desire to have one conceived in the appropriate way. Passing on one's property is thus held to be more important than passing on one's genes.

The significance of this point lies not in what is said about legitimacy itself but in the light it throws on the nature of the desire for children. To what extent is it a socially produced desire?

The Desire for a Child: Natural or Artificial?

Peter Singer and Deane Wells, in *The Reproduction Revolution*, take the view that "the desire for children is . . . something very basic and cannot be overcome without great difficulty, if at all. There are obvious evolutionary reasons why this should be so."[10] On the other hand, Fanny Lines, in a letter to the *Guardian*, writes:

> You talk of "infertility blighting the happiness of couples." Others speak of the desperation of childlessness. These are emotive, strong words. The fundamental problem is the desire for a child. Why? These people have been pressured by our culture, conditioned by a society that values inheritance, woman's mothering role and man's role as provider.[11]

So, is the desire biological or is it social? Singer and Wells stress the evolutionary reasons why it might be thought that the desire is basic to human beings. But if the desire for children is so basic, why has it evolved in connection with a very strong desire for sex to back it up?

According to Plato, the desire for children is natural as a desire for immortality:

> [T]here is a sense in which nature has not only somehow endowed the human race with a degree of immortality, but also implanted in us all a longing to achieve it, which we express in every way we can. One expression of that longing is the desire for fame and the wish not to lie nameless in the grave. Thus mankind is by nature a companion of eternity, and is linked to it, for ever. Mankind is immortal because it always leaves later generations behind to preserve its unity and identity for all time: it gets its share of immortality by means of procreation. It is never a holy thing to deny oneself this prize, and he who neglects to take a wife and children does precisely that.[12]

The fact that Plato in the *Laws*, however, felt obliged to suggest penalties for non-participation in this enterprise suggests that it may not be as natural as it is cracked up to be by him.[13]

There is also plenty of evidence to suggest that the desire for children is affected by social circumstances.[14] For example, family size has been correlated with social status, and with social circumstances such as provision for looking after the elderly. Then we also have to consider the fact of large-scale abortion—what does this say about the desire for children? Germaine Greer has argued that it, among other things, shows that modern Western society is profoundly hostile to children.[15]

To say that there is a very large element of social determination in the desire that people have for children is not to deny that there may be some biological element in it; it is simply to point out that we cannot assume that the desire for a child is a very basic fundamental one natural to human beings and that that is the end of the story.

It is also important to bear in mind that even if the desire to have children is to a large extent socially induced, that need not imply that it is any less *strong* than it would be were it an integral part of human nature. A socially induced desire may be just as strongly felt. This will be important if we find that the strength of desire as opposed to its origin is an important consideration.

It is important to make these distinctions, as the way in which we describe the desire can influence the way in which we think about it. Paul Ramsey has made the point that the very fact that we use the term "reproduction" rather than, for example, procreation is significant: "a significant move toward in vitro fertilization and all the rest was made when first we began to use a manufacturing term—'reproduction'—for procreation."[16] Just as it may be important whether we speak of reproduction instead of procreation, just so it may be important whether we speak of begetting or rearing.

With our distinctions made, we can go on to assess whether we should assign a right to reproduce on the basis of a desire to do so.

THE ARGUMENT FROM DESIRE

We have seen that the desire for a child may be one of a number of different desires, or perhaps a combination of them. What we have to consider now, however, is whether the fact that such a desire exists constitutes a good argument for the use of reproductive technology.

On the face of it, it does not follow from the fact that someone wants something, that (s)he ought to have it. This is clear not only from reflection on experience but from the gap between what is the case and what ought to be the case that was pointed out by David Hume. . . . Further argument is required to show that the desire necessitates action, rather than a response of "Too bad."

One way in which the desire argument could be backed up would be by a utilitarian framework. For obviously within an ethical perspective that advocates desire satisfaction in general, such as preference utilitarianism, the presence of this desire will provide prima facie grounds for satisfying it. It would, of course, have to be weighed against the satisfaction of other desires claiming consideration, but those who use the desire argument seem to accept that it is a very strong one. Thus Warnock says: "For those who long for children, the realization that they are unable to found a family can be shattering. It can disrupt their picture of the whole of the rest of their future lives."[17] . . .

. . . [The] fact of a desire does not necessitate the conclusion that we ought to seek its satisfaction: on the contrary, those who have the desire may find that they can achieve just as much fulfilment by looking for alternatives.

But proponents of the desire argument who, like Warnock, do not want to be utilitarians, may argue that of course we do not think that the simple fact of a desire necessitates its satisfaction. But there is something special about the *content* of the desire. Perhaps it is the fact that the desire is a desire *for a child* that wins it such support. Then of course the basis of the argument has shifted from the fact of desire to its concern with children. Perhaps the idea is that children are a good thing to have around; why is this?

Of course, there have been societies, and still are, where *governments* want to try to encourage reproduction (especially by certain sections of the population, as we shall see later), but if this is the case, it might be unwise to concentrate on this particular method (that is, the use of artificial means). If government is serious about wanting to encourage people to have more children, to avoid a shortage of citizens, or soldiers, more care facilities might have greater practical results than technology.

However, perhaps this is not the point. It may be that there is a very deep-seated belief among people generally that children are a good thing, a blessing. Perhaps it is felt that the hope and future of the species lies in its children. For we must remember that in this argument we are no longer thinking in terms of the desires of individuals.

There are well-known difficulties in explaining why we should value the creation of new people, but even if for some reason children are felt to be a good thing, so that the more the merrier, it would not necessarily indicate reproductive technology.[18] We could cut down on abortions and thereby ensure that more children were produced. But that would involve overriding the desires of those who want abortions, which brings us back to the argument from desire. . . .

CONCLUSIONS

We have argued that it is difficult to take as a starting point for addressing these issues the claim that all adults have a right to reproduce. This right may, however, be assigned as the result of argument. The central argument seems to be the argument from the desire for a child, which seems to be very strongly felt, although it manifests itself in various ways and may be to a certain extent socially determined.

However, we have also argued that since not all desires can be satisfied, some form of selection must be operated. In this context it is appropriate as a matter of public policy to give priority to an assessment of what the desires of the children produced as a result of our practices will be. . . .

At present we have a broad distinction between interference in rearing and interference in begetting. In our society, historically, there has for a long time been public intervention in the question of rearing. It is well established and much publicized in the media that we think it right to remove children from parents who abuse them. So the desire to rear is thought to carry less weight than the desire of children not to be abused, and the desire of other members of society not to tolerate this kind of behavior. We also exercise stringent controls on adoption.

There are arguments to the effect that this kind of interference should be extended to the desire to beget. Hugh LaFollette, for example, has argued that we should introduce a system of licensing parents to have children, on the basis of predictive tests designed to pick out those who are liable to abuse their children. This suggestion has gained little support. We have another principle, that one is innocent until proven guilty, and there are obvious problems in the suggestion that guilt can be predicted.

However, there is also the suggestion that we should interfere with the desire to beget on the grounds of overpopulation. Again, it has been argued that some people possess undesirable genes that they should not be allowed to pass on to children. . . . It has not only been argued but has informed social policy in some societies.

Some hold that all reproduction, including begetting and rearing, should be private; others hold that it should all be a matter of public concern. A third position is to draw a distinction between rearing and begetting, and to say that society, through the law, has to concern itself with child-rearing and abuse. But once reproductive services are provided, begetting becomes public too. . . .

NOTES

1. Quoted in S. Lederberg, "State Channeling of Gene Flow by Regulation of Marriage and Procreation," in *Genetics and the Law*, ed. A. Milunsky and G. J. Annas (New York: Plenum Press, 1976), p. 255.

2. *Times*, August 4, 1986.

3. Mary Warnock, *A Question of Life: The Warnock Report on Human Fertilisation and Embryology* (Oxford: Blackwell, 1985), para. 2.2.

4. "The Men Who Want to Be Mother," *Daily Mail*, May 19, 1986.

5. Germaine Greer, *Sex and Destiny: The Politics of Human Fertility* (London: Secker & Warburg, 1984), p. 11.

6. I am using "cloning" here in the popular sense of producing an exact copy of a presently existing adult individual.

7. Warnock, *A Question of Life*, para. 8.13.

8. *NACK* 39 (1985): 14.

9. Warnock, *A Question of Life*, para. 2.2.

10. Peter Singer and Deane Wells, *The Reproduction Revolution: New Ways of Making Babies* (New York: Oxford University Press, 1984), p. 67.

11. Fanny Lines, *Guardian*, January 16, 1985.

12. Plato, *Laws*, trans. Trevor J. Saunders (Harmondsworth, England: Penguin, 1970), p. 183.

13. Ibid., pp. 253–56, 266–69.

14. Marilyn French, *Beyond Power: Women, Men and Morals* (London: Jonathan Cape, 1985), p. 468. She writes, "Women may ardently desire children—especially sons—in cultures in which their own identity or well-being depends on it. . . . But that wish is . . . not great enough to counter the lack of esteem for reproduction that pervades our society."

15. Greer, *Sex and Destiny*, pp. 1 ff.

16. Paul Ramsey, "Shall We 'Reproduce'? II: Rejoinders and Future Forecast," *Journal of the American Medical Association* 220, no. 11 (1972): 1480–85.

17. Warnock, *A Question of Life*, para. 2.2.

18. See Jonathan Glover, *Causing Death and Saving Lives* (Harmondsworth, England: Penguin, 1977), pp. 69–71.

STERILIZATION OF THE MENTALLY SEVERELY HANDICAPPED

A VIOLATION OF THE RIGHT TO HAVE CHILDREN?

Eike-Henner W. Kluge

INTRODUCTION

*T*he Universal Declaration of Human Rights (1948) stated, and the Declaration of Teheran (1968) reiterated, that every person "of full age" has the right to have children and "found a family." The right thus enunciated is usually interpreted as being universal, inalienable, and indefeasible; and it is at least in part on this basis that many jurisdictions have rejected the nonconsensual sterilization of the mentally severely handicapped as being both discriminatory and unethical when performed for reasons other than to safeguard the health and welfare of the handicapped person. It is on this basis also that most commentators have rejected such sterilization.

However, both the general thesis, as well as its application to the mentally severely handicapped, may be challenged. The general claim may be challenged on three grounds: the nature of the right claimed, as well as its legitimacy, is extremely dubious; the grounding of the alleged right presents severe ontological problems; and the claim that such a right is indefeasible ignores the contextual nature of all rights. As to the particular claim as advanced for the mentally severely handicapped, three further arguments may be raised against it: the mentally severely handicapped cannot meet the basic precondition for such a right; insistence on such a right would violate the rights of children; and, finally, it would also violate the rights of other people.

Reprinted from *Ethical Problems in Reproductive Medicine* 1, no. 1 (1989): 12–15.

While none of these considerations, even if successful, entail that the mentally severely handicapped should be sterilized as a matter of course, they do entail that under circumstances where conception and procreation of the mentally severely handicapped can reasonably be prevented only in this fashion, sterilization is ethically permissible.

THE NATURE OF THE CLAIM

To begin with the nature of the claim itself: what precisely does the alleged right to have children amount to? Several possibilities come to mind, but one is generally taken to be central: the right to have biological progeny of one's own. In the interest of clarity, however, it should be noted that such an interpretation is rather simplistic. In the first place, one cannot have a right to what it is impossible to provide. Many persons are irremediably sterile and cannot have biological progeny. In their case, therefore, the alleged right would fail for want of its logical precondition. Whence it would follow that, contrary to the initial claim, the alleged right would not be universal (unless, of course, it were to be argued that the right is universal after all, and that in cases such as these, society has an obligation to develop and employ techniques of artificial reproduction that would overcome this problem. We shall not pursue the issue here.)

Second, the right, no matter how construed, centrally involves children. Children, however, are not objects. They are persons. Therefore it follows that if there is a right to have progeny at all, it could not ethically be interpreted in a proprietary or dispositionary fashion. It would have to be understood in some other way. But how?

Finally, the right to have biological progeny of one's own would not ordinarily be considered to be satisfied by the mere existence of such progeny without any contact and association on part of the progenitor. A direct and personal interaction of an ongoing and formative sort is also taken to be implicated. An acceptable interpretation of the right claim, therefore, must include this associative parameter.

How to combine all this into a reasonable whole? The Universal Declaration of Human Rights, in its insistence on the right to "found a family," points the way. Whatever its cultural idiosyncracies of constitution, the family context is one of nurturing, of education, and of raising children. In short, insofar as the person context is concerned, it is one of parenting. Therefore in keeping with the preceding considerations, we suggest that the claim of a universal right to have children amounts to this: everyone has the right to (attempt to) have biological progeny and parent without undue state interference.

GROUNDING THE RIGHT

If we assume that this is an appropriate interpretation, the next question is, "How could such a right be grounded?" The literature, and indeed pure reasoning itself, suggest several possibilities: in the biological survival needs of the human species, the fact of individual desire, the requirements for the realization of a truly human potential, and the fact of social policy. We shall not here examine these possibilities in detail but merely sketch some considerations.

No purely material fact, and a fortiori no fact of biology, can establish an ethical right. That requires an ethical premise, which is here not given. Less abstractly, it is one thing to say that the human species will not survive unless its members reproduce; but is another to say that it ought to reproduce, or that it has the right to do so. Furthermore, even if the right were granted, it would not follow that every member of the species therefore had a right to progeny. Logically, such an inference would commit the fallacy of division because materially, the facts of biology would deny it. At best, what would follow from this basis would be that all and only those whose progeny could reasonably be expected to advance species survival would have such a right. The biological argument, therefore, would only allow for a limited right conditioned by evolutionary considerations.

The argument from individual desire fares no better. To put it bluntly, the connection between desire and right must be shown. It cannot merely be assumed. Otherwise it begs the question. As to the argument from the realization of personal potential, it faces the same problem. The existence of a fact, in this case, personal potential, does not establish a right. As it stands, the argument assumes that the connection between the fact (desire) and the right is established independently, in some other fashion; but that is not the case. The argument requires that children be considered as objects, as entities whose function it is to assist in the development of others. That, however, is ethically anathema. What one can argue is that *if* there is a particular potential and *if* there is a child, then ceteris paribus whoever has that potential has a prima facie right to use the child's existence to realize the potential. But *only if* the child will not be treated as an object. That, however, is quite different from the right claimed in the first instance. It is not the right to bring about a child for that purpose.

The argument from social existence has two versions, one legally oriented, the other ethical. The former focuses in the law extant in a given society. We shall not deal with it here. The latter is based on the thesis that society, whether it recognizes this explicitly in its laws or not, de facto guarantees each of its members certain fundamental rights as a condition of membership, and that the right to procreation and to parenting is one of these. However, while we may grant that society does indeed guarantee certain fundamental rights to its members, this does not establish that the right in question is one of them.

Furthermore, even if we did allow that there was such a right and that it was grounded in the fact of social existence, this would not show that it was absolute and unconditioned. The very fact that it was grounded in the social context would entail that like all other rights thus grounded, it would be subject to conditioning constraints. For one thing, it would be conditioned by the competing rights of others. Therefore if the exercise of this right interfered with the exercise of another person's more fundamental right, e.g., the right to life, then the right would become ineffective. For another, it would be conditioned from the perspective of society as a whole. That is to say children, both as persons and as biological organisms, have needs. Providing for these, however, is not simply a parental function. No matter how wealthy, well-endowed, or positioned, no set of parents can meet these conditions alone. Directly or indirectly, meeting them involves whole social institutions such as health, education, and welfare, which no one is wholly able to defray. The coming-into-being of a child, therefore, is a social affair; and society, by allowing someone to claim the right to have a child, acquires the obligation to provide for its needs if, when, and as it becomes necessary. Justice, however, entails that no one can have an obligation unilaterally thrust upon him or her. There must be some ethically acceptable way for the individual to escape the obligation. This means that it must be possible for society to avoid being locked into the relevant obligations vis-à-vis the new child. This would be possible only by preventing the child from coming into existence in the first place. It therefore follows that although there may be a socially guaranteed right to have children, that right is not absolute but defeasible from the side of society itself.

Finally, the right also is defeasible from the side of the child. That is to say, there are situations in which the conditions governing the genesis of a child are the beginning of a causal chain that predictably will eventuate in such a qualitative state for the child that, were it imposed de novo upon a person who is already present, it would constitute the infliction of harm. To procreate under such circumstances would be tantamount to a temporally protracted infliction of harm. Therefore while the act of procreation per se may be morally blameless, the act *under such circumstances* would be blameworthy and constitute an injury. Under such circumstances, therefore, the right to have a child fails.

THE MENTALLY SEVERELY HANDICAPPED

The right to have a child, therefore, even if it is granted, is neither universal, absolute, nor unconditioned. So far, we have argued this only for persons in general. How does it apply to the mentally severely handicapped?

To avoid confusion, we shall define a mentally severely handicapped person as someone who is congenitally so severely impaired that he or she cannot look after his or her needs as an independent and autonomous being but requires continuous supervision and assistance in order to allow him or her to survive and function; and furthermore as someone who cannot grasp the nature of a child as a person, and who fails to comprehend the requirements inherent in providing for a child. Does such an individual have a right to have a child in the sense discussed above? And is there a right on the part of society to sterilize such an individual in order to prevent him or her from having children?

If our preceding analysis is correct, then the answer to the first question is negative. There are two reasons for this: one logical, the other ethical. Ex hypothesi, the mentally severely handicapped cannot perceive, relate to, or otherwise treat children as persons. Consequently, they cannot fulfill the requirements of a parenting role. Since the ability to fulfill such a role is a precondition of the right to have children, it follows that the right itself fails from a purely logical perspective. As to the ethical reason for its failure, the very nature of the handicap entails that a child born into such a situation would play the role of an object of personal development and self-gratification for the severely handicapped. However, as we said before, no right can involve the use of persons purely as objects in an instrumental fashion. The right, therefore, fails once again.

It might be argued that while the inabilities of the handicapped to parent and to see children as persons may be admitted, this does not entail that they do not have a right to have children. Instead, it entails that society has an obligation to provide for the services of someone who will take over those areas of parenting that the severely handicapped are constitutionally unable to provide: to act, as it were, in loco parentis toward the children. The inability of the handicapped is thus being made up, their right is preserved, and they will be able to benefit from and enjoy the remainder of the parenting experience.

But such an argument would fail. The central precondition ineluctably associated with the right to have a child is that the individual who claims the right must be able to experience, relate to, and otherwise interact with the child as a person. The proposal at hand would not allow the mentally severely handicapped to meet this precondition. It would be the parent-proxy, the individual who is provided by society to act in loco parentis, who would relate to the children in the requisite manner. Short of changing his or her nature, nothing can be done for or to the mentally severely handicapped that would allow him or her to meet this condition. For him or her, the children will still remain objects. In more formal terms, if a's having quality ϕ is a necessary precondition of having right R, then the fact that b has quality φ does not establish that therefore *a* has *R* after all. The only way in which *a* can acquire *R* is for *a* to acquire φ. In this case it would mean that the mentally severely handicapped would have to cease being mentally severely handicapped. If that were possible, there would be no ethical problem. As it stands, however, it is not the case.

STERILIZATION

If the foregoing is correct, then the mentally severely handicapped do not have a right to have children in the sense we have developed. Society has both a right and a duty to step in. But in what fashion? Surely sterilization is too restrictive? Surely contraception and even abortion are less permanent, less irreversible, and less intrusive alternatives?

As to abortion, it is almost as intrusive as tubal ligation and since it does not prevent future conceptions, it is a potentially repetitive procedure. Given that it does have an intrusive nature, it follows on the last count that any advantage it might have over sterilization would have to be sought in the fact that it did not bring about an irreversible condition. That, however, prompts the following question: Under what circumstances would reversibility be a relevant consideration? The answer is only in those cases where the factor that mandated interference in the first place, the severe mental handicap, was not a permanent characteristic of the individual in question. However, instead of telling against sterilization per se, this surely means that sterilization is unacceptable *in those cases*. It does not mean that in cases where the severe mental handicap is permanent, sterilization should also be withheld, in the expectation of a miracle, as it were.

Turning to contraception, since it is the least permanent and least intrusive alternative, it appears to be the method of choice. However, those methods of contraception, which under the circumstances would be the most appropriate—subcutaneous implants, IUDs, and so on—while they are indeed least intrusive in a mechano/physiological sense, emerge as quite intrusive when it is considered that they are biochemically active on the person as a whole. In any case they do have quantifiable risks of morbidity and mortality that exceed those of sterilization. Their attractiveness on this count, therefore, wanes. As to their lack of permanence and irreversibility, not only do they also have long-term effects in that direction but relevance of the criterion of reversibility should also be reexamined.

We suggest, therefore, that there are cases in which sterilization is appropriate. All and only those, namely, where according to all appropriate standards of medical certitude the severe mental handicap is a permanent feature of the individual.

However, a fundamental question remains: Does the state have the right to breach the principle of inviolability and commit trespass to the person in the pursuit of its right and in order to prevent perceived harm to future persons?

There must be a proportion between a right/duty that is claimed and the method used to pursue it. And here the following consideration seems germane. Sterilization by vasectomy or tubal ligation is currently being used by competent people on a voluntary basis to control their own fertility. Nor is sterilization deemed ethically inappropriate or indefensible in this context. The method itself, therefore, is ethically acceptable per se. The only reason an objection might arise is that in the case of the mentally severely handicapped it would be imposed in a nonconsensual manner. Here, however, we should like to suggest the following as a particularization of the principle of equality. If a particular method or procedure is unobjectionable when employed by a competent individual on a voluntary basis in order to control a particular activity or bodily function, then the fact that it is employed by a proxy decision-maker for an incompetent individual for reasons that are ethically defensible in their own right does not render it ethically objectionable. If this principle is false, then nothing that a proxy decision-maker decides on the basis of comparison with normal situations will ever be ethically defensible. On the other hand if, as we have suggested, it is correct, then in many cases sterilization will be an ethically appropriate way to proceed.

THE RIGHT TO PROCREATE

WHEN RIGHTS CLAIMS HAVE GONE WRONG

Laura Shanner

*C*lassifying the desire to have children as a need or as a mere desire is complicated and politically charged. The perception of something as a need usually gives it legitimacy and importance not granted to mere desires. . . .

It seems clear that in biological or medical terms, having a child is not a need in any sense comparable to the need for lifesaving treatment, food, water, oxygen, sleep, or other factors that keep a body alive and healthy. . . .

Following John Rawls, we could envision primary social goods as fundamentally important hypothetical needs, since they are the sorts of things that allow an individual to compete with others for secondary social goods or to pursue chosen life plans.[1] Freedom, education, fair access to material resources, and, perhaps, access to health care are all basic goods that make it possible for a person to acquire other desired goods. While having children is generally considered a positive element of one's life, it is a secondary good, a chosen life plan, rather than a primary good that enables one to choose life plans at all. Basic goods are those necessary for one's continued existence and success in the community, but a child (unlike adequate shelter, nutrition, and health care) is not necessary for one's continued existence. A child might aid in achieving success in a community, but this result is contingent upon the social value and social pressures placed upon procreation. Having a child is often a necessary requirement for *women* to achieve other goods in society, since they are less likely than men to be rewarded for nonreproductive and

From "The Right to Procreate: When Rights Claims Have Gone Wrong," by Laura Shanner, *McGill Law Journal* 40 (1995): 823.

nonsexual roles. This observation says less about children, though, than it does about gender role inequalities. . . .

Procreation and parenting, by definition, involve relationships between parents and children. Procreating is not simply a matter of my seeking to complete my own life plan by having a child, as it would be by having a career; if I succeed in the attempt to reproduce, I have produced another person and substantially shaped that other person's life. In other words, my procreative actions affect *our* lives, not just my life. Having children thus fits into a category of establishing relationships rather than a category of pursuing individual goals. . . .

Our understandings or the term "having children" should also be clarified. We may speak of having children (or friends, or lovers, etc.) in several different ways, and most of their meanings can be located on a gradient of contrasting attitudes toward, or images of connection with, the other. At one extreme, the child is perceived to be an element or extension of oneself, perhaps as one might have brown eyes or a rapier wit. People who are unable to recognize the child as a separate individual, and who attempt to live through their children, often suffer from psychological immaturity or maladjustment, and may inflict serious emotional damage on the child.

At the other end of the gradient is a distanced attitude of acquisition that characterizes children as items to be had and collected rather like cars or houses. This acquisitive notion of "having" children reduces them to the status of desirable objects rather than persons, reinforces the image of women as baby machines, and is often accompanied by an attitude of control over others.

A third attitude toward having children may be found between the extremes of self-identification and distanced, objectified acquisition: the child is recognized as external to oneself, but also as part of an existentially self-defining relationship. In this third sense, the child is brought into the world and is connected in a unique way to the parent. Recognition of the child as an other who defines oneself captures a quality of transcendence; while not entirely of oneself, as are the brown eyes or rapier wit, the child is of the parent, reflects the parent, and allows the parent to revisit his or her own past. In this sense, the "having" statement is interchangeable with a "being" statement; "having children" is phenomenologically equivalent to "being a parent," much as having true friends is experienced as being a friend, or having a lover involves loving.[2] This attitude of transcendental recognition opens many positive possibilities for interaction, response, appreciation, and understanding of the child as a unique, developing individual.

A key problem with claims of a right to procreate is that they too often sound like claims to objects or material resources. It is significant that English lacks a gender-neutral personal pronoun, leading us commonly to refer to a fetus or infant as "it"—the word reserved for objects—which is a practice we avoid when speaking about unspecified adults. Expressing reproductive options in terms of a right to procreate fails to encourage the relational notion of having children over an objectifying one.

Procreative relationships are different from friendships, romances, partnerships, and even adoptions in the sense that the other with whom one establishes the parenting relationship is *created* specifically to form this relationship. In all other relationships, the partner is encountered, after which the relationship is recognized, defined, or consciously initiated. It would be absurd to suggest that every act of reproduction is morally suspect just because children are being produced in order to form parental relationships. Nevertheless, persons who otherwise would not have existed come into being when we exercise our reproductive capacities; this fact ought to give us moral pause. In reproducing I am not making decisions only for myself but necessarily for another who not only cannot consent or refuse but who would not even exist if not for my choices.

It is implausible to suggest that any birth under any circumstances is to be considered positive, such that not coming into existence is itself a harm. If conception has not yet occurred, who exactly is harmed by not coming into existence? Accepting a claim that nonexistence is a harm to unconceived children undermines any attempts to prevent teen pregnancies, promiscuous men who father multiple unsupported children, and other known predictors of harm to children. The supposed harm of nonconception would also undermine the extensive support for contraception and fertility control. Thus, while we indeed have the capacity to bring others into existence, capacities do not justify their exercise. Procreation therefore seems better described as an awesome responsibility rather than as a right. A need for third-party assistance in the enterprise does not alter the underlying moral weight of the act. . . .

[Ed. note: The following discussion responds to a 1995 U.S. case in which a man was charged with beating to death the five-week-old infant delivered by a hired surrogate mother.]

It is commonly observed that persons with all sorts of dysfunctional relationships, dire socioeconomic situations, and indicators of poor parenting skills are nevertheless able to have children, and we do not prevent them from doing so; is it not discriminatory, then, to prevent someone from having a child through new reproductive technologies [NRTs] simply because of infertility?

I agree that there is a hard-to-define line between preventing child abuse and negative social consequences and, alternatively, establishing dangerously restrictive legal definitions of "acceptable" parents. I am extremely suspicious of people who claim to have a clear sense of who is fit or unfit to be a parent, and I worry about the political context of controlling such decisions; the reluctance to judge others or unfairly limit their options is thus generally a good thing. We must exercise this reluctance to judge very carefully, however, and avoid turning such reluctance into an all-or-nothing acceptance of, and even promotion of, irresponsible procreation. The desire not to restrict reproduction unfairly or coercively should not evolve into a tacit acceptance or even vigorous defense of irresponsible reproduction and incompetent parenting. Despite my hesitation to identify people who might be qualified to make such judgments, and the specific grounds upon which such judgments might be made, I reject the claims that such judgments ought never to be made, and that if they are, that they require the same level of justification as does interference with coital reproduction. . . .

We are faced with an unavoidable choice: either every infertile adult has an equal right to assisted conception because any healthy person could initiate a pregnancy if they wanted to, or we must establish some notion of responsible parenting and concern for the well-being of future children. Reluctance to judge whether some people should be parents may prevent abuses of power, but it too easily falls into an irresponsible compliance with demands made by people who make bad choices. . . .

Children are the only parties to reproductive decisions who cannot voice their interests, and after birth they are the most vulnerable to abuse, neglect, and injury. However, I have shown that they cannot claim any rights prior to their conception, and framing reproductive decisions as matters of competing rights claims between adults and possible future children leads to absurdities. Thus, while we cannot say that children have a right not to be conceived if they will be harmed in life, we can certainly say that people who are unable to meet the responsibilities of parenting should not be assisted in procreating. Bringing children into the world is a profound action, and responsibility for doing so must rest on all who participate in it. . . .

. . . The complaint that fertile people are not equally subjected to parenting evaluations should not hold sway: fertile people are not asking for assistance, and it would be extremely intrusive to restrict their procreative options. Their mistakes must be their own responsibility. . . .

NOTES

1. John Rawls, *A Theory of Justice* (Cambridge, Mass.: Belknap Press, 1971), pp. 62, 90–95.

2. The self-identification attitude may also sometimes be expressed with "being" statements, such that having a rapier wit is equivalent to being witty. Yet the relational sense of "having" and "being" is a more active sense of both terms: having children = being a parent = parenting = to parent; having a lover = being in love = loving = to love; etc. Having brown eyes is clearly not active at all; I am brown-eyed, but not brown-eyeing.

2. Is Legislation the Best Response?

*P*erhaps an equally strong objection to licensing parents concerns the "coercive" nature of legislation (though surely we don't consider all forms of legislation to be coercive). For this reason, many people advocate alternatives such as education, economic incentives, and various other social policies.

A parent-licensing policy might regulate parent*a*ge in a number of ways, and the authors in this section examine some of these possibilities. First, it might prohibit conception (mandate contraception), and it might do so because of concerns either for quality, which is the focus of Robertson's piece, or for quantity, which is the focus of Chasteen's piece. Robertson acknowledges that state control of reproduction has, in the past, been subject to abuse, but insists that the matter be addressed in the public forum. The state's responsibility to protect its citizens justifies social policies, but what kind of social policies? Robertson discusses education, incentives, and penalties, and argues that the first two are preferable to more coercive policies.

Like Robertson, Chasteen notes our reluctance even to discuss legislative population control (indeed, he wrote his book thirty years ago and no one since has addressed the topic as thoroughly), but, he says, it is "untenable" that reproduction should be controlled only by private interests (p. 286). He argues that, with regard to population control, support for traditional policies and programs, and opposition to legislation, is based on several myths or mistaken assumptions. He presents and examines each of these, then argues for compulsory contraception as "vital to our collective survival" (p. 299).

Second, a parent-licensing policy might mandate genetic engineering, for the eradication of genetic disease and/or for the provision of genetic enhancement. Both Singer and Wells and Kitcher provide comments on this matter. Singer and Wells compare the laissez-faire/free-market approach to genetic engineering decisions with the central-planning/government-control approach and suggest a sort of middle road: decisions should be left up to the parents except for "adventurous" proposals which would require society's permission through application to the government.

Kitcher also rejects the current laissez-faire approach (by which people simply decide with whom to have reproductive sex) because it doesn't honor individual reproductive freedom as much as we think it does, because individual decisions affect the whole, and because individual decisions may be morally misguided. He suggests replacing it with a slightly different laissez-faire approach, "utopian eugenics," in which prenatal testing is equally available to everyone and in which there is widespread public education and discussion about the decisions to be made by the individual parents. Such an approach would not be problem-free, however, as is shown by his "Modern Civics Class" story.

Third, such a policy might regulate (or prohibit) gestation, and this is the subject of Mathieu's analysis. She presents three arguments that support such regulation: consideration of the consequences, the rights of the future child, and the obligations of the pregnant woman. However, she argues, coercive state intervention is justified only when certain conditions of proportionality are met.

While none of the forementioned pieces considers the merit of regulating parent*ing*, many of the issues are the same: rights and responsibilities, consequences, and the relative effectiveness of alternatives. They can, therefore, provide insights from which we can benefit. The last piece, however, does focus on licensing parenting: Westman presents a very thorough examination of no fewer than nineteen arguments against licensing parents, many of which either explicitly or implicitly suggest responses other than legislation. He finds, however, that every argument is flawed—and maintains his advocacy of licensing parents.

NORPLANT, FORCED CONTRACEPTION, AND IRRESPONSIBLE REPRODUCTION

John A. Robertson

*N*orplant offers safe and effective [and reversible] contraception for up to five years, thus increasing options for women seeking to control their fertility. Yet shortly after FDA approval in 1990, proposals surfaced to have Norplant implanted in child abusers, welfare mothers, and teenagers. Because the contraceptive effect is reversible at any time, Norplant appeared to offer an acceptable technological solution for harmful or irresponsible reproduction.

However, the notion of state intervention to limit reproduction is anathema to many people. If procreation is a basic right, then people must be allowed to reproduce as they wish and the consequences tolerated, just as the consequences of free speech or the due-process rights of criminals must be tolerated. Still, the possibility of temporary interference with irresponsible reproduction is an attractive option. At the very least, this technology forces us to address issues of reproductive responsibility that have long been ignored. This chapter discusses irresponsible reproduction and the social policies that may be adopted to discourage it. . . .[1]

Norplant Controversies

As a voluntary method of contraception that has met regulatory standards of safety and efficacy, Norplant presents no major ethical or legal issues, beyond

J. A. Robertson, *Children of Choice*. Copyright © 1994 by Princeton University Press. Reprinted by permission of Princeton University Press.

making it available to all women who want it and assuring that women are informed of its side effects. Voluntary use by adolescents raises issues of parental consent and impact on nonmarital sexual activity, but these issues arise with any contraceptive use by minors.

Norplant has become controversial, however, because of attempts by judges, legislators, and others to require that certain women use Norplant to avoid reproduction that is alleged to be irresponsible or harmful to children and society. Within a month of FDA approval, for example, a trial judge in California offered to release from prison a woman convicted of child abuse, if she would consent to use of Norplant. Other judges have offered similar deals to women, and legislation authorizing involuntary insertion of Norplant in alcoholics and drug addicts who have given birth to children has been introduced.[2]

Legislators have also been quick to offer Norplant to women on welfare. In 1991, a Kansas legislator introduced a bill that would pay $500 to any mother on welfare who had Norplant implanted, and $50 a year to maintain it. Lousiana state representative David Duke introduced a similar bill in his home state, with a $100 reward. A 1990 editorial in the *Philadelphia Inquirer* proposed making use of Norplant a condition of receiving welfare as a way to reduce the size of the "underclass."[3] In January 1993, the governor of Maryland proposed that use of Norplant be made mandatory in certain cases.[4]

Mental health professionals have considered use of Norplant with retarded and mentally ill women who are at risk of sexual exploitation in residential facilities. Others have proposed that Norplant be required of or offered to women who are HIV-infected, and to women who are at risk for offspring with severe genetic disease. Still others would provide Norplant to teenagers at school clinics.[5] Proposals to have Norplant inserted in all girls at puberty have also surfaced.[6]

Reactions to such proposals have varied from enthusiastic approval to horror and outrage. Approval comes from those persons who believe that certain kinds of reproduction are irresponsible, and that the state may take steps to prevent irresponsible reproduction with an easily reversible device such as Norplant. Others see proposals to offer, entice, or compel women to use Norplant as a violation of basic human rights—a racist or elitist response to problems that should be resolved by other means. They also oppose such an approach, because women vary in their tolerance of Norplant's irregular bleeding and other side effects.

Whatever one's views about these proposals, it is clear that Norplant has succeeded in reintroducing a discourse of reproductive responsibility into public life. Because Norplant is easily inserted and fully reversible, it appears to be much less intrusive of personal rights and dignity than is compulsory sterilization, which is now widely opposed. Moreover, many of the proposals are not directly coercive but merely provide incentives for target groups to use Norplant. The result is a long overdue discussion of reproductive responsibility and the state's role in promoting such responsibility.

REPRODUCTIVE RESPONSIBILITY

[An earlier chapter] presented the case for recognition of both a moral and legal right to reproduce. Arguing that reproduction is important to individuals because of the personal and social meanings that surround it, the chapter concluded that decisions to reproduce should be viewed as presumptive rights that are subject to limitation only upon the showing of substantial harm to the interests of others. The development of Norplant now requires us to address what kinds of harm would constitute a sufficient basis for limitation of that right.

Any discussion of reproductive responsibility and governmental action to limit reproduction is a touchy subject, however.[7] The history of attempts to limit "irresponsible reproduction" is replete with abuse and discrimination. From 1920 to 1960, more than sixty thousand "mental defectives" were forcibly sterilized on eugenics grounds, even though the risk of transmission of genetic disease was low and diagnostic errors of mental deficiency abounded.[8] Poor and minority women have also been sterilized without consent under both public and private programs well into the 1970s.[9] As a result, there is an extreme reluctance to even discuss the idea of irresponsible reproduction, much less propose public policies, for fear that it will be viewed as racist or lead to coercive state policies that will replicate earlier abuses.

Nevertheless, it is essential that conversations about reproductive responsibility take place. Reproduction always has moral significance because it leads to the birth of another person, whose needs for love, nurturing, and resources have to be met. Clearly, one can act responsibly or irresponsibly in reproducing, because of the impact that one's actions will have on offspring and others, including existing children. A dialogue about the circumstances that make reproduction desirable or undesirable, advised or ill-advised, responsible or irresponsible is needed to help us determine the parameters of morally and socially acceptable conduct, and to guide or limit governmental action that affects reproductive choice.

Any judgment about the reproductive responsibility of individuals must pay attention to four issues: the importance of the reproduction in question to the person(s) reproducing; the ease or difficulty with which they could avoid that reproduction; the burdens that reproduction will cause resulting offspring; and the burdens or costs imposed on society and others.[10] Clarifying these parameters is necessary before they are applied to individual cases and questions of public policy are addressed.

Reproductive Interest

Reproduction is often said to be irresponsible because of the costs imposed on others. Implicit in such a judgment is the assumption that the person reproducing has little or no reproductive interest to justify those costs. What counts as a reproductive interest? What distinctions can be made on this score?

An important issue here is whether the persons will be involved in rearing resulting offspring. Although reproduction may occur without rearing, one reason reproduction is highly valued is because of the rearing and family experiences it makes possible. A person who reproduces but has no contact with offspring may have a lesser interest in reproduction than a person who reproduces with the intent to rear children. Whether the reproduction of either is undesirable will depend on the costs imposed on offspring and society. However, in balancing those costs against the value of the reproductive experience, the capacity and likelihood of rearing is a relevant factor.

On this parameter a man who fathers many children with different women but who has no contact with any of them and provides no support is more easily open to a charge of irresponsibility. At the opposite extreme would be the cases where the person reproducing is seeking to nurture and rear her offspring. HIV women, welfare mothers, and unmarried teenagers may fit this category. Although their reproduction may be undesirable because of consequences for offspring and the welfare system, they have substantial reproductive interests at stake when they will also rear their offspring. Because reproduction with rearing is presumptively protected, a correspondingly high level of harm will have to be shown to justify overriding their procreative freedom.

Other cases will fall in between these two extremes with many variations among them. Some persons may have minimal contact with offspring, rear intermittently, or require the assistance of other rearers. Some may rear fully but die while offspring are still young. Also relevant in assessing the value of the reproductive interest at stake will be whether the person has previously reproduced, or will be able to reproduce in the future if a present opportunity is denied.

The key question in each case will be the value to the person and others of the precise reproductive experience that is occurring. Answering this question, however, will pose many problems beyond merely determining whether genetic reproduction *tout court* should be valued as much as genetic reproduction cum rearing. If the question is pushed, questions of the worth of the experience to the person will have to be faced, and distinctions must be drawn based on previous and likely future reproductive experiences, expected life span, the amount of rearing, and the like. Because of these complications, it may not be possible as a practical matter in most cases to go beyond whether the persons reproducing will be aware that they have reproduced and whether they will have some rearing role or contact with offspring.

Burdens of Avoiding Reproduction

Judgments of irresponsible reproduction will also have to factor in the ease or burdens of alternatives open to the person to avoid reproduction. Even if reproduction imposes high costs on others and the person has only a minimal reproductive interest at stake, a charge of irresponsibility will fit only if the person has reasonable alternatives to reproduction. A person who could have been abstinent, used birth control, or terminated pregnancy would be acting irresponsibly if their failure to do so imposes high costs on others, particularly if they have no intention or ability to rear resulting offspring. On the other hand, if they have been raped, cannot reasonably remain abstinent, or birth control or abortion is dangerous, not available, or morally repugnant, then their responsibility is less.

The hard cases here will arise over whether alternatives to reproduction are reasonably available. For example, should a conscientious belief about the immorality of birth control or abortion justify actions that produce little or no significant reproductive experience and impose high costs on others? Must a woman insist that she or her partner use contraception? The lack of moral accountability for undesirable reproduction does not lessen the costs that reproduction imposes on others, nor does it increase the significance of marginal reproductive interests. Of course, questions about the burdens of avoidance do not determine whether the reproductive outcome is desirable or advised, but merely whether a person can be held responsible for undesirable outcomes. It also does not prevent society from acting to prevent the reproduction in question.

Impact on Offspring

Reproduction is said to be irresponsible when it is reasonably foreseeable that the parents will be unable to produce healthy offspring or will otherwise rear them in circumstances that deny them a minimum level of care, nurture, and protection. Parents who abuse their children by prenatal or postnatal conduct, rear them in disadvantageous circumstances, or pass on genetic or infectious disease would appear to fit this category.[11] The consequences for offspring, when coupled with an unwillingness or inability to rear and reasonable alternatives to reproduction, would arguably make this reproduction irresponsible.

There is, however, a major problem with finding harm to offspring in these circumstances, and hence with claiming that the reproduction is irresponsible. The problem is that in many cases of concern the alleged harm to offspring occurs from birth itself. Either the harm is congenital and unavoidable if birth is to occur, or the harm is avoidable after birth occurs, but the parents will not refrain from the harmful action. Preventing harm would mean preventing the birth of the child whose interests one is trying to protect. Yet a child's interests are hardly protected by preventing the child's existence. If the child has no way to be born or raised free of that harm, a person is not injuring the child by enabling her to be born in the circumstances of concern. The overwhelming majority of courts faced with this question in wrongful-life cases brought on behalf of the child have reached the same conclusion.[12]

Of course, this objection would not hold if the harmful conditions are such that the very existence of the child is a wrong to it. Such a case would arise where from the perspective of the child, viewed solely in light of his interests as he is then situated, any life at all with the conditions of his birth would be so harmful to him that he would prefer not to live. In such a case existence itself is a wrong. In theory cases of wrongful life could exist, but it is doubtful whether most of the cases of concern fit that extreme rubric. For example, children born with a genetic handicap or HIV might have years of life that are a good for them, as would children born in illegitimacy, poverty, or to abusive parents, even though it is less good a life than they deserve. In fact, if true cases of wrongful life did arise, one's duty would be to act immediately to prevent continued existence in order to minimize the harm. Protecting offspring by preventing their birth thus prevents the birth of offspring whose life is a net benefit to them, and is not always necessary to protect them in cases where their life is truly wrongful.[13]

This point about wrongful life is key to any claim that reproduction is irresponsible because it harms offspring by bringing them into the world in a diseased, handicapped, or disadvantaged condition. If offspring are not injured because there is no alternative way for them to be born absent the condition of concern, then reproduction is not irresponsible because of the effect on offspring who are born less whole than is desirable. This is true both in cases in which the harms are congenitally unavoidable because of genetic or infectious disease, and cases in which the harm is avoidable after birth but parents will nevertheless not avoid injuring their offspring. If there is no injury to offspring from their birth alone, then reproduction is not irresponsible solely because children are born in undesirable circumstances.

Yet one may still morally condemn giving birth to offspring in such circumstances. Derek Parfit captures this point well in his example of a woman who is told by her physician that if she gets pregnant while on a certain medication she will give birth to a child with a mild deformity, such as a withered arm, but if she waits a month, she can conceive a perfectly normal child.[14] If the woman refuses to wait and has the child with the withered arm, she has not harmed that child, because there is no way that this *particular* child could have been born normal. Still, many would say that she has acted wrongly because she has gratuitously chosen to bring a suffering child into the world when a brief wait would have enabled her to have a normal, though different, child. Now one could argue that her action is morally justified by the net good provided the child born with the withered arm. However, if one concludes that her actions are wrong, it is not because she has harmed the child born with the withered arm, but because she has violated a norm against offending persons who are troubled by gratuitous suffering.[15]

Burdens on Society

A main ground for charging that reproduction is irresponsible is the costs or burdens imposed on others. These burdens may take a financial or nonfinancial form. A common kind of nonfinancial burden is the sense of outrage or offense felt when someone gratuitously has children who are born with disease or disadvantages, as in Parfit's example of the withered arm. Even though bringing children into the world who have no other practical way to be born healthy does not in itself injure them, it does injure the sensibilities of those persons offended by the action, particularly when the person reproducing could have easily avoided that outcome. In this case, the person reproducing is harming only those whose sensibilities are affected by this experience.

But there is a problem in using this notion of offense to condemn those who bring unavoidably handicapped children into the world. The sense of offense is grounded in the undesirability of handicapped or disadvantaged children, and is inescapably a judgment about their worth. A claim of irresponsibility that rests on the undesirability of handicapped persons will not be a strong basis for moral condemnation or public action to prevent such births, particularly if those reproducing plan to rear or have other strong reproductive interests in the birth in question, and cannot reproduce without risking the handicapped birth.

The most significant burdens on others thus turn out to be the rearing burdens and financial costs that reproduction will impose on others and on the public treasury in welfare payments, medical costs, educational costs, child-abuse monitoring, social workers, and so on. Unspecified costs such as the costs of crime and social disintegration that such reproduction helps cause could also be included here.

Now this category of costs is significant only if it significantly exceeds the costs that *any* birth imposes on society. It may be that any additional child makes demands on societal resources and incurs public subsidies to some extent. It may also be that only some children subsidized in this way repay those costs over their lifetime through their own contributions. Only where the costs imposed or the subsidies demanded exceed a reasonable level might one be said to be harming others by their reproduction.

It is difficult to say which cases fall into that category and thus may be deemed irresponsible. Persons who reproduce knowing that they will depend on the welfare system or the charity of others to support their children will be imposing costs on others. The question is, however, whether those costs are beyond what we reasonably expect children to cost, or which we are willing to pay to enable persons to have offspring. If the costs do exceed that ceiling, there may be grounds for charging them with irresponsible reproduction because their reproduction requires others to pay more than can be reasonably expected to enable reproduction to occur.

The size of the cost will be determinative when the reproductive interest at stake is small, as in cases where reproduction will not lead to rearing, and will be less important as the reproductive interest mounts. Of course, how great that reproductive interest must be, and how the interests compare in individual cases, will require close judgments. Such judgments will affect the validity of state efforts to minimize the costs by discouraging the reproduction.

Another important issue of burdensome and possibly irresponsible reproduction is reproduction in the face of overpopulation. When are additional births irresponsible because of the large number of existing persons? To answer this question, we must first decide how many people there ought to be, and then allocate future reproduction accordingly. Parfit has shown that a number based either on the highest possible average level of happiness in the community or the highest total amount of happiness in the community will be inadequate.[16] Such questions raise complex questions that are beyond the scope of this book. Although reproduction may be irresponsible due to overpopulation, this is not the source of the concerns that have led to proposals to require use of Norplant to prevent allegedly irresponsible reproduction in the United States.

The Parameters Applied

With this account of factors relevant to judgments of undesirable or irresponsible reproduction, one can assess the reproductive decisions of particular individuals. The judgment in any given case will reflect a balancing of the reproductive interests at stake, the ease or burdens of avoiding reproduction, and the effects on others. A careful assessment of these factors will often be difficult because of factual uncertainties and normative imponderables about the weight to be assigned to each factor. Yet this is the task that anyone who fairly attempts to judge reproductive responsibility must undertake.

SOCIAL POLICY ISSUES

The question of social policy to discourage irresponsible or undesirable reproduction presents a different set of issues. Even if we agree that reproduction in certain cases is undesirable or irresponsible, the question remains
what to do about it. Should reproduction always be left to the individuals
involved, or are governmental actions to discourage or prevent irresponsible
reproduction appropriate?

Excluding the government as an actor/participant in the dialogue about
reproductive responsibility is not justified. The state has responsibilities to
protect citizens and to facilitate exercise of their rights. Because reproduction
so directly affects others, and the state is often called upon to pay the costs of
reproduction, there is a legitimate role for the state to speak on these matters.

More controversial, however, are the steps that the state may take to implement its views of reproductive responsibility. These range from providing
subsidies, information, education, and access to the use of positive incentives,
penalties, and seizures. An important distinction is between governmental
programs that support or encourage voluntary choice and those that are
more coercive. Programs that inform, educate, assist, and subsidize will be
more easily accepted than more coercive actions. However, voluntarism may
have dangers, even in purportedly benign government programs. Information can be delivered in settings or in styles that might be perceived as threatening. The very fact that the government is involved constitutes a judgment
about the undesirability of conduct and may offend some persons. Charges
of genocide or discrimination may arise because a voluntary program appears
targeted to a particular ethnic or minority group. In general, however, programs designed to inform women or to provide access to Norplant are desirable and acceptable. This is true even if only particular groups are targeted,
such as welfare mothers, teenagers, women with AIDS, or those convicted of
child abuse.

More controversial governmental actions involve programs that offer
incentives or condition program benefits in return for certain reproductive
choices. In general, incentive programs are designed to preserve autonomy,
even though they attempt to influence how the autonomy in question is exercised. However, offering rewards to use Norplant or conditioning the receipt
of welfare benefits on its use may be perceived as burdening or coercing individual choice, especially when the choice is presented to welfare mothers,
teenagers, and other vulnerable groups. As the discussion below will show,
however, the legality of such offers and conditions should be distinguished
from their wisdom as social policy. If the incentive offer or condition does
not deprive a person of what she or he is otherwise entitled to, it will usually
be legally permissible. However, one can question whether irresponsible

reproduction is so serious a problem that focusing on these groups is a sound answer to serious social problems.

More coercive measures, such as penalties for reproducing irresponsibly or refusing birth control, have a strong presumption against them. Prudential questions aside, there may be legal or constitutional barriers against such policies. The power of the state to coerce or force people not to reproduce turns on whether its actions violate a fundamental right, and if so, whether there is a compelling interest to justify it. If the state's action interferes with or limits coital reproduction by a married couple, it would ordinarily be found to infringe a fundamental right to procreate, and thus require strong justification.[17]

An unresolved question at this point is whether courts evaluating such a claim would assess the relative importance of the reproduction at issue to the individuals involved. If the parents would rear, mere offense at what they are doing or costs to the taxpayer probably would be insufficient to justify intruding on their right. However, if the parents would not rear, because of unfitness, past neglect, impecunity, or other factors, the courts in particular cases could find that the reproductive interest is so slight as to allow a lesser state interest to justify intrusion.[18] Of course, direct seizures to implant Norplant or to sterilize individuals would require a very strong justification because of the intrusion on bodily integrity alone.

Policies directed at reproduction by unmarried persons or minors might have a lesser constitutional hurdle to surmount. Because the Supreme Court has not held that persons have a right to reproduce outside marriage, a lesser justification may be needed to uphold such policies.[19] In that case, costs to the community might justify laws that could not be justified against married persons. However, unmarried persons would still have rights against bodily intrusion. Thus state policies that required physical burdens or sacrifice, such as forcible implants or sterilization, would have to meet the compelling interest standard. In those cases saving money or preventing insults to community sensibility may not be sufficient, even if the legally protected reproductive interest is less than in the case of married persons.

It appears that coercive sanctions will be rarely available to states seeking to minimize or discourage irresponsible reproduction. In most instances, the harms sought to be averted are costs to the community or to a sense of offense, because children themselves, who have no way to be born without the disadvantage in question, would not be harmed. These kinds of concerns will not justify coerced intrusions on the body, much less on strong reproductive interests. However, they could justify limitations on lesser reproductive interests, such as genetic reproduction *tout court*, when persons have no protected reproductive interest because of age and marital status. Other than the severely retarded, there may be no group that fits the criteria for coercive action. In the end, government policy will almost invariably have to rely on information, education, counseling, subsidies, and incentives so that the freedom of choice in matters of reproduction is protected.

FIVE PROBLEMATIC CASES

With the parameters of reproductive responsibility and the range of policy options as background, we are now ready to discuss five problematic situations for which Norplant has been urged. In each case, we must balance the benefits of the questionable reproduction to the person involved against the claims of irresponsibility. The availability of state policies to discourage undesirable reproduction will depend on the extent to which those policies that interfere with fundamental rights can be justified by harmful effects on offspring, taxpayers, and society. The discussion will show that in most instances the alleged irresponsibility will not support coercive policies, though it will permit voluntary measures that use education, information, subsidies, and incentives.

Contraception as a Condition of Probation

The question of compulsory use of Norplant has been most frequently raised in cases involving women convicted of child abuse or homicide of their children. In these cases, the sentencing judge is faced with a problem. Although a prison sentence is justified, the judge recognizes that the woman might be better rehabilitated in the community. However, she also knows that if the woman has more children, rehabilitation will be more difficult and that there is a real danger that abuse of a new child might occur. In these situations, some judges have offered women the option of probation on condition that they consent to Norplant or other contraception as an alternative to the prison sentence that would otherwise be imposed.[20]

The most widely publicized case of mandatory contraception, *People* v. *Johnson*, involved a twenty-seven-year-old woman sentenced to two to four years in prison for child abuse.[21] She had been convicted of severely beating two of her four children with a belt. Toward the end of her first year, the trial judge offered to release the woman on probation if she would agree to have Norplant implanted for three years of probation. The woman initially agreed. Later she sought to appeal this sentence on the ground that it was coerced, that it violated her fundamental right to procreate, and that it was medically contraindicated.

In a rehearing after the woman revoked her initial agreement to the sentence, the judge noted that she had shown herself incapable of caring for her children and stated: "It is in the defendant's best interest and certainly in any unconceived child's interest that she not have any more children until she is mentally and emotionally prepared to do so. The birth of additional children [before] she has successfully completed the court-ordered mental health counseling and parenting classes dooms both her and any subsequent children to repeat this vicious cycle."[22] He further noted: "Although the right to procreate is substantial and constitutionally protected, it is not absolute and can be limited in a proper case. The compelling state interest in the protection of the children supersedes this particular individual's right to procreate and does not interfere with her right of sexual expression."[23]

In considering the validity of contraception as a condition of probation, an important preliminary issue is whether the judge's sentencing power includes the power to impose contraception as a condition of probation. If the law does not authorize such a sentence, then such conditions are invalid.[24] If such probation conditions have been authorized, the question then is whether the authorized sentence is unconstitutional.

Ordinarily a state requirement or coercive offer that a woman take Norplant would require a compelling justification, for it intrudes into her body and limits her reproduction. A convicted child abuser could still have an interest in reproducing. She may wish to have and rear more children, precisely because of guilt she feels for her past behavior. However, if she will lose custody of any child upon birth because of her past record as an abuser, her reproductive interest may be reduced. If custody will not automatically be removed, or if she will be permitted to have some limited contact with offspring, her reproductive interest increases in importance. Even if she has no rearing role, she may still get important satisfaction from having produced another child. Although the facts of individual cases will vary, convicted child abusers will often retain the reproductive interests that enjoy presumptive protected status.

If that is so, any coercive state efforts to prevent her from reproduction would have to meet the compelling interest test. In this case the asserted state interest—protection of future offspring who will be injured by future abuse—may not exist. If the woman retains custody of future children, she may have been rehabilitated and no longer be an abuser. Or social workers may more closely monitor her to prevent abuse from occurring.[25] Even if she does abuse future children, it is not clear that they will enjoy such a horrible life that they never should have been born at all, and thus are harmed by being born to an abusing mother.[26] In short, the need to protect future offspring does not appear to justify overriding her right to procreate, because the means of protection prevents the birth of the children whom one is trying to protect.

Nor could limitations on her reproduction be justified by the need to protect society and the community. Child abusers who reproduce will cost the community more money and services in monitoring, treatment, and other services. If children are born and later injured, many people will experience outrage at the mother's repetitive conduct. More demand on scarce foster parent resources will occur, at a time when those resources are severely strained. Costly medical and psychological treatment may be needed for the child.[27] In addition, people may lose confidence in a system that permits a woman who has severely beaten or murdered her children to produce more children. But these costs would ordinarily not support coercive sanctions that limit exercise of a fundamental right, and probably will not support coercive sanctions for failure to use Norplant.

However, the woman in question is a convicted child abuser and could be sent to prison. A condition of imprisonment is that men and women are ordinarily prevented from reproducing—from begetting and bearing children while in prison.[28] They have no constitutional right to conjugal visits, and no right to hand their sperm out for artificial insemination.[29] Since prisoners are ordinarily deprived of procreation during the term of imprisonment, could not the state place a person subject to imprisonment on probation with contraception, on the ground that the greater power to imprison implies the lesser power to impose contraception?

If the greater power to imprison does not imply the lesser power to impose contraception, then interfering in reproduction in this way will be a punishment that must satisfy Eighth Amendment standards against cruel and unusual punishment.[30] This provision bars punishments that are excessive or barbarous.[31] Because temporary loss of reproduction via Norplant does not appear to be excessive for the crime of abusing children, the question will turn on whether imposition of Norplant is inherently cruel or barbarous. Here the method is a choice—probation with Norplant or prison—that is akin to the choices presented defendants deciding whether to plead guilty, but one that focuses on their body and its functions. It causes them to accept a minor surgical intervention into their body, some side effects of varying intensity, and the loss of procreative ability for a period of time.

One cannot predict with certainty how courts would rule on a claim that such a punishment violates the Eighth Amendment. Bodily and reproductive intrusions are clearly disfavored, yet Norplant is not so highly intrusive or shocking, given the restrictions that usually occur with imprisonment, that offering the persons a choice that will temporarily limit their reproductive ability for a period of time as punishment for crime would necessarily be found to be unconstitutional. However, the question is a close one, and cannot be decided without more particular facts. Because the restriction is rationally related to rehabilitation and to preventing the very crimes being punished, the ultimate decision will hinge on perceptions of the need for the state to mandate reproductive restrictions.[32]

In sum, the validity of compulsory contraception for convicted child abusers depends on whether the limitation of procreation must be independently justified or is a rational, nonbarbarous punishment for serious crime. If the former, the state justifications are insufficient. Neither the interest in protecting unborn offspring from harm nor in saving social welfare resources justifies limiting procreation. Only if persons subject to imprisonment but placed on probation have fewer procreative rights would such a condition of probation be acceptable. Even then, one can question whether a technological solution to the problem should be sought

Compulsory Contraception to Prevent Congenital Disease

The case for compulsory contraception to prevent the birth of offspring with congenital disease is also hard to sustain. One target of such efforts would be couples who are at risk for having children with genetic handicaps and insist on reproducing. Ordinarily, they would have a one in two or one in four chance of having a child with the defect in question. Depending on the disease, the child could die early or have a lifetime of chronic illness and medical care. However, this is a relatively small group, whose overall numbers do not justify such an intrusive intervention.

A more likely target would be women who are HIV positive. They have a 25 to 35 percent chance of passing HIV to offspring.[33] If they do, the child may die early or be maintained at high cost for many years. Even if children are not infected, the parents still are at risk of dying and leaving their children parentless. Indeed, the problem of children who are parentless due to AIDS is a growing social problem, with eighty thousand such children predicted by the year 2000.[34]

In either case, however, the compulsory use of Norplant cannot be justified. To begin with, members of both groups have substantial interests in reproduction. The couple that has had a handicapped child may hope for a healthy child, but be willing to raise and care for another child with the handicap in question. Moreover, the risk of a child with handicap will ordinarily be one in four. Preventing the birth of the handicapped child would also prevent the greater likelihood that offspring will not have the disease in question. Avoiding the birth of an affected child may also require prenatal testing and abortion, to which the parents are opposed.

Similarly, women with HIV may still find procreation immensely meaningful, both because it is a prime source of meaning and validation in their social-cultural context, and because it meets their need for continuity after the death looming over them. As Nancy Dubler and Carol Levine note, in the view of these women, "having babies . . . may be the most reasonable and available choice, a natural outcome of all the forces in their lives, in which avenues for self-definition and expression other than mothering are largely absent."[35] Even if particular individuals will not rear affected offspring or will not rear for long, core interests of reproduction are at stake for both groups.

The case for claiming that their reproduction is irresponsible must therefore rest on the burdens it imposes on offspring and society. The burden commonly cited is that they are knowingly having or risking having children who are born with serious genetic or infectious disease. The children who are born with HIV may face an early death, or a period of health and normal growth until symptoms arise. They will then face repeated hospitalizations and an early death. If they do not themselves have HIV, they are likely to be born into circumstances in which their parents will soon die, and may end up orphaned in foster care or other disadvantageous circumstances.

Similarly, children born with serious genetic handicaps may face repeated surgeries and hospitalizations, significant mortality and morbidity, social stigma, and the suffering that arises from their mental and physical limitations. While their parents may rear them, some of them will be placed in poorly funded state institutions or group homes.

Yet in both cases one cannot say that these children have been harmed by being born, because they have no way to be born free of the congenital diseases or social circumstances that are so disadvantageous.* Unlike Parfit's case of the risk of a withered arm, the persons procreating here cannot produce a healthy child by postponing conception. All their offspring are at risk for the conditions of concern. Few of those conditions would make the child's life so horrible that its interests would have been best served by never being born.[36] Thus it is unlikely that the goal of preventing harm to offspring by preventing them from being born would justify a coercive contraceptive policy toward their parents.

Nor will the significant costs that they may impose on the public treasury and charity. In some instances the parents will not impose rearing costs on others, because they will bear the cost themselves, either directly or through insurance. However, in most cases the persons reproducing with this risk will end up requiring large subsidies from the state for medical care and other services for their children. If the children's diseases are serious enough, as AIDS and some genetic conditions will be, they will be demanding subsidies greater than those ordinarily provided to persons who reproduce. In addition, there may be other social costs, from the degradation of many orphans in impoverished settings to the offense felt at the actions of persons who do not attempt to avoid reproduction when the risks of an abnormal birth are great.

---

*This case is thus to be contrasted with those in which the procreator could make offspring healthy and whole but chooses, out of perverse malice or narcissism, to make the child worse than she need be.

None of these costs, however, is sufficient to justify directly imposing Norplant or other contraception on women at risk for offspring with these conditions. Because these women's reproductive interest is generally a strong one, only very compelling needs would justify overriding their fundamental right to procreate. Saving money and preventing offense ordinarily would not rise to the required level. However, a closer analysis of their reproductive interest could on occasion yield a different conclusion. For example, if they lack the capacity or interest in rearing, will institutionalize the child at birth, or face a short life span due to their own illness, required contraception would not violate as significant a reproductive interest than if they intended to rear for long periods.[37] If the bodily intrusion associated with compulsory contraception is relatively minor, it may be that compelled contraception in rare cases could be justified, though such policies would be highly controversial.

At present, however, this discussion is largely hypothetical, because no one has proposed that HIV women or those at genetic risk should be penalized for reproduction or failure to accept Norplant. These remedies seem so extreme because of the seriousness of the intrusion and the lack of sufficient justification for it. They would also be open to charges of racism and discrimination against those who are less than able-bodied.

The more immediate policy question concerns the lengths to which the state may go to persuade these groups voluntarily to avoid reproduction. In both cases the state could support or conduct programs to make sure that persons at risk are aware of the potential consequences of their reproductive behavior, and that contraception and abortion to avert reproduction is available. Included in such information would be facts concerning prenatal or other tests to inform them of their risk status or the status of a fetus.[38]

Much more controversial is whether the state or private parties should engage in directive counseling with prospective parents, urging that they not reproduce because of the risks of affected offspring and the other problems thereby caused. Health-care providers, counselors, and ethicists are currently split over whether directed counseling can be justified in these cases.[39] This debate is largely prudential rather than ethical. As long as directed counseling leaves the woman free to make her own choice, it would not violate her autonomy. Indeed, it may be useful to make her aware of the serious consequences of her actions. However, any mandatory or directive program will be controversial, whatever its ethical or policy justification, because of the perception that it is singling out women who are already stigmatized, and because of the risk that it denigrates the worth of the children whose birth it is trying to prevent.

Welfare Issues

Compulsory contraception through Norplant has also emerged as an issue of welfare policy. Shortly after the FDA approved Norplant, legislators in Kansas, Oklahoma, and Louisiana introduced bills offering financial rewards to welfare mothers who agreed to Norplant implants. The rewards ranged from $100 in Louisiana to $500 in Kansas, with Kansas also offering a yearly maintenance fee of $50. Welfare would also pay the costs of the Norplant. Similar proposals are likely in other states.

Although none of these proposals has passed, the appeal of Norplant as a way to control costly reproduction by poor women is obvious. A common perception is that high welfare costs are the result of poor women having children to cash in on welfare benefits. The editorial board of the *Philadelphia Inquirer* fell prey to this myth when in an editorial entitled "Norplant and the Underclass" it praised Norplant as an answer to problems of welfare associated with a high minority birth rate (when the black community protested, the newspaper quickly apologized).[40] A common sentiment is that poor women are acting irresponsibly when they have children that the taxpayers will have to support. If so, the idea of encouraging them to contracept makes sense.

But is reproduction when one will require public assistance to support offspring irresponsible? A person who intends to rear such offspring, as most welfare mothers do, will have a significant reproductive interest at stake. However, to realize their reproductive goal they will be demanding that the community pay rearing costs that those who reproduce are usually responsible for. Is it unreasonable to ask the community to do so? A good argument can be made that it is, particularly if one has already reproduced and could do so at some point in the future. Only if there are no reproductive alternatives for that person, or avoidance is not reasonably possible, might that action be reasonable.

Yet even if a mild judgment of irresponsibility can be lodged, it would not follow that compulsory contraceptive measures are justified. Indeed, as a legal matter, the state probably could not penalize persons for giving birth to children who need welfare, even if moral culpability could be shown. The injury to the community's resources and norms of proper reproduction is simply insufficient to justify coercive intrusion on a fundamental right. Nor have such proposals been seriously made.

Instead, the focus of policy has been on proposals to encourage women on welfare to use Norplant voluntarily. While no one objects to informing welfare mothers of the Norplant option and providing it free of charge, proposals to pay women to have the implant, or to require it as a condition of receiving welfare, are more controversial. Neither idea unconstitutionally infringes procreative liberty. However, one may question whether the costs of excessive births by welfare mothers are such a serious problem that direct state intervention into reproductive decisions is advisable. . . .

Compulsory Contraception for the Retarded

Controlling the reproduction of mentally retarded persons has a checkered history in the United States. In the early twentieth century the American Eugenics Society actively lobbied to sterilize "mental defectives" and "feeble-minded persons" because of a perceived threat to the gene pool and social welfare. The result was compulsory sterilization laws passed in over thirty states, which the United States Supreme Court upheld in 1927 in *Buck* v. *Bell*.[41] With this imprimatur, more than sixty thousand persons were sterilized over the next thirty years.

In the 1960s a strong reaction to compulsory eugenic sterilization occurred, impelled by awareness of the excesses of Nazi eugenic practices and the scientific unsoundness of the hereditary assumptions underlying these laws. It also became clear that many persons had been sterilized who were neither mentally ill nor retarded, including Carrie Buck, the original plaintiff in *Buck* v. *Bell*.[42] Although that case has never been reversed, compulsory sterilization is now generally viewed as a gross violation of human rights and no longer performed for eugenic reasons.

In the mid-1970s, however, it became clear that there were some circumstances in which sterilization was justified to protect the retarded from pregnancy rather than to serve eugenics or save money. For example, retarded women in state institutions or group homes are vulnerable to sexual exploitation or rape. Pregnancy, especially in women who lack comprehension, poses serious health risks. Delivery by cesarean section may be necessary. Often parents restrict participation in group homes and other opportunities to avoid having their retarded daughters risk pregnancy.

Faced with parents seeking to have retarded daughters sterilized, state courts began authorizing such procedures. Since few states still had statutes authorizing such sterilizations, the main issue before the courts was whether a probate court's inherent *parens patriae* power over incompetent patients authorized them to order sterilization in the absence of statutory authority when it seemed in the incompetent ward's interest.[43] While some courts preferred to wait for legislative authorization, influential state supreme courts, including those of New Jersey, Massachusetts, and Washington, devised tests that allowed sterilization when it could be shown to benefit the incompetent ward.[44]

Norplant presents an attractive alternative in situations in which sterilization would otherwise be appropriate. Because there is usually no serious reproductive interest at stake, the main question is whether implantation of Norplant will cause harm. If sterilization is justified, a fortiori Norplant should be used, because it is less intrusive and reversible. Indeed, it would seem preferable to sterilization. Thus parents or guardians who petition for sterilization should show that less restrictive contraceptive measures such as Norplant are contraindicated or not available.

In fact, it may be acceptable for parents or caretakers who are concerned about the risk of pregnancy to have Norplant routinely implanted in mentally retarded and institutionalized women. Because surgical insertion is required, the consent of parents or guardian is necessary, though the judicial review required for sterilization should not be. Norplant may thus provide a technological solution to the risk of pregnancy faced by mentally retarded women.

Controlling reproduction in severely retarded women with Norplant limits procreation without limiting procreative choice. For the notion of reproductive choice is no more meaningful for severely retarded women than is electoral choice. If they are so mentally impaired that the concept of reproduction and parenthood has no meaning, then limiting their reproduction does not infringe their procreative liberty. The concept of procreative choice simply does not apply to them.[45] If mistakes are made about reproductive interest, the Norplant can simply be removed.

Of course, the retarded do have rights of bodily integrity and rights to be treated with respect. They should not be burdened merely to serve the needs of others. Limiting their reproduction, however, does not harm them, and actually serves their interests by protecting them from the physical risks of pregnancy. If done with a minimal intrusion on their body, as occurs with Norplant, it should be socially acceptable as well. However, careful monitoring of how Norplant is used with this population, including indications, side effects, and length of use, is needed before implantation routinely occurs. With these protections, the use of Norplant with the retarded at the request of parents and guardians may be acceptable.

Norplant and Adolescents

Norplant has also been suggested as an answer to teenage pregnancy. If informed consent is obtained, the use of Norplant poses no issues beyond those raised by teenage contraceptive use generally. The chief issue here is whether teenagers can obtain contraceptives without parental consent or notification. If state law permits adolescent females to obtain medically prescribed contraceptives, then they should be able to obtain Norplant as well.

Also, there should be no barrier to parents or guardians providing Norplant to adolescent girls who desire it. The discretionary power of parents to rear their children entitles them to obtain medical care that is in their child's interests. Postponing pregnancy until a more mature time serves the interests of child and parent. While parents should not be able to have doctors insert Norplant against a teenager's wishes, there should be no objection if the child agrees with the parent's desire for Norplant.

Programs that offer Norplant in school clinics are more controversial, however, because the state appears to be taking a more active role in controlling adolescent reproduction. The Baltimore school system, which now provides Norplant along with other contraceptives, has been careful to preserve choice in offering Norplant to a teenage population with an exceedingly high pregnancy rate.[46] The young women are informed of the risks and benefits of the implant, and are not pressured in any way to accept it. Parents are notified if the teenager consents to such notification. However, some people are troubled by the idea of city authorities trying to influence female reproduction, and doubt whether such programs are truly noncoercive.

A more hypothetical question is whether the state could require that teenage girls have an antifertility vaccine or Norplant implanted shortly after puberty, after one illegitimate birth, or some other risk marker in order to make pregnancy a matter of deliberate choice.[47] This policy would prevent teenage pregnancy, but would not prevent girls who wish to have children from regaining fertility by having the implants removed or the vaccine rendered inactive.

Given the very high rates of unintended teenage pregnancy, such a policy would no doubt have many supporters. It would not necessarily violate the procreative liberty of its targets, for it only temporarily postpones pregnancy and is aimed at unmarried adolescents who do not have the same legal right to conceive and reproduce that adults do. If the intrusion is viewed as minor, they will have ample time to have and rear children when they decide to do so.[48] Such a policy would prevent many illegitimate births and the cycle of dropping out of high school, poor employment opportunities, and welfare that adolescent pregnancy often brings. Also, it would prevent the birth of children who themselves are often doomed to repeat that cycle, or who grow up without male authority figures in their life. Although such children are not wronged by being born, society may still prefer that children be born with more advantages.

Although the purpose is commendable and teenagers may lack a right to reproduce, a policy of compulsory contraception will face high constitutional barriers. Teenagers do have a strong interest in bodily integrity. The insertion of the device may be viewed as minor, but the potential side effects are serious enough—many women cannot tolerate Norplant—to make the bodily intrusion substantial. Overriding this interest may be difficult to justify, despite the worthiness of the goal.

A further problem would arise in identifying the target of such an intrusive policy. If directed at all female adolescents, it would be grossly overbroad, intruding upon the many to prevent pregnancy by a few.[49] If targeted to subgroups that have high rates of pregnancy, it risks actual or perceived discrimination on racial or ethnic grounds. In its most defensible form, it would apply only to teenagers who already had a teenage pregnancy and refused to use contraception. Yet even there the intrusiveness of forcing a contraceptive implant on an unwilling subject would be a difficult barrier to overcome, particularly if parents objected.

In short, such an intrusive policy of social engineering sounds too Orwellian to be acceptable, even if the state possessed the raw constitutional power to implement it. As with most instances of allegedly irresponsible reproduction, it is far preferable to rely on education and choice rather than on mandatory measures. Indeed, a fair attempt to encourage contraceptive use by adolescents would probably obviate the need for involuntary implantation.

CONCLUSION

Procreation is a basic right, but it is not an absolute right. Its protected status does not relieve individuals of the moral obligation to reproduce responsibly. When they do not, public pressure arises to use reversible technologies such as Norplant to limit their reproduction.

Unless voluntarily chosen, however, the use of Norplant or other contraceptives can rarely be justified as a solution to problems of allegedly irresponsible reproduction. Its most defensible application is with severely retarded females who are at risk of sexual exploitation or rape. In the other situations discussed, however, its intrusiveness and effect on procreation make it highly suspect. Child abusers, HIV women, welfare mothers, and teenagers have interests in procreation or bodily integrity that mandatory use of Norplant violates. Neither protection of future offspring nor conservation of public funds are compelling enough reasons to justify intrusions on such basic rights. In addition, there is the danger of discrimination or antipathy toward targeted groups.

This conclusion should not prevent the state from informing women of the Norplant option, subsidizing its provision, or even offering financial incentives to use it. If these alternatives are pursued, the need for compulsory contraception through Norplant further weakens. Forcible limitations on reproduction need a much stronger justification than these cases present.

NOTES

1. Norplant illustrates well the theme of autonomy and ambivalence that arises with new reproductive technologies. The ambivalence is strong because it involves the state in mandating a particular reproductive outcome and directly interfering with choice. Even if justified in particular circumstances, state involvement sets a dan-

gerous precedent that could lead to instances of forced contraception and other interventions that are less compelling.

2. State of Washington, 52nd Legislature, 1992 Regular Session, House Bill 2909.

3. Editorial, "Poverty and Norplant: Can Contraception Reduce the Underclass?" *Philadelphia Inquirer*, December 12, 1990. A vehement protest from black journalists and the black community led to an apology. "Apology: The Editorial on 'Norplant and Poverty' Was Misguided and Wrongheaded," *Philadelphia Inquirer*, December 23, 1990.

4. "Governor's Welfare Plan Pushes Free Birth Control," *New York Times*, January 17, 1993.

5. Tamar Lewin, "Baltimore School Clinics to Offer Birth Control by Surgical Implant," *New York Times*, December 4, 1992.

6. Matthew Rees, "Shot in the Arm," *New Republic*, December 9, 1991.

7. There is more willingness to impose limitations on noncoital reproduction, usually because the connection with the freedom to procreate is not recognized.

8. Phillip Reilly, *The Surgical Solution* (Baltimore: Johns Hopkins University Press, 1991).

9. *Relf v. Weinberger*, 386 F. Sup. 1384 (D.C. Dist. Ct. 1974). As a result of the *Relf* litigation, informed consent and a thirty-day waiting period are now required for sterilization in federally funded programs. Note, "Coerced Sterilization under Federally Funded Family Planning Programs," *New England Law Review* 11 (1976): 589–614. See also Reilly, *The Surgical Solution*, pp. 150–52.

10. One could also talk about the reproductive responsibility of society—its obligation to make sure that safe and healthy means of reproduction or its avoidance are available, including resources that children brought into the world need to have a healthy and productive life.

11. Here we must distinguish between prenatal harm that is unavoidable with their birth and prenatal or postnatal harm that is avoidable but which in the circumstances may not be avoided.

12. See *Smith v. Cote*, 128 N.H. 231, 513 A. 2d 341 (1986); *Becker v. Schwartz*, 46 N.Y. 2d 401, 386 N.E. 2d 807, 413 N.Y.S. 2d 895 (1978); *Nelson v. Krusen*, 678 S.W. 2d 918 (Tex. 1984).

13. Of course, there is no guarantee that the remedial action that will mitigate the harm of wrongful life will occur.

14. Derek Parfit, "On Doing the Best for Our Children," in *Ethics and Population*, ed. Michael D. Bayles (Cambridge, Mass.: Schenkman, 1976).

15. In this example, unlike most of the situations discussed here, the woman has an alternative way to have a healthy child. She can simply wait a month.

16. Derek Parfit, *Reason and Persons* (New York: Oxford University Press, 1984); David Heyd, *Genethics: The Moral Issues in the Creation of People* (Berkeley and Los Angeles: University of California Press, 1992).

17. Although not enumerated in the text of the Constitution, such a belief doubtlessly has constitutional status. Reproduction is so basic to human life and meaning that deprivation without consent would be widely acknowledged as a violation of a fundamental liberty. Indeed, the Supreme Court has acknowledged the existence of such a right in dicta in several cases.

18. Whether it will be determinative that they have reproduced already, or could reproduce in the future in more felicitous circumstances, is unclear.

19. Note that the issue is whether unmarried persons have the right to engage in coitus or have access to noncoital means of reproduction, such as in vitro fertilization. Once conception occurs, they clearly have a right to go to term, and once birth occurs, to rear offspring. But it does not follow that they have a constitutional right to conceive in the first place, even though they cannot be denied the right to gestate a formed fetus or rear a born child.

20. Because Norplant is easily monitored and requires a one-time intervention, it is preferable to a general condition to use birth control or to avoid pregnancy.

21. Tamar Lewin, "Implanted Birth Control Device Renews Debate over Forced Contraception," *New York Times*, January 10, 1991.

22. Michael Lev, "Judge Firm on Forced Contraception," *New York Times*, January 11, 1991.

23. Ibid. See Stacey Arthur, "The Norplant Prescription: Birth Control, Woman Control, Or Crime Control," *UCLA Law Review* 40 (1993): 1.

24. At least one court has struck down such a condition on this ground. See ibid.

25. A major limitation with this point, however, is that most child welfare agencies are so overworked and underfunded that they may not be a reliable monitor of the offender's behavior with future children. Also, adequate foster care to protect the child may not be available. The less restrictive alternative of monitoring and removal to foster care may be more a theoretical than real protection of future children from convicted child abusers.

26. The claim that contraception is justified to protect unborn offspring has cogency only if the offspring would have a life so burdened with suffering that its life, from its own perspective, would not be worth living. But even serious child abuse does not appear to cause a life of such unremitting suffering that its life is wrongful, e.g., that the child would have preferred no life at all and would commit suicide at the first available opportunity. For example, from the perspective of the child, even a life in which one has been abused by parents would seem preferable to no life at all.

27. For example, offspring of cocaine-addicted women cost the medical care system many times what other babies do.

28. Of course, if the woman is pregnant when she enters prison or manages to get pregnant while there, she cannot be forced to have or prevented from having an abortion.

29. *Goodwin* v. *Turner*, 908 F. 2d 1395 (8th Cir. 1990).

30. It may be that loss of the greater power to imprison and prevent reproduction while in prison is based on an essential feature of prison administration, and is not an inherent or necessary part of punishment.

31. *Gregg* v. *Georgia*, 428 U.S. 153 (1976); *Rummel* v. *Estelle*, 445 U.S. 263 (1980).

32. If Norplant as a condition of probation surmounted previous hurdles, it would still face equal protection problems. All of the mandatory contraception crises to date have involved women, even though men also are convicted of child abuse. Perhaps this is because women are more likely to care for children, and thus are more likely to be in a position to repeat their abusive behavior. But men sentenced to prison for child abuse could claim a violation of equal protection if they are not given the

same option of temporary contraception that women are. This challenge would be especially powerful if both a husband and wife were convicted of child abuse, and the woman were offered the option of Norplant and the husband sent to prison.

33. John Arras, "AIDS and Reproductive Decisions: Having Children in Fear and Trembling," *Milbank Quarterly* 68 (1990): 353, 367.

34. David Michaels and Carol Levine, "Estimates of the Number of Motherless Youth Orphaned by AIDS in the United States," *Journal of the American Medical Association* 268, no. 24 (1992): 3456. The authors argue that ignoring this problem "invites a social catastrophe of the greatest magnitude" because the "death of a parent . . . is one of the most traumatic experiences any child can suffer. When that death is accompanied by stigma and isolation and is followed by instability and insecurity, as it is in AIDS, the potential for trouble, both immediately and in the future, is magnified." Ibid., p. 3460.

35. C. Levine and N. Dubler, "Uncertain Risks and Bitter Realities: The Reproductive Choices of HIV-Infected Women," *Milbank Quarterly* 68 (1990): 321, 323. For women trapped in poverty, illness, crime, and other humiliations, "[a] baby is the chance to have something concrete to love, or, as important, to be loved by. It is proof of fertility and the visible sign of having been loved or at least touched by another." Ibid., p. 334. The importance of reproducing is even greater if the woman will die of her disease, because of her need to "leave someone behind for a mother or husband to care for in the future . . . the link to immortality that genealogy presents." Ibid., p. 335.

36. The strongest case for such a claim might be Tay-Sachs disease, but that disease would also present a strong case for nontreatment early in the onset of the disease, so that any harm to the child from mere existence could be mitigated.

37. Such persons may still have a substantial interest in reproducing. For example, HIV women who will die in a short time may still find great meaning in having a child whom they will not rear for long. See Levine and Dubler, "Uncertain Risks."

38. While the state could require that providers inform at-risk persons of the availability of such tests, it is less clear whether the state could require that such testing occur. It may be that minimally intrusive tests that leave the person free to act on the results would not interfere with procreative choice, and would serve a useful function. By contrast, requiring that known carriers of genetic disease use birth control or that they abort affected fetuses would clearly interfere with procreative liberty.

[Ed. Note: Robertson says in an earlier chapter that "[m]andatory carrier or prenatal tests would, however, interfere with privacy or liberty rights not to know certain information. Any mandatory test more invasive than a simple blood test is also likely to violate rights of bodily integrity. . . . It is unlikely to decrease appreciably the incidence of handicapped births beyond voluntary measures and will incur a heavy cost in personal liberty."]

39. Arras, "AIDS and Reproductive Decisions," 353.

40. "Apology," *Philadelphia Inquirer*, December 23, 1990.

41. *Buck v. Bell*, 274 U.S. 200 (1927).

42. Paul A. Lombardo, "Three Generations, No Imbeciles: New Light on *Buck v. Bell*," *New York University Law Review* 60 (1985): 30, is an insightful and intriguing historical analysis of the deficiencies in the factual basis of that decision.

43. *In re Guardianship of Eberhardy*, 102 Wis. 2d 539, 307 N.W. 2d 881(1981).

44. See, e.g., *In re Grady*, 85 N.J. 235, 426 A. 2d 467 (1981); *In re Moe*, 385 Mass. 555, 432 N.E. 2d 712 (1982); *In re Guardianship of Hayes*, 93 Wash. 2d 228, 608 P. 2d 635 (1980).

45. This argument is developed in John A. Robertson, "Procreative Liberty and the Control of Conception, Pregnancy and Childbirth," *Virginia Law Review* 69 (1983): 405, 411–13.

46. Tamar Lewin, "Baltimore School Clinics to Offer Birth Control by Surgical Implant," *New York Times*, December 4, 1992.

47. An antifertility vaccine has not yet been developed, though it is an important area of future research. To be acceptable, it would also have to have a limited duration of efficacy and be reversible when one wished to restore fertility. See Carl Dejerassi, "The Bitter Pill," *Science* 245 (1989): 356, 359.

48. One may disagree with this assessment, particularly because of the side effects that many young women would experience.

49. Even though there is a high rate of teenage pregnancy, only a very small percentage of female adolescents become pregnant.

THE MYTHOLOGY
OF FAMILY PLANNERS

Edgar R. Chasteen

It is imperative that we give all our citizens, regardless of income, the right
to plan the size of their families. . . . However, let me make it perfectly clear
that these services are offered on a strictly voluntary basis. No one must
ever be forced to practice birth control.

—Senate Bill 2108, May 8, 1969

No couple should have to produce more children than they want;
family planning is a basic human right. Fifty years ago these notions
of Margaret Sanger's were revolutionary. Prior to that time, parents had little
choice but to accept the unplanned and sometimes unwelcome consequences
of their sexual drives. As a nurse in a Brooklyn slum, Sanger witnessed the
daily misery of women frequently but unwillingly pregnant. She listened to
their pleas for help, and watched them die because it was not given. The
Comstock Laws and the medical profession conspired, the first by intent, the
second by indifference, to deny women the control of their own fertility.

Because she attempted to emancipate women from the bondage of unwanted pregnancies, Margaret Sanger invoked the wrath of government,
church, and school. Her willingness to accept imprisonment and public disapproval in order to make contraceptives available to women who needed
them shall long stand as an example of personal courage and social relevance.

The origin of all family planning agencies in this country today may be

Reprinted from *The Case for Compulsory Birth Control*, by Edgar R. Chasteen (Englewood Cliffs,
N.J.: Prentice-Hall, 1971).

traced, directly or indirectly, to the philosophy and programs of Margaret Sanger. However, times change, and Margaret Sanger's philosophy is today not revolutionary, but reactionary. Family planning has become such a conventional idea, so pursued by powerful and respectable organizations, that we have been blinded to its inadequacy. The proliferation of people since World War II has distorted Margaret Sanger's compassion for individuals into a conspiracy against humanity. So preoccupied have family planners been with individual pregnancies, their prevention and spacing, that they have had too little time or thought for the ominous and astronomical increase in U.S. and world population.

In 1883, the year of Margaret Sanger's birth, world population stood at 1.4 billion and the U.S. population at just over 50 million. At her death in 1966, world population had reached 3.4 billion and that of the United States exceeded 195 million. Family planners usually claim a high degree of success for their programs, but that success is usually measured in terms of pills distributed, patients seen, and speeches made. I would suggest, however, that any program having to do with the prevention of pregnancy is less than successful when measured against the above statistics. Personally, I will count my efforts at teaching, program design, and political pressure as a total failure if world population growth is not completely stopped during my lifetime.

The population of the world, now totaling 3.6 billion, is rocketing toward its rendezvous with disaster aboard the good ship "family planning." If its trajectory and velocity are to be altered, we must quickly reverse our uncritical acceptance of "parental rights" and exert the full force of reason.

As our waters become undrinkable, our air poisoned, our resources depleted, our countryside littered, our cities ugly and ungovernable, we are beginning to realize that we can no longer tolerate such massive numbers of people. During Margaret Sanger's lifetime, world population increased more than 240 percent, and U.S. numbers almost quadrupled. Family planners then and now helped resolve individual problems associated with too many children, but they were and are irrelevant to societal problems associated with too many people. In fact, family planners aggravate society's problems by opposing new organizations and ideas designed for population control, such as compulsory birth control and zero population growth. A letter written in 1969 by a national leader of a family planning program to agency personnel across the country accuses those working for zero population growth of "zealotry, hysteria, and paranoia." The letter ends with the warning: "With friends like these, we don't need enemies."

In 1934 Margaret Sanger said, "There can be no justification for violating the right of every married woman to decide when and how often she shall undertake the physical and far-reaching responsibilities of motherhood."[1] In the 1930s these words expressed an emerging viewpoint, one that recognized the possibilities of a rapidly developing contraceptive technology. These same words today represent an established philosophy and millions of dollars in programs. Rather than attacking a problem as Margaret Sanger did, family planners now use her own words to defend a program, to justify their inability or their unwillingness to anticipate new contraceptive developments and the changes in philosophy and program that must accompany them.

The philosophy of family planners is like the insecticide DDT. Twenty-five years ago, both were important breakthroughs, promising a better and safer life for all. Now both have turned on us, threatening to destroy what they helped to create.

The usual reaction of society when it recognizes the existence of a problem is to pass a law restricting the behavior that produces the problem. When American society some fifty to one hundred years ago sought to attack illiteracy and disease, laws were passed requiring school attendance and immunization. Economic insecurity and housing inadequacy were alleviated with social security legislation and building and zoning regulations. For half a century, family planners have insisted that parents have the right to the number of children they desire; it is now, therefore, difficult, if not impossible, for them to consider the limitation of family size by law.

U.S. Representative Morris Udall of Arizona wrote a generally excellent article on population for the December 1969 *Reader's Digest*. Titled "Standing Room Only on Spaceship Earth," the article argued for a halt to U.S. population growth. After endorsing President Nixon's 1969 proposal for a Commission on Population Growth and the American Future and suggesting that the "Congress and the President declare it the goal of the United States to encourage, by decent, humane, and voluntary means, a stabilized U.S. population," Representative Udall added, "But no government will or should ever undertake to tell people when to have, or not to have, children. The solution, if there is one, must come from individuals changing certain basic attitudes."[2]

I suggest that this reluctance even to examine the merits and precedents for legislative population control arises from the historical commitment of organizations concerned with population problems to parental freedom of choice. Margaret Sanger, matriarch of the family planning movement, believed that every child should be wanted, and so dedicated her considerable energies and talents to ensuring that every couple could, through application of efficient contraceptive technology, give birth to exactly the number of children they desired.

In 1920—even as late as 1960—this desire to free married couples from physiological accidents was part and parcel of a liberal humanitarianism that sought to deliver the individual from the capriciousness of politics, religion, and his own biology. Events of the past ten or fifteen years, however, have rendered this initially liberal doctrine conservative, if not reactionary.

It is untenable to argue that human fertility—a condition fraught with potential for either societal destruction or deliverance—should be governed only by private interest. Since World War II, world society has been engulfed by political and racial turmoil. Automation has assumed the physical tasks for which men were once needed, and cybernation promises to appropriate much of the mental. Ignorance and poverty have erased the minds and crippled the bodies of increasing millions as world population has mushroomed. Unless the births that occur to the hundreds of millions of world families are governed by considerations beyond the immediate and the personal, we shall plunge ever deeper into the jungle of political ineffectualness and racial madness from which only a stable and manageable population size will permit our extrication.

We should have learned by now that a complex and intricate social system composed of multifarious racial, religious, and cultural groups cannot maintain itself except by law. The history of labor relations and civil rights offers graphic proof that good intentions, private motivations, and emotional rhetoric all eventually give way to Taft-Hartley laws, Supreme Court decisions, and civil rights acts. In commenting upon current population problems, Colorado State Representative Richard Lamm says, "Like other new social problems, they probably will have to be solved by law. The development of law, strong enough to be enforced, wise enough to be acceptable, will be the challenge of the new generation of lawyers and law makers."[3]

To justify their opposition to law as a means of population control, family planning organizations have constructed an elaborate mythology to support their belief in the ability of their traditional programs to abort the population explosion. At least seven different but converging myths are contained in the mythology. The first three are explicitly stated in family planning literature; the last four are implicit assumptions that motivate family planning personnel and programs:

1. Parenthood is a right rather than a privilege.
2. The objective is to make every child a wanted child.
3. Individuals are free to choose whatever method of birth control they desire.
4. People see the relationship between their own behavior and the good of their society.
5. People always do what is good for them.
6. Education can solve the population problem.
7. Individual family planning equals national population control.

Mythology has peculiar powers over its believers. So convinced are they of the rightness of their cause that they are able to dismiss or reinterpret all objective evidence or personal experience that tends to cast doubt upon their faith. Rather than rethinking their assumptions, true believers redouble their efforts. The more the real world is unlike the mythology holds it to be, the greater its power to motivate its adherents. For they see the discrepancy between what is and what ought to be as their personal failure to keep the faith. Through periodic meetings at which they confess their shortcomings and rekindle their enthusiasm, believers perpetuate the mythology, and in the process they build in their own eventual demise. As with all true believers, so with family planners.

There was a time in man's quiet past when mythology was sufficient to sustain him, but no longer. The desperate present demands that we live by reason or we will not live. Humankind is now in the throes of an experiment in which man made himself the subject. The question to be decided is man's intelligence. Is he capable of solving, with his gadgets and his audacity, the many problems confronting him? Can he wrench from a reluctant Nature the secrets of longer life and greater happiness, or will his medical and industrial successes serve only to overburden and eventually destroy those political, economic, and social structures that keep him from anarchy? Man is intelligent, but he may be intelligent enough only to demonstrate his essential stupidity.

Let us see how the mythology of family planners fares when examined.

PARENTHOOD AS A PRIVILEGE

Myth Number One—Parenthood is a right rather than a privilege.

Americans are accustomed to think in terms of rights as being inalienable and unchanging. This is, however, a politically naive view, fashioned from an ignorance of history and an inability to understand societal needs. Rights must have a source; they must be created. There are no natural rights conferred upon man by virtue of his being human. Rights are derived from the law and the law is manmade. Rights are, in the last analysis, simply a recognition of that which is seen as necessary in a certain place at a given time. Laws are not sacred and immutable, but practical and dynamic. Their purpose is to enable us to live together at an acceptable level of decency and decorum. But if we are to understand the function of law as a regulator of human conduct, we must first briefly recall the history of civilization.

When men lived in small groups of two to ten families, there were few laws because few were needed. They all agreed on what was good and necessary behavior for their small group. In today's world of giant cities, with their divergent racial, religious, political, educational, and cultural groups, however, there is little common consent about proper rules of conduct. So law replaces group consensus as a regulator of behavior, its purpose being to reduce to an absolute minimum the frictions that would otherwise overheat the melting pot.

The history of civilization is the process of translating absolute rights into conditioned privileges. Roman fathers two thousand years ago had the power of life and death over their children.[4] If they so chose, they could leave a child on a hillside to be stolen by animals or killed by the elements. Likewise, Chinese fathers had the right to trade female children in exchange for some needed household item.[5] Up to the turn of the century, American parents had the right to put children to work rather than to send them to school.

But all this has now changed. Laws have been passed that severely restrict the rights of parents over their own children. Compulsory school attendance laws, health laws, delinquency laws, housing laws—all have translated parental *rights* into *privileges*. The next logical extension of this process is to make it a privilege to *have* children. Such laws would serve not only to defuse the population bomb, but also to protect firstborn children against the too prolific reproduction of their parents.

Following a group discussion of the need for control of population size, I received a phone call from a man who had been in attendance. "Could you come out to see my wife and me this afternoon?" he asked. Several hours later the three of us were seated in his living room. He began, "I was born into a miserably poor family of thirteen children. I was number eleven, and nobody ever had any time for me. I didn't get much education, and now I have to work ten hours a day, seven days a week, on an assembly line just to get by." Nodding at his wife, he said, "We couldn't hardly make it if she didn't work. Even with both of us working, we have to farm a little on the side to get by."

The conversation with this couple in their early thirties ended with the husband's emphatic statement: "We have three children, and that's all we're going to have."

Recent studies have shown that one of the most crucial factors associated with the economic status of a family is its size; the larger the family, the more likely it is to be poverty-stricken.[6] The chance of a child's acquiring an education, a healthy body, adequate shelter, and a decent job decline as the number of his brother and sisters increases. Approximately 70 percent of all those rejected by Selective Service for reasons of mental deficiency come from families of four or more children. Close to half of the rejectees (47 percent) are from families of six or more.[7]

In today's world, conditions demand that we recognize parenthood as a privilege extended to citizens by the society in which they live. If we continue to insist that parenthood is a right, we shall so inundate our world with people that the very concept of "rights" becomes unintelligible. As Garrett Hardin has written, "The only way we can preserve and nurture other and more precious freedoms is by relinquishing the freedom to breed, and that very soon."[8]

Some will object to defining parenthood as a privilege, contending that it smacks of Big Brother and George Orwell's *1984*. On the contrary, it would seem that such Orwellian conditions are inevitable *without* such a policy. It is the freedom "to be" rather than the freedom "to have" that is essential to human fulfillment. The more children a couple has, the less freedom they all have to realize the full limit of their potential "to be." If having is elevated in importance over being, those characteristics we cherish as most human—compassion, courage, conviction—inevitably lose out to our baser instincts: selfishness, ignorance, cowardice. This fact was poignantly captured by a sixteen-year-old drug addict in Chicago: "You're a fool if you believe what people try to tell you. Everybody is just out for himself. Nobody really cares about anybody else. The way things look for the future, most people would be better off if they never were born."[9]

Complete freedom is anarchy. If freedom may be thought of as the right to swing one's fist, then freedom stops where someone's nose begins. This crude but picturesque analogy serves to illustrate both the relative nature of freedom and its relationship to the population explosion. The more people there are, the less freedom there is.

The essence of man's present predicament was caught by Walter Lippmann, the dean of American political commentators, in an interview on his eightieth birthday:

> This is not the first time that human affairs have been chaotic and seemed ungovernable. But never before, I think, have the stakes been so high. I am not talking about, nor do I expect, a catastrophe like a nuclear war. What is really pressing upon us is that the number of people who need to be governed and are involved in governing threatens to exceed man's capacity to govern. This furious multiplication of the masses of mankind coincides with the evermore imminent threat that, because we are so ungoverned, we are polluting and destroying the environment in which the human race must live. The supreme question before mankind—to which I shall not live to know the answer—is how men will be able to make themselves willing and able to save themselves.[10]

THE WANTED CHILD

Myth Number Two—The objective is to make every child a wanted child.

The 1967 conference of the International Planned Parenthood Federation proclaimed "the individual's right to plan and limit the family's size . . . to be a basic human right."[11] In 1968, designated as Human Rights Year by the

United Nations General Assembly, thirty heads of state, representing two-fifths of the human race, presented a resolution to the UN urging that "the opportunity to practice family planning be recognized as a basic human right."[12] In May 1969, Sen. Joseph Tydings of Maryland introduced a bill in the U.S. Senate entitled "Family Planning: A Basic Human Right."[13] The ultimate purpose of the proclamation, the resolution, and the legislation is to ensure that all future children will be wanted rather than accidental. All three naively assume that once it is possible for parents to give birth only when they want to, all family and social problems related to population size will be solved. This assumption was made explicit by a 1969 Planned Parenthood brochure that maintains that Planned Parenthood is working "to reduce the number of unwanted pregnancies and *thus curb excessive population growth*" (emphasis added).[14] Alan Guttmacher, President of the Planned Parenthood Federation of America writes, "The underlying philosophy of Planned Parenthood is a very simple one, that is, only to have 'wanted children' born to parents who feel they can be responsible for their upbringing. If this goal is ever realized, it would eliminate many of the social ills which beset us."[15]

But it is entirely possible for every family in the United States and the world to give birth only to wanted children yet the population explosion continue or even accelerate. George N. Lindsay, 1968 board chairman of Planned Parenthood-World Population, asserted that "it is mainly the more fortunate Americans, confirmed contraceptive users, who are causing U.S. population growth by producing 'wanted babies' so abundantly."[16] A 1966 Gallup Poll indicated that 41 percent of all American women wanted four or more children,[17] a condition that, if realized, would make the baby boom of the forties seem like a lullaby.

Contrary to public opinion, it is not the poor who most aggravate the population problem; it is the middle class. Demographer Alice Day says,

> By far the major portion of our United States population growth comes from middle- and upper-middle-class families who account for 80 percent of the children born. If poor families, whose childbearing rate is higher, had had only the same number of children the middle and upper groups did, the total number of children would have been only 4 percent less.[18]

The Committee on Population of the National Academy of Sciences reports that "there seems little doubt that the rise in fertility in the United States is caused more by the preference for larger families among those who consciously choose the number of children they have than by the high fertility in the impoverished segments of the population."[19] In an article titled "A Limit to 'Wanted' Babies," *Medical World News* reported in December 1968 that "the main source of population overloading isn't the poor or near poor but the middle class and the rich who produce seven out of ten babies in the

U.S. each year." Richard Day, M.D., writing in the *American Journal of the Diseases of Childhood*, traces the population crisis to the fact that so many affluent families who practice birth control nevertheless give birth to three or more children.[20]

By insisting that contraceptives are to be used only to allow parents to have the number of children they want, family planners unnecessarily restrict their efforts to narrowing the gap between anticipated and actual fertility. Seldom do they ask why parents want a certain number of children. For some reason that desire is assumed, at least implicitly, to be immutable. Therefore few programs to change attitudes are undertaken, and family planners give almost all of their attention to improving contraceptive technology and distribution.[21]

Some future historian will look back on the twentieth century and write that in the year 19—, laws were passed in the United States that struck down forever that anachronistic practice to which we had too long adhered—the right to have as many children as we wanted. That "want" after all is socially created and may be socially redefined. No one is born wanting a certain number of children any more than one wants at birth to speak English or to eat with a fork. The desire to give birth to one, four, seven, or fifteen children is thus exposed for what it is—an accident—conditioned by the time and place of our own birth. That future historian will consider us as uncivilized for having permitted unregulated births as we do the Romans and Chinese for their "irresponsible" behavior.

FREEDOM, RESPONSIBILITY, AND EDUCATION

[Ed. note: Myth Number Three (omitted here), deals with the coerciveness of family planning organizations regarding choice of contraception.]

Myth Number Four—People see the relationship between their own behavior and the good of their society.

"Social responsibility" is an intriguing concept. It has long been upheld in the United States by religion and government as a desirable goal for the individual citizen. We are urged to vote, to attend meetings, to pay taxes, to defend our faith and our country, to choose an occupation, to set an example for the young—all in the name of "social responsibility." Certainly a democracy, more than any other form of government, is dependent upon the involvement and the allegiance of its people. However, some decisions and actions of the individual have traditionally not been defined as part of one's social responsibility. Family planners like to believe that social responsibility is a consideration in parenthood, affecting the number of children born to a husband and wife. Not so! Parenthood has so long been thought of as unlike any other condition that we do not apply the same reasoning to it. With the categorical assertion that "parenthood is private," we make it immune to appeals for reason and responsibility.

But for another reason, also, it is unrealistic to expect individual parents to act in the best interest of society. Our social system is far too intricate and much too large for any individual fully to understand the consequences of his own behavior. In deciding to have another child, the well-to-do couple thinks only of their ability to support the child and their desire for one. They do not think about the fact that their new child will consume five times as much of the world's resources as a baby born in India or an American slum.

There seems to be in operation a "law of universal exclusion" by which individuals convince themselves that they are somehow different from all other human beings, not subject to the same emotions and irrational actions. It is "other" people who litter the countryside with waste thrown from automobiles. In disposing of those bottles along the roadside, "we" were avoiding possible injury to our children resulting from a sudden stop. Our neighbor does not vote because he is indifferent to the problems of government. We did not vote, however, because we were involved on election day with other good causes that kept us from the polls. A friend bought a fancy color television to impress us; we bought the same set because it gets all 84 channels. The family "across the tracks" has a houseful of kids because they don't know any better. We have too many because we love children.

It is difficult for people to see the relationship between their parental behavior and the good of their society, for the societal consequences are neither immediate nor direct. Thus it is impossible for individual parents to realize that they are part of the population problem. Because of their inability to see this relationship, the question of social responsibility involved in parenthood is seldom raised. A recent bumper sticker announced that "The Population Bomb Is Everybody's Baby," but I daresay the truth of that statement went unnoticed by most of those who saw it and many of those who displayed it.

Myth Number Five—People always do what is good for them.

The very fact that people have problems would seem sufficient to refute this assumption. Hundreds of millions of dollars are spent yearly by Americans on quack medicines, youth elixirs, stimulants, depressants. The more far-fetched the claim for a product, the greater its demand.

Russell Lynes wrote a book some years ago called *The Taste Makers* in which he argued that how we spend our money and our leisure is determined for us by the advertising industry and the mass media.[22] This argument is best caught in the familiar phrase "What's good for General Motors is good for the country." Somewhat more recently in *The Affluent Society*, John Galbraith contended that the supply of goods today creates its own demand rather than the other way around, as has been true historically.[23]

To contend that people *do* what is good for them assumes that they first *know* what is good for them. So complex and complicated is today's world that no individual can possibly comprehend all the options available in any particular situation. Neither can we anticipate all the possible consequences of our actions. We are like the four blind men trying to describe the elephant by touching different parts of its anatomy. One of the most frustrating characteristics of our age is the competing and often contradictory claims made by products, politicians, and pressure groups. We are bombarded by so much information, so poorly integrated, that rather than enlightening and motivating, it tends to obscure and neutralize. Overwhelmed by all those who "tell it like it is," and intimidated by others who urge us to "keep the faith, Baby," the ordinary citizen simply withdraws into the cocoon of noninvolvement, from which we are then impervious to the outside world. We exercise our freedom by choosing to surrender it; we find our personal good at society's expense—a fool's bargain that time and events will unmask!

During 1969 conflicting statements were issued by knowledgeable and responsible individuals concerning the proper course of action to take on the population problem. Scientists meeting at the John Muir Institute in Aspen, Colorado, in September termed voluntary birth control "insanity" and called for some kind of official action to restrict the birth rate.[24] In December 1969 the president of Planned Parenthood–World Population, testifying before the Senate Committee on Labor and Public Welfare in support of a pending family planning bill, attacked this point of view:

> In the last year, a number of prophets of doom have rushed into the headlines to pronounce the verdict that voluntary fertility control is "insanity." These men have little knowledge of the potential of improved family planning programs and improvements in the delivery of services and techniques. They believe that population growth can be brought under control only through governmental coercion and decree.
>
> I do not share their despair. The appropriate response, in my view, is to mobilize rapidly a total, coordinated U.S. program by government, in collaboration with voluntary health services, in an all-out maximum effort to demonstrate to the world what voluntary fertility control can accomplish in a free society.[25]

It is understandable that the ordinary citizen is confused by such contradictory positions from reputable sources. However, it should be noted that family planning organizations have a vested interest in voluntarism, both because those who use their services choose to do so and because the bulk of their workforce is made up of volunteers donating their time. This means that we must somewhat discount the attachment of family planners for voluntarism as an example of their instinct for organizational survival rather than a dispassionate response to society's need. Critics of voluntarism, on the other hand, risk their professional reputations and their future careers by insisting that compulsion is the only adequate response to the population dilemma.

Myth Number Six—Education can solve the population problem.

It has always been said of whatever problem man has faced, "Education is the answer." But it has never been sufficient. In fact education alone cannot solve even the education problem, and laws are passed to correct deficiencies in the educational process itself. It seems a little naive then to suggest that we rely solely on education to persuade individual parents not to have too many children. Certainly education is necessary in our effort to check population growth, but it is by no means sufficient.

Even though attempts have been made to educate smokers on the dangers of cigarettes, more people are smoking now than in 1964 when the surgeon general's report linking cigarettes to cancer was issued.[26] Drivers continue to sit on their seat belts despite the educational campaign by the National Safety Council, which urges us to "buckle up for safety." A similar fate awaits our well-intentioned efforts to educate for "responsible parenthood." Education is individual; the population explosion is societal. A societal problem cannot be solved by a technique designed for individual development. To say that education can solve the population problem is as unreasonable as saying that crime prevention, labor relations, social security, and land use can be sufficiently controlled by education, without recourse to the legislative and judicial processes.

In fact there is a danger in education. It is that we will become so accustomed to discussing a thing, so adept at analyzing and recommending, so fascinated with our verbal facility, so busy with meetings and resolutions, that we never do anything. The *Population Bulletin* published by the Population Reference Bureau characterized population trends in 1969 as "The 'Talk-No Do' Syndrome." The *Bulletin* said:

> The population movement in the United States, the United Nations, the majority of the world's developing nations—is still bogged down in talk. . . . If the "Talk-No Do" syndrome of 1969 was merely a phase that any social revolution must pass through, then it was a step forward. But it can easily become a habit, a substitute for getting on with the job.[27]

Those of us who teach are continually disheartened at the difficulties encountered in trying to teach what people do not want to learn. It used to be commonly assumed that education could do away with most if not all of the irrationalities and inconsistencies of the human mind. It was thought that as education increased, hate and prejudice would decline. But it has not turned out to be so. Rather than eliminating prejudice, education has modified its method of expression. No longer so violent or so obvious, it is no less vicious or destructive. To contend that education can do more with the population problem than with the race problem requires a kind of blind faith ill suited to our day.

FAMILY PLANNING AND POPULATION CONTROL

Myth Number Seven—Individual family planning equals national population control.

In his 1967 *Science* article, "Population Policy: Will Current Programs Succeed?" Kingsley Davis points out that the United States has no policy in regard to population. As director of international population and urban research at the University of California at Berkeley, Davis shows that none of the more than thirty countries now trying to curb population growth seems to have any idea what their goals are. All of them equate individual and voluntary family planning with national population control. But Davis says, "There is no reason to expect that the millions of decisions about family size made by couples in their own interest will automatically control population for the benefit of society. On the contrary, there are good reasons to think they will not do so."[28]

Since current family planning programs have no clear-cut and identifiable objectives, any decline in fertility, no matter how short range, is seized upon as justification for the programs. Some point to the United States' present growth rate of 1.0 percent per year, compared to Africa's 2.4 percent or Latin America's 2.9 percent, as proof that the United States has solved the problem. What is not pointed out, however, is that population growth occurs in waves, and this nation is currently at the foot of an ominous new wave. As the baby boom of the forties and fifties comes of age, the number of births will increase. If we may judge from several recent studies that show an increasing number of third- and fourth-children suburban families, then we are forced to conclude that not only will the absolute number of births go up, but so will the rate of increase. In fact, the U.S. birth rate rose three-tenths of 1 percent during the twelve-month period ending in September 1969 as compared to the same period in 1967–68.[29]

The year 1969 may have been the beginning of the end for family planning organizations. Despite the fact that the federal government was much more receptive to them than ever before, "many respected authorities in 1969 began to question whether family planning could offer much more than humane and badly needed help to the tiny minority of American families which are classified as poor or near-poor—that is, whether it could have a major impact on U.S. population growth."[30]

In a controversial *Science* essay, demographer Judith Blake criticized family planning organizations for not attacking the fundamental cause of United States population growth, which she defined as the desire of the majority of Americans for families of more than three children. She accused family planners of having goals related only to means of contraception and none having to do with family size.[31]

Planned Parenthood is a service program designed to provide contraceptive assistance to individuals in order to further whatever personal goals they may have. The evidence is abundant that the accomplishment of these individual goals will do little to achieve a manageable rate of population growth. Planned Parenthood of Greater Kansas City, for example, had 2,136 new patients during 1969. Of this total, 566 (38 percent) already had three or more children and 212 (10 percent) already had five or more.[32] Regardless of how well the program operates, it is too little too late when applied to families who already have more children than is consistent with society's welfare.

A related inadequacy of voluntary family planning programs is that not enough people volunteer. Planned Parenthood operates approximately 500 clinics nationwide yet they report serving only 350,000 women (and apparently no men) each year. Of this number 275,000 are poor, yet Planned Parenthood's own estimate puts the number of medically indigent women who want to avoid pregnancy at five million.[33]

At present none of the organizations working in the population field would restrict the number of children parents could have. All of them—from Planned Parenthood to the Association for Voluntary Sterilization and the Campaign to Check the Population Explosion—are committed philosophically to parental freedom of choice. This position was succinctly stated in a letter written to me in 1968 by the director of a national population organization:

> Neither this organization nor any of the others you have mentioned would support a policy of compulsory birth limitation. It is our view that parents in the United States and overseas must be provided with access to the latest medical information and methods to limit conception, to make a free choice with regard to family size. We can and do argue that smaller families are desirable for a variety of reasons, but we would not join any efforts to devise or impose limits on the family size in the United States or elsewhere.

Aside from a philosophical commitment to parental choice, however, family planners find themselves opposed to legal controls for strategic reasons.

In order to gain wider public acceptance, every effort is made to pacify religious and political opposition by repeated insistence that contraceptives are produced and disseminated only so women may have the number of children they want. This unwillingness to evoke opposition undoubtedly has made family planning less controversial than it might have been, but it has thereby been made less effective as a method for the control of population size.

The one organization that has at least discussed restrictions on parenthood is Zero Population Growth, Inc. (ZPG). At its September 1969 board meeting, ZPG passed the following resolutions, the intent of which was to encourage governmental action to restrict the number of children born to individual parents:

1. It is resolved that parenthood is not an inherent right of individuals, but a privilege extended by the society in which they live. Accordingly, society has both the right and the duty to limit population when either its physical existence or its quality of life is threatened.
2. We further resolve that every American family is entitled to give birth to children, but no family has the right to have more than two children.
3. We further resolve that the Congress of the United States must (a) enact legislation guaranteeing the right of parenthood to all Americans but restricting the number of natural (not adoptive) children to two, and (b) adopt and finance a "crash" program to develop a birth control technology sufficient to accomplish this objective without using criminal sanctions.[34]

At its April 1970 board of directors meeting, ZPG passed another resolution having to do with family size. This one was directed to parents:

> ZPG recognizes that even if an average family size of two children were instituted immediately and maintained in the U.S., population would continue to grow until after 2000 A.D.; and that the only way to achieve faster population stabilization would be to bring down average family size below two natural children. Therefore, the Board of Directors urges all Americans to limit their children to a maximum of two natural children.

As a charter member of ZPG and as a member of the executive committee of the national board, I introduced the first three resolutions described above, and they were adopted after considerable discussion. Since their passage, however, ZPG has backed away from any hint of compulsory birth control. Many of our directors and members believe that our political effectiveness would quickly disappear if we were to endorse compulsion. They may be right. Senator Joseph Tydings, speaking at the First National Congress on Optimum Population and Environment, argued that "strong resistance still exists in Congress to programs promoting voluntary family planning, much less compulsory population control. Indeed, at this time, talk of compulsion constitutes the greatest threat to the success of the voluntary population stabilization movement."

I respect the senator's judgment of congressional attitudes toward population programs. But history has demonstrated that there is often a distinct difference between the politically attractive and the socially necessary. The popularity of an idea at a point in time is more a reflection of public opinion than of human need. And those opinions change as the needs become more apparent.

Perhaps the biggest reason for compulsory birth control being politically unattractive at present is that no one has carefully examined the need and the precedents for it. Nor has it been shown to be directly related to the very survival, much less the welfare, of all the human race. Jumping to conclusions has always been a favorite recreational pastime of Americans. Accordingly, we have always concluded that only a racist or a eugenicist would recommend compulsory birth control. That is patently ridiculous. It's like saying that only a dictatorship would deny people the right to die.

"Don't confuse me with the facts, my mind is made up," so heralded a popular little saying of several years back. Intended to be humorous, it may well have been prophetic.

In March 1968, I received a letter from the director of a Planned Parenthood office in a major U.S. city. The letter said in part:

> I read your paper about the government limiting births with great interest. I think you are right, but I hope that you are wrong. The great fear that has kept the government from getting into the field of family planning has been the thought of compulsory limitations of births. Even to me, an old hand at this game, I dislike the idea of compulsory limitation. At the present rate of growth something will have to be done. This might be the last generation where free choice will be possible.

Old myths cannot cope with new realities. Those who think otherwise simply compound society's problems and intensify their personal frustrations.

Sleep well, family planners, for you live in a dream world, and awake in a madhouse of your own design.

[Ed. note: The following is excerpted from the end of "Birth Control as Preventive Medicine," chapter 6 of Chasteen's book. Earlier in that chapter, he describes a reversible vaccine to immunize against fertility, which he assumes will soon be available.]

Writing in the April 1970 issue of *Sexology*, Richard Stiller, associate director of the Information Center on Population Problems, asked himself the rhetorical question "Why not, then, in the interests of all of us, restrict by law each family to two children to keep our population stable?" He then replied to his own question, "Because it won't work. Since we cannot put policemen in every bedroom, we should not put policemen in some bedrooms."[35]

The picture of the policeman in the bedroom, while designed to frighten the unthinking, is a misrepresentation of what would actually be required. More appropriately, compulsory birth control should make us think of the chemist in the laboratory or the statesman in his chambers. Surely those who advocate family planning, "wanted" children, and "responsible" parenthood would not contend that parenthood is a spontaneous act committed in the bedroom rather than a decision reached jointly in less sexually designated areas of the home.

There is not a doctor in every living room or an accountant in every study, but vaccination and taxation are compulsory. And they certainly are necessary in society's effort to maintain itself. Compulsory birth control is just as vital to our collective survival.

⑨   ⑨   ⑨

[Ed. note: The following is excerpted from "A Population Policy for America," Chapter 10 of Chasteen's book. He is referring, I believe, to a brief piece by Kenneth E. Boulding, titled "Marketable Licenses for Babies," which first appeared in *The Meaning of the 20th Century*.[36]]

It has been suggested that fertility could be controlled through the issuance of marketable licenses to have children. Under this provision couples would be licensed to give birth to a certain number of children, depending upon the need of society and the language of the law. If a couple did not wish to have the number of children to which their license entitled them, they could offer their unwanted fertility for sale to the highest bidder. Such a system as this would result in an invidious discrimination against the poor, for they would be priced out of the market. They would not be financially able to purchase fertility on the open market, and it is unlikely that government would subsidize their buying power.

The poor would also be under strong economic pressures to sell rather than to exercise the fertility to which their own permits entitled them. The ready market for their potential children would provide a temporary escape from their poverty. By driving their birth rate down, this system would also enhance the long-range economic outlook for the poor. But the discriminatory features of such a policy make it unworkable and politically unattractive. It would also be inefficient, since affluent Americans contribute most to the pregnancy epidemic. The conventional wisdom has long recognized that "the rich get richer, and the poor get children." Under a system of marketable fertility licenses, the rich would get both.

[Ed. note: Boulding writes, "This plan would have the additional advantage of developing a long-run tendency toward equality in income, for the rich would have many children and become poor and the poor would have few children and become rich."[37]]

. . . If more than two children are born to a woman, we could take those children from the parents and offer them for adoption and/or fine or imprison the parents. Laws presently governing parenthood provide certain punishments for parents deemed by the courts, for reasons of abuse, neglect, or inability, to be unfit. Such laws could be extended to include overly prolific parenthood as a type of unfitness. . . .

NOTES

1. Margaret Sanger, in S. Hanan, *Nation* 138 (January 31, 1934): 129–30.
2. Morris Udall, "Standing Room Only on Spaceship Earth," *Reader's Digest* (December 1969): 134.
3. Richard D. Lamm, "The Reproductive Revolution," *American Bar Association Journal* 54 (January 1970): 44.
4. Naphtal Lewis and Meyer Reinhold, *Roman Civilization* (New York: Columbia University Press, 1951), p. 1.
5. Kenneth Scott LaTourette, *The Chinese: Their History and Culture*, 3d ed. rev. (New York: Macmillan, 1946).
6. Kingsley Davis in *Poverty in America*, ed. M. E. Gordon (San Francisco: Chandler, 1965), pp. 229–319; Lee Rainwater, *And the Poor Get Children* (Chicago: Quandrangle, 1960); A. A. Campbell, "The Role of Family Planning in the Reduction of Poverty," *Journal of Marriage and Family* 30 (May 1968): 236–45.
7. E. James Lieberman, "Preventive Psychiatry and Family Planning," *Journal of Marriage and Family* 26 (November 1964): 471–77.
8. Garrett Hardin, *Planned Parenthood News* 1, no. 2 (May 1969): 3.
9. John M. Murtagh and Sara Harris, *Who Live in Shadow* (New York: McGraw-Hill, 1959), p. 36.
10. H. Brandom, "A Talk with Walter Lippmann at 80 about This Minor Dark Age," *New York Times Magazine* (September 14, 1969): 140.
11. L. Miller, "Toward a World of Wanted Children," *Reader's Digest* 91 (October 1967): 89.
12. The Victor Fund for the International Planned Parenthood Federation, no. 8 (spring 1969): 3.
13. Congressional Record, Proceedings and Debate of the 91st Congress. First Session.

14. Planned Parenthood–World Population, "When More Is Less."

15. Alan F. Guttmacher, "Family Planning, The Needs and the Methods," *American Journal of Nursing* 69 (June 1969): 1230.

16. D. Dempsey, "Dr. Guttmacher Is the Evangelist of Birth Control," *New York Times Magazine* (February 9, 1969): 82.

17. *Gallup Poll Research Text* (April 1966), p. 17.

18. From a speech by Alice Taylor Day, May 7, 1965, at a Planned Parenthood meeting, Milwaukee, Wisconsin.

19. Committee on Population, National Academy of Science–National Research Council Publication no. 1279, p. 6.

20. Richard Day, "Society's Stake in Responsible Parenthood," *American Journal of the Diseases of Childhood* 113 (May 1967): 519–21.

21. See Judith Blake, "Population Policy for Americans: Is the Government Being Misled?" *Science* 164, no. 3879 (May 2, 1969): 522–29.

22. Russell Lynes, *The Tastemakers* (New York: Houghton Mifflin, 1958).

23. John Galbraith, *The Affluent Society* (Boston: Houghton Mifflin, 1958).

24. "The 'Talk-No Do' Syndrome," *Population Bulletin* 25, no. 6 (December 1969): 119.

25. Testimony of Alan Guttmacher, M.D., President, Planned Parenthood–World Population, before Senate Committee on Labor and Public Welfare on S.2108, December 8, 1969.

26. *Statistical Abstract of the United States*, 90th annual ed. (1969), p. 731.

27. *Population Bulletin*, p. 1.

28. Kingsley Davis, "Population Policy: Will Current Programs Succeed?" *Science* 158 (November 10, 1967): 732.

29. "The 'Talk-No Do' Syndrome," p. 124.

30. Ibid., pp. 125–26.

31. Judith Blake, "Population Policy for Americans," p. 528.

32. The total of 4,739 patients served by Planned Parenthood in 1969 includes 2,603 former patients and 2,136 new ones.

33. Alan Guttmacher, "Family Planning, The Needs and the Methods," pp. 1229–34.

34. Passed September 30, 1969; for information, contact Zero Population Growth, Inc., 330 Second Street, Los Altos, California 94022.

35. Richard Stiller, "Compulsory Birth Control: Yes or No," *Sexology* 36, no. 9 (April 1970): 30–34.

36. Kenneth E. Boulding, *The Meaning of the 20th Century* (New York: Harper & Row). Reprinted in *Population, Evolution, and Birth Control: A Collage of Controversial Ideas*, ed. Garrett Hardin (San Francisco: W. H. Freeman and Company, 1964).

37. Garrett Hardin, *Population, Evolution, and Birth Control* (San Francisco: W. H. Freeman), p. 341.

GENETIC ENGINEERING
GOALS AND CONTROLS
Peter Singer and Deane Wells

*I*t would be well to pause here and recognize that what we are talking about [genetic engineering] is different only in degree, and not in kind, from the human behavior with which we are all familiar. The genetic constitution of our population is determined by human choices to a far greater extent than we like to admit. Whenever people choose one marriage partner rather than another, they affect the gene pool of the future. It would be foolish to deny that tall people often choose other tall people, particularly attractive people often choose others similarly fortunately endowed, sporting people often choose other sporting people, artistic people often choose other artistic people, and so on. Sometimes we seek genetic consequences quite deliberately: when we make these choices of marriage partners we often have, decently interred at the back of our minds, the thought that a person with certain characteristics would make a good mother, or father, for our children. But even if this is the last thing in our minds when we choose our spouse, our choices will nevertheless determine the genetic constitution of the next generation.

What is new is the extent of the intervention that genetic engineering will make possible. The genetic lottery, which individuals have deliberately influenced since time began, will become a much less risky game of chance. To a far greater extent than ever before, the procreating generation will be able to determine the constitution of its successors. The question is: who should decide the genetic constitution of the next generation?

From *The Reproductive Revolution: New Ways of Making Babies*, by Peter Singer and Deane Wells (Oxford: Oxford University Press, 1984). Reprinted by permission of Oxford University Press.

There is a central planning approach and a laissez-faire approach to handling disagreement over the desirability of a particular form of genetic engineering. The centralized approach would have the government, presumably acting through some expert committee, make the decisions. If the government considered high intelligence desirable, prospective parents would be offered the opportunity to have their embryos treated so as to raise the intelligence of the resulting child.

The government would, no doubt, find it difficult to get consensus on the qualities to be considered desirable, and that is one strong objection to this approach. A still more powerful reason against it, however, is that it puts a frightening amount of power into government hands.

To avoid this, one could take a "free market" approach. Couples would make their own choices about the genetic constitution of their children. The problem of obtaining agreement about what is desirable is thus overcome, for agreement is unnecessary. All we need is tolerance of other people's choices for their own offspring. Individual freedom would be maximized, the state kept out, and the opportunities for misguided bureaucratic planning, or for something still more sinister, eliminated.

Neither the free market approach nor the central planning approach seems to us particularly satisfactory. The latter is far too much like *Brave New World*. Citizens should choose the constitution of their government; governments should not choose the constitutions of their citizens.

The free market approach is unsatisfactory for a different reason. It puts too much power in the hands of individuals who might use it irresponsibly or even pathologically. It is hard to imagine any parent using genetic engineering to produce a bodyguard of mindless clones, but it is just possible to imagine the sort of parents who might want to genetically engineer a nice, uniform football team.

We don't need to multiply instances to illustrate this point. There is, however, one aspect of individual choice in a competitive society that is worth noticing. If there is pressure on individuals to compete for status and material rewards, the qualities that give children a winning edge in this competition are not necessarily going to be the most socially desirable. For instance, above-average drive and ambition might make a child more likely to succeed—but too much striving for individual success will not make for a harmonious and cooperative society. Now consider the logic of leaving to individuals the choice of the type of children they will have. Suppose that genetic engineering has advanced to the stage at which we could significantly increase the drive and ambition of our children. Then any parents who wished their children to achieve high status and earnings would do well to make use of genetic engineering to produce an above-average level of drive and ambition. If many parents were to have such desires for their children, however, and to take the course that would give their children the best prospects of making it to the top, the result would simply be an increase in the average level of drive and ambition. Since this increase could do nothing to increase the number of winners—by definition, only a few can make it to the top—the result could only be greater frustration all round. So parents might try to engineer an even *greater* increase in drive and ambition for *their* children, thus leading to an upwards spiral in these characteristics that would be difficult to reverse. For although the increased emphasis on personal success might so reduce public-mindedness as to endanger the very existence of society as a communal enterprise, no parents could withdraw from this damaging spiral without condemning their own children to the lower ranks of the society. It would not be within the power of individuals to stop the accelerating rush to a society of supremely ambitious individualists. Such is the logic of rational self-interest—or family-interest—in a free-market situation.

Those still skeptical about the desirability of any state interference with individual choice in this area should remember that we are talking now of decisions that will (to a much greater degree than contemporary human procreation decisions) alter the public human environment. It is generally acknowledged that a society has the right to exclude certain types of people by the use of immigration laws. Some criteria of selection we do consider wrong—race is the obvious example—but selection on the basis of needed skills, or exclusion because of known criminal associations, is not considered objectionable. If a society is justified in thus selecting those who will become its members, surely it is also justified in excluding certain types of people its own members are proposing to create.

Our suggestion therefore is this: the genetic endowment of children should be in the same hands it has always been in—the hands of parents. But parents who wished to use genetic engineering to bring about a characteristic that had not previously been sanctioned by the society through its government should have to apply for permission. The public should know what such adventurous parents are proposing to do, and should equally have the right to say "no."

The machinery for such a system would not be too hard to devise. A broadly based government body could be set up to approve or reject particular parents' proposals for genetic engineering. It would consider whether the proposed piece of engineering would, if its practice became widespread, have harmful effects on individuals or society. If no harmful effects could be foreseen, the committee would license the procedure. This would mean that parents who wished to use it were free to do so. The committee would keep track of how many people were using each licensed procedure, and with what results. It could always withdraw a license if unexpected harmful results emerged. Because the committee would need to agree only on the absence of harm, its deliberations would not be as difficult as they would be if agreement on positive benefit were required—though they would still be difficult enough.

The selective cloning of people with special abilities . . . could be handled in the same manner. In addition to keeping an eye on the problems of adjustment of the cloned individuals, the committee would also place strict limits on the number of clones that could be made from any one person, and on the extent of cloning in general. Thus a potentially harmful reduction of the diversity of the human gene pool could be avoided.

What concrete decisions might such a committee make about the genetic engineering procedures it licensed and the individual from whom cloning would be sanctioned? Presumably it would license proposals to increase intelligence (but cautiously, by small steps) and refuse to license proposals, if there were any, to diminish it. Presumably it would favor proposals that promoted the health of the future member of the society, and reject any that put it at risk. It might refuse to allow genetic engineering that would determine even for some positive characteristic (such as physical strength) if it was thought to be associated with some negative characteristic (such as propensity to heart attack). If it happened that scientists found genes associated with altruism or malice, it might license proposals to determine for the former, but not the latter. But what it should never do is make positive directions as to what should be done. It should confine itself to exercising the power of veto. In our view, choosing the positive content of the gene pool should remain the preserve of those who have always done it up until now—the parents.

INESCAPABLE EUGENICS

Philip Kitcher

T he brutal compulsion of the Nazi eugenics prompted an important
change in postwar efforts to apply genetic knowledge. Everyone is
now to be her (or his) own eugenicist, taking advantage of the available
genetic tests to make the reproductive decisions she (he) thinks correct. If
genetic counseling, practiced either on the limited scale of recent decades or
in the more wide-ranging fashion that we can anticipate in the decades to
come, is a form of eugenics, then it is surely *laissez-faire eugenics*. . . . Ideally,
citizens are not coerced but make up their own minds, evaluating objective
scientific information in light of their own values and goals. . . . As for the
traits that people attempt to promote or avoid, that is surely their own business, and within the limits of available knowledge, individuals may do as they
see fit. Laissez-faire eugenics, the "eugenics" already in place and likely to
become ever more prominent in years to come, is a very different form of
eugenics from the endeavors of Charles Davenport [who amassed studies to
show the genetic inferiority of people from eastern and southern Europe],
Henry Goddard [who combined official immigration policy with the use of
intelligence tests], and Hitler's minions [who introduced compulsory sterilization to achieve racial purity].

. . . Naively, we might try to avoid the smear of eugenics by insisting that
nobody use this information [genetic information gained by prenatal testing]

---

for selective abortions—we shall not interfere with the genetic composition of future populations. But once we have the option of interfering, this allegedly "noneugenic" decision shares important features with eugenic practices. Tacitly, it makes a value judgment to the effect that *unplanned* populations are preferable to *planned* populations. . . .

Molecular knowledge pitches us into some form of eugenic practice, and laissez-faire eugenics looks initially like an acceptable species. Yet its character deserves a closer look.

The most attractive feature of laissez-faire eugenics is its attempt to honor individual reproductive freedom. Does it succeed? Are the resources of prenatal testing in affluent societies equally open to all members of the population? Do they help people to make reproductive decisions that are genuinely their own? And is that really a proper goal? Since individual reproductive decisions have aggregate consequences for the composition of the population, should there not be restrictions to avoid potentially disastrous effects? Finally, because individual decisions may be morally misguided—as with those who would select on the basis of sex—will laissez-faire eugenics foster evil on a grand scale? . . .

Individual choices are not made in a social vacuum, and unless changes in social attitudes keep pace with the proliferation of genetic tests, we can anticipate that many future prospective parents, acting to avoid misery for potential children, will have to bow to social attitudes they reject and resent. They will have to choose abortion even though they believe that a more caring or less prejudiced society might have enabled the child who would have been born to lead a happy and fulfilling life. Laissez-faire eugenics is in danger of retaining the most disturbing aspect of its historical predecessors—the tendency to try to transform the population in a particular direction, not to avoid suffering but to reflect a set of social values. In the actual world unequal wealth is likely to result in unequal access, and social attitudes will probably prove at least partially coercive. How are these problems to be solved? . . .

Prenatal decisions do not affect only the parents; they have a consequences, very directly, for the cluster of cells within the uterus and, more remotely, for other members of society who may have to contribute to support for the child who is born. . . .

In the presence of practical constraints, attractive ideals conflict. Reproductive freedom is important to us; providing support for all members of society, including people with expensive genetically imposed needs, is equally important. But our resources are finite. In a callous society, as we have seen, individual reproductive freedom is severely constrained. In a caring society, individual reproductive freedom may lead to social disaster. . . .

Today's enthusiasts for the use of molecular genetics in prenatal testing rarely call themselves "eugenicists," but their vision of future reproductive practice depicts a particular version of laissez-faire eugenics—*utopian eugenics.* . . . Utopian eugenics would use reliable genetic information in pre-natal tests that would be available equally to all citizens. Although there would be widespread public discussion of values and of the social conse-quences of individual decisions, there would be no societally imposed restric-tions on reproductive choices—citizens would be educated but not coerced. Finally, there would be universally shared respect for difference coupled with a public commitment to realizing the potential of all those who are born . . .

Most basic is the task of clarifying utopian eugenics, uncovering the con-siderations that should guide our reproductive choices . . .

⑤   ⑤   ⑤

The Modern Civics class, taught by a young woman of serene warmth, uses the most up-to-date materials, including the fifteenth edition of the famous text *Your Reproductive Responsibilities,* published just last year in 2069. The teacher starts with the darkness of prehistory, the days before prenatal testing was available to responsible citizens. Once, she tells her students, many babies were doomed to die in infancy, there were special institutions for "defective" children, and the more enlightened nations diverted large sums from other health and education projects to provide special care for children with genetic disabilities. But the progress of the reproductive responsibility movement has been heroic: Tay-Sachs is a thing of the past, Down syndrome is virtually eliminated, congenital forms of heart disease are now extremely rare, there are far fewer people with mutant tumor-suppressor genes, far fewer fat people, far fewer homosexuals, far fewer short people. All this is the work of molecular geneticists, doctors, counselors, and—she smiles mod-estly—of the teachers who have helped teenagers recognize their reproduc-tive responsibilities.

A student raises her hand: she has heard that "mental defectives" are still sometimes born, that not everybody takes the tests or acts appropriately. Indeed, the teacher sadly acknowledges, education sometimes fails to convey the important message, and sometimes people who have sat through the class form different opinions; we must respect these differences and not condemn those who do not behave as we would have done. But the student persists; she has heard stories of people who went too far, who terminated pregnan-cies because the fetus was female, even, in one case, because it carried a gene for dark eyes. Unfortunate but true, the teacher admits, using the question as an opportunity to present the historical data on uses of amniocentesis to select for sex. The class agrees that this is barbaric; their society would never countenance any such practice.

With student interest high, the teacher raises a question of current controversy. The fifteenth edition of the text already embodies the accepted ideas that homosexuality, mutant tumor-suppressor genes, and obesity have personal and social costs, but debate rages over what the planned sixteenth edition should say about left-handedness, whose genetic basis is now thoroughly understood. Left-handers can function quite normally—so long, of course, as special support is available—but they continue to have reduced life expectancy. One student points out that the resources used to make the world safe and easy for left-handers could be channeled toward different projects, improvements in support for higher education, for example. The students are moved by his argument, and though the class is divided, a majority believes that responsible procreators would promote dexterity and avoid the sinister. . . .

⑨   ⑨   ⑨

. . . The fear made vivid in this fantasy—Modern Civics 2070—far-fetched though it may appear, is that no line can be drawn, that objectivism about disease cannot be sustained, that decisions . . . must ultimately turn on a social consensus about what kinds of lives are valuable. . . .

Utopian eugenics attempts to mix individual reproductive freedom with education and public discussion about responsible procreation. Our problem has been to understand whether any talk of reproductive responsibility could be more than the expression of our likes and dislikes. Convinced that there is a moral gulf between terminating a pregnancy because the fetus carries alleles for neurofibromatosis and aborting because the fetus is female, we have explored the possibility of grounding the distinction in an objective notion of disease. I believe the exploration has led us to a better perspective, one that acknowledges the need for making special types of value judgments, those that focus on the quality of human lives.

From this perspective, we can begin to see how Modern Civics 2070 might be taught. A different teacher would start with fundamentals. Responsible reproductive decisions, she suggests, involve thought about the qualities of lives. What kind of a life could a child who developed from this fetus have, given what is known about its genotype and the environments that could be provided? What effects would its life have on the quality of other lives that have already taken shape—on the lives of the parents, of their other children, of people in the broader society to which they belong? Sometimes the decisions are easy. When certain allelic combinations occur, the parents know that neurodegeneration will set in during infancy, that the child can be supported for a few years with elaborate care, that there will be no opportunity for the development of a self. By contrast, in affluent societies, although discrimination against women persists, its impact is not so severe as to make it impossible for those who have two X chromosomes to live happy and fulfilling lives. Nor *should* similar opportunities be out of reach for homosexuals, the congenitally obese, or the left-handed. If prospective parents correctly judge that the presence of a genotype for any of these characteristics signals greatly diminished prospects for a life that will go well, then their judgment indicts the social milieu, not the genotype or the trait. Their predicament is exactly that of the Northern Indians who reluctantly abort their daughters to save them from the fate of being female: The moral problem attaches to the social prejudice. The young utopian eugenicists who imbibe the lessons of Modern Civics 2070 should be moved to fight the social and environmental conditions that artificially cramp the quality of lives that might have blossomed.

But there are bound to be many hard cases. Some women, or couples, will have obligations to others—to children already born or to aging parents—which could not be met if a child with great needs demanded their constant attention. Sometimes time and love are not enough, and prospective parents must consider both whether their society can provide the support required to compensate for a combination of alleles and whether they have the right to demand that support. Modern Civics 2070 does not dictate how decisions are to be made in such cases. Instead, the teacher insists on the importance of attending to the quality of future lives, recognizing the constraints and the competing obligations.

Taught in the more adequate way, Modern Civics 2070 presupposes our ability to make judgments about the quality of human lives. That ability, I suggest, is the foundation of a solution to the problem that has hung over the present and previous chapters. To find the moral compass that the enterprise of utopian eugenics needs, we should turn not to the notion of disease but to the concept of the quality of life. As yet, I have introduced that concept in an impressionistic way, relying on our power to make comparisons between lives that unfold very differently. Ultimately, we shall need more refinement, but for the moment we have sufficient clarification: Utopian eugenics envisages a world in which molecular genetics helps people make free and educated reproductive decisions and in which the education is directed toward enhanced understanding of the likely quality of a nascent life.

. . . There is an important challenge here. It is time to meet it.

ARGUMENTS IN FAVOR AND AGAINST LEGALLY REQUIRING A PREGNANT WOMAN TO ACT IN THE INTERESTS OF HER FUTURE CHILD

Deborah Mathieu

ARGUMENTS IN FAVOR

*W*e earlier argued that a pregnant woman is morally obligated to act in the interests of the child she will bear. . . . Now, however, our concern is with the grounds for believing that at least some of a pregnant woman's moral obligations should also be regarded as legal obligations. In other words, are there good reasons for holding that the state may interfere in the life of a pregnant woman in order to prevent prenatal harm? If there are not—if we conclude that state involvement should not even be considered—then a characterization of a woman's moral obligations to act in the interests of the child she intends to bear, while valuable, will have no policy implications.

. . . Three types of supporting arguments [justifying coercive state intervention to prevent prenatal harms] are available. The first is a consequentialist argument: Preventing certain types of prenatal damage creates more good than harm overall. The second type of argument involves the rights of the future child: One could argue, for instance, that a child has a right to begin life with a sound mind and body, or one could base an argument on the more general right not to be harmed, a right that is enforceable as to conduct occurring before birth. For those who remain unconvinced by assertions of rights, a third type of argument is available. This position is based on the premise that a pregnant woman is obligated to meet certain standards of care for the sake of her future child, even if the child has no corresponding rights to such care, and that these obligations should be enforced by the state. We shall deal, in turn, with each of these types of arguments.

An Appeal to Consequences

The basic consequentialist argument is simply that if we permit pregnant women to do as they please—to ingest alcohol or cocaine, to refuse prenatal care, to work with chemicals known to cause teratogenic damage—then we at the same time permit grave harm to befall tens of thousands of innocent beings each year: the children to whom the women give birth. Much of this harm could be prevented and, because it causes so much suffering, many people conclude that it *should* be prevented.

Consider, for example, the case of a pregnant woman who pays insufficient attention to controlling her diabetes. Not only is her own health at risk, but she greatly increases the chances that her child will be born prematurely and with severe malformations. Since both the woman and her child reap the benefits of her adherence to a strict treatment regimen, and since the serious harms to both can easily be avoided, it makes sense, according to a utilitarian calculation, to require the woman in this instance to take her medications and keep to her diet.

This type of utilitarian reckoning, which is concerned with the benefits to individuals in particular, is buttressed by considerations of the benefits to society in general. The high costs of treatment in neonatal intensive care units (which average approximately $2,000 a day) would be reduced, mitigating the financial burden on private insurance companies, the hospitals that often must absorb much of the cost, and the taxpayers who fund Medicaid programs (which cover the hospital costs for many indigent children).[1] In addition, the expense and difficulties of institutionalizing mentally and physically handicapped individuals would also decrease—as would the demands for special education programs—as the numbers of severely handicapped individuals dwindle. At the same time the numbers of productive, self-supporting, tax-paying citizens would increase.[2] Thus, it could be argued, society would benefit more were the state to intervene in the activities of pregnant women than were it to allow pregnant women the freedom of choice they have enjoyed in the past.

On these grounds, then, one could argue both that a pregnant women has a moral obligation to refrain from causing prenatal harm (because the benefits to the child outweigh the disbenefits to her), and that the state may enforce this obligation (because the benefits to society at large outweigh the disbenefits to pregnant women). So there are good utilitarian arguments for permitting state intervention in order to prevent at least some cases of serious prenatal harm.

But how much weight should we give these arguments? The answer, of course, is a matter of great controversy. One set of countervailing considerations involves the rights of the pregnant women: Many people in our society believe that an individual's fundamental rights may not be abridged for utilitarian purposes, since these rights outweigh considerations of social benefit. State intervention into the lives of pregnant women, according to this line of thought, would be permitted only insofar as it does not interfere with the women's constitutional rights. But it should be noted that the debate does not end here, for we first must determine which rights a pregnant woman enjoys, and whether these rights indeed outweigh the social benefits of preventing prenatal harms. In addition, the rights of the pregnant women are not the only rights at stake. If children have rights that accrue during the fetal stage, and if pregnant women have corresponding obligations to honor those rights, then the consequentialist arguments in favor of limiting the mother's choices will be strengthened considerably.

The designation of the scope and limits of these rights thus plays an important role in our discussion, and it is fair to say that the consequentialist arguments can be assessed accurately only in light of them. Later, we shall explore the rights of the pregnant woman; here, we examine the alleged rights of future persons.[3]

ARGUMENTS BASED ON THE RIGHTS OF FUTURE PERSONS

Our increased awareness of the causes of prenatal harms and the development of new techniques for preventing the maturation of serious defects while the child is in utero have led some people to assert two rights of the future person: the right to begin life with a sound mind and body, and the right not to be harmed. Either (or both) of these rights might be invoked to justify state intervention into the lives of pregnant women without their consent.[4]

In *Smith* v. *Brennan*, a 1960 case involving a child who was born with deformed feet and legs caused by the effects of an automobile accident that occurred while he was still in utero, the New Jersey Supreme Court ruled that

> [j]ustice requires that the principle be recognized that a child has a legal right to begin life with a sound mind and body. If the wrongful conduct of another interferes with that right, and it can be established by competent proof that there is a causal connection between the wrongful interference and the harm suffered by the child when born, damages for such harm should be recoverable by the child.[5]

In this ruling, the court appeared to go beyond the usual finding of prenatal harm to posit a "legal right to begin life with a sound mind and body." Similarly, the New York Supreme Court in *Park* v. *Chessin* held that there is a "fundamental right of a child to be born as a whole, functional human being."[6]

One important question, of course, is whether or not a person does indeed have an inalienable and primary right to begin life with a sound mind and body. Although the *Smith* court announced the right, the actual holding states that damages were recoverable because the automobile accident caused harm to the child while he was still in utero. In other words, the court recognized a fairly straightforward tort and probably did not mean to create a new category of right separate and apart from traditional tortious acts that cause identifiable harm.

It has been proposed, however, that the right to begin life with a sound mind and body should be interpreted more broadly and more dramatically. One commentator, for instance, suggests that the court's ruling "would seem to establish the principle that the child's right to a healthy life takes precedence over the parents' right to reproduce."[7] Understood in this manner, the right to begin life with a sound mind and body would potentially be a powerful means of championing the welfare of children and limiting the freedom of parents (especially pregnant women).

How should the parameters of such a right be set? It seems reasonable to suggest that recognizing a right to begin life with a sound mind and body would require that a child be made better off than he otherwise would be: A fetus with a treatable genetic anomaly, for example, would receive the appropriate medical care so that he could be born unimpaired.[8]

If the right to be born with a sound mind and body is construed to imply a right to be made better off than one otherwise would be, then this right is necessarily a limited one: I can think of no sound reason for recognizing a right to be made beautiful, or a genius, or a star athlete—or even pretty, smart, or strong. The right to be born with a sound mind and body should not be interpreted in terms of perfection (however that is construed), or as implying that the goal of childbearing is similar to the U.S. Army's promise to help each recruit to "be all that you can be." Instead, the right should be more modestly regarded as a right to be as free as possible from significant pain and dysfunction. . . .

The Right Not to Be Harmed

The right not to be harmed is a widely accepted and fundamentally important right that serves as a foundation for our moral and legal codes. Indeed, it is generally accepted in our society that one of the most important goals of state action is to prevent harm to persons, and that this goal may legitimately involve interfering with individual liberty. As the philosopher Joel Feinberg states,

In short, state interference with a citizen's behavior tends to be morally justified when it is reasonably necessary (that is, when there are reasonable
grounds for taking it to be necessary as well as effective) to prevent harm or
the unreasonable risk of harm to parties other than the person interfered
with. More concisely, the need to prevent harm (private or public) to parties other than the actor is always an appropriate *reason* for legal coercion.[9]

Some theorists argue that the sole legitimate reason for the state's limiting a
person's liberty is to prevent him or her from harming another person. It is
significant to note, however, that even if you do not agree that an individual's
liberty may be limited only to prevent harm to a third party, you may still
believe that the need to prevent harm provides a stronger reason for limiting
liberty than any other value.

The right not to be unjustly harmed is even regarded as being enforceable by the state against conduct occurring before birth. The argument for
this is one that the tort law recognizes as legitimate: The harm with which
we are concerned is suffered by the child after birth, not by the fetus in utero.

Practically all aspects of a pregnant woman's life take on moral significance
because of the potential to harm another person, her future child. There is considerable evidence, for instance, that consuming alcohol, using narcotics, and
eating improperly may cause fetal damage; even everyday activities such as
drinking coffee and smoking cigarettes may be harmful. A woman who abstains
from these activities during pregnancy, however, greatly improves her fetus's
health and chances for survival, as does one who alters her lifestyle during pregnancy.[10] Therefore, it makes sense to offer pregnant women information about
the effects of lifestyle choices on the outcome of a pregnancy and encourage
them to behave differently. The difficult question is whether more should be
done. Those who are disturbed by the plight of impaired, low-birth-weight
infants—infants who would have been born healthy had their mothers behaved
differently—argue that a pregnant woman should be required to change her
lifestyle for the sake of the child she is carrying. The argument is fairly straightforward: By indulging in substance abuse, for instance, the pregnant woman
who intends to carry her pregnancy to term is harming another and is thereby
violating one of the most fundamental rights of a person, the right not to be
harmed; the harm to a woman occasioned by her abstinence would be minor
compared with the great benefit to the future child; thus coercing a pregnant
woman to alter her lifestyle may be justifiable under some circumstances.

This argument is buttressed by the contention that the state has certain
obligations to protect the well-being of individuals, obligations that should
be applied equally to all (including newborns). Indeed, one primary obligation of the state is to provide equal protection to all persons. This obligation
may be regarded as being grounded in utilitarian concerns (society will benefit most this way) or as being grounded in the principle of equality; the

foundational arguments are not really germane here. What is important is that most people would agree that the state does have, and should have, a commitment to the equal protection of all persons.

Arguments Based on a Pregnant Woman's Obligations

Our society is characterized by a high regard for individual rights, and persons on every side of an issue can be expected to couch their arguments in terms of one or more rights. But what are they really talking about? What is a "right"? What types of beings possess rights? Which rights do they have? Are there rights that outweigh considerations of utility? If so, what are these rights? How should we argue for them? What does it mean to say that a right carries a correlative obligation? How should we resolve conflicts among rights? In sum, the issue of rights is an enormously complex and controversial one, and a host of fundamental questions remain open.[11]

Because so many issues regarding the scope and power of rights are matters of continuing debate, and some people are thereby unpersuaded by appeals to rights, we also need to consider arguments that avoid references to rights altogether. We have explored one of these so far: the argument based on consequences. Another type of argument is available that also refrains from appealing to the alleged rights of the future child; this one is based on the claim that a pregnant woman has certain obligations to her future child—obligations that may or may not carry correlative rights—and that these obligations are similar to her obligations to other people. While these obligations are not grounded on the rights of the future person, they are related to its interests. . . .

A parent's legal duties toward his or her child are based in large part on the interests of the child, but they are limited by the interests and rights of others (including those of the parent herself). Thus a parent is not obligated to do what is in the child's best interest, but rather the parent must act within some acceptable range of these interests, a "range of reasonableness." This range is necessarily flexible, given the economic and social variances (and inequities) across society, the range of values and beliefs within society, and the broad scope of a typical parent's responsibilities: to her other children, her spouse, her employer, herself. In application, then, this standard may be very similar to a "minimum needs" standard, which holds that a parent must satisfy at least certain minimum needs of his or her child. Should a parent fall below this range, creating significant risk of serious and long-lasting harm to his or her child, then the state may step in to protect the child. The California Supreme Court has proposed that the fundamental question to be asked in these cases is: "What would an ordinarily reasonable and prudent parent have done in similar circumstances?"[13] . . .

State Intervention

So far we have explored arguments in favor of recognizing that a woman has some legal obligations to act in the interests of her future child. But other factors must be considered to determine whether or not legal coercion may be allowed . . .

Proportionality

Although the factor motivating state intervention in the lives of pregnant women is the prevention of serious harm to future persons, it does not follow that the appropriate social policy would be to interfere in every instance in which a pregnant woman is posing significant harm to her future child. Administering such a program would no doubt prove unworkable: inefficient, awkward, and unreasonably intrusive. Other factors must also be considered, especially proportionality: The intervention should not create more harm than it is aimed to alleviate. Allowing legal interference in every instance in which a future child is or could be harmed might create more harm than good, and thereby would defeat the whole point of intervening. This stands as a powerful reason for limiting state intervention. It also leads us to conclude that state interference would be justifiable only if four conditions can be met: (1) The harms to be prevented to the future person greatly exceed the degree of invasion to the pregnant woman, (2) the intervention is expected to be successful, (3) the intervention involves the least intrusive means available, and (4) a policy permitting such interventions will be, on the whole, beneficial to society in general. A few words on the first two conditions are in order here.

Weighing Particular Harms and Benefits

Determining whether the harms to be prevented to the future person in fact greatly exceed the degree of invasion to the pregnant woman is not an easy task, and involves weighing three interrelated factors: magnitude of harm, probability that the harm will occur, and probability that the harm can be prevented or removed. No simple formula for the application of these factors in all situations exists; at best, one can give a general outline of their scope and relevance.[14]

The question of the magnitude of the harms involved has two parts: (1) To what extent will the future child be harmed by his mother's actions? and (2) to what extent will the pregnant woman be harmed if her decision is overruled and her body is invaded? Answering these questions requires determining which interests are at stake (e.g., a woman's interest in making her own decisions, a child's interest in not being disabled), and the degree to which each interest will be invaded (a matter of duration times severity). One interest at stake, for instance, would be the woman's interest in bodily integrity, and different actions would invade it to different degrees: The extent of harm to this interest caused by a mandatory inoculation is substantially less than that caused by a forced cesarean section. Since it makes a difference how important the interest is and whether it is being only slightly thwarted or downright defeated, these two actions would require different types of justification.[15]

Determining the probability that the pregnant woman's actions will in fact cause grave harm to her future child is also an important and troublesome factor. There should be ample evidence to indicate that there is a high probability of serious harm to the future child if steps are not taken to intervene on its behalf, but this certainty is often lacking. For instance, the probability of the risk of harm is especially difficult to determine in instances of environmental or workplace hazards because many of the harms in question have a multitude of contributing causes and often are the result of cumulative or synergistic influences. And although we may have significant evidence that drinking alcohol during pregnancy may cause serious prenatal harm, for example, there is no evidence that this is always the case. Hence it is often difficult in any particular instance to determine with certainty whether or not the future child is at grave risk of serious harm.

The third factor to be considered is the probability that the harm to the future child can be avoided or removed. Intervention makes sense only when there is a significant or high probability that a harm can be prevented or at least ameliorated. One is obligated neither to make futile efforts to prevent harm nor to suffer especially risky or experimental measures. The central question is easily discerned: What constitutes a "significant" probability that intervention will be successful?

With respect to fetal therapies, the answer involves three factors: (1) the general reliability of this type of therapy as determined by prevailing standards of the medical profession; (2) its estimated efficacy in this instance; and (3) the value of the expected results (for example, the value of a generally healthy life or of a brief life filled with great pain).

It is appropriate to allow the pregnant woman the discretion to choose any of various treatment options when the proposed medical care is a matter of debate within the medical community and there is no medical consensus regarding the appropriate treatment for the child. The difficult questions regarding the scope of her discretion do not concern a choice among ordinary therapies, but rather involve a decision to reject them entirely or to forgo a less than satisfactory conventional therapy in favor of a promising but unorthodox one. This issue cannot be decided in isolation from the other interests mentioned, but it does point to the importance of one factor: the value of the expected results. It makes a difference whether the treatment can be expected to cure the child, to mitigate the symptoms without curing, or to save the child's life but leave her in a permanently comatose state. The general principle is intuitive: The obligation of a parent to utilize a particular therapy decreases in direct proportion with the tentativeness of the desired results of that therapy.

The problem of determining the scope and limits of the obligation to provide "effective" therapy is not a problem unique to fetal therapy: It is present throughout medicine. Reflection on this factor, however, does lead to the conclusion that social and legal policy must be selective. To assert that no fetal therapy should be mandated, or that all should be, would be unreasonable. Different therapies promise different outcomes, and only those that are likely to be effective in avoiding or ameliorating severely deleterious conditions may be required. The final decision, of course, cannot be made without balancing the severity of the harm to the future child against the risk to the pregnant woman of intervening.

Preliminary Conclusions

So far, we have argued that there are good moral and prudential reasons for trying to prevent prenatal harms, reasons based on three types of considerations: (1) utility (i.e., more good than harm will result), (2) the future person's positive right to receive adequate medical care and his negative right not to be harmed, and (3) the pregnant woman's general obligations to refrain from harming another and to aid another, as well as her special obligation to care for her future child. In other words, it makes good moral sense to argue that a pregnant woman does not have carte blanche to act any way she wishes, at least if her actions will cause harm to her future child. In addition, we have contended that it may be justifiable for the state to intervene to prevent some prenatal harms, but that there are two important factors that ought to be taken into account before doing so: due process and proportionality.

While there may be good arguments in favor of limiting the liberty of pregnant women in order to protect their offspring, these arguments are far from justifying any and all types of state intervention. First is the practical matter of proportionality: Allowing the state to interfere in every instance in which a future child is or could be harmed would no doubt create more harm than good, and this stands as a powerful reason for limiting state intervention. And second, we have argued that there are two distinct levels of obligation to which pregnant women may be held—the first involves minor duties of due care, while the second level involves more stringent duties similar to those in a parent-child relationship—and that the burdens a pregnant woman may be expected to bear grow as the pregnancy advances. The implications of this for state intervention are profound: The state would not be justified in intervening to prevent some very troubling prenatal harms simply because they are caused during the early stage of pregnancy and dealing with them would place an unwarranted burden on the pregnant woman.

The discussion so far has been fairly abstract, and necessarily so. We cannot make reasonable conclusions about concrete cases until all of the relevant moral, legal, and public policy issues have been addressed. And so far we have considered only a small subset of those arguments that bear on the issue at hand: Only the arguments in favor of coercing a pregnant woman to behave in certain ways have been advanced. We have been looking, in other words, at the rights of the future child, the duties of the pregnant woman to the future child, and possible benefits—to the children and to society in general—of preventing prenatal harms. But there are many other arguments to examine before a final determination can be made. We must, for instance, consider a pregnant woman's duties in conjunction with her rights and liberties, and we must examine other sorts of factors that militate against state intervention in these cases, such as the disbenefits that might result.

Thus although the thrust of the discussion so far has been that it is reasonable to impose some legal limitations on the choices open to pregnant women, these conclusions are only preliminary because other important relevant ingredients have yet to be taken into account. The arguments against state intervention into the lives of pregnant women, which will be examined next, are at least as strong as the arguments in favor of state intervention.

ARGUMENTS AGAINST

... Proponents of state intervention look to cases like these to support their arguments. In the Pamela Rae Stewart case, for example, her physician's list of instructions does not seem unduly burdensome: She was told to take a certain medication for a couple of weeks, refrain from having sexual intercourse, refrain from ingesting illegal drugs, and get as much rest as possible. Advocates of state intervention question which is likely to cause more harm: requiring her by law to follow these instructions or not requiring her to do so. We must weigh the relatively minor inconvenience and discomfort to Stewart, it is contended, against the death of a child who, had his mother behaved differently, would presumably be alive and healthy today. This is a utilitarian calculation: We weigh the possible harms and benefits, and choose the alternative that would produce the least harm and/or the greatest benefit.

A legitimate goal of state intervention with pregnant women is the prevention of harm to their future children. And the guiding concern behind the intervention is in principle the welfare of these children. But as we shall see from a closer examination of the above cases, efforts to act on these laudable intentions must be scrutinized carefully: State intervention may cause more harm than it prevents; it may discriminate unfairly against pregnant women; and a professed interest in the welfare of children may mask a more controversial attitude toward the place of women in society.

Of those who argue against state intervention to prevent prenatal harms, most hold that *no* interventions should be allowed. They would probably agree with Martha Field's contention that "No maternal action, not even drug abuse, should justify pre- or postbirth sanctions for pregnant women's behavior."[16] As with arguments in favor of state intervention to prevent prenatal harms, there are a variety of arguments available against state intervention. We shall analyze four of the strongest positions: (1) those that appeal to the rights of pregnant women, (2) those employing consequentialist calculations, (3) those based on a claim of unfair discrimination, and (4) those appealing to the problems of drafting and implementing fair, workable laws. . . .

Rights of Pregnant Women

. . . There are many considerations that must be taken into account before reaching a conclusion regarding which infringements with a pregnant woman's rights of liberty and privacy would be inappropriate and unfair. As demonstrated earlier, for instance, there are good reasons to assert that a woman does not have carte blanche to do whatever she wants while pregnant and that she may have certain moral and legal obligations toward her future child. In other words, because the proper response to the issue at hand— overriding a pregnant woman's preferences in order to protect the interests of her future child—calls for a balancing of interests, consequences, rights, and obligations, it is premature to conclude that a pregnant woman's rights of bodily integrity and private decision making may never be overridden. Yet since these rights are of such fundamental importance to our society, it should be clear that they may be abridged only in order to uphold something else that is of even greater importance. Thus the question for us—whether the protection of the interests of her future child is ever reason enough to override her rights of self-determination and privacy—remains open.

Consequentialist Arguments

It was argued earlier that the state has a legitimate interest in the prevention of prenatal harms, and that this interest may be important enough to outweigh the pregnant woman's right to be left alone. If this were so, it would be the case only when state intervention could be expected to be successful: that is, only when state intervention would indeed prevent harm to the future child. Although there are potential benefits to children of attempts to prevent prenatal harms, there is also a plethora of potential negative effects on them and on their mothers.

Critics of state intervention claim that, instead of reducing suffering, state intervention in these cases will only increase it. A pregnant woman who fears that her physician will report her to state authorities might be unwilling to divulge the details of her life, for instance, to avoid unwanted limitations on her choices. She may even refrain from seeking medical care altogether. Many of these women have what are considered to be high-risk pregnancies, and they are precisely the women who need medical care the most.

It is conceivable, then, that coercive measures designed to help a child could result instead in discouraging his drug-abusing mother from obtaining prenatal care, or encouraging her to refrain from telling the truth about her condition to the physician. Other negative possibilities abound: "Coercive measures may lead to concealed pregnancies, nonassisted births, an upsurge in abandonment, and even infanticide."[17] Were this the case, the big losers would be the children. In response to these and other "potentially regrettable consequences of forced medical or surgical procedures," the Committee on Bioethics of the American Academy of Pediatrics recommends that court intervention should be sought only "in rare cases" and "should be seen as a last resort to be undertaken with great caution."[18]

Although opponents of state interference take the possibility of these negative consequences as conclusive, it is important to note that instituting state involvement in prenatal matters may not have these effects. All fifty states require by law that many professionals—pediatricians, emergency room physicians, teachers, social workers—report suspected cases of child abuse to state authorities and thus initiate mechanisms designed to remove children from the custody of their parents, yet the efficacy of these professionals has not been destroyed. However, because there is a real possibility that something could go drastically wrong were pregnant women required by law to behave in certain ways, careful exploration of the social consequences is warranted before action is taken on a public policy level.

Methods of dealing with prenatal damage after it has occurred may also cause more harm than good. Bringing criminal charges against a woman for fetal abuse, for instance, may not have much deterrent effect, for the choices of many pregnant women are often not amenable to rational incentives. And criminal sanctions may be counterproductive: The newborn of a woman in jail would be without his mother during crucial bonding stages, and a mother who is imprisoned after the birth of her son because of harm she caused him while pregnant may thereby resent him and may mistreat him should she regain custody.[19]

It is also important to note that other methods exist for reducing the incidence of prenatal harm, methods that are likely to be more successful than the coercive measures discussed above. Many prenatal harms are not caused intentionally but instead are the result of the mother's ignorance about the special circumstances of pregnancy: the nutritional requirements, the effects of certain drugs, the consequences of maternal infections, and so on. Health education, then, is an important element in the prevention of prenatal harms. It should be required of all school children, and made available to everyone else (and for girls, at least, the classes should emphasize the special needs of pregnant women).

Education will not solve the problem of preventable prenatal harms, of course, for some pregnant women will continue to pay insufficient attention to the welfare of the children they will bear even though they are aware of the consequences of their acts. One likely explanation for this behavior is that the women do not wish to be pregnant. And the proper response to this is obvious: Improve methods of contraception, make them more easily affordable and more widely available, and reduce the barriers to abortion during the first trimester of pregnancy. A consequentialist calculation of the net benefits of these measures in relation to more coercive measures (such as threatening to imprison a mother after the birth of an impaired child) would no doubt rank the former as preferable: They will reduce the incidence of prenatal harm with few negative repercussions.

The "Slippery Slope" Arguments

A different sort of consequentialist argument is called the "slippery slope" argument. There are two parts to this argument, what we may call the *logical* version and the *practical* version.

The logical version of the slippery slope argument says, in effect, that it is not possible to formulate a principle that will permit just the actions we want to permit while also excluding all those we want to exclude. Thus, unless we wish to allow the state to interfere in every aspect of a pregnant woman's life, we must not take the first step—we must not permit any intrusion at all into a pregnant woman's liberty—for that would also logically commit us to permitting the most severe and most unjust interferences with her liberty as well.

The strength of this argument lies in the accuracy of the statement that there are no good reasons for accepting some intrusions with a pregnant woman's liberty while rejecting others. But is this true? Are there really no rational grounds for distinguishing one type of state interference from another in these cases? The answer lies in an examination of a set of related factors that must be considered before the conclusion can be drawn that any intervention is truly justified. These include the requirements of due process of law and proportionality (which weighs the nature and extent of the harm to be prevented, the probability that it will occur, the probability that it can be avoided, and the degree of the intrusion). Limits have been set in other types of cases: The Supreme Court makes a distinction, for instance, between the minor invasion of taking a blood sample from a suspect and the major invasion of pumping his stomach, and legislators of every state in the nation believe that a line can be drawn between the legitimate exercise of parental discretion and the illegitimate infliction of child abuse. Rational limits can be set in pregnancy cases as well, but no doubt these limits would not satisfy those who oppose all state interventions into the activities of pregnant women.

The other version of the slippery slope argument—which is characterized as the practical version—is based on predictions of outcomes, not logic. The basic contention of this argument is that once we allow any intrusion at all into the lives of pregnant women, even intrusions of the most minor sort, then other, more morally questionable intrusions will in fact follow: We will continue to change and loosen our principles as we become psychologically accustomed to what previously seemed extraordinary and unacceptable. First a pregnant woman might be forbidden to take certain illegal drugs known to cause fetal damage, then she might be forbidden to use other, otherwise legal, teratogenic substances such as alcohol and tobacco. Then the state might require her to take certain vitamins and eat certain foods: The importance of maternal nutrition during pregnancy has been well documented.[20] Eventually the state would prohibit her from taking some over-the-counter drugs (such as cough medicines and aspirin), require her to get a certain number of hours of bedrest, monitor her sexual activity, and so on. Indeed, the argument goes, potentially almost everything a pregnant woman does will be open to state control (since almost everything a pregnant woman does may cause prenatal harm).

How could conformity to these strictures be ensured? George Annas suggests that "[e]ffectively monitoring compliance would require confining pregnant women to an environment in which eating, exercise, drug use, and sexual intercourse could be controlled. This could, of course, be a maximum security country club."[21] After all, could we trust a pregnant woman who is addicted to nicotine to cease smoking simply because a judge ordered her to do so? And would not a drug addict be more likely to hide than to submit to weekly urine tests? The only way we can be certain that pregnant women are not doing anything that will harm their future children is to monitor their every activity.

But, as Annas points out, "such massive invasions of privacy can only be justified by treating pregnant women during their pregnancy as nonpersons."[22] This is not paranoia speaking. The history of women is fraught with domination and subjugation and denial of basic rights: In the past, women in this country could not hold public office, serve on juries, or bring suit in their own names; women could not practice law, or bartend, or work extended hours; women could not even vote. All of these restrictions have since been lifted in the United States, but the worry remains that the attitude behind them—which views men and women as fundamentally dissimilar, with distinct social roles to play—still persists.

The view that men and women are intrinsically different is an old and familiar one. And the implications drawn from it—that men belong in the public world of work while women belong in the home caring for their families—is one many people find appealing. But while this view of the distinctive spheres of men and women reflects a very common worldview, it is not a worldview that is universally accepted or appreciated. And it is certainly not a worldview that should be imposed on those who do not share it, at least in our pluralistic society, where many people believe that, with regard to social roles, there are no significant differences between men and women. It would be unfair, then, to impose one set of values on people who do not share them, to treat all women as though their primary function were to propagate the species and thereby to deny them access to alternative lifestyles. . . .

Difficulty of Drafting and Implementing Legislation

Legitimate state intervention into the lives of pregnant women presupposes that the women have been put on notice that society expects them to meet a reasonable standard of due care and will not tolerate certain activities. One effective way to do this is through legislation: Certain behaviors of pregnant women could be legally proscribed through a body of "crimes against the fetus' statutes."[23] Indeed, such laws are necessary if criminal penalties are to be imposed, since crimes in this country are set by statute, not through the common law (as are torts).

Statutorily prohibiting prenatal harms in general would not work, in part because some prenatal harms simply cannot be avoided: There are certain deleterious conditions for which no medical treatment exists, for instance, or that cannot be detected in time to permit intervention.[24] The law, then, should speak only to that set of prenatal harms that can be prevented. Ideally, the law would include all and only those whose behavior we wish to change and exclude those whom we believe it is improper to coerce.

As a point of departure, consider the actions of Pamela Rae Stewart, as described by the prosecutor:

> Defendant's concealed argument is that a mother, with impunity, may ignore the warnings of her doctor despite the knowledge that she is experi-

encing a problem pregnancy. She may ply her body with dangerous, illegal and harmful drugs with no thought to its effect on the helpless human being growing in her womb. She may subject herself to the rigors of sexual intercourse without concern for the effect on the baby. And even though specifically warned, she may lay bleeding for hours without seeking available medical attention as her baby is deprived of its only source of nourishment. Such extreme disregard for any other human life, not to mention one whose only chance of survival depends upon the mother who carries him, approaches the level of maliciousness and conscious disregard for human life, which would properly support a second-degree murder conviction, not to mention one for a violation of Penal Code section 270.[25]

Let us assume for the sake of argument that the prosecutor has accurately described the facts. What precisely did Ms. Stewart do that was so terribly wrong? She stopped taking her prescribed medication, she had intercourse with her husband, she took some sort of drug (the prosecutor claims amphetamines, Ms. Stewart claims antihistamines), and she postponed seeking medical care. Except for taking amphetamines (which she denies), Ms. Stewart's actions were not especially troublesome, yet the combination of factors resulted in the birth of a severely brain-damaged child who died in infancy.

Could we devise a law (or set of laws) that would speak to analogous cases yet exclude women who have good reasons to engage in similar activities? Surely we do not want to prohibit by statute sexual relations between consenting adults (especially married couples); nor can we reasonably put limits on how much time may lapse between the realization that medical care may be needed and the seeking of such care: There are, after all, a large number of quite acceptable reasons for postponing medical care, one of which is the sensible judgment that whatever is wrong is not wrong enough to warrant the bother and expense of professional treatment.

So the proposal for dealing with cases such as Ms. Stewart's through a set of laws dealing with particular activities—sexual relations between consenting adults, judgments about the need for medical care, and so on—is untenable. Such laws would intrude too much on the privacy and autonomy of all of us. Instead, it might make sense to address these cases in light of her one over-arching failure: She failed to follow her physician's instructions. The proposal, then, is to require pregnant women to conform to their physicians' recommendations.

But would we really want to make criminal all failures to follow a physician's advice? After all, physicians are not invariably correct. In the past, they routinely prescribed X-rays and diuretics for pregnant women, for instance, practices that are discouraged today. And medical interventions accepted today are fraught with uncertainties as well, as the American College of Obstetricians and Gynecologists points out:

Medical knowledge and judgment have limitations and fallibility, which the obstetrician must recognize when assigning clinical risks and benefits in order to advise patients. Methods for detecting fetal distress or deterioration are not always reliable indicators of poor outcome; therefore, assigning a degree of risk to the fetus is difficult. In addition, expected benefits for the fetus cannot always be achieved.[26]

The prevalence of uncertainties in medicine stands as a strong disincentive for requiring by law that a pregnant woman follow her physician's advice.

Perhaps, though, it should be illegal for a pregnant woman to ignore a physician's recommendation when doing so causes prenatal harm. The woman, in other words, could be punished after the fact. But even when a physician's diagnosis is accurate and his or her recommended treatment course is the standard one, a policy of punishing a woman for having failed to conform has serious problems. The first is that, unless medical care is provided free of charge, we must expect that there will be legitimate financial reasons for not following some physicians' instructions. We could hardly fault a pregnant woman for not purchasing a prescription drug she believed she could not afford, or for not quitting the job she needs to support her family in order to obtain the recommended number of hours of bedrest. In addition, if we permit physicians to make decisions for pregnant women, we give them unprecedented power over one group of people, power that they do not have over any other. Physicians have the legal and moral duty to obtain the informed consent of all competent patients, including pregnant women. To make an exception to the informed consent rule in the case of pregnant women would be to discriminate unfairly against them.

The type of law we have been considering is too dangerously vague to be taken seriously. It would also probably be unconstitutional. As the Supreme Court has noted, "A vague law impermissibly delegates basic policy matters to policemen, judges, and juries for resolution on an ad hoc and subjective basis with discriminatory application."[27] The worry that such laws would be open to discriminatory implementation and abuse is not an idle one. The case of Kay Smith is instructive. First, her rights of due process were violated when her case was heard in a juvenile court—which is not constituted to handle cases of the mental competence of adults—and so she was not judged according to the specific statutes that determine the state's right to restrict her liberty due to her mental illness. Second, although lawyers for the state argued in court that Smith's pregnancy was very near term and that her detention would therefore last approximately only two weeks, she in fact remained institutionalized for more than six weeks. One has to wonder if the stage of her pregnancy was misrepresented so that the state's proposal would appear less onerous to her.[28]

And it is probably not a coincidence that many such cases involve women who are poor: Almost all of the pregnant women who have been subject to state intervention have been indigent or disadvantaged in some way. A national study conducted in 1987 showed that of the twenty-one cases in which court orders were sought to intervene in the decisions of pregnant women, all of them involved women who were receiving public assistance or who were treated in a teaching-hospital clinic. In addition, 81 percent of the women were minorities (African, Asian, or Hispanic), and 24 percent spoke English as a second language.[29]

Another study—this one conducted on women who enrolled for prenatal care in one Florida county in 1989—raises the question of discriminatory implementation of the law even more pointedly.[30] The researchers concluded that, although white women are just as likely to use drugs and alcohol during pregnancy as black women, blacks are much more likely to be reported to state authorities for drug use than whites:

> The proportion of white women reported for any drug use (48 of 4,290 who delivered live-born infants) was 1.1 percent, whereas the proportion of black women reported for any drug use (85 of 793) was 10.7 percent. Thus, a black woman was 9.6 times more likely than a white woman to be reported for substance abuse during pregnancy. The difference was evident despite the fact that in the population we surveyed the frequency of positive results on toxicologic testing of urine samples obtained at the first prenatal visit was similar for white women (15.4 percent) and black women (14.1 percent).[31]

The authors of the study were unable to explain their results—but unfair discrimination would not be a bad guess.

One alternative to instituting vague laws that are open to discriminatory implementation and abuse is to spell out precisely what activities are prohibited and/or required. To accomplish this, however, we must abandon the goal of developing laws that would include a wide variety of prenatal harms—since, as pointed out above, the state's power to interfere with individuals' lives would be too great—and instead adopt the less onerous task of developing laws that cover a few specific prenatal harms. The case of Margaret Reyes is relevant here. Ms. Reyes ingested heroin during her pregnancy, and her twin children were born with heroin addictions. Since heroin is already considered to be an illegal substance, and since ingesting an illegal substance while pregnant is a straightforward action easy to describe, designing a statute prohibiting it seems relatively unproblematic.

The trouble with this proposal, however, is that we again run the risk of being arbitrary: Only those activities that we are able to describe satisfactorily in a statute will be prohibited or required, while equally harmful behavior goes unchallenged simply because it cannot be codified adequately.

Finally, before we decide to invoke the criminal law as a social response to prenatal harms—before we decide to create a new class of criminal—we should be certain that there is a strong preponderance of reasons in favor of doing so, for to be given a criminal status in our society is to be given a condemnation; indeed, we often refer to it as being "branded" a criminal. Joel Feinberg calls this the "expressive function [of punishment]: punishment is a conventional device for the expression of attitudes of resentment and indignation, and of judgments of disapproval and reprobation."[32] We have argued that there is no such preponderance of reasons in favor of criminal legislation; indeed, we have argued that the balance falls against regarding pregnant women as potential criminals. But even if the arguments fail to persuade that the balance of reasons lies against criminalizing certain activities of pregnant women, at least it should go far in showing that a clear preponderance of reasons in support of criminal legislation does not exist.

Conclusion

We have argued that there are compelling reasons against allowing the state to intervene with the activities of pregnant women even when it is clear that their children will be carried to term: The state should not monitor a pregnant woman's activities in order to prevent harm to or promote the well-being of her future child, nor should it criminalize certain activities of pregnant women because they cause prenatal harms. These conclusions are based on a variety of arguments: (1) a woman's fundamental rights of bodily integrity and private decision making should not be subordinated to the welfare of someone else; (2) requiring pregnant women to behave in certain ways will have seriously negative consequences: pregnant women will be unwilling to be candid with their physicians or they will not seek prenatal care at all, the number of abortions will increase, or grave hardships will be imposed on already burdened pregnant women; (3) a few reasonable limitations on the activities of pregnant women will lead inevitably to many unjust and onerous limitations (the "slippery slope" arguments); (4) it is not fair to demand things of pregnant women that are demanded of no one else in society, so requiring pregnant women to behave in certain ways or risk legal penalties is unfairly discriminatory; and (5) the obstacles to drafting and implementing fair, workable laws seem insurmountable.

Of course, not all of the arguments presented here are compelling. One could argue, for instance, that it is not impossible to draft responsible laws that would make at least some of a pregnant woman's obligations to her future child clear and not unduly burdensome: After all, other laws considered by many people to be necessary—including child abuse and neglect laws—require equal subtlety and raise similar concerns. And the fact that all prenatal harms cannot be prevented is not reason enough to forgo preventing any of them.

In addition, we should be cautious about concluding that laws limiting the liberty of pregnant women are bound to be abused: It is not clear that imposing some minimal legal requirements of due care on pregnant women would inevitably lead to the imposition of unfair burdens. We previously argued for the opposite position, that a legal duty of due care on the part of a pregnant woman with regard to the child she will bear should be recognized and that this duty—which is based on a standard of reasonableness—would not be unduly onerous. Indeed, while "slippery slope" arguments should be taken seriously, since the potential for abuse in these cases is real, they should not be taken too seriously: It is possible to conjure up potentially terrible consequences for every public policy initiative, even the most benign.

So some of the arguments are stronger and more reliable than others. An important question at this juncture is whether any combination of them is strong enough to justify the position that state interference into the activities of pregnant women is always wrong (because such interference would violate important rights of pregnant women), unfair (because the rules cannot be enforced impartially), or useless (because more harm than good would be produced in the process). If this is the case, then it would be consistent to advocate as a public policy position that state intervention into the lives of pregnant women in order to prevent prenatal harms should *never* be allowed. The arguments here, however, may not have shown that all types of state intervention to prevent prenatal harms are improper, but only that many of them are. Indeed, I believe that I have presented a strong array of reasons to conclude that even though a pregnant woman has moral obligations to act in the interests of her future child throughout her pregnancy, there are compelling reasons against legally requiring her to meet certain standards of due care before it is uncontroversially clear that she intends to bring the pregnancy to term. This conclusion has far-reaching implications for state intervention: The state would not be justified in acting to prevent some very serious prenatal harms during the early stage of a woman's pregnancy.

The issue now, then, is the strength of the arguments against state intervention during the later stage of pregnancy (the stage at which a woman's moral duties are most strong because she clearly will be carrying the pregnancy to term). Perhaps some state interventions to prevent prenatal harms at this stage are warranted.

NOTES

1. The National Commission to Prevent Infant Mortality estimates that for every low birth weight prevented, the general health care system would save between $14,000 and $30,000. "Disease: The Focus of Programs to Reduce Infant Mortality," *Infectious Disease in Children* 20 (1988).

2. The National Commission to Prevent Infant Mortality estimates that if the 1985 U.S. mortality rate had been 5.5 per 1,000 births (instead of 10.6 per 1,000 births), and if the number of low-birth-weight infants had been reduced by half, an additional $6.4 billion to $12 billion would have been earned over the children's lifetime—approximately $1.4 billion to $2.6 billion of which would have been paid in taxes. Ibid.

3. Since we assume nothing about the moral status of the fetus, and are acquiescing to the legal principle that the fetus has no legally protectable interests, it follows that the fetus has no rights strong enough to outweigh its mother's rights.

4. It should be noted, however, that these rights do not necessarily imply that there is also a right to be born. The duty to provide medical treatment, for example, to the fetus who will be carried to term is a duty to the post-fetal person she will become *if* she is carried to term, and it need not entail a duty to carry her to term.

5. *Smith v. Brennan*, 31 NJ 353, 157 A2d 497 (1960).

6. *Park v. Chessin* 400 NYS 110 (1977). While "the right to begin life with a sound mind and body" has been adopted by other courts (*In re Baby X*, 97 Mich App 111, 293 NW 2d 736 [1980]; *Womack v. Buckhorn*, 384 Mich 718, 187 NW 2d 218 [1976]), the right of a child to be born as a "whole, functional human being" has held little sway, and indeed was rejected almost immediately by the New York Court of Appeals. *Becker v. Schwartz*, 46 NY 2d 401, 386 NE 2d 807, 413, NYS 2d 895 (1978).

7. M. W. Shaw, "Conditional Prospective Rights of the Fetus," *Journal of Legal Medicine* 5 (1984): 95.

8. There is another possible interpretation of this right: that a child who cannot be born healthy may have the right not to be born at all.

Consider the following hypothetical case. Diagnostic procedures performed on Mrs. D. reveal that the fetus she is carrying is severely impaired: the fetus has spina bifida (an open spinal column), hydrocephalus (excess fluid on the brain), microcephaly (an abnormally small head and brain), and an improperly formed brain stem. Although it is anticipated that the child will survive past infancy, it is clear that he cannot be born with, and will never enjoy, "a sound mind and body," nor will he ever be a "whole, functioning human being." If the child has a right to be born sound and whole, and this right cannot be met, does it follow that he has a right not to be born at all?

The existence of such a right would have profound effects. If a child has a right to begin life with a sound mind and body, then any action that interferes with that right would be prima facie wrongful, even if the action does not worsen the condition of the child. This means that bringing an impaired child into the world—even if it is not possible under the circumstances to produce a healthy child—would be wrong, since it violates his right to be born healthy. Some commentators have argued for such a position, and have suggested that legislators at least consider prohibiting certain acts by pregnant women: exposing a fetus to "the mother's defective intrauterine environment caused by her genotype," for instance, and carrying a seriously defective child to term. M. W. Shaw, "The Potential Plaintiff: Preconception and Prenatal Torts," in *Genetics and the Law II*, ed. A. Milunsky and A. J. Annas (New York: Plenum, 1980).

There are several ways for the state to recognize this right. One method of protecting a right not to be born unhealthy is to monitor all potential parents and refuse to permit those individuals who are likely to pass on severely deleterious genes to reproduce. We could, in other words, create a legal duty to refrain from passing on certain genes (M. W. Shaw, "Genetically Defective Children: Emerging Legal Considerations," *American Journal of Law and Medicine* 3 [1977]: 333–40). The state could screen all men and women of childbearing age: Those who are fertile and who are at high risk of having seriously impaired children could be sterilized.

A second method of protecting the right not to be born would be to monitor all pregnant women and to require those who are carrying severely impaired fetuses to obtain abortions. This would mean compelling some pregnant women to get abortions against their wills and against their most fundamental beliefs.

Another alternative is to utilize the tort law: The child could be allowed to sue for compensation for having been born severely impaired, or someone could sue on the child's behalf. Courts have been confronted with the difficult task of addressing these suits—usually referred to as "wrongful life" cases—since the early 1960s. In a wrongful life suit, the child argues that her being born with serious impairments (even though there was no possibility that she could be born without the impairments) was a harm that calls for compensation, and she claims damages for having to live with her permanent and severe handicaps. In a way, the child claims that her suffering is so great that it would have been better had she not been born.

And finally, infanticide could be legalized. Infanticide is an option insofar as the desire to prevent prenatal harms is motivated by the desire to reduce human suffering, and one way to reduce human suffering is to eliminate the people who suffer the most. Infanticide for any reason at all is not the issue here; we are considering infanticide as a means of mitigating human suffering in the same way we are considering state intervention into the lives of pregnant women to prevent prenatal harms as a means of mitigating human suffering. In other words, infanticide may be considered to be an alternative means of dealing with devastatingly severe prenatal harms, and it offers the potential for reducing the suffering occasioned by some prenatal harms without intruding on the autonomy of pregnant women.

While theoretically plausible, none of these alternatives offers a viable solution to the dilemma at hand. Most courts continue to reject wrongful life suits, for instance, and states are increasingly moving to prohibit them by statute. And given the serious shortcomings of the other proposals—the invasions of privacy, the overtones of prejudice, the negation of individual liberty, the assault on self-determination, the lack of respect for human life, the unacceptable increase of state control, and the inevitable abuse of such discretionary power—these options are likely to be anathema to most people. They are not being recommended here.

9. J. Feinberg, *The Moral Limits of the Criminal Law, Volume One, Harm to Others* (Oxford: Oxford University Press, 1984), p. 11.

10. M. Aronson and R. Olegard, "Children of Alcoholic Mothers," *Pediatrician* 14 (1987): 57–61; C. D. Cole et al., "Neonatal Ethanol Withdrawl: Characteristics in Clinically Normal, Nondysmorphic Neonates," *Journal of Pediatrics* 105 (1984): 445–71; Department of Health, Education, and Welfare, *Smoking and Health: A Report of the Surgeon General* (Washington, D.C.: U.S. Government Printing Office, 1979); R. E. Little et al., "Fetal Alcohol Effects in Humans and Animals," *Advances in Alcohol and Substance Abuse* (1982): 103–25; C. Orstead et al., "Efficacy of Prenatal

Nutrition Counseling: Weight Gain, Infant Birth Weight, and Cost-Effectiveness," *Journal of the American Dietic Association* 85 (1985): 40–45.

11. L. E. Lomansky, *Persons, Rights, and the Moral Community* (Oxford: Oxford University Press, 1987); L. W. Sumner, *The Moral Foundation of Rights* (Oxford: Oxford University Press, 1987); C. Wellman, *A Theory of Rights* (Totowa, N.J.: Rowman and Allanheld, 1985).

12. R. Veatch, "Limits of Guardian Treatment Refusal: A Reasonableness Standard," *American Journal of Law and Medicine* 9 (1984): 427–70.

13. *Gibson v. Gibson*, 3 Cal3d 914, 479 p2d 648, 92 Cal. Rptr. 288 (1971).

14. D. Mathieu, "Respecting Liberty and Preventing Harm: Limits of State Intervention in Prenatal Care," *Harvard Journal of Law and Public Policy* 8 (1985): 19–55.

15. Feinberg, *Moral Limits of the Criminal Law.*

16. M. A. Field, "Controlling the Woman to Protect the Fetus," *Law, Medicine, and Health Care* 17 (1989): 114–29.

17. J. Gallagher, "Position Paper: Fetus as Patient," in *Reproductive Laws for the 1990s*, ed. S. Cohen and N. Taub (Clifton, N.J.: Humana Press, 1989), p. 214.

18. American Academy of Pediatrics, Committee on Bioethics, "Fetal Therapy: Ethical Considerations," *Pediatrics* 81 (1988): 898–99.

19. Someone who believes that punishment is justified because the guilty deserve to be punished (who holds, in other words, a retributivist theory of punishment) would most likely be indifferent to these potential negative effects of punishing a mother for having caused prenatal harms, and would instead argue that if she wrongfully caused harm, then she should be punished, regardless of the consequences. This is not the position presumed here.

There are two telling criticisms of this type of retributivist stance. One could argue that even though the woman may deserve punishment, it does not follow that she should be punished, since countervailing considerations—such as the disbenefits to her child—may be more important. Thus one may reasonably conclude that it is better not to punish her at all but to deal with the problem in some other way. Alternatively, one could claim that punishment is never morally good (since it is an infliction of harm), and it is justified only if its "good" consequences (e.g., deterrence of undesirable activity) outweigh its "bad" consequences (e.g., the punished women are harmed and their infants are left without their mothers). I am suggesting here that punishing women for having caused prenatal harm is likely to have more disbenefits than benefits.

20. Committee on Nutrition, *Nutrition in Maternal Health Care* (Chicago: American College of Obstetricians and Gynecologists, 1974); Committee to Study the Prevention of Low Birthweight, Institute of Medicine, *Preventing Low Birthweight* (Washington, D.C.: National Academy Press, 1985); R. L. Naeye et al., "Effects of Maternal Nutrition on the Human Fetus," *Pediatrics* 52 (1973): 494–500; C. Phillips and N. Johnson, "The Impact of Quality of Diet and Other Factors on Birthweight of Infants," *American Journal of Clinical Nutrition* 30 (1977): 215–21; R. Rosso, "Nutrition and Maternal-Fetal Exchange," *American Journal of Clinical Nutrition* 34 (1981): 744–81.

21. G. J. Annas, "Pregnant Women as Fetal Containers," *Hastings Center Report* 16 (1986): 13–14.

22. Ibid.

23. "Comment: Criminal Liability of a Prospective Mother for Prenatal Neglect of a Viable Fetus," *Whittier Law Review* 9 (1987): 363–96; J. Parness, "Crimes against the Unborn," *Harvard Journal on Legislation* 22 (1985): 97–172.

24. This raises the issue of the value of recognizing a right not to be born, mentioned briefly in note 6.

25. *People* v. *Stewart*, No. M508197 (San Diego Municipal Court, 1987), E. L. Miller Jr. and R. C. Phillips, "Points and Authorities in Opposition to Defendant's Demurrer and Motion to Dismiss."

26. Committee on Ethics, "Statement of the Committee on Ethics," American College of Obstetricians and Gynecologists, Washington, D.C., 1987.

27. *Grayned* v. *City of Rockford*, 408 US 104 (1971), p. 109.

28. I am not arguing that Smith should have been released before the birth of her child. A homeless, mentally impaired, near-term pregnant woman who cannot care for herself should be a legitimate exception to a rule forbidding state intervention. The point is, rather, that the procedure for deciding her fate was seriously flawed, and so her rights of due process were violated. Even though the presence of due process very likely would have produced the identical outcome in Smith's case, the state should have adhered to the requirements of due process under the theory that following the correct procedure will produce the desired (i.e., fair) outcome considerably more often than will ignoring the requirements of due process.

29. V. E. B. Kolder et al., "Court-Ordered Obstetrical Interventions," *New England Journal of Medicine* 316 (1987): 1192–96.

30. I. J. Chasnoff et al., "The Prevalence of Illicit-Drug or Alcohol Use during Pregnancy and Discrepancies in Mandatory Reporting in Pinellas County, Florida," *New England Journal of Medicine* 322 (1990): 1202–1206.

31. Ibid., p. 1204.

32. J. Feinberg, "The Expressive Function of Punishment," in *Doing and Deserving* (Princeton, N.J.: Princeton University Press, 1970), p. 98.

ARGUMENTS AGAINST LICENSING PARENTS

Jack C. Westman

███████████████████████████████████

If men were angels, no government would be necessary. If angels were to govern men, neither external nor internal controls on government would be necessary.

—James Madison, *The Federalist*, 1787[1]

I wrote *Licensing Parents: Can We Prevent Child Abuse and Neglect?* because of the image in my mind of the millions of children who are being neglected today. That image contains faces I know. They will not leave me, and I cannot turn away from them. I know that these children have no political constituency. I know firsthand the enormous resistances to helping them, even on the part of well-intentioned people. But I also know that truth and logic are on the side of these children. I know that we live in a nation in which justice for them has a chance to prevail.

No reasonable person would deny that children should not be neglected and should be competently parented. Yet any effort to ensure that children have competent parents meets strident objections. Such an effort encounters the strongly held sentiments that family life is a private matter and that government already interferes in our lives too much. We are loath to point fingers at parents. Underneath these sentiments lies a disguised but deep-seated presumption that children are the possessions of their parents.

Even more fundamentally, we Americans resist constraints on our lives. We do not like to think of ourselves as controlled by forces that limit our choices. We do not like to think of ourselves as dependent on other people. We prefer to think of ourselves as independent actors free of constraints. We do not want anyone looking over our shoulders as we do anything, especially parent our children. Many people also are weary of our society's emphasis on rights and feel that we do not need additional claims for rights for children now.

The very notion of setting expectations for parenting can readily be construed as "blaming" those of us who are parents. We already are stressed by living in a society that does not support us. We feel stretched to our limits as we try to do our best in meeting the demands of child-rearing. We may well fear that if there were public expectations for parents, our own lives would be made even more difficult.

Furthermore, most of us who are or have been parents have acted in ways that have fallen short of our images of ideal parenting. We feel guilty and inadequate when we make mistakes or let our children down. For this reason, the mere mention of parental competence in itself might evoke the fear that we would not qualify as competent.

Actually, a statement by society that parenting is important would have the opposite effect. Because only the most obviously abusive and neglectful parents would not meet the simple expectations of minimal competence, the vast majority of parents would be affirmed. Rather than being taken for granted as a secondary or minor role in our society, parenting would be more realistically appreciated and valued as an essential social institution. Because the requirements for licensing would not be met only by parents who clearly are incompetent, the vast majority of parents would be reassured that they are competent. Furthermore, the due process of law and appeal procedures would ensure that a competent parent would not be denied a license.

From the political point of view, those of us who are liberals might be concerned that the emphasis on individual responsibility inherent in licensing parents could be used as an excuse to curtail government support programs. Those of us who are conservatives might regard parent licensing as an objectionable intrusion into our private affairs. Most likely, a parent licensing process really would call attention to foundering parents and provide objectives for government programs designed to help them. It would no more invade the privacy of families than do existing child abuse and neglect statutes.

There is an overwhelming list of reasonable arguments against parent licensing. That list includes the following categories: the imposition of majority standards on minorities; the fear of violating the sacred nature of the parent-child relationship; the fear that licensing would foster blaming parents; the fear of restricting the personal freedom of adults, even to behave unwisely; the fear that licensing would accompany financial child support; the fear of according adult rights to children; the fear of enforcing conformity in child-rearing; the political rejection of the family; the belief that rearing a child in itself produces maturity; objections to the prior restraint of adult freedom; the fallibility of prediction and education; the unfeasibility of administrating licensure procedures; the fear that licensing would replace aid to parents; the lack of adoption opportunities; the fact that research on social problems is incomplete; the belief that education and training in parenting are sufficient to ensure competent parenting; the belief that children should not be accorded favored legal treatment; society's inherent need for incompetence; and the belief that drastic social changes cannot occur.

Unless each one of these arguments is carefully analyzed, the sheer number of them seems to be enough to summarily dismiss even the mention of licensing parents. That reaction neatly conceals juvenile ageism because each of these arguments is flawed.

THE IMPOSITION OF MAJORITY STANDARDS

Fears that a licensing process could be used to impose the standards of the majority on minority groups are not to be taken lightly. To dispel fears of this form of intentional manipulation, a parenting licensing system would have to be based upon simple standards free from cultural and socioeconomic biases.

The experience of Nazi Germany stands as a warning that the powers of the state can be used against minorities. Eugenics, or "racial hygiene," became popular and academically respectable in Europe in the late nineteenth century.[2] Until the 1920s racial hygiene focused primarily on counteracting the declining birthrate and on reducing mental and physical degeneracy. Thereafter, the presumed Jewish threat to Aryan supremacy preoccupied the racial hygiene movement in Germany and resulted in a distinctively Nazi category—"life unworthy of life."

Germany's ills at that time were attributed by the Nazis to threats to the "folk body" from the growing number of the "unworthy"—the handicapped, criminals, and the inferior yet dangerous races. By medicalizing social problems in the name of improving their race, the Nazis justified the isolation or elimination of those whom they considered to be undesirable. The Nazis encouraged the procreation of people they called Aryans and the rearing of children by the state.

The possibility of such abuse of government powers is remote in the United States because of constitutional guarantees and the modus operandi of our democratic government. More specifically, licensing parents to raise children would not limit the ability of individuals to conceive or to give birth to children, nor would it necessarily affect the lifestyles of individuals.

In fact, because their right to competent parenting is not recognized, incompetently parented children in disadvantaged minority groups are the victims of racial, sex, and age discrimination now. Incompetent parenting forecloses the opportunities of these children and perpetuates their disadvantaged minority status. Licensing parents actually would enhance, rather than threaten, the survival and the quality of life of minority groups.

VIOLATING THE SACRED PARENT-CHILD RELATIONSHIP

Some people might protest that licensing parents would be like licensing cars, bicycles, and dogs. It would demean children by treating them like property and demean parents by treating them like animals. Comparing licensing parents with these other forms of licensing certainly does trivialize the sacred bond between parents and children. Parenting is a much greater responsibility and deserves even more attention by society than anything else that we license.

Yet simply mentioning parent licensing can evoke the image of taking a baby away from a weeping mother and completely block rational consideration of the matter. This actually happens when an irresponsible but tearful mother sways a jury in a termination of parental rights proceeding more than the facts of the case and the pursuit of the child's and the parent's actual interests. It is difficult for many people to accept the fact that mothers can seriously harm their own children. The powerful emotional investment of a mother in the image of having a child, even though she is unable to care for one, is one of the most important barriers to social service and legal efforts to act in the interests of neglected children.

There is no question that the emotional resistance of a mother who has given birth to a child to relinquishing that child can override both her own and her child's interests. That emotional reaction is not sufficient, however, to assure her competence as a parent or that an affectionate attachment bond exists between her and her child. The strength of the emotional feeling of a mother for her child at a particular time cannot be the sole basis for judging her parenting competence or the bonding of her child with her.

A mother who truly loves her child and recognizes her inability to rear her child is more likely to desire placement for the child than an emotionally immature or disturbed mother who is unrealistic about her capabilities and disregards the child's needs. Most adopted children have been placed voluntarily by parents who desire a better life for their children.

Another circumstance that is mistakenly construed to indicate that a child should remain with an abusive or neglectful parent is that many abused and neglected children suggest through their words and their behavior that they want to remain with their incompetent parents. The reasons for this vary, but these children usually are clinging to an idealized image of their parents and are fearful of alternatives that are unknown to them and that mean leaving a familiar situation, however inadequate it may be. Some older children may feel a responsibility to care for their foundering parents. As with the motives and statements of parents, those of children in abusive and neglectful circumstances need to be evaluated clinically, particularly in the light of a strong social policy bias toward family preservation.

The tension between the right to bear children and judgments about the competence required to rear them is illustrated by the case of Debra Ann Foster.[3] In the summer of 1988 in Mesa, Arizona, she was sentenced to use birth control for the rest of her childbearing years because she had repeatedly neglected her sons. The court concluded that she was incapable of rearing children. The American Civil Liberties Union protested that the order violated her reproductive freedom, and the Roman Catholic Church objected because it violated her religious beliefs.

Because people have rights to free speech, free religious expression, and to conceive and bear children, one can argue that people have a right to parent children as well. The right to free speech does not include slander, the right to freedom of religion does not include the mistreatment of human beings or animals, and the right to bear children does not include harming them.

All rights are limited and entail responsibilities in order to protect the innocent. Most importantly, in reality the sacred parent-child relationship is earned through affectionate attachment bonding between parent and child over time. It does not automatically follow the biological conception of, and giving birth to, a child.

LICENSING WOULD FOSTER PARENT BLAMING

There is an understandable reason to fear that licensing might increase parental guilt because parents are susceptible to feeling guilty—and they already consciously or unconsciously feel guilty enough.

Licensing would hold parents responsible for their children. Some parents might fear being wrongly blamed for their children's misbehavior. At the same time those parents may well be the ones who are inclined to blame their children for their own child-rearing difficulties. They are likely to believe that the behavior problems of children are caused solely by factors in the children, such as by diseases, brain damage, or chemical imbalances in their brains, not by parental influences.

Underlying these sentiments lies a juvenile ageist rejection of the contribution parents make to the fate of their offspring. This comes in the context of a general abdication of personal responsibility for our own actions in our society. This attitude is reflected when the responsibility for problems in child-rearing is placed on institutions other than families or on factors within the children themselves. Because they are helpless and unable to protest, children are ready targets for this form of scapegoating. They, not their parents, are regarded as the causes of their own problems. This attitude is reinforced by the reactions of the children in the form of withdrawing from, or rebelling against, the scapegoating. The children thereby confirm their culpability by further misbehaving. The circle is tightly closed as abused and neglected children are seen as thorns in the sides of their parents and are blamed for their own situations. Historically, the same dynamics of the acquiescence or rebelliousness of victims have justified discriminatory practices of the prejudiced against their victims in general.

Acceding to the fear that licensing would encourage blaming parents and heighten parental guilt might relieve the anxieties of some parents, but it would ignore the interests of children. A more humane and realistic approach to relieving parental anxiety and guilt is through social policies that support rather than undermine parenting and by recognizing parental competence through a licensing process that would affirm the vast majority of parents as competent.

RESTRICTING THE RIGHTS OF ADULTS TO FREEDOM OF ACTION

There is a fundamental and necessary resistance in the United States to forcing well-intentioned ideas for personal behavior on other people. The civil right to freedom of action has been construed to include the right of adults to live dangerously, and even foolishly, provided their actions do not injure others. This point has been raised successfully as an argument against laws mandating the use of automobile seat belts and motorcycle helmets.

The purpose of parent licensing is not to restrict the freedom of parents by prescribing parenting behaviors. It is simply to protect children from harm. The principles that parents are not free to harm their children or intentionally permit children to harm themselves are well accepted in the United States.

Still there is an understandable reluctance to restrict the actions of a person unless there is a "clear and present" danger that harm to others will result from those actions. Actually the degree of harm required to evoke a sanction depends on public sentiment. The regulation of smoking did not take place until public sentiment rose to a level that justified intervention on the basis of inconvenience without a "clear and present" danger to the health of each nonsmoker. The grave import of incompetent parenting for society justifies interventions before there is clear and present danger of abuse or neglect, and certainly before abuse and neglect actually occur. As it now stands, interventions occur after abuse and neglect have taken place.

Another freedom-based objection to licensing parents is an outgrowth of the argument that our society is moving toward less formal forms of cohabitation and that even marriage constitutes too much restriction of individual freedom. To the extent that this trend continues without the contractual relationship of marriage, the need for protecting the civil and legal rights of children becomes more, not less, important. The interests of children are not inherently recognized or assured when the liaisons of their parents shift. It is the contemporary lack of commitment to parenting and the irresponsibility of a few parents that has created the current impetus for licensing parents.

An obtuse freedom-based resistance to licensing parents involves fear of the loss of the freedom of adults to use corporal punishment in the parent-child relationship. On the one hand, physical child abuse is deplored, but on the other hand, parents know that some form of physical management of children is necessary. The idea of licensing parents might evoke the fear that there would be an increased risk that someone will allege child abuse whenever a parent lays a hand on a child. This possibility would be no greater with licensing than it is now.

LICENSING WOULD ACCOMPANY FINANCIAL CHILD SUPPORT

The basic thrust of parent licensing is to encourage the formation of child-parent affectionate attachment bonds by drawing upon the natural affinity of parents for their offspring. The tragic fact for children, however, is that avoiding parental responsibilities can be the primary aim of a biological parent. Many fathers, and some mothers, do not wish to parent their children and must be legally forced to financially support them.

In the light of mandatory child support, a parent license might be construed as being automatically given to a biological parent who provides financial support for a child. This would not be the case. Financial responsibility for a child's support and the privilege of parenting the child are separate issues that do not necessarily overlap. Financial responsibility for a child does not make one competent to parent nor does it necessarily mean that the interests of a child are served by a relationship with that parent. Equating financial support with custody or visitation treats the child as chattel for which financial responsibility implies the rental or possession of the child as property.

The separation of financial responsibility and a child's relationship with a parent rests on a fundamental distinction between a monetary relationship with a child and an affectionate attachment bond relationship. The purpose of licensing a parent is to foster the affectionate attachment bonding aspect of the parent-child relationship that may or may not accompany financial responsibility. Eligibility for licensing would not be based solely on financial responsibility for a child. It would be based upon the simple licensing criteria: majority age, commitment to parent and to not abuse or neglect the child, and possibly completion of parenting education.

The licensing of parents is a separate issue from mandated financial support of a child. The appropriate procedure, from a child's point of view, when a parent wants to avoid financial responsibility for a child, is to terminate that parent's parental rights and release the child for adoption, thus relieving the biological parent of unwanted financial responsibility for the child.

FEAR OF ACCORDING ADULT RIGHTS TO CHILDREN

Some people fear that according civil rights to children would mean giving them all of the rights of adults. This attitude reflects a misunderstanding of child advocacy based on the literal transfer of the legal concept of advocacy for adults to children. It construes child advocacy as following the wishes of children. This fear is a reaction against those who mistakenly believe that children should be treated as adults. Actually equating adults' and children's rights represents a subtle juvenile ageist position that ignores the differences between childhood and adulthood and that ignores the need of children for nurturance, protection, and guidance.

The civil rights of children include both freedom from oppression and access to the adult guidance and limit setting inherent in competent parenting. Appropriate and informed child advocacy involves advocating the developmental needs of children, not their immediate wishes; it is not a question of according them all of the rights of adults. A child's civil right to competent parenting reified by a licensing process would not inappropriately accord children adult rights.

Still there is the argument that the children's rights approach is not the most appropriate way to recognize the needs of children in our society. That argument holds that resources should be redistributed so as to equitably support all children and parents as contributing members of society. It envisions a society in which resources are allocated according to humane priorities rather than by the advocacy of competing rights. It reflects ideals that favor the common good side of the individual versus collective rights equation.

Reallocating resources according to society's priorities can be achieved through entitlement programs and through tax relief and credits. In the United States, as a capitalistic democracy, those priorities are determined by the vigorous representation of the interests and rights of affected groups. But the allocation of financial resources is less important than society's values in determining how children are parented.

Because financial entitlements for children and parents can be abused, as illustrated by some of the effects of the Aid to the Families of Dependent

Children program, standards are needed for the quality of parenting that society is willing to support financially. The reallocation of financial resources more equitably for parents and children in itself would not ensure that children would be competently parented.

ENFORCING CONFORMITY IN CHILD-REARING

For some people the idea of licensing parents conjures up images of a totalitarian state in which parents are forced to raise their children in a uniform way with the prospect of producing conforming masses of adults who lack originality and creativity. That scenario would have no room for the mavericks and creative geniuses who are so essential to the evolution of a democratic society. That feared outcome of conformity is particularly envisioned whenever prosocial values are mentioned as a desirable ingredient of competent parenting.

The criteria for licensing parents would only restrain those who abuse or neglect their children. Licensing would not prescribe child-rearing practices. It would not affect those who seek to change society or who are unhappy with the status quo. It probably would facilitate social change by fostering the development of adults with the characters and coping skills needed to effect change.

THE POLITICAL REJECTION OF THE FAMILY

In recent years the family has been portrayed as a repressive institution that fosters the dependency of women. It also has been recognized accurately as the main site of violence against women and children. Domestic relationships have been unpleasant, painful, and even damaging for many people.

For critics of the family, the abuse and neglect of children by their parents is seen as signaling the need to shift the responsibility for the care of children from parents to society in a collective sense.[4] More fundamentally, through the years there have been persistent tensions between political ideals of equality and the elitism of families. This tension is based on the fact that the opportunities of children raised by their families can never be equal when they become adults, because families vary so much in their access to resources. Even when the access to resources is equal, the motivations of parents to further the interests of their children vary widely.

Equal treatment in a society, in a strict sense, probably is incompatible with family ties. Family loyalty treats people on the basis of kinship and affection. Family members usually make no pretense of treating people outside of the family the same as themselves for better or for worse. For these reasons, some people hold that families are incompatible with modern life and represent archaic holdovers from the past that need not be taken seriously. For them licensing parents would prolong the natural death of the family. They would favor an emphasis on the societal rearing of children in standardized ways rather than supporting parents in different styles of child-rearing.

The realities of family life cannot be dismissed so simply. Some degree of family feelings are essential, biologically based parts of the lives of all but a few human beings. The ethics that govern relationships between people who love or care for each other inevitably intrude into public life, coloring people's perceptions of what they and others ought to do. It is appropriate to expect public officials to avoid favoritism, but it is a completely different matter to expect all human beings to relate to each other with emotional detachment, whether or not they are related by family ties. To imagine stripping human relationships of their emotional and familial components is to imagine a world of robots rather than human beings. Family relationships really do not assure success in life nor does the lack of family ties assure failure.

When oppressive discrimination is minimized, our ability to deal with the differences in opportunities and in the treatment we receive in life makes it possible to progress in a competitive world that depends on each one of us to shape our own destinies. Among those differences in opportunities in life are those determined by personal relationships. Each one of the many political efforts to abolish the family as a social institution from the time of ancient Greece to the present has failed because it did not face this reality. The family as a cultural institution probably will survive with or without the licensing of parents.

THE MATURING INFLUENCE OF CHILD-REARING

Another objection to parent licensing is that it is not needed because the presence of a child in itself will cause a mother or father to become a competent parent.

Not all jurisdictions have been willing to prohibit parents from taking custody of their infants when circumstances indicate that the infants' safety or health would be jeopardized if placed in the parents' custody, as illustrated by the opinion of a Washington Appellate Court:

> A parent's right to custody and control of his or her child should not be abridged except for the most powerful reasons. . . . It may well be, as the social workers and psychiatrists opined below, that the odds do not favor that a petitioner because of youth and a history of avoiding responsibility will become a good parent. Fortunately for the preservation of the human

species, however, a lot of people who would rate poorly on any scale of parental prospects have done rather well at it when confronted by the reality of a baby, in a crib, in the home. . . .[5]

There is no question that the presence of a baby can stimulate personal growth in a parent. There also is evidence that significant changes in some women and men do occur following childbirth, such as the discontinuation of substance abuse.[6]

Our culture encourages an optimistic belief in the future for all Americans. This is the land in which anyone can succeed if given the opportunities to do so. If anyone can become president, certainly anyone can become a competent parent. This optimism fosters hope for improvement in the lives of incompetent parents, but it also blocks awareness that there are some people who are incapable of changing their lives in time to benefit their children.

The courts are beginning to recognize the need to intervene in the lives of children when the likelihood of abuse or neglect exists. In the case of *In re East* the Court of Common Pleas of Ohio held that a child should not have to endure harm in order to give a mother an opportunity to prove her ability to parent the child.[7] The court held that the law did not require courts to experiment with a child's welfare to see if the child will suffer "great detriment or harm."

The idea that the welfare of a child should be risked solely because of the possibility that the presence of that child might cause an incompetent parent to become competent in the face of evidence to the contrary is a clear-cut expression of juvenile ageism.

OBJECTIONABLE PRIOR RESTRAINT

Because of its preventive purpose, a parent licensing program would deny licenses to people judged to be incompetent even though they had never maltreated children and, therefore, such licensing could constitute objectionable prior restraint of the freedom of adults. Prior restraint is used commonly, however, when the restricted activity is one that could lead easily to serious harm.

We hospitalize people judged as potentially harmful to themselves or others, and we withhold professional licenses prior to an individual making errors as a practitioner. The potential of harm to a child and society by an incompetent parent is a much more serious matter than either of these examples.

THE FALLIBILITY OF PREDICTION AND EDUCATION

A major objection to licensing is the presumed difficulty in identifying incompetent parenting. Other than age, demographic factors in themselves are not sufficiently reliable to identify potentially incompetent parents.

When demographic data are supplemented by the use of individualized screening methods, such as the Child Abuse Potential Inventory, the combination seems to have predictive power.[8] Testing instruments, however, assess knowledge rather than skills. They also are subject to all of the issues of fairness and distortion inherent in testing procedures. Basing licensing parents on knowledge testing alone would introduce an unacceptable degree of unreliability. Even a license to drive a motor vehicle does not depend solely on knowledge testing; a demonstration of actual driving skill is necessary.

There is no assurance that making education in parenting a requirement for licensing would reduce the risk to children. Parenting involves more than knowledge; it requires intuition and mature judgment.

Still, by developing a body of family life knowledge, by training teachers of parenting skills, by promulgating parenting curricula, and by certifying mastery of this knowledge, we might hope for a change in prospective parents' appreciation of the importance of competent parenting. Some might learn enough about children's needs to decide to defer child-rearing until they were ready to meet its demands. Many might profit from an introduction to parenting skills prior to having to use them.

For all these reasons, parent licensing criteria should be simple and straightforward, rather than based on knowledge testing procedures. The analog is a marriage license rather than a license to practice a profession. The objection of fallibility can be raised for all licensing procedures, which essentially are audits of present knowledge and performance to decrease potential harm and thereby are predictive. The fact that they are not infallible does not detract from their usefulness. No licensing program is completely successful. Licensing motor vehicle operators has not eliminated hazards on the roads or ensured the competence of drivers. Without such regulation, however, motor vehicle hazards would be much greater.

THE UNFEASIBILITY OF ADMINISTRATION

Another objection to licensing parents is the unfeasibility of its implementation. The specter of an enormous and inflexible bureaucracy needed to deal with the myriad of issues surrounding licensing is frightening enough in itself. But the prospect of dealing with millions of existing incompetent parents all at once is absolutely overwhelming.

Any kind of parent licensing program would encounter many problems and exceptions. What about a situation in which one parent qualifies for licensing, but the other does not? What if a mother is licensable, but she lives with a man who abuses her and her child? Should licensing be repeated at intervals, or does a single licensing permanently qualify one as a parent?

Not all children are alike in temperament; in the simplest terms, some are "easy" and some are "difficult" to parent. It is plausible that some parents could rear an "easy" child, but would be likely to neglect and abuse a "difficult" child. Would we license a parent only to bring up an "easy" child? Another consideration is the situation of handicapped children who have special needs and pose challenging parenting issues.

These practical questions highlight the importance of basing licensing on simple criteria, as we do marriage licenses, rather than upon detailed definitions of competence or incompetence and upon specific testing procedures. Using the simple criteria of age, parenting pledge, and possibly educational certification accomplishes this.

Most of the complications that would arise from licensing parents would be the result of the inconvenience of introducing the rights and needs of children into situations and activities now dominated by juvenile ageism that leads society to behave as if children do not have these rights. The whole idea of licensing is based upon the interests of children. Our society would profit from addressing, rather than avoiding, questions raised by the issue of licensing parents.

A new bureaucracy would not be needed for licensing parents because specific situations that require individual judgments would be handled by child protective service systems that are already available and most likely are already involved with questionable parents. The credentialing process itself could be handled by the existing birth and marriage registration and licensing processes.

The fear that licensing parents would make it easier for bureaucratic social workers to remove children from their families is not justified because legal safeguards and appeal procedures would remain in place as they are now. The same safeguards apply to fears that social workers would be given inordinate powers to dictate child-rearing practices.

As it commonly is for other credentialing procedures, a parent licensing system would need to be prospective rather than retroactive. It could be applied first to parents who receive governmental financial support for rearing children to ensure that incompetent parenting is not encouraged and actually supported by public funds.

If parent licensing were to be seriously undertaken, it would take years to develop the system. Decisions also would have to be made about ways of handling the transition from the present situation in which there are no parental expectations to one in which expectations for parents would be implemented. The fact that reducing the federal debt takes years of planned adjustments should not preclude the mission of protecting the national economy. The prospect of a lengthy process in developing a parent licensing system should not preclude protecting our economy and the quality of our lives in a much more fundamental and enduring way.

LICENSING WOULD REPLACE HELPING PARENTS

An important concern about licensing is that in itself it could be regarded as the solution to the personal and social problems associated with incompetent parenting and thereby permit bypassing the obvious needs for the support and treatment of foundering parents and for the improvement of their socioeconomic conditions.

An example of a superficial legislative approach to human behavior problems is the West Virginia school attendance law that suspends the driver's licenses of students who drop out.[9] This law has been criticized because it does not address and deflects attention from the school-based reasons for dropping out, even though it does provide an incentive for students to remain in school and actually has reduced school dropout rates. In contrast with this kind of legislative sanctioning, licensing parents would address fundamental family problems.

Because of the possibility that it could be regarded as the only necessary governmental response to incompetent parenting, it is essential that licensing be seen as a standard-setting vehicle for deploying resources to help parents to become and remain competent.

INSUFFICIENT ADOPTION OPPORTUNITIES

Another important concern about licensing parents is that there would be no adoptive parents for the children who would be made available for adoption when parents were found to be intractably incompetent. There are even those who question the validity of adoption itself as an institution.[10]

A definitive answer to the adoption question is not possible now. The contemporary pool of potential adoptive parents is large, and there is considerable interest in transracial adoptions.[11] On the positive side, there are about 200,000 women who begin actively seeking to adopt children each year. On the negative side, in 1986 the nation's foster care system harbored at least 36,000 adoptable "special needs" children, but only 13,500 found families.

Yet, according to the National Council for Adoption, there are 1 million infertile couples and 1 million parents who seek an additional child. The Council estimates adoption possibilities for 2 million children, particularly if adoption occurs shortly after birth rather than after children have been damaged and are designated as having "special needs." As it is now, homes must be found for seriously impaired babies because of brain damage, physical handicaps, and AIDS.

At the present time there are only about sixty thousand legal adoptions annually in the United States; fifty thousand of the children are from the United States, and ten thousand from foreign countries. About one-quarter of all of these adoptions are transracial. These data suggest that the adoption pool seeking 1 million children is large enough to absorb the number of neglected children and that the races of the children would not pose insurmountable barriers if a shift in attitudes toward adoption took place.[12] To illustrate this point, in the most unlikely event that all babies born to mothers between the ages of fifteen and nineteen were placed for adoption, the total number according to 1990 statistics would be about 227,000 Caucasian, 96,000 African American, and 43,000 Hispanic children.

Serious questions have been raised about the advisability of transracial adoptions. There is anecdotal evidence that some transracially adopted children have experienced adjustment problems. There is a strong belief within some minority groups that in order to preserve their cultural heritage their children should not be raised by parents from other racial backgrounds. This viewpoint was codified in the 1978 Indian Child Welfare Act that generally gives tribal courts exclusive power to make custody and foster care decisions for children considered to be legal residents of a reservation, regardless of where they live. The argument also has been made that only an African American family can equip an African American child with the psychological armor needed to fight racial prejudice.[13] This may be feasible because of the finding that, when properly recruited, there are substantial numbers of African American adults who seek to adopt African American children.

On the other hand, longitudinal studies of transracial adoptions reveal that they generally have been successful and that transracial adoption, although posing problems in our society, is a viable means of providing stable homes for children.[14] The adoption of high-risk children also has been more successful than anticipated during its early trials; their adoption disruption rate has been reported to be between 8 and 13 percent in long-term follow-up studies. Adoption also has been found to be superior to long-term foster care and residential placement. Waiting for a same-race adoption can be an injustice to the affected children.

In the light of all of this evidence and the contemporary political climate, the Child Welfare League of America has taken the following position on transracial adoptions: "Children in need of adoption have a right to be placed into a family that reflects their ethnicity or race. Children should not have their adoption denied or significantly delayed, however, when adoptive parents of other ethnic or racial groups are available."

The point also can be made that maintaining racial and cultural purity is contrary to the pluralistic values of the American culture and is negated ultimately by the inevitability of interracial marriages in the United States. Furthermore, the birth mother has emerged in many instances as a significant participant in selecting the adoptive parents of her child.

The evidence suggests that ample opportunities for the adoption of children from all backgrounds exist in the United States, particularly by identifying incompetent parents before children are damaged and thereby become "high-risk" candidates for adoption.

Licensing parents would raise the question of parental competence before or at birth and would result in larger numbers of babies available for adoption. It would serve the needs of both the babies and the competent parents who seek to adopt children.

RESEARCH IS INCONCLUSIVE

You have two choices. You can accept the conclusion of some researchers, such as the authors of *Pathways to Criminal Violence*, that we do not know enough about why people become criminals or welfare dependent and wait for the results of further research.[15] You also can rely upon your own judgment about the effects of parental incompetence.

Although some hardy individuals do not seem to be adversely affected by abuse or neglect, the mistreatment of children is neither to their advantage nor to society's advantage. Further research will help us to understand the details, but it certainly is not needed to prove that incompetent parenting is harmful to both children and adults. It is a reflection of juvenile ageism that research questions are framed in terms of whether or not there is evidence that abuse and neglect harm children rather than in terms of whether or not it is in the interests of children to be abused and neglected.

Another viewpoint of some researchers is that values should not interfere with empirical research in child development. This is reflected in the following statement by the child psychologist Jerome Kagan:

> The findings of future empirical inquiry may affirm the popular belief that surrogate care of infants has psychological dangers [but] even the most traditional student of child development would admit that these beliefs remain largely unproven. . . . A combination of emotional conviction and frail evidence often betrays the fact that a deep value is being threatened. . . . I

believe that the possibility that the biological mother might be partially replaced bothers a great many citizens.[16]

This statement reveals the underlying belief that cultural values should not play a governing role in establishing child-rearing objectives, in influencing child-rearing methods or in evaluating parental competence. This viewpoint has been interpreted by those who disparage parenting to imply that child-rearing should be guided by "scientific" rather than "sentimental" factors. They hold that establishing sentimental affectionate attachment bonds between parents and children is not a valid objective in child-rearing.

The ethical question for social scientists is the same as for environmental scientists. Do we have to wait for future research to show that the environment or society has been damaged before concluding that environmental pollution or incompetent parenting are harmful? The answer to this question must consider the readiness of many people to use the need for more research as an excuse for inaction or as a justification for funding the research enterprise.

EDUCATION, TRAINING, AND CLINICAL SERVICES ARE SUFFICIENT

Most thinking about improving parental competence focuses on education, training, and clinical services. The reasoning is that the positive reinforcement of voluntary behavior is more effective than coercive regulation. There is a reluctance to legislate expectations of parents because the educational and clinical approaches are seen as more humane and as potentially more effective.

Yet the fact that educational and clinical services are necessary but are not enough to prevent damaging others because of addiction to alcohol, drugs, and smoking is well known, so public regulation of those activities is accepted. School-based educational programs can be useful in reducing undesirable behavior, such as smoking, alcohol consumption, and substance abuse, for many children and adolescents.[17] However, there is a core group for whom adhering to antisocial peer pressures has overriding importance in spite of the persuasive and educational efforts of adults. Those youngsters, who are more susceptible to peer pressure than to the influence of parents and schools, are either unaffected by educational efforts or are more strongly motivated to pursue self-defeating behavior by them. They are the youngsters who are prone to become incompetent parents. The most effective approach to them is to ensure that they receive competent parenting themselves. When that is not available, law enforcement is necessary.

Persuasion and education also are recognized as insufficient to protect the public from incompetent motor vehicle operators, so laws that license them are necessary. No one questions that the licensing of professional activities is required beyond the education of the professionals.

The damage to other persons by incompetent parenting far exceeds in scope and severity the damage caused to others by alcohol, drug, and smoking addictions; by incompetent motor vehicle operation; and by incompetent professionals. Yet the call for remedies to incompetent parenting usually is limited to education and professional services with the glaring omission of placing expectations on parents through regulation. This is particularly ill-informed in the case of teenage parents, because it overlooks the inherent sense of invulnerability in adolescents that impairs their judgment and that in itself in other aspects of their lives requires parental and societal regulation.

Any activity that can adversely affect other people is subject to some form of regulation beyond persuasion and education—except parenting. For example, our society financially and educationally supports parents who are not permitted to operate motor vehicles. That the devastating and widespread consequences of incompetent parenting, for children and for the incompetent parents themselves, go unrecognized is an obvious expression of juvenile ageism.

FAVORED LEGAL TREATMENT IS UNDESIRABLE

The political and legal systems of the United States are strongly biased against providing favored treatment for any particular individual or group and toward favoring equal treatment of everyone.

The exception to the equal treatment principle is that all individuals are presumed to be equal unless they have "disabilities." This legal doctrine has been applied to the obvious inequality of children, who are regarded as growing progressively out of the "disabled" state of legal "infancy" and gradually acquiring the rights of adults by being "emancipated" from the "disabilities" of childhood.

The doctrine of disability has justified the protection of children from responsibilities and from dangers. It has given rise to child labor and child abuse and neglect laws, but it also has been used inappropriately. For example, the mistreatment of children can be concealed because they are regarded as "disabled" dependents on their parents. In those instances the child's dependence on the parent conceals the parent's oppression and abuse of the child.

From the theoretical point of view, confusion arises when the legal and political rights of children are equated with their human and civil rights. The legal principle of equal treatment does require the limitation of children's legal and political rights because of the inherent "disability" of their immaturity. It does not require limitation of their human and civil rights, which should apply to anyone regardless of age.

The principle of equal treatment can be used spuriously to avoid the restriction by society of adult behavior in order to accommodate children because such restriction would "favor" children. Restricting adult behavior that is harmful to children actually would give children equal treatment in accordance with the same human and civil rights that now apply only to adults. It would not accord children favored treatment in legal and political matters.

The doctrine of avoiding favored treatment underlies the segregation of children from undesirable adult influences. Rather than providing favored treatment for children by restricting adult behavior, children are segregated from adult influences that are harmful to them. The result is that adults are accorded favored treatment over children. If, as with antismoking laws that protect nonsmokers, public sentiment favored regulation of adult behavior that was inimical to children, the society of the United States could accommodate the presence of children, as do the majority of other societies, without giving them favored treatment in the legal sense. Both adults and children could be accorded equal treatment by restricting the behavior of each class that is offensive or harmful to the others.

From another perspective, licensing parents might be construed as according parents favored status over adults who are not parents. If that did occur, it would be an appropriate outcome, because the contribution that competent parents make to the greater good of society would be more formally recognized.

SOCIETY'S NEED FOR INCOMPETENCE

The communications expert Lee Thayer pointed out that if thousands, if not millions, of people are not to be thrown out of work, future parents must be at least as incompetent as present parents.[18] The deficiencies of their offspring provide employment for legions of social service, mental health, educational, law enforcement, legal, and correctional personnel and for related businesses. Incompetent adults further reduce competition in the workforce.

All prevention efforts meet covert but formidable resistance from professions and industries. In this instance, professionals need not fear the loss of employment, as health care workers have found in the effective prevention of physical illnesses. A societal emphasis on competent parenting would not reduce the need for human services because of the continued need for services to help parents be competent. Competition in the workforce also is not an issue because projections are for future labor shortages rather than surpluses.

There is another factor that favors employing professionals to repair damage rather than placing expectations on people to prevent problems. It is the thinking of the Industrial Age that has led us to believe that scientific methods and technological devices and services are the solutions to human problems. We rely excessively on experts to provide services and to answer questions that really can only be answered by ourselves. Prime examples are what kind of a life we want to lead, what kind of society we want to live in, what kind of environment we want to surround us, what kind of citizens we want in our society, and how we should raise our children. These are value-based rather than science-based questions.

If our society wants to improve the quality of its citizens and the competence of its parents, the answers lie in the realm of social values and public policies, not just in professions that repair damage and in the methods of experimental science. On the contrary, science and technology need ethical guidance. In addition, the industries and professions that service incompetent parents and their products need to consider their ethical responsibility to include prevention in their aims and practices.

Professional interventions are inadequate when whole populations do not follow, or do not even want to follow, competent child-rearing practices.[19] The answers for them lie in changing their values and living conditions. The rapid assent of Asian Americans up the economic ladder without public or professional assistance in the face of racist resentment against them is an affirmation of cultural values that serve that group well: respect for the family, valuing education, and bootstrap entrepreneurship.

The responsibility lies with our society, not with scientists or professionals, to develop and implement proparenting policies to reduce incompetent parenting. If that happens, the service professions and industries certainly still will have enough to do. Contractors can shift from building prisons to family homes.

DRASTIC CHANGES IN PUBLIC POLICY DO NOT OCCUR

The argument is advanced that a change in public policy, such as licensing parents, is too drastic, and therefore, cannot occur. Contradicting this belief are a number of examples of major shifts in public policies occasioned by changes in social attitudes.

The most comprehensive examples of changes in public policy have been stimulated by women's movements from the turn of the century to the present time.[20] Earlier in this century, women's movements were responsible for the passage of legislation that benefited women and children. In recent years they have pressed for affirmative action and equal rights legislation that has dramatically changed the role of women in our society. Similar innovations have improved the status of children.

The most recent example of drastic change in public policy is the regulation of smoking, so that an activity that once was regarded as socially desirable has become socially undesirable. Significantly, that change involves persuasion and education but ultimately requires local and national regulation for its implementation.

A similar shift has occurred in the public attitude toward the degradation of the environment. One indication of the intensity of this sentiment is the success of the Nature Conservancy, which has become a powerful private resource for acquiring land in conjunction with local, state, and federal agencies.[21] Even with many voluntary efforts such as this, however, legislative regulation of environmental pollutants has been required with substantial enforcement provisions.

ARE THESE ARGUMENTS OBSTACLES OR HURDLES?

The most important obstacle to recognizing the civil rights of children by licensing parents is the implication that doing so entails additional responsibilities and burdens for adults. The expectation of competency in parenting runs counter to our yearning to lessen our personal responsibilities and to our distaste for external regulation.

Our society, devoted as it is to the free pursuit of adult interests, already has enough difficulty expecting us to be responsible for our actions. The dominant sentiment is one of feeling overburdened and stressed, particularly for those of us who are parents. Many of us have had painful experiences in our own families and do not want to even think about the interests of other parents and children. Yet our society's support of the competent parenting of children would relieve much of that stress, which is caused by the social and economic problems of our nation that result from incompetent parenting.

All of the objections to licensing parents can be regarded as insurmountable obstacles, or they can be seen as hurdles to be taken into account in designing and implementing licensing procedures. If undertaken, a process for licensing parents should carefully consider all of the potential problems. It should not be ruled out simply because it has not been done before or because it would be too much trouble. The excuse that according parenting the same status as marriage or the same status as operating a motor vehicle would be too difficult or is unnecessary is a clear expression of juvenile ageism.

Even if the ideas that children have a right to competent parenting and that licensing parents would be useful are accepted, both can be dismissed as idealistic and impractical. That attitude betrays a lack of vision for the future that depends upon the competent parenting of children at the present time.

NOTES

1. Benjamin F. Wright, ed., *The Federalist by Alexander Hamilton, James Madison, and John Jay* (Cambridge: Harvard Library, 1961), p. 356.

2. Robert Proctor, *Racial Hygiene: Medicine under the Nazis* (Cambridge: Harvard University Press, 1988).

3. Tamar Jacoby, "Is Sterilization the Answer?" *Newsweek*, August 8, 1988, p. 59.

4. The family as an institution is critiqued by Michel Barren and Mary McIntosh, *The Antisocial Family*, 2d ed. (London: Verso, 1991); Delores Hayden, *The Grand Domestic Revolution* (Cambridge: MIT Press, 1985), pp. 1–29, 47–49, 96–105; and Harriet Fraad, "Children as an Exploited Class," *Journal of Psychohistory* 21 (1993): 37–51.

5. *In the Matter of the Welfare of Baby Boy May*, 14 Wash. App. 765; 545 P. 2d 25, 1976.

6. Denise B. Kandel and Victoria H. Raveis, "Cessation of Illicit Drug Use in Young Adulthood," *Archives of General Psychiatry* 46 (1989): 109–21.

7. *In Re East*, 32 Ohio Misc. 65, 288 N.E. 2d 343, 1972.

8. Claudia Pap Mangel, "Licensing Parents: How Feasible?" *Family Law Quarterly* 22 (1988): 17–39, 25–26; Doyle C. Pruitt and Marilyn T. Erickson, "The Child Abuse Potential Inventory: A Study of Concurrent Validity," *Journal of Clinical Psychology* 41 (1985): 104–11; Michael J. Sandmire and Michael S. Wald, "Licensing Parents—A Response to Claudia Mangel's Proposal," *Family Law Quarterly* 24 (1990): 53–76; D. P. Sommerfeld and J. R. Hughes, "Do Health Professionals Agree on the Parenting Potential of Pregnant Women?" *Social Sciences and Medicine* 24 (1987): 285–88.

9. Jill Rachlin and Joseph R Shapiro, "No Pass, No Drive," *U.S. News & World Report*, June 5, 1989, pp. 49–50.

10. Elinor Rosenberg, *The Adoption Life Cycle: The Children and Both Their Families Through the Years* (New York: Free Press, 1992).

11. Christine Bachrach, Kathryn London, and Penelope L. Maza, "On the Path to Adoption: Adoption Seeking in the United States, 1988," *Journal of Marriage and the Family* 53 (1991): 705–18; National Committee for Adoption, *Adoption Fact Book* (Washington, D.C.: National Committee for Adoption, 1989).

12. Ibid. Bureau of the Census, *Current Population Reports, series P-20, no. 454: Fertility of American Women, June 1990* (Washington, D.C.: U.S. Government Printing Office, 1991), pp. 29–31.

13. Beth Brophy, "The Unhappy Politics of Interracial Adoption," *U.S. News & World Report*, November 13, 1989, pp. 72–73; Maria Douglas, "Fostering Black Adoptions: Private Agency Finds Lots of Willing Families," *Wisconsin State Journal*, November 17, 1991; Andrew Billingsley, *Climbing Jacob's Ladder: The Enduring Legacy of African-American Families* (New York: Simon & Schuster, 1993).

14. Rita Simon and Howard Alstein, *Transracial Adoptees and Their Families* (New York: Praeger, 1987); Ruth McRoy and Louis A. Zurcher, *Transracial and Interracial Adoptions* (Springfield, Ill.: Thomas, 1983); Arnold R. Silverman and William Feigelman, "Adjustment in Interracial Adoptions: An Overview," in *The Psychology of Adoption*, ed. David M. Brodzinsky and Marshall D. Schechter (New York: Oxford

University Press, 1990), p. 199; Rita Simon and Howard Altstein, *Adoption, Race, and Identity* (Westport, Conn.: Praeger, 1991), pp. 1–36; Child Welfare League of America, *Standards for Adoption Service, Revised* (New York: Child Welfare League of America, 1988). The vicissitudes of transracial adoptions are described in Elizabeth Bartholet, *Family Bonds: Adoption and the Politics of Parenting* (Boston: Houghton Mifflin, 1993); and J. Douglas Gates, *Gift Children: A Story of Race, Family, and Adoption in a Divided America* (New York: Ticknor & Fields, 1993).

15. Neil Alan Weiner and Marvin E. Wolfgang, *Pathways to Criminal Violence* (Newbury Park, Calif.: Sage, 1989).

16. Jerome Kagan, "Family Experience and the Child's Development," *American Psychologist* 34 (1979): 886–91.

17. Phyllis L. Elickson and Robert M. Bell, "Drug Prevention in Junior High: A Multi-Site Longitudinal Test," *Science* 247 (1990): 1299–1305.

18. Lee Thayer, "The Functions of Incompetence," in *Vistas in Physical Reality*, ed. Ervin Laszlo and Emily Sellon (New York: Plenum, 1976), p. 178.

19. Richard Carlson and Bruce Goldman, *20/20 Visions: Long View of a Changing World* (Palo Alto, Calif.: Stanford University Alumni Association, 1990), p. 245.

20. Theda Skocpol, *Protecting Soldiers and Mothers: The Political Origins of Social Policy in the United States* (Cambridge: Harvard University Press, 1992).

21. John Barbour, "New Groups Are Protecting Land by Buying It," *(Louisville, Ky.) Courier-Journal*, 1990, pp. D1–2.

EPILOGUE

S uperficially, what motivated the column (reprinted below) that led to
Steven Mitchell's invitation for an edited anthology on the topic of
licensing parents was the possibility of cloning humans and the realization
that we'd probably have rules and regulations about who could and who
couldn't, and when, and why. "But we don't have that for other kinds of
reproduction," I thought. And because such rules and regulations seemed
appropriate, instead of thinking then, "So we *shouldn't* have them for
cloning," I thought, "We *should* have them for the other!"

However, on a deeper level, what motivated the column—and this book
—is my experience of broken kids. As a teacher, as a residential worker for a
child and family agency, as an adolescent worker in an observation and
detention center, I have seen broken kids. Kids who have been so betrayed,
they don't trust. Period. Kids who didn't get what they needed at a critical
stage in their development, so they go through life thinking the world owes
them something. And indeed we do. But sadly, tragically, we can't give it to
them—no matter how hard we might try. That critical window of time has
passed: we can't go back and flush from the fetus the chemicals that interfered with its development; we can't go back and provide the baby with the
nutrients required for growth; we can't go back and give the child the safety
and attention in its formative years that would have led to a secure personality.[1] Every year millions of children all over the world are seriously abused;
thousands die. And that doesn't count the ones still walking around.

For these broken kids grow up—they become broken adults, with the

357

attendant increased potential for action, much of it detrimental to society, some of it severely so. And so because we have to pay for someone else's mistake, anger is added to the sadness. Unless, of course, it's our mistake—in not requiring a license to parent.

NOTE

1. I don't mean to disparage teachers and social service workers: they often do fix what's broken, and that's nothing short of amazing. They have my deep and sincere respect, praise, and gratitude.

PARENTING LICENSES

We have successfully cloned a sheep; it is not unreasonable, then, to believe we may soon be able to create human life. Despite Frankensteinish visions of a brave new world, I'm sure we'll develop carefully considered policies and procedures to regulate the activity.

For example, I doubt we'll allow someone to create his own private workforce or his own little army.

And I suspect we'll prohibit cloning oneself for mere ego gratification.

Doing it just because it's fun will certainly be illegal. And I expect it won't even be imaginable to do it "without really thinking about it," let alone "by accident."

I suspect we'll enforce some sort of quality control, such that cloned human beings shall not exist in pain or be severely "compromised" with respect to basic biological or biochemical functioning.

And I suspect one will have to apply for a license and satisfy rigorous screening standards. I assume this will include the submission, and approval, of a detailed plan regarding responsibility for the cloned human being; surely we won't allow a scientist to create it and then just leave it on the lab's doorstep one night when he leaves.

Now the thing is, *we can already create human life*. Kids do it every day.

And though we've talked ourselves silly and tied ourselves in knots about *ending* life—active, passive, voluntary, coerced, premeditated, accidental, negligent—we have been horrendously silent, irresponsibly laissez-faire about *beginning* life.

We would not accept such wanton creation of life if it happened in the lab. Why do we condone it when it happens in bedrooms and backseats?

It should be illegal to create life, to have kids, in order to have another pair of hands at work in the field or to have someone to look after you in your old age.

It should be illegal to create a John Doe Junior or someone to carry on the family name/business.

It should be illegal to have kids because, well, it just happened (and it felt so good) and you didn't really think about it.

And it *isn't* possible to create life "by accident"—men don't accidentally ejaculate into vaginas and women don't accidentally catch some ejaculate with their vaginas. (As for failed contraception, there's follow-up contraception.)

And it should be illegal to knowingly create a life that will be spent in pain and/or that will be severely substandard.

As for the screening process, we already do that for adoptive/foster parents. Why do we cling to the irrational belief that biological parents are *necessarily* competent parents—in the face of overwhelming evidence to the contrary? We have, without justification, a double standard.

Oh, but we can't interfere with people's right to reproduce! *Right* to reproduce? Merely *having* a capability does not entail the *right to exercise* that capability. (Re)Production, with its attendant responsibilities, should be a privilege, not a right.

And yes, of course, this proposal, this argument for parenting licenses, opens the door for all sorts of abuses. For starters, who will design and administer the screening process? But look around: it's not as if the current situation is abuse-free. In fact, millions of the little human lives we've created so carelessly are being starved, beaten, or otherwise traumatized. Millions.

To be succinct: The destruction of life is subject to moral and legal examination; so, too, should be the creation of life, whenever and however it occurs.

Peg Tittle, June 1997

NOTES ON THE CONTRIBUTORS

Elizabeth Bartholet is professor of law at Harvard Law School. She writes, lectures, and consults widely on issues involving adoption and reproductive technology. Among her publications are "Beyond Biology: The Politics of Adoption and Reproduction," *Nobody's Children: Abuse and Neglect, Foster Drift, and the Adoption Alternative* (2000), and *Family Bonds: Adoption and the Politics of Parenting* (1993).

Dan W. Brock is currently professor of philosophy and biomedical ethics and director of the Center for Biomedical Ethics at Brown University. Among his publications are "Cloning Human Beings: An Assessment of the Ethical Issues Pro and Con" and *Life and Death: Philosophical Essays in Biomedical Ethics* (1993).

Ruth F. Chadwick is professor of moral philosophy and head of the Centre for Professional Ethics at the University of Central Lancashire. She has coordinated a number of multinational and multidisciplinary research projects funded by the European Union focusing on genetic screening, genetic counseling, cultural and social objections to biotechnology. Her publications include *Ethics, Reproduction and Genetic Control* (1992).

Edgar R. Chasteen was professor of sociology and anthropology at William Jewell College in Missouri from 1965 to 1995. At the time of writing *The Case for Compulsory Birth Control* (1971), he was on leave from the Institute of Community Studies in Kansas City, Missouri.

Katherine Covell is professor of psychology and director of the Children's Rights Centre at the University College of Cape Breton. Among her publications is "A New Role for the Psychologist in Custody Disputes" and, with R. Brian Howe, *The Challenge of Children's Rights for Canada* (2001).

Joseph Fletcher (d. 1991) was visiting scholar of medical ethics at the University of Virginia and Robert Treat Pain Professor Emeritus at the Episcopal Theological School (Harvard University). He is author of numerous works, including *The Ethics of Genetic Control* (1988), *Humanhood* (1979), *Moral Responsibility* (1967), *Situation Ethics* (1966), and *Morals and Medicine* (1954).

S. L. Floyd, with degrees in philosophy and law, has taught philosophy at Dickinson College and is now senior trial counsel in the U.S. Justice Department.

R. Brian Howe is associate professor of political science and director of the Children's Rights Centre at the University College of Cape Breton. Among his publications are "Do Parents Have Fundamental Rights?" and, with Katherine Covell, *The Challenge of Children's Rights for Canada* (2001).

Leon R. Kass is a professor in at the College and the Committee on Social Thought at the University of Chicago, and a founding fellow of the Hastings Center. Among his publications are "Making Babies: The New Biology and the 'Old' Morality," "Preventing a Brave New World: Why We Must Ban Human Cloning Now," and *Ethics of Human Cloning* (1998). In August 2001 he was appointed by President Bush to chair the President's Council on Bioethics.

Philip Kitcher teaches in the department of philosophy at Columbia University. Among his publications are *The Lives to Come: The Genetic Revolution and Human Possibilities* (1996) and *Vaulting Ambition: Sociobiology and the Quest for Human Nature* (1985).

Eike-Henner W. Kluge currently teaches at the University of Victoria, and is founder and past director of the department of ethics and legal affairs for the Canadian Medical Association. Among his publications are *Readings in Biomedical Ethics: A Canadian Focus* (1991) and, with Carole Lucock, *New Human Reproductive Technologies: A Preliminary Perspective of the Canadian Medical Association* (1991).

Hugh LaFollette is professor of philosophy at East Tennessee State University. Among his publications is *Personal Relationships: Love, Identity, and Morality* (1995), and he is currently writing *The Practice of Ethics*, which integrates ethical theory and discussion of practical ethical issues.

Ruth Macklin is professor of bioethics in the department of epidemiology and social medicine at Albert Einstein College of Medicine in New York, and past president of the International Association of Bioethics. Among her publications are *Surrogates and Other Mothers: The Debates over Assisted Reproduction* (1994) and numerous articles on human reproduction and health policy.

Claudia Pap Mangel has degrees in public health and law. She is currently an assistant general counsel for a North Carolina pharmaceutical company, and has practiced food and drug law for fifteen years.

Deborah Mathieu is associate professor in the department of political science at the University of Arizona. Among her publications are "Mandating Treatment for Pregnant Substance Abusers," *Preventing Prenatal Harm: Should the State Intervene?* (1996), and other works in the area of medical ethics.

Roger McIntire is professor emeritus of psychology at the University of Maryland. He is a columnist and a frequent guest on radio and television talk shows. Among his publications are *Teenagers and Parents* (2000), *Raising Good Kids in Tough Times* (1999), and *Enjoy Successful Parenting* (1996).

Christine Overall is professor of philosophy and associate dean of the faculty of arts and science at Queen's University in Kingston, Ontario. Among her publications are *Thinking Like a Woman: Personal Life and Political Ideas* (2001), *Human Reproduction: Principles, Practices, Policies* (1993), and *Ethics and Human Reproduction: A Feminist Analysis* (1987).

D. Pomerantz taught philosophy at the State University of New York and is now on the staff of the U.S. House Appropriations Committee.

Laura M. Purdy is professor of philosophy at Wells College. Among her publications are *Reproducing Persons: Issues in Feminist Bioethics* (1996), with Anne Donchin, *Embodying Bioethics: Recent Feminist Advances* (1994), and *In Their Best Interest? The Case against Equal Rights for Children* (1992).

David Resnik is an associate professor of medical humanities at East Carolina University. He has published numerous articles in the philosophy of science and ethics, and is coauthor, with Pamela Langer and Holly Steinkrauss, of *Human Germ-line Gene Therapy: Scientific, Moral, and Political Issues* (1999), and author of *The Ethics of Science: an Introduction* (1998).

John A. Robertson is professor of law at the University of Texas School of Law at Austin. He has served on or been a consultant to many national bioethics advisory bodies, and is currently cochair of the ethics committee of the American Society for Reproductive Medicine. Among his publications is *Children of Choice: Freedom and the New Reproductive Technologies* (1994).

Laura Shanner is associate professor in the department of public health sciences and the John Dossetor Health Ethics Centre at the University of Alberta. Among her publications in ethics, law, and policy in reproduction are "The Supreme Court of Canada on Reproduction: Private Matters and Conflicting Interests" and "Procreation."

Peter Singer is professor of bioethics at Princeton University's Center for Human Values, founding president of the International Association of Bioethics, and founding coeditor of *Bioethics*. Among his publications are, with Helga Kuhse, *Practical Ethics* (1989), and with Deane Wells, *Making Babies: The New Science and Ethics of Conception* (1985) and *The Reproductive Revolution: New Ways of Making Babies* (1984).

Diane A. Trombetta has degrees in cultural anthropology and counseling, and has taught in the Graduate School of Professional Psychology at John F. Kennedy University. She has been a mediator, psychotherapist, and custody evaluator in private practice, and has written extensively on the subjects of joint custody, mediation, and custody evaluation.

Lawrence P. Ulrich has degrees in philosophy, education, and counseling, and is professor in the philosophy department at the University of Dayton. He is also a bioethics consultant for various health care institutions, and has written extensively in the fields of bioethics and social philosophy.

Deane Wells taught philosophy in Australia and the United Kingdom; he then held various positions in the government of Australia and is currently the Minister for Environment. Among his publications are "Priorities in Medical Ethics," "A Proposal for a National Bioethics Consultative Committee," and, with Peter Singer, *Making Babies: The New Science and Ethics of Conception* (1985) and *The Reproductive Revolution: New Ways of Making Babies* (1984).

Jack Westman is professor emeritus of psychiatry at the University of Wisconsin Medical School. He has been editor of *Child Psychiatry and Human Development* and is president of Wisconsin Cares. Among his publications are *Licensing Parents: Can We Prevent Child Abuse and Neglect?* (1994) and *Child Advocacy: New Professional Roles for Helping Families* (1979).